EX LIBRIS

By the same author

FICTION

All in the Mind

Maya

My Name Is . . .

NON-FICTION

The Blair Years

The Alastair Campbell Diaries
Volume One: Prelude to Power

The Alastair Campbell Diaries
Volume Two: Power & the People

The Alastair Campbell Diaries
Volume Three: Power & Responsibility

The Alastair Campbell Diaries
Volume Four: The Burden of Power: Countdown to Iraq

The Irish Diaries

The Happy Depressive:
In Pursuit of Personal and Political Happiness

ALASTAIR CAMPBELL

WINNERS

And How They Succeed

With special thanks to my son
RORY CAMPBELL
who pressed me to write this book,
and helped me every step
of the way

HUTCHINSON
LONDON

1 3 5 7 9 10 8 6 4 2

Hutchinson
20 Vauxhall Bridge Road
London SW1V 2SA

Hutchinson is part of the Penguin Random House group of companies
whose addresses can be found at global.penguinrandomhouse.com.

Penguin
Random House
UK

First published by Hutchinson in 2015

www.randomhouse.co.uk

A CIP catalogue record for this book is available from the British Library.

ISBN 9780091958855 (Hardback)
ISBN 9780091958862 (Trade paperback)

Printed and bound by Clays Ltd, St Ives plc

Typeset by Palimpsest Book Production Ltd, Falkirk, Stirlingshire

Penguin Random House is committed to a sustainable future for our business,
our readers and our planet. This book is made from Forest Stewardship
Council® certified paper.

MIX
Paper from
responsible sources
FSC® C018179

CONTENTS

ACKNOWLEDGEMENTS

One of the best things about working on *Winners* was doing so with my son Rory. Indeed, along with my agent Ed Victor, as ever a great support, Rory was foremost in pressing me to write the book. We have many similarities, not least our shared obsession with winning and winners; but whereas I would cite language and creativity as my strongest areas, his are a mathematical mind and a deep understanding of data, backed by an encyclopedic knowledge of most sports. Rory's has not been the most conventional career path, but whenever I have raised an eyebrow that an Oxford degree in Politics, Philosophy and Economics has led to professional gambling, his riposte is that 'you wouldn't be saying the same if I was playing chess'.

He has simultaneously pursued a separate career in football, qualifying for FA and UEFA badges, and has worked with a number of professional clubs in coaching, scouting and player recruitment. He completed a master's dissertation on the use (or rather misuse) of data in the football transfer market, a piece of work commissioned by Chelsea FC's then director of operations Mike Forde, and now works at the University College of Football Business at Wembley. We did many of the interviews together, and in some parts of the book, particularly those which call on his specialist knowledge in the use of data in sport and innovation, the work is as much his as mine, and I am hugely grateful.

I had further terrific research assistance, and boundless enthusiasm, from Kevin Keith, a Liverpudlian, ex of Burnley Council and now making a new life for himself in Australia, and Sam Nurding, so sincere thanks to them too.

My ten previous books have been political diaries, novels and a short memoir on mental illness. This book was a new kind of challenge, and one for which I was lucky to have Nigel Wilcockson as editor, given his experience editing business books and autobiographies. This is a long book, but it was a lot longer and less coherent before he put his scissors and restructuring skills to work. Thanks also to copy editor Katherine Fry, meticulous as ever, editorial manager John Sugar, publicist Najma Finlay, Jason Smith for the superb cover, Simon Rhodes who handled production and text design, Rose Waddilove who looked after the proofs, and also to Alison Urquhart of Random House Australia, who put me in touch with some of my Australian interviewees.

Gail Rebuck, friend as well as publisher, was among those who read drafts at various stages and made helpful suggestions, as did her daughters Georgia and Grace Gould, Ed Victor, Charlie Falconer, David Mills, Brendan Foster, Humphrey Walters and my partner Fiona. I want to thank my son Calum, not least for his constant exhortations to 'get Mayweather' (and American PR Kelly Swanson who 'got him' for me), and my daughter Grace, who does not share the male Campbells' mania for sport but nonetheless helped me with transcribing the interviews.

The people who have made the book what it is, though, are the winners and their teams who have given me their time. I feel privileged to have met so many people at the top of their chosen fields, sharing their insights and experience. This includes people who do not normally speak to outsiders, such as past and present advisers to the royal family who not only spoke to me but also helped with fact-checking in my profile of the Queen.

Finally, I want to thank Jean Afterman, assistant general manager of the New York Yankees, the highest ranking woman in baseball, who guided me through US sport and who, after reading a few draft chapters, gave me the title, originally planned as *Winning*. 'This book is about people not things,' she said. 'It should be *Winners*, not winning.' She was right. So here it is.

INTRODUCTION

'You always get a buzz from winning. Winning is everything.'

A.P. McCOY

I have two great passions in my life: politics and sport. I have a lot of experience in the former, a lot of knowledge about the latter, and a fascination bordering on obsession with the one thing that most obviously unites those passions – the importance of winning.

Winners explores that fascination. Given some of the remarkable people who flit in and out of the following pages, offering their wisdom and insight, and also their lessons on defeat – an important ingredient in most recipes for winning – I hope those who share my interest in politics and sport will enjoy reading it. But more than that, especially considering the business figures who have joined in the debate, I hope it will prove useful for entrepreneurs, community leaders, campaigners, people running public services, performers, students, anyone trying to take on a challenge – from losing weight to changing the world – and win.

Writing the book has been something of a journey. One of the first impulses to embark on it came as a result of work I have done with businesses since leaving front-line politics, and the discovery that many of them are poor at strategy, campaigns, communications and crisis management, the things I know best. So when I began mapping out the book, I had in mind a guide to these areas, as well as teamship, leadership, resilience, decision-making and all the other things that go to make political winners, as seen through the prism of personal political experience, and thousands of hours watching and playing sport, and talking to some of the greatest sports winners of our time.

But as the book developed, it dawned on me that there was an arrogance in the view that simply because I had helped put together winning machines and strategies in politics, and knew lots of winners in sport, I could write a guide for CEOs, or head teachers, or charity general secretaries, let alone elite sports teams, in the art of winning. The reason is that the more I delved into it, the more I learned that there is an awful lot that the best of business does better than the best of politics; and there is lots done by the best of elite sport that is better than both. So instead of this being my guide to winning, it is more an analysis of winners – who they are, how they do it, and how we can all apply some of their lessons to our own lives.

Despite this turnaround, I am still arrogant enough to believe that what I have to say about how to win elections will be of use to people in politics and elsewhere. But in talking to people outside politics, and in studying the great entrepreneurs of our time, I wish I had known some of what I know now when I was working for the Labour Party and the government.

One of the lessons that comes through from great sportsmen and women, and great businessmen and women, is that you can always do better. That certainly goes for New Labour, good though I believe we were. But more generally, I'm concerned that politics in the advanced democracies is trapped inside its own comfort zone, aware of public disengagement and disillusion but seemingly unable to rebuild a strong democratic relationship, which in turn is helping the less democratic countries of the world to win further political and economic strength. I was quite shocked while researching this book to discover how many people in the West saw Russian President Vladimir Putin as the most effective modern leader. 'I may not like him, but. . .' the refrain begins, followed by criticism of leaders we might expect Western business people or politicians to admire. Add in the fact that terrorism and extremism are winning more battles than they should and world politics becomes a worrying place.

Most people in business and sport accept that politics, especially government, is harder because it is so vast and the challenges so complex. But as I went, chapter by chapter, through all the elements I consider essential to winning, I learned that, almost without exception, those in elite sport and business are better at them than those in politics. In fact, the only areas where I feel others might have something to learn from politics are communications and crisis management – perhaps because these are such an integral part of political life. Elite sport gets better, and its presentation to the public better still. Even with the financial crash, business continues to break new frontiers in the technological age. Democratic politics is staying largely the same, and the world may be the loser as a result.

Of course, there is no such thing as a single 'recipe for success', and nobody is likely to win anything simply by following the formula of another winner. But studying success in other worlds is not a bad way to try to improve in your own.

I am now more sure than ever that there are principles and values and techniques that can be applied across any winning mind or winning organisation; that the rules of strategy applied to successful political projects have relevance today to businesses taking on a competitor or starting a new venture, and to coaches trying to get the best out of a team; that any worthwhile venture in life will emerge from teamship, and that there are lessons for all of us – business, politics, public services, NGOs, individuals – in studying the great team-builders of sport; that anyone who wants to win needs to know how to lead in their own environment.

The focus in *Winners* is on those who have stood out in a particular area, who have demonstrated the ability to win or to gain competitive advantage, and the analysis will centre on whether the tools and strategies they use can be transferred to other areas. Do baseball legend Billy Beane's skills as an innovator and team-builder, or Ben Ainslie's skills as a leader at sea, have any relevance to political leaders as they put together their teams for election campaigns? Could finance ministers still struggling to recover from the fallout of the global financial crisis learn anything from Dave

Brailsford's obsession with 'marginal gains' in cycling or José Mourinho's ferocious attention to detail in preparing for a football match? As coaches prepare for a major international tournament, might they learn more from reading about how Abraham Lincoln built his Cabinet from a team of rivals than from another ghosted memoir or video compilation of opponents? Indeed, could politicians today learn more from looking at figures of history than their own generation? Could managers and owners, in the notoriously short-term world of football, where a long-serving Ferguson or a Wenger is an exception not the norm, learn from business leaders who have brilliantly managed their own longevity, such as a Branson or a Buffett or a Wintour? Would the bankers have handled the global financial crisis better had they learned from the crisis management experience of political leaders?

The book starts with an examination of what I call 'The Holy Trinity' – strategy, leadership and teamship – and is followed by interview profiles of individuals who have excelled in each category: José Mourinho, Anna Wintour and Albanian Prime Minister Edi Rama, the only current head of government to have played international sport. In the second part, 'It's All in the Mind', I turn to the various component parts of a winning mindset, drawing on interviews with top sports people who in my view excel in this key area. I also look at the 'extreme mind', and I consider the power of visualisation with the help of Diego Maradona, before moving on to an interview with a boxer who has never lost a pro fight, Floyd Mayweather. The third part, 'Standing Out from the Crowd', looks at what I think are the three vital ingredients in getting ahead: a willingness to think boldly, a hunger to innovate, and a preparedness to be guided by hard facts and data and not prejudice or received wisdom. Formula One and Indian Prime Minister Narendra Modi are masters here. The fourth part, 'Changing Setbacks into Advantages', considers how great crisis managers operate – Bill Clinton among them – and the various facets of resilience. I also profile one of the most extraordinary women I have ever come across, Australian surfer Layne Beachley. Her country is the subject of one of two profiles, where I examine the history, mindset and winning habits of a nation I hugely admire. The other profile is of the most famous woman in the world, the Queen. Finally, I seek to bring everything together with the help of Haile Gebrselassie, an outstanding sportsman and businessman who now has his eyes on the political arena.

As a lifelong republican, I did not imagine when starting out on this book that I would end up realising Elizabeth II is one of the great enduring winners of our lifetime. But like I said, it has been a journey. I hope you enjoy reading the book as much as I have enjoyed writing it; and I hope you get as much from reading it as I did from researching and writing it.

PART 1

THE HOLY TRINITY

1
STRATEGY

'Too many coaches teach technique when they should be teaching strategy.'

MARTINA NAVRATILOVA

Strategy is God. That is why it has to come first in the holy trinity of Strategy, Leadership and Teamship. This is not meant to offend believers, but to stress the importance of strategy to achieving success. Good leaders excel at devising strategy. Good teams excel at implementing strategy. You can have all the talent and ambitions you need, but without clear strategy, understood by everyone from the top of the organisation to the bottom, the ambition will not be fulfilled. So: strategy first, last, always.

'We don't do God' is one of my most quoted sound bites. That wasn't meant to be offensive either. It was a throwaway remark to an American journalist, but once it stuck, I thought, 'Why not use it?', so the words 'We don't do God, but we do do strategy' were on a card on my desk for the 2005 election campaign two years later, alongside my perennials: 'By failing to prepare, you are preparing to fail' (Benjamin Franklin), and 'It is amazing what you can accomplish if you do not care who gets the credit' (Harry Truman). By then, my co-strategist Philip Gould and I were long-time co-believers in 'SIG' (Strategy is God) and we had our SIG rules.

Like God, strategy is open to different interpretations and so has become one of the most misused words and concepts. Many 'strategies' turn out to be vague goals or wild tactical gestures. It's therefore essential to understand from the outset what the concept does and does not involve. It's also essential to appreciate that strategy incorporates distinct phases and principles, and that if you fail to appreciate them or – as many people do – confuse them, it's a recipe for defeat and disaster.

OST, THE ABC OF WINNING

The simplest way to view strategy is to consider three letters, letters which have been on my desk and on the inside cover of my notebooks since 1994.

> **O** for Objective
> **S** for Strategy
> **T** for Tactics

Objective comes first because it's the most important initial step, and to an extent it's also the easiest one to define: it's where you want to get to, what you want to achieve. It's the 'what' in Margaret Thatcher's famous injunction to a senior civil servant: 'I know the what. Don't tell me the what. Tell me the how.'

Getting to where you want to end up doesn't automatically entail 'winning' pure and simple. Winning requires definition or, at least, calibration, according to circumstances. A struggling football team might start the season with the objective not of winning every match but of avoiding relegation. If Manchester United or Barcelona fail to win their domestic title or the Champions League, as happened in 2014, they have 'lost' over the season. But if a team that struggled the previous season loses numerous matches but staves off relegation this time around, it has achieved its objective and 'won'. Crystal Palace manager Tony Pulis was one of the standout English Premier League performers of the same 2014 season, taking a club from the bottom of the league when he took over to a comfortable position. He 'won', and was named Premier League manager of the season by his peers. Barca and United 'lost', despite winning more games. Costa Rica 'won' their World Cup 2014 journey. Spain and England, out in the early stages, left as losers.

Or compare the world of Formula One, where according to McLaren chairman and chief executive Ron Dennis, 'The objective is not merely to win a Grand Prix or a championship but to dominate' – in other words, it's about the here and now, winning the race, then the title, and staying at the top – with the even more long-term view of a business leader such as former BP CEO John Browne who believes that the definition of winning in business is 'Sustainably making money better than others in the sector; it is all about the long-term value of the company'. Browne acknowledges that it hasn't always been thus: for a man like Jack Welch at General Electric, winning involved ensuring all the divisions within his empire were number one or number two in the market. But Browne argues that these days, when there are 'more inquisitive boards, shareholders, activists, employees, and people hear so much about corporate pay that they assume all the time they are being ripped off', a more nuanced business approach is required when striving for success and measuring it.

> 'I skate to where the puck is going, not where it has been.'
> **WAYNE GRETZKY**

Deciding where and how to set the bar applies to personal performance too. When I took up running in my forties, and entered the 2003 London Marathon, I knew I wouldn't 'win' the race, not least because some of the greatest runners on the planet were also running – indeed, Britain's Paula Radcliffe set a new women's world record that year. But I needed motivation to 'win' against the clock, against myself, against people of my age and standard. So I took advice, from athlete turned commentator Brendan Foster, from Sebastian Coe, and from my near neighbour Hugh Jones, the first Brit to win the London Marathon back in 1982, who helped with my schedule, and trained with me for hundreds of miles. They agreed that for someone closer to fifty than forty, who had taken up running only recently, breaking four hours was a 'win'. So that was the objective, and the training – my strategy, developed and overseen by Hugh – was geared towards it. When I crossed that finishing line in 3 hours, 53 minutes and 1 second, I knew I had 'won', and felt delirious and fulfilled.

Even political campaigns, essentially all about winning elections, involve careful consideration of objectives to define winning. Working once in Bosnia and Herzegovina, I quickly learned just how complicated its political system, born out of the Dayton Agreement of 1995, actually is. This is scarcely surprising: the authors of Dayton were grappling with the aftermath of a barbarous civil war so they created a system in which straight 'winning' by one side is virtually impossible (unfortunately, this makes governing pretty well nigh impossible too). To devise a strategy for a campaign, therefore, a party needs a clear idea of what winning actually looks like. In the case of the main parties in Bosnia it means getting the biggest share of the vote (20 per cent is about as good as it gets) and securing a share of the top jobs. Whatever your walk of life, it's only when you are SMART (specific, measurable, attainable, relevant and time-limited) about your objective that you can begin to design and implement a clear strategy to meet it.

So how ambitious should you be when setting an objective? Set the bar unattainably high and the result may simply be disillusionment and criticism when the hoped-for results don't transpire; at worst, you end up being remembered for what you didn't achieve rather than what you did. Nicklas Bendtner is a case in point. The man who described himself as 'one of the best strikers in the world' is likely to be remembered more for his boasts about his objectives – playing for Barcelona or Real Madrid instead of Arsenal reserves – than for what he has achieved (he's now with Wolfsburg, a mid-table German side). Over-ambition can also lead to dangerous levels of risk-taking, particularly in the spheres of business. Lehman Brothers is no longer with us because they overreached. The Co-op Bank was similarly plunged into crisis thanks to inflated objectives that could not be realised.

And yet setting an objective that fails to inspire is to risk mediocrity. 'I like to think of seemingly unachievable goals and then work backwards,' says Dave Brailsford, who set himself the target of leading the first British team to win the Tour de France. 'Sometimes I set a target and then get home and say "Did we really decide to do that?" Then fear kicks in and the fear of defeat makes me do the things we need to do to win. I won't allow anyone to imagine an obstacle is insurmountable.' Perhaps the only way to judge whether an objective is pitched at the right level is to assess the extent to which it sets the pulse racing. It should be ambitious enough that winning really will feel like an achievement. It should also be ambitious enough that failure will feel truly galling. That latter point is worth emphasising. Time and time again, I've been struck by just how many very successful people say that what motivates them ultimately is not a desire for success but an absolute dread of losing. 'I hate losing more than I love winning,' says Brailsford. 'That philosophy was always in me,' says Leigh Matthews, Aussie Rules 'Player of the Century', 'hate losing more than love winning.' Certainly, in the political sphere the Blair campaign team felt an almost visceral fear of failure, and a belief right to election day that it could happen, whatever the polls said. But this fear of failure made us more, not less, ambitious about our objectives.

FROM OBJECTIVE TO STRATEGY

Having decided what your objective is, you need to put in place the strategy to achieve it. Again, absolute clarity of thinking is required. Above all, there is one lethal but common mistake to be avoided: the confusion of strategy with tactics. Asked to advise a German financial services company recently, I presented board members with identical postcards. On one side of the card were printed the words 'Our objective as an organisation is . . .', on the other, the words 'Our strategy to meet this objective is . . .'. What emerged from their responses was a lack of clarity about both. Some of them clearly did not know the difference between an objective and a strategy, and, worse, several laid out a strategy that was actually nothing more than a set of tactics. 'We should do a regional tour to rebuild relations with local banks' was one suggested strategy. A strategy, I pointed out, would be 'regionalisation'. A tour is a tactic.

They had approached me because they thought they had a communications problem. This particular company, though, had a reality problem, and they were using their poor communications – also a reality – as a shield from facing up to the void in strategy. This is another common mistake, and a symptom of a failing organisation. A business plan is not a strategy; it is one of the means of securing a strategy. As John Browne says: 'Strategy is the bit between your purpose and your business plan. People with a clear view of winning know that strategy is everything. You have to have a strategy and stick to it, and never lose the plot.'

> 'Strategy is like putting together a gigantic puzzle, hard to assemble, but easy to understand once it's done.'
>
> **JOE TORRE**

In fact we set strategies for ourselves all the time, but we're often not very good at delineating them as such. Take dieting, for example. It's not difficult to turn a vague 'I want to lose weight' into a campaign with a clear O and S and a credible set of T. Objective: lose ten kilos. Strategy: diet (eat less, exercise more). Tactics: record calorie intake and exercise output; visualise 'thinner me', possibly with photos on fridge; use stairs not lift; join up with other dieters. Expressed like this, a real sense of purpose is injected into what is being planned. The problem is that, in most situations, we tend not to strive for this clarity of thought.

But great strategists do, constantly, instinctively. Ben Ainslie, seen by many as the world's most competitive sailor, is a man with a very clear sense of OST. The objective in a race is clear enough, and the strategy, he says, is all about defining how you believe the wind and currents are going to act. 'We would have in-depth models of what the wind and the current might do, and you define the strategy before you start: if this happens, we do this; if this happens, we do that.' He makes a clear distinction between this strategic thinking, and the tactical thinking that goes alongside it and which, as far as the world of racing is concerned, is entirely about the competition and what rivals are doing. 'Strategy is how we manage the weather and the environment. Once you are into the race, it is pretty much all tactical, but within your strategic frame.'

Good strategies can sometimes be almost breathtakingly basic and straightforward. When in 1997 Steve Jobs returned to Apple, the company he had founded but from which he had been ousted in 1985, just two words defined his immediate objective and strategy: *survival* (the phenomenal success came later) and *simplification.*

That simplification meant an overhaul of everything – products, style, management systems, team structures. It became a philosophy of leadership. 'That's been one of my mantras,' he said, 'focus and simplicity. Simple can be harder than complex. You have to work hard to get your thinking clean to make it simple. But it's worth it in the end because once you get there, you can move mountains.' Returning to his company after years away, he complained they had 'a zillion and one products' – well, more than forty – and he reduced it to four. 'Simplicity is the ultimate sophistication,' he said. As strategies go, it was astonishingly powerful, helping to create one of the great modern industrial success stories. Apple also took a strategic shift to put design rather than engineering as its driving force, and great innovation followed.

Such clarity of thought, however, is not that easily won. Steve Jobs was brilliant at drilling down to the essentials, but many people struggle to separate the essentials from the white noise. So how do you arrive at that light-bulb moment?

One route is, of course, the Jobs approach – looking within, discovering what is wrong and establishing a strategy to fix it. Arguably, that's easier to do when things are bad (and they certainly were at Apple when he returned for his second spell there): problems sometimes bring things into sharp focus. That does seem to have been the case with the supermarket chain Sainsbury's under their former CEO Justin King. He was only too aware how much the company had slipped when he took over, and his objective was therefore a very clear and stark one: 'Make Sainsbury's great again.' To achieve this he came up with three strategic planks: universal appeal (to stop Sainsbury's being seen as narrowly focused on the more affluent); fix the basics; and understand the customers better. 'We had grown very complacent,' he says. 'We were a number three behaving like a number one, refusing to take responsibility for years of failure and neglect. Better to be a number one behaving like a number two.' A Manchester United fan, he took inspiration from Alex Ferguson: 'He would always try to play the underdog even when they were clearly the best.'

> 'If you do not have a clear objective, you have no definition of winning. If you do not have a clear strategy, you have no chance of winning. And if all you have are tactics, you have no right to win.' **AC**

King's overall response, however, shows that his strategic approach derived not just by looking within the organisation but also by studying what was going on outside too. 'I came from ASDA and M&S,' he points out, 'and I wanted Sainsbury's to match ASDA for price and M&S for quality, so everyone would think they could shop with us, because of our approach to pricing, quality, choice.' And there's no doubt that seeing what your competitors are doing, and being honest about their merits, can be a powerful aid to strategic thinking. This is most obvious in sport, with the competitive element present in every event. But, as the Sainsbury's recovery demonstrates, it can work in business too. 'Getting the right strategy means you have to assume your competitors are damn good, or at the very least as good as you are, and that they are moving just as fast or faster,' Jack Welch said in his autobiography. 'When it comes to peering into the future, you just can't be paranoid enough.'

'Paranoia' was the same word used by John Browne, who quintupled the size of BP and turned it into Britain's biggest company by market capitalisation before being felled by revelations about his personal life. 'I assumed our competitors were plotting BP's downfall every moment of the day. I thought it because that is what we were doing to them.'

My own route into this mindset – never underestimate your opponents and always hold on to the visceral fear of defeat – partly came from a presentation I saw on Prozone, a system which allows coaches to analyse in microscopic detail the performance of individual athletes on a team. It was launched in Britain in 1998, and has created an environment in which, as Chelsea manager José Mourinho put it to me: 'Everyone knows everything about everybody, so you have to be cleverer in the analysis.'

Prozone inspired me to suggest that in devising New Labour strategy we should formalise the analysis we made of the Opposition. Philip Gould and I would meet weekly to ask this question: 'If we were them analysing us, assuming that they had the same information about us that we do, what we would do with that information?' and based upon that, send a note to Tony Blair. It was, in effect, a reverse political Prozone analysis. Some call it 'the mirror test' where you subject yourself to brutal analysis, with a touch of self-hate thrown in. By imagining we were our political opposites, we could better understand their strengths and our weaknesses. It was hard to get Tony to take seriously the idea that William Hague – and even more so Iain Duncan-Smith and Michael Howard when they led the Conservative party – would ever be elected prime minister. But it was important that we were better at working out our weaknesses than they were, because then we could hopefully do something about fixing them before they got on to them.

Such an approach – deriving a strategy from an opponent's potential strength – was brilliantly demonstrated by Pete Carroll, the head coach who led the Seattle Seahawks to a remarkable win in the 2014 NFL Super Bowl Final. It was a clash between a side renowned for its defence (Seattle) against one renowned for its offence (Denver Broncos, complete with Peyton Manning, one of the sport's greats, at quarterback).

Objective: win the Super Bowl.

Strategy: defensive strength, limit Manning.

Carroll realised that his strategy had to be to curtail Manning's effectiveness, and play to his own side's defensive capabilities, but in a way that created counter-attack opportunities. Tactically that meant that Manning could be allowed to play lots of short passes, but be stopped from making long ones. In the event, Manning broke the Super Bowl record for completion of passes, thirty-four out of forty-nine. However, these passes averaged just 8.2 yards, the third worst mark in Super Bowl history. The Seattle players didn't 'blitz' Manning – in other words, send defenders other than linemen to crowd him – because, although this is a standard tactic, they knew he thinks well under pressure. Instead they dropped into coverage, so they had more people deep to limit the quarterback's options – almost unheard of in the NFL.

Seattle did not just beat Denver; they blew them apart, by 43–8. Carroll came up with a plan and coached the execution of that plan in a way that nullified his opponents' strengths and maximised his own team's strengths in line with their season-long objective and strategy.

Note that while Carroll studied Denver's strong points he didn't seek to emulate them. Similarly, once ambition and fear were driving Dave Brailsford to build his Tour de France team, he didn't look at past winners and say 'Let's do what they do'. He looked at past winners and said 'Let's do things differently because then we might beat them. If we do the same as them, they win, because they've been doing it for longer.' The ability to think big when attempting radical strategic overhaul is essential, and that requires imagination, analysis of every area and the ability to base strategy on both knowns and unknowns, not out-of-date changes by others. As Brad Pitt, aka Billy Beane (of whom much more later), says in *Moneyball*: 'If we play like the Yankees in here, we lose to the Yankees out there.'

It's a point that chess grandmaster Garry Kasparov makes too. 'You certainly need to take account of who your opponent is and how they play,' he argues, 'and you need to be adaptable (as the saying goes, "chess is an attempt to paint a masterpiece while someone tugs at your sleeve"), but you can't be defined by how your opponent plays. Thus a grandmaster is constantly making calculations to themselves along the lines of: I can play move A, which is objectively better but leads to the type of positions my opponent enjoys, or I can play move B, which isn't anything special but leads to the type of positions in which I excel.' This existence of style and areas of preference and competence in grandmasters, Kasparov suggests, is why chess is still a human game despite super-strong computers.

Kasparov, world champion at the age of twenty-one, number one for two decades, is one of the most strategic minds I have ever come across. He applies his chess strategies to life in general – appropriate for someone who is also a leader of the United Civil Front, the pro-democracy movement in Russia, and an activist in the game's global governing body, FIDE. 'You may want to match your competitor's offering simply because he is your competitor,' he tells me, 'but what if it distracts your resources away from what you are best at, or what you are best known for? Should Microsoft have gone into building tablet hardware? Such reactions can serve a purpose or they can be like a sushi restaurant starting to sell pizza just because a pizza place opens up next door. It's a delicate balance. If you change your strategy all the time you really don't have one.' He cites the popular quote attributed to Churchill: 'However beautiful the strategy, you should occasionally look at the results.' And every politician would do well to delete the word 'chess' and insert the word 'politics' in the following telling remark: 'In chess if you play without long-term goals your decisions will be purely reactive and you'll be playing your opponent's game, not your own.'

Kasparov agrees with me that Bill Clinton was a past master in this regard. During the 1992 Democratic primaries his candidacy was under pressure from a host of scandals eagerly lapped up by media and opponents. His team reacted instantly to each unfolding disaster, but in every statement made and every press release published they also made sure to hammer home their candidate's message. Clinton maintained a similar approach in the presidential election against George Bush Sr. Against each attack the Clinton team responded with a defence that also refocused the debate on their own strategy – the now famous 'It's the economy, stupid' – constantly reinforcing the fundamentals of their own campaign. By contrast, four years earlier, the Democrat candidate Michael Dukakis, totally thrown off course by the Republicans' aggressive tactics, was on the defensive. In campaigns, winners have to make the weather, even when surrounded by storms.

Running through everything Kasparov says is the idea that winners have to be good at strategy and at tactics, as Clinton was. The good strategist who lacks the ability to exploit opportunity will not win. The good tactician who can seize on opportunities but lacks the ability to make progress when no obvious opportunities present themselves will not win. 'And another thing,' he says, 'hoping for your opponent to make mistakes is not a strategy.' Indeed, opponents must never be underestimated.

Another winning strategist, Clive Woodward, who led England to Rugby World Cup victory in Australia in 2003, has talked me through the journey the England team made. 'You're not doing this in a vacuum,' he says, 'because there are other countries who think they can win too. I used to say, "OK, we are in this room, and in that room over there you have New Zealand, there is Australia, that room France, over there South Africa. They all have talent, so talent alone is not a prerequisite for success." So you have to say to yourself, "What do we need to do to be better than them?" And it meant we had to look at what we did, and what they did, from top to bottom, analyse every part of it, where we were strong, get stronger, where we were weak, address the weaknesses, energise all the organisations involved to think and act differently. It's always a risk to set public goals because you might not meet them but I really believed if we set that goal, and did everything required, we could give it a shot.'

I suggest that if there is a single word for the strategy it's 'excellence' and he nods. 'In everything we did, I was determined that every individual, and every part of the organisation, should be the best they could be.' From a standing start – he was the England team's first full-time professional coach, and didn't even have an office on his first day – that pursuit of excellence was turned into a revolution for English rugby and its attitudes to team-building, science and innovation, the winning mindset. In Woodward's experience, rugby still had the English public-school world view that 'it's the taking part that matters'. 'It is great that teams can tear lumps off each other, then shake hands and have a beer, but don't let that read across into people thinking winning doesn't count. In professional sport, winning counts for everything.' Woodward's strategy, then, didn't just involve building a team but also changing a culture.

IT'S NOT STRATEGY UNTIL IT'S WRITTEN DOWN

This is an absolutely vital SIG rule. Think in ink, as Marilyn Monroe said in one of her poems. In politics, it's easier, because so much of political debate is forged through words. These words matter. Yet sometimes the pressures of a hectic life mean that people do not commit to print in the way that they should. The leadership of New Labour tried to ensure that strategy was written down, and communicated as widely as possible. That could be overall strategy – such as deciding the main slogan would be 'New Labour, New Britain'; or the explanation of a specific act of strategy, such as the decision to alter the party's constitution as a way of signalling our determination to change, and the plan to bring that about; or the thinking behind a particular speech or interview. If the words didn't speak to the overall strategy, they were wasted words.

At Apple, according to Sally Grisedale, former manager of the company's Advanced Technology Group, writing everything down became part of the company's culture. 'It's all written down. It has to be. There are so many moving parts.' Warren Buffett's annual reports are much more than yearly accounts; they are expressions of ongoing strategy, pointers to the future as well as analysis of the past. Sir Richard Branson goes everywhere with a school notebook, and habitually writes in it, impressions, observations by others. It is a useful way of clarifying thoughts. As the American writer Joan Didion says: 'I write entirely to find out what I'm thinking, what I'm looking at, what I see and what it means. What I want and what I fear.' I do the same, whether writing diaries, books or, more importantly, sketching out strategy.

'Think in ink.'

MARILYN MONROE

The best strategies can be expressed as a word, a phrase, a paragraph, a page, a speech, and a book. There have been many books about New Labour. But the single word back at the beginning was 'modernisation'. The phrase was 'New Labour, New Britain'. The paragraph said that New Labour existed to deliver power, wealth and opportunity to the many not the few; we would provide leadership not drift; our focus would be on the future not the past; and education was our number one priority.

The page would take each of those themes and show what they meant in policy terms, concentrating on the issues that mattered most to people – the economy, health, schools and crime. But instead of focusing on grand claims (though there were plenty of these in the big speeches), we opted to prioritise specific limited pledges, which were turned into the first of our pledge cards, an exercise repeated successfully at subsequent elections. The pledge card was a tactic to illustrate the concrete nature of the policy promises; using these specific policies was a tactic designed to show we got people's priorities, and were realistic about how we could meet them.

It's during – and not after – the writing stage of a strategy that any necessary internal debates need to be had. Just days before the 1994 conference, for example, even Tony Blair and Peter Mandelson, both at the modernising end of modernisation, felt it might be pushing things too far to launch 'New Labour' so soon into his leadership. Tony was worried about John Prescott, the deputy leader, whose instincts were to be loyal, but who was wary of Tony's modernising zeal. Over the next few days, persuading John to support Tony's plan to change the constitution and replace the old Clause

4, getting rid of the commitment to wholesale nationalisation of the economy, something Labour had not believed in for years, was essential. Because if Tony had made that announcement, and John had been against it, and said so, we would have been dead from day one. The great thing about John was that the only way he knew how to have an argument was really to have the argument. If you tried to humour him or, worse, kept him out of the debate, you had no chance. If, however, you set out honestly what was intended, and why, he would have his explosions, but that was his way of testing the argument to destruction in his own mind. So we had the argument, day and night, in between Tony and me trying to write the section of the speech in which this bombshell was to be dropped. We were intending to do it subtly, and it was John, finally won round to the argument, who said that if Tony was going to do it, he should be clear and straight with people, not beat about the bush.

That debate with a key member of the team was crucial. Being a control freak is not incompatible with wanting and welcoming tough internal debate. When arguments are driven by ego and position they are tedious, but when they are real, about important issues, they are invigorating, and the means by which policy and strategy are made. Ultimately, decisions have to be made, but there is nothing wrong with big arguments along the way, provided that once agreed, everyone goes along with it.

The Northern Ireland peace process was replete with similar examples, where some participants passionately wanted something, others passionately opposed it, and yet, via the heat of argument, decisions and deals were made. The Bloody Sunday Inquiry springs to mind. Nationalists wanted it. Unionists didn't. Mo Mowlam as Northern Ireland Secretary wanted it. The Ministry of Defence didn't. Tony was on balance against but persuaded to go for it. It became a hugely expensive running sore, but its conclusion, under the next government and one of David Cameron's best parliamentary performances, was seen by almost everyone as a good and healing moment. We got there by argument. A strong leader and a strong organisation will welcome those arguments rather than try to pretend that the possibility of a strategy or policy exists which pleases everyone. Interestingly, Jack Welch of General Electric puts candour right at the top of his list of ingredients for success, and yet lack of candour permeates almost every level of business, he says. It can kill a business, and the opposite – genuine openness at every level – can make a business flourish.

Once strategies have been agreed and have been written down, they need to be repeated – endlessly. One of my SIG rules was 'just when the communicator is getting bored with saying something, that is when there is an outside chance of it reaching the outer radar of public opinion'.

Particularly in Opposition, you have limited opportunities to set out your stall. When shadow ministers rebelled at what some saw as excessive command and control systems from the centre, I would endeavour to explain. 'We are trying to persuade people who did not vote for us last time, to vote for us this time. The strategy that has been agreed is New Labour, New Britain. That means that we are a changed Labour Party. We will show how we have changed, through a new constitution, a new approach to policy, and new ways of campaigning and communicating. In Opposition we cannot make an active difference to people's lives in the way the government can, so showing we are capable of change in these ways is vital to earning the trust of people to believe we can change Britain. But how are they to know other than through how we tell them?'

> 'Strategies must be repeated endlessly.'
> **SIG RULE**

I would describe strategic communication as like painting a picture. Every piece of action or communication lands a tiny dot. Over time the dots come together. Counter-messages distort, even destroy it.

Here I call Steve Jobs as a witness, having learned he was a fellow dot-lander, albeit in a different way. 'You can't connect the dots looking forward; you can only connect them looking backwards,' he said.

And on the message delivery point, I also call Jack Welch as a witness in support of my rule. He finds it as annoying as I do, but obeyed it nonetheless. 'You have to talk about vision constantly, basically to the point of gagging. There were times I talked about the company's direction so many times in one day that I was completely sick of hearing it myself. But I realized the message was always new to someone. And so, you keep on repeating it. And you talk to *everyone*.'

The sad fact is that most companies have, hanging on their walls, vision statements that are never applied in practice; and they change a message if it doesn't work quickly, when in fact – assuming they have done their strategic homework properly – they should keep going with the same message until it gets through. I used to love it when the press groaned as I recited my oft-repeated mantras.

NEVER CONFUSE TACTICS WITH STRATEGY

I've already mentioned the dangers of confusing strategy and tactics, but it's a point that needs to be emphasised. Good strategies are big, bold and consistent. Tony Blair wanted 'modernisation', Steve Jobs wanted 'simplicity', Clive Woodward sought 'excellence' through attention to detail. Not all strategies can be expressed in just one word, of course, but the great ones have a clarity to them that rings out.

When tactics win over strategy, the result is a muddle; with this in mind it is worth considering what happened in the British general election of 2010.

Remember the context. Labour had been in power a long time. The Blair/Brown narrative had dominated politics since 1994, and while Gordon Brown brought his own style to government and handled some problems well – not least the global economic crisis – there was a palpable sense among the electorate of 'time for a change', stoked inevitably by government fatigue and the scandal surrounding MPs' expenses claims that did most damage to Labour as the governing party.

David Cameron, then, was in a powerful position, and his

objective couldn't have been simpler or, arguably, more achievable: get Labour out of power and establish a Conservative government. But what was his strategy? Pre-1997, Tony Blair would say in speech after speech, interview after interview: 'We are running as New Labour. We will govern as New Labour,' and then in government he would say repeatedly: 'We ran as New Labour, we are governing as New Labour.' I've sometimes asked Conservatives to fill in the blanks on an equivalent statement. 'David Cameron said: "We ran as — Conservatives, we are governing as — Conservatives.' They have invariably struggled. Modernising? Traditional? Right-wing? Centrist? Compassionate? Austerity? Thatcherite? Heir-to-Blairite? Take your pick. Mine would be that he ran as a strategic butterfly, and went on to govern as a strategic butterfly.

The public aren't daft. They may not be peering at politicians through my OST lens, but they do get the point. They see things, and they notice. What they noticed about Cameron, I believe, was that 'yes, he looks and sounds the part, but I'm not really sure what he's all about'. And that is why they decided to send an uncertain result and 'instruct' the politicians to create a coalition from the mess.

To my mind, much that David Cameron did after he became prime minister confirms the electorate's initial view: quite clear about O, pretty handy with T, but all over the shop on S. Clarity on O or skilfulness with T doesn't add up to a winning formula unless there is equal clarity and skilfulness regarding S. He proved good at posing for a fabulous picture in a stunning ski suit being pulled by huskies on an Arctic sledge to highlight climate change and promising to lead 'the greenest government ever'; and promoting his plans for the Big Society, his way of saying he was not as right-wing as Margaret 'no such thing as society' Thatcher. Both good tactics. Both memorable. But what was the strategy underpinning them? And how did it relate to what he would do in government, if he met his objective and won?

What's more, how do you square the inevitable contradictions to which his short-term tactics led? You can't talk about 'the greenest government ever' but then never make a single major speech on the environment as prime minister. You can't go for a short-term public relations 'win' by opposing airport expansion if you know deep down that this is essential if Britain is to recover, prosper and 'win' in a globalised economy. 'Incredibly frustrating, just wrong, big mistake and they will regret it,' says Willie Walsh, CEO of International Airlines Group. 'Sad,' says Richard Branson. 'Just sad for Britain, because business that would come here is going to go elsewhere because of the short-term trumping the real long-term need.'

As for the Big Society, Cameron essentially dropped it, confirming suspicions that it was not a thought-through strategy for government, but a short-term tactical distancing from Margaret Thatcher, a distancing he reversed dramatically amid the tributes surrounding her death, which if anything served to underline the difference between them – the clarity of her political message and priorities, and the lack of clarity of his. The Big Society was also fatally compromised by Chancellor George Osborne's austerity strategy – though he, at least, has shown signs of having a strategy and sticking to it. The referendum on Scottish independence also revealed Cameron's strategic weakness. SNP leader Alex Salmond ran rings around him in setting the terms, chiefly a two-year campaign, the framing of the 'Yes' question, and votes for sixteen and seventeen-year-olds. Cameron seemed relaxed because at the time 'No' was 20 points ahead of 'Yes' in the polls. Complacency set in, and ministers did not galvanise themselves until two weeks before the vote when a poll showed 'Yes' moving into the lead. Cameron rushed out measures to give extra powers to the Scottish Parliament, then ceded the idea of more power for England and the regions, all driven tactically as a result of strategic failure. By not doing enough to win the argument, he ended up giving away too much. And when it came to a key issue like Britain's place in Europe, he essentially subcontracted strategy to another party altogether – UKIP – which is a bit like a football team asking one of the other team's players to take a penalty for you.

When you say you're not sure what someone is all about, you

are basically saying they do not have a clear strategy. They are 'trying anything'. Companies whose employees' complaints go beyond the usual whingeing inside any organisation, into the zone of constant questioning of their superiors' actions and attitudes, tend to be revealing strategic failure. The sports fan who complains 'I can't see where we're going' is making the same point, and if Joe Public cannot see a sense of strategy, that could be a failure of leadership and communications, but more likely it is exposing a lack of one. Strategy expert Michael Porter's quote below applies to businesses, but it can apply to parties and governments too.

> 'A company without a strategy is willing to try anything.'
>
> **MICHAEL PORTER**

It's what Garry Kasparov meant when he said a constantly changing strategy is not a strategy at all. 'You may have to adapt,' he adds, but 'you should only change strategy when the whole environment and the funda-mentals change'.

The fact is that tactics on their own are invariably short-term and can easily trip you up. I recall how defiantly New Labour stood in the centre ground, resisting our opponents' tactical attempts to push us off it ('From Bambi to Stalin' was Tony's memorable summary of the ways the Tories tried to characterise him). Conservative leaders William Hague, Iain Duncan Smith and Michael Howard felt squeezed for space and so ultimately they either went right or went opportunistic. Opportunism, as Howard in particular learned to his cost, is never a strategy, always tactical.

NEVER LOSE SIGHT OF STRATEGY

In November 2005, for many Manchester United fans the unthink-able happened. Roy Keane, for years one of the club's most impor-tant players, had his contract terminated. Had they read Professor Douglas McGregor's book, *The Human Side of Enterprise*, published in 1960, and applied it to Alex Ferguson's management style, they would have seen it coming. 'If there is a single assumption that pervades conventional organisation theory, it is that authority is the central, indispensable means of managerial control,' says McGregor. As Arsenal manager Arsène Wenger puts it: 'If the manager is not the most important man at the football club, then why do we sack the manager if it doesn't go well?'

Ferguson's objective for Manchester United had been clear from the day he arrived in 1986 from Aberdeen: to win games and win titles, consistently, first in England, then Europe. 'Conveying authority is essential in order to be an effective leader,' he tells me. 'Every time I went into a team talk I bounded in, chest out, making sure I conveyed authority and control. I never slunk in without anyone noticing.'

The key words in his strategy were 'control' and 'talent'. That might seem obvious. But choosing to focus upon those as acts of strategy, alongside an emphasis that no individual is bigger than the club, is far from universal. Indeed, the all-powerful manager has declined considerably in the Roman Abramovich era of super-wealthy foreign owners who do think they are bigger than the club. Ferguson, with the board's backing, had a clear and consistent management structure that acknowledged him as the single most important person in the organisation. His talent strategy was focused on the recruitment and development of world-class young players who understood that the winning mindset was an essential part of being at Manchester United.

Keane had the winning mindset, for sure, but in attacking his teammates in an interview for the club's TV channel, MUTV, he was behaving in a way that challenged the authority – control – of the manager. As for talent, Ferguson saw the attacks as seeking to instil a culture of fear way beyond Keane's remit as captain. Fans who were always quick to praise Ferguson's strategic approach should have known Keane was on the way out the moment that interview was in the can. Ferguson has always believed 'values' have to run through an organisation, and that in building a team 'you must recognise the value of the team as one in order to achieve your goals'. When Keane criticised the team in public, he challenged the strategy, betrayed this fundamental principle, and therefore had to go.

His exit might have been one of the reasons Manchester United failed to win the Premier League that season. But they went on to win three in a row, and the Champions League in 2008 with arguably Ferguson's best ever side, spearheaded by his best ever player, Cristiano Ronaldo. Ferguson made a short-term sacrifice in moving Keane on, but he did so with the club's long-term objective and strategy in mind.

Terry Leahy, CEO at Tesco when it rose to market dominance, points out that working within a clear framework of strategy and values will always gain you respect with employees. Sackings and restructurings will cause resentment and create a reputation for being tough. 'Yet if that reputation is based on your unremitting focus on the truth, and people see you act according to the values you espouse, then that is no bad thing for a manager, your integrity will grow.'

Unswerving focus on strategy can be found among successful leaders in all walks of life. Take the German Chancellor, Angela Merkel – to my mind the world's most impressive current national leader, as I will explain in the next chapter – and her handling of the eurozone crisis. She was under enormous pressure to be much bolder and more dramatic than she wished to or she thought sensible. Her objectives were to save the eurozone, while also preserving Germany's continued pre-eminence. Her strategic moves were all designed to ensure this. She could have made short-term tactical wins by courting popularity in struggling eurozone countries (think how unpopular she became in Greece, for example), but she never lost sight of her own objective and strategy, and emerged strengthened in the longer term as a result.

When Vladimir Putin has faced international attack, all his experience as a judo black belt comes into play. He turns the attacks to his benefit, by playing the victim, showing that Russia matters again, while also increasing fear of himself abroad. Garry Kasparov may loathe him, but the grandmaster in him surely has to recognise that Putin operates more like a chess player than most of his fellow world leaders. He has a long-term objective – to rebuild Russian power. His core strategy is the assertion of his and Russian power. His tactics vary from Olympic Games and World Cups to land-grabs, from muzzling the media to rewarding cronies and keeping oligarchs on board. His pawns include Dmitry Medvedev, the president who filled in for Putin while he had a spell as prime minister before returning to the top job. He is in numerous ways a bad man, as Kasparov will be the first to allege, but he is a very strategic leader, and has – so far – outwitted his many opponents at home and abroad. It is hard to like Putin – I speak as someone who did when we first met – and some of his actions have been repulsive, but from the Machiavellian perspective that to exercise power you must hold power, develop power, use it to your own advantage, he is something of a winner. Angela Merkel is convinced Putin lowers and deepens his voice when they speak, and if the intention is to remind her of his days as a KGB interrogator, he succeeds.

So, like him? No. But looked at coldly, analytically, it is impossible to dismiss the skills he has shown in driving home his own strategic message and what he sees as his strategic advantage. He certainly doesn't. Indeed I learned via a world leader who was at the G20 summit in Brisbane in 2014 of a remarkable outburst by the Russian president, who told other leaders he was the only one in the room with a strategy, and that they were all tactical, adding 'you think your tactics will bring me to my knees but you will be on your knees first.' He had been subject to a succession of public attacks and had decided to boycott the dinner, adding 'all you do is eat.' His risk may be over-reach – and the rouble crisis not long afterwards was an indication that sanctions as well as the falling oil price were hitting him hard. But at another summit, this time NATO, a Polish minister echoed Putin's point, saying to the Americans and others that 'nobody knows what your strategy is, everyone knows what his is. Yours seems to be weakness. His is strength.' Whether he sustains his current standing depends in part on things beyond his control, but he has certainly made the weather. Looking at the world through Western eyes, we might think Putin commands respect at home and considerable revulsion abroad. However, Simon Anholt, who specialises in nation branding, and tracks how countries are seen around the world, says that whenever Putin makes what the West sees as an illiberal move, his standing rises in public opinion globally, not just at home. 'Even if people don't agree with them, they respect leaders who stand up for what they believe,' he says. 'People see a leader exercising his authority.'

Compare this with the muddle that too often governs Western strategic thinking. President Assad of Syria uses chemical weapons. President Obama, who has described this as a 'red line', says there has to be a strong response, and asks David Cameron for UK support in military action. The prime minister agrees. But this is a short-term tactical move for which there has been no long-term strategic planning. Cameron can't follow through on his promise, Obama takes much the same tack, Assad remains in place, and the West's strategic thinking is exposed for what it is, a vacuum. Politicians left and right congratulate themselves for stopping 'the rush to war', yet what has followed is in some ways even worse: as ISIS has grown in power and territorial presence, the West finds itself sharing an enemy with Syria, but is unable to share a strategy; and because Cameron was overturned on military action once, and because leaders see how George W. Bush and Tony Blair remain dogged by the Iraq war of 2003, he finds himself unable to take the action he probably thinks he should. So bombs are dropped on Iraq but not the main ISIS bases in Syria, and ground troops are ruled out in any event. There are no easy choices here, but if there is no clear strategy, the choices become harder. If the red lines are actually a watery pink, don't be surprised if pressure is ignored. Putin, in particular, has a stock response to strategic weakness – strength. ISIS has been showing the same approach, in different circumstances. And, as the satirist Jon Stewart told me, the rhetoric of leaders is that 'this is the gravest peril of our times', but they want to pretend to the public that 'it can be fixed without sacrifices such as a military draft, loss of Western life, or higher taxes'.

Part of the problem in all walks of life, and particularly in democratic politics, is that strategic thinking and communication take place under relentless and fierce scrutiny. It explains why Putin saw media control as a strategic priority, something that would of course rightly be impossible in a fully-fledged democracy. At one level, given the way the media has changed, it's therefore not surprising that leaders are becoming more not less tactical, less not more strategic. But it's a fatal mistake. The move should be in the opposite direction.

> 'Even if people don't agree with them, they respect leaders who stand up for what they believe.'
> **SIMON ANHOLT**

Some get the change better than others. Who, do you think, gave this brilliant analysis of the impact of social media and the World Wide Web on leadership, and the fear it can create among decision-makers under its relentless and hostile scrutiny?

We have gone from a vertical society to a horizontal society where everybody has an opinion about every decision you make, everybody has an opinion on the Internet straight away. Basically the respect for people who make decisions is gone because every decision is questioned. So one of the most important qualities of a good leader now is massive resistance to stress. Under stress you become smaller and smaller until you cannot give out a message any more and that, of course, is something that is vital. Many people underestimate this challenge.

I read out those words at a conference in London, and asked who the author might be. People variously guessed Clinton, Obama, Prince Charles, Mandela, Mark Zuckerberg, Tim Berners-Lee, Sergey Brin. In fact, it was Arsène Wenger, speaking to Mike Carson, the author of *The Manager*, a book for the League Managers' Association. He is right.

The mindset to hold now, compared with 1994 when we first built the New Labour communications machine, is that you can only control what you say and do; you cannot control what people say and do about it. What you say and do is more important than how others react, so long as what you do and say is consistent with overall strategy. This applies also to 'one-on-one leadership'. In their different worlds, both Wenger and Tesco's Terry Leahy argue that face-to-face communication and contact is perhaps even more important than it was before because it is the element you can best control. 'A leader cannot delegate this role to another person,' says Leahy. 'People want to see you, the leader – to look at how you behave and see whether your actions match your words.'

Many high-profile people make the mistake of confusing good press or positive social media with good reputation or outcome. One of the ironies of the media age is that its great barons have almost universally ended with their reputations in a worse place than when they started, whatever power and wealth they have enjoyed en route. On a speaking tour of Australia, I made a point at each engagement of asking for a show of hands on whether they thought one of their most famous children, Rupert Murdoch, now an American national, had a good or bad reputation. At every stop on the tour, virtually every single person said 'bad'. There was an exception of one table at a dinner in Melbourne, and it turned out the table was hosted by one of his newspapers. It is a reflection of this changed media landscape that someone with so much control of broadcast and print content around the world has nonetheless lost control of how he is perceived. Others who have endured huge quantities of negative press, not least from Murdoch's titles, have emerged stronger, by understanding this basic notion that what they say and do is more important than how others react to it, provided they are good at what they do, and there is a clear set of values and OST underpinning it all. The Queen (objective: keep the monarchy; strategy: tradition, slow adaptation – though as we will see in a later chapter, the S-word is banned by some at Buckingham Palace), Bill Clinton (objective: stay relevant; strategy: post-power politics), David and

Victoria Beckham (objective: to be global brands; strategy: fashion) are examples of people who have endured negativity, and emerged stronger, by excelling at OST.

The Sage of Omaha, Warren Buffett, a long-time critic of the 'greed and short-termism of Wall Street', has a fine way of explaining reputation. 'You can't build it in a day or a week or a month. You do it one grain of sand at a time. You can destroy it fast but build it slowly.' The same goes for strategy. The hard work is having one, and sticking to it, and landing the dots effectively.

MIXED STRATEGIES NEVER WORK

As important as not losing sight of strategic goals is rejecting goals that turn out to be contradictory. Here we're back to the need for simplicity and clarity of vision. As Tom Peters and Robert Waterman argue in *In Search of Excellence*: 'One of the key attributes of the excellent companies is that they have realised the importance of keeping things simple despite overwhelming pressure to complicate things.' Rene McPherson, when he took over at the Dana Holding Corporation, dramatically threw out 22½ inches of policy manuals and replaced them with a one-page statement of philosophy focusing on 'productive people'. The economist Jim O'Neill says that when he was working for Goldman Sachs, as head of asset management, there were never more than two or three major strategic priorities. Once out of full-time banking, with a portfolio life, he became a non-executive board member at the Department of Education, and says he was shocked on arrival to be given a list of priorities for the department. 'It was a long list. There were too many, and they didn't hang together.'

For a classic example of the dangers of mixed strategies, look no further than the fate of the England football team, predictably exiting early from the 2014 World Cup (this is not hindsight, I said publicly they would not get through the group stages, and that Germany would win). Here we have two organisations – the Premier League and the Football Association – theoretically working together for the English game, but with entirely incompatible strategies. The

Premier League is an extraordinary success story, and its chief executive, Richard Scudamore, has a very strategic mind, and power within the game sufficient to survive a storm over puerile sexist emails that would have brought down others. Objective: be the best and richest league in the world. Strategy: build a global brand through TV, delivering the revenues to attract the best players.

What that strategy means in practice is that individual clubs benefit financially and strategically and use their income to hire the best coaches and players, develop elite training grounds and sport-science systems. There's little room here for the national side the Football Association is so keen to promote, and if club coaches are being totally honest, they couldn't care less about that. Compare that with the way Clive Woodward and Dave Brailsford led a whole sport to change its ways. Or with the far more aligned and long-term strategies to be found in Spain, the dominant force in world football until their last disastrous World Cup (they failed because they stopped innovating and fought the last campaign rather than the next one, and because their key players were mentally exhausted); or in German football where the Bundesliga and the German FA work closely together, and are more strategically aligned. Is it surprising that England has failed to win the World Cup since 1966?

Changes the FA are trying to put in place, in the way coaches are educated, players evaluated and talent developed, started in Germany more than ten years ago, and they have now moved on to the next stages. Interestingly, before Germany's World Cup triumph, head coach Joachim Löw was being criticised in parts of the German media for being 'too obsessed with strategy'! Yet strategy is what gained German football its success. England's position is not going to change without strategic realignment. As he is now part of the England coaching set-up, former player Gary Neville has to be a little careful what he says about the FA, but in his autobiography, he was scathing. 'When it comes to grand strategy, the FA has not been blessed with dynamic leadership. There's been a lack of real substance at the top addressing the bigger issues of player and coach production.' He says during his long England

career, the only time FA chairman Geoff Thompson spoke to him
was to ask why he didn't sing the national anthem.

FROM STRATEGY TO TACTICS

Once a strategy is clear, it must become part of who and what you
are; this helps ensure, to borrow Jack Welch's phrase, that you 'don't
overbrain things to the point of inaction'. Overbrain! Great verb.

Now it's time to put tactical flesh on the strategic skeleton.

One way of exploring the sequence from objectives through
strategy to tactics is to look at New Labour's approach over three
successive elections.

1997
Objective: win.
Strategy: New Labour, New Britain.
Tactics: anything and everything that said we were a
changed Labour Party, e.g. sticking to Tory spending limits
for two years. No rise in the basic and top rate of tax.
New approach to business and the unions. A pledge card
setting out limited promises in five key areas.

2001
Objective: win.
Strategy: New Labour, New Britain, with focus on schools
and hospitals.
Tactics: anything and everything which showed New
Labour was beginning to deliver change according to the
promises made in 1997. Lots done. Lots to do. Lots to
lose if the Tories come back.

2005
Objective: win.
Strategy: New Labour, New Britain, with focus on
economy, Tony/Gordon back together.

Tactics: anything and everything which showed that Labour had delivered two terms of growth and prosperity, and the Tories would wreck it.

Note here that neither the electoral objective nor the core strategy ever changed. Where we were flexible, though, was in the tactics we adopted, moving on from the previous period in office, adapting where necessary, responding to new challenges. The economy is always central to an election campaign. In 1997, the tactics were all about reassurance, persuading businesses and people that we could be trusted. In 2001, with the economy doing well, the tactics focused more on using the wealth of the nation to invest in schools and hospitals. In 2005, the economic reputation was fairly well cemented, and we were able to portray the Tories as a risk, but only after we managed to get Tony and Gordon working together again. By 2010, of course, the economic debate was defined by the global crisis, so the landscape changed.

'Don't overbrain things to the point of inaction.'

JACK WELCH

One tends to associate tactics most closely with sport, so it's not surprising to find some of the finest tacticians there. Pep Guardiola, manager of two wonderful football teams, Barcelona and then Bayern Munich, was only thirty-seven when he was appointed Barca manager in the summer of 2008, and quite a controversial choice: someone who had been a very good but not a great player and whose only managerial experience was a year with Barcelona B team. He was also assuming the helm at a club that had an intimidating record. Objective: win everything. Guardiola's strategy was to play better football than anyone else. Do that, he said, and the medals and trophies follow. All his training was directed at that goal. As Guillem Balagué records it in his book *Pep Guardiola: Another Way of Winning*: 'When we have the ball, we can't lose it. And when that happens, run and get it back. That is it basically.'

Guardiola accepts that the first of his two Champions League Final wins against Manchester United, in Rome in 2009, could have gone either way. They won but it was much closer than his 3–1 win two years later, by which time he had created 'his' side with 'his' way of playing, based on guiding principles. One was that in possession they would create a 'free man' or 'numerical overload' in any area where a passage of play might start. This depended on the technical ability of the players, but there were grounds for confidence about that: most of the players had come through the club's famous La Masia academy; and those brought in from outside were recruited largely because of their technical ability. What he had to do was give them the tactical knowledge to make sure they always had a numerical superiority. This had two main advantages: first, there was always a 'safe' pass because one man was free, and second, if they were to lose the ball they had the numbers to press it and get it back quickly. In training and in matches, Guardiola enforced a five-second rule on regaining possession in tight areas, with fitness and technical training geared to that. Listening to Guardiola, it is almost as though a tactical method becomes a form of ideology. 'Always accumulate more players than your rival right from the start of a move to gain the initiative. So, having three players near the ball if the other team have two, or four players if they have three.'

Prior to the 2011 final in London, Ferguson was aware of Guardiola's strategy and in training focused on how to avoid Barcelona gaining numerical superiority in central areas. This worked early in the game with United stifling Barcelona. Realising this, Guardiola adjusted tactics slightly, with the grand strategy remaining the priority. Two key cogs in the Barcelona possession machine, Xavi and Lionel Messi, dropped a lot deeper to get possession between United's well-drilled defensive lines and they created their numerical superiority, even if it did mean they had to give up, in the short term, a slight territorial advantage. Suddenly United were on what a crestfallen Ferguson described to me as 'their carousel', the one thing he wanted to avoid, as he saw the defeat that followed as inevitable once that had happened. On the day, Guardiola's strategy was always going to be implemented, no matter how hard they had to work to do it.

GETTING THINGS DONE

Strategy and tactics are all very well, but they are meaningless if the drive and discipline are not there to enact them. Great teams and organisations therefore always make sure that there is a dynamic flow through the OST stage to putting plans into action.

For New Labour, this is where 'The Grid' came in. The Grid is a single page, one vertical column for each day, on which all the planned activities of a given week are laid out. Main government item at the top, lesser items below, other activities – for example, release of official statistics or select committee reports, plans of opponents or major events outside politics – below that.

When used badly (my German financial services friends had a grid of sorts), it is little more than a diary of events. Used properly, it is a key driver of strategy. When we arrived in Downing Street, I was shocked to discover that no such function really existed. Departments were to a large degree able to do their own thing, which meant that in terms of feeding into an overall strategy, even if they wanted to, they were operating almost by guesswork. We had exploited the lack of strategic cohesion in Opposition, and were therefore determined to ensure we repaired it, because the tactical execution of a strategy requires the people and the systems needed to give you the best possible chance of making it happen. That sounds obvious. But often it is not done.

We took organising ideas from Opposition and applied them to government – the Grid, proper media monitoring, meeting and planning structures which brought greater coherence to government as a whole. We set up new structures to make a reality of strategic communications, against considerable resistance but with some success.

On the Grid, my on-field leader was a mild-mannered civil servant named Paul Brown who, eventually, probably knew more about what was happening across government than anyone else. His job was to keep tabs on everything, and order it on the Grid in a way that suited our strategic priorities. Of course, at times this meant clashes between departments and ministers. But as the system bedded in, the realisation grew that by planning what ministers were doing, and coordinating individual actions to have their own space and impact, everyone benefited. This was about much more than dominating the news agenda. It was about bringing order to seemingly disparate events and actions. I made sure Paul understood what the overall strategy was. He made sure that the Grid reflected it.

One of the principles we operated was 'maximum openness for maximum trust'. I can see why corporations, worried about industrial espionage and the loss of intellectual property, might reject that. Perhaps Apple's notorious focus on secrecy of 'need to know' planning has been a factor in that success. But the more that can realistically be shared within an organisation, the better for the organisation as a whole. To Jack Welch, for example, the secret to running a successful business is to make sure that all key decision-makers in that business have access to the same set of facts.

Very few parties anywhere now operate without something similar to the Grid. It is a tool used by many businesses too. It seems so obvious and yet sometimes things are so obvious people assume someone else must be taking care of it. That is another SIG rule. Never assume that anything is done automatically. Make sure it gets done.

'EVENTS, DEAR BOY, EVENTS'

I doubt Harold Macmillan ever imagined that this would become one of his most famous quotes, up there with 'you've never had it so good', and the 'wind of change' blowing through Africa, in the almanac of Supermac sound bites. But the reason it stuck is the basic veracity at its heart. No matter how hard you work to stay on your own strategy, things happen all around you, all the time, which force you to adapt.

Perhaps the most dramatic example of events driving strategic change in government is the attacks on the World Trade Center, which I examine further in the chapter on crisis management. In virtually every one of the business interviews I have done, and in the business biographies I have been devouring of late, 9/11 gets a mention, not just because it was one of those moments where people like to say where they were when . . . but because it had a direct impact on their businesses: Richard Branson and Willie Walsh immediately seeing the potential crisis for their airlines; Warren Buffett fearing the impact on his insurance conglomerate; Jeff Immelt of General Electric, who had taken over as CEO just four days earlier, looking ahead to what would become a $600 million hit on their insurance business, and a huge hit on their airline engine sales; Jeff Bezos of Amazon about to do wall-to-wall media on a new deal with Target, realising it would be inappropriate, and nobody would be interested; oil companies fearing the sudden impact on prices; banks and other financial institutions losing lives, including some of their best New York talent. 'A day which changed the world' cannot be said of many days. But that one did, for just about everyone. I was with Tony Blair at the Trades Union Congress in Brighton. He rarely got a warm welcome from them at the best of times, but in 2001 he was taking forward fiercely opposed public service reforms and the airwaves were filled with talk of him heading into the lion's den. In fact, he ended up getting his first and only standing ovation from the TUC – because when he went onto the platform it was to say he could not stay because he had to get back to London to deal with the fallout of the attacks.

World leaders, whenever a terrorist attack occurs, say: 'We will

> 'Strategy is the place to have arguments, not avoid them. Strategy is a team game. Strategy is about action, not theory. The best strategies are consistent, but have flexibility to adapt.'
>
> **AC**

not be deflected and we will not change our ways.' But they are, and they do. I reflect on that every time I go through airport security. Terrorism from Northern Ireland led to a changed security culture. Al-Qaeda and other violent Islamist groups have led to even greater change, which is likely to be a part of our lives forever. 9/11 led to the war in Afghanistan. There then followed the war in Iraq, the consequences of both still reverberating. We had won the election a few months before 9/11 as New Labour, promising to put schools and hospitals first, with major investment to be backed by significant reform. We had planned for the second term to be much more about mainstream domestic policy than the first, where we had been forging new relations in Europe, taking the presidency of the G8 and the EU, prioritising Ireland, focusing on the war in Kosovo. It was not to be. Foreign policy defined the term instead.

This is the reality of government. Trying to take your own strategy forward, but also dealing with events and unexpected challenges as they arise. When it came to the 2005 election, there is little doubt that we lost some support because of Iraq. We won though. Not with as big a majority as 1997 and 2001, but a majority we would have lived with back in 1997, before the landslide. And one of the reasons we won was that even when Tony was totally consumed with foreign policy, we had the systems in place to make sure work was still being done across the public services, though not always with the grip and vigour he wanted, and when he returned to the domestic scene, he could slip back very easily into the basic New Labour strategy because it was authentically him.

Businesses and people whose reputation and success endure have a core strategy that gets stronger with time. But in a world of change, even that may not be sufficient. Famously, Kodak failed to see how camera phones were impacting on their core. Where Kodak under-reacted, Lego for its part over-adapted, almost crashing out of fear that the online world would destroy them. In reality, their core was the real physical appeal of putting the Lego parts together, and they refocused and flourished.

In South Africa in 2013, I spoke at a conference on innovation at which the speaker before me told the story of his alarm clock company. I never realised it was possible to be so passionate about alarm clocks, but he was. He gave a brief history of his life and his firm, and showed the press release he had put out in excited welcome of the advent of mobile telephony, which he said would make doing business 'so much easier as we move into new markets'. He then explained how in fact the mobile phone – eventually with in-built alarm – came close to destroying him. It was going through an airport check, and a security woman saying 'we don't see many of those any more' as she saw his travel alarm clock in his luggage, that made him realise he had to adapt to the change. He was determined to stay in alarm clocks though, so went back in time, and has now built up a successful vintage alarm clock company.

His objective was always to sell alarm clocks. His strategy and tactics changed as the world changed, but both were always rooted in knowing that he loved what he did, and that it mattered.

I started the chapter with a quote from an interview I did some years ago with Martina Navratilova. Let me end it the same way.

Do what you love and love what you do, and everything else is detail.

That might be an idealist's view of the world. But when she told me that too many people put technique ahead of strategy, when it should be the other way round, she was showing herself to be practical, pragmatic and right.

2

LEADERSHIP

'A leader never stops learning, never stops teaching, never stops looking to the future.'
BILL CLINTON

THE MERKEL FACTOR

Angela Merkel seems, in some ways, an unlikely leader of the EU's most powerful nation-state. The German Chancellor places pragmatism ahead of grand gestures, and values political and administrative competence above bold statements about changing the world. She lacks Obama's soaring rhetoric or Clinton's charisma. She doesn't enjoy – hates, even – big set-piece speeches. She does not inspire outbursts of hysterical enthusiasm. Nor, at the opposite end of the spectrum, does she provoke the sense of apprehension or fear that Putin can produce when he enters a room, with or without the dog to unleash the canine phobia Merkel developed as a child. In other words, she resembles a competent manager rather than a great leader. One wouldn't speak of her in the same breath as, say, an Abraham Lincoln or a Nelson Mandela.

But she is a winner, with three federal election victories behind her. She is also rare in modern politics in being both successful and widely respected by public opinion and by her peers. And when many of her character traits are examined closely, they turn out not to be dull or ordinary but carefully considered and brilliantly used. Let's start with the seemingly trivial. For women leaders – to the irritation of someone serious like her – there is a greater focus than with men on how they look, how they dress. Yet when was the last time you saw a feature on Merkel's fashion choices? You don't. You may be surprised to know that she travels with a stylist, a key member of her fairly small and extraordinarily tight-knit entourage. But it is more to avoid comment on how she looks than to inspire it. The stylist's task is to make sure the Merkel look is unchanging, same hair, same make-up, same style; it is a deliberate tactic that speaks to her strategic seriousness. She has a wardrobe of different-coloured jackets and trousers of the same design. Her look reinforces her political and strategic message – steadfast, serious, constant. It is also very hard to imagine her stylist recommending – or Merkel ever agreeing to – the cosmetic surgery or Botox use that some male politicians have indulged in, especially in the US, though Putin seems to get younger with age too.

A scientist by training, Merkel is also a gifted linguist, speaking fluent Russian and excellent English. This too surprises people, as she usually speaks German in public, which means that most people in the world know her through an interpreter. That approach, though, has served her well on the world stage: it has proclaimed that what she does is more important than what she says or how she says it, but what she says about a topic is more important than what others say about it.

Merkel is conscious of her strengths, and of her limitations. She will watch Barack Obama give a speech and be as moved as the next spectator by the power of his voice and the beauty of his lyricism. She doesn't waste time wondering whether she could develop such oratorical powers, because she knows she can't. But she has been known to reflect that, though she cannot orate like Obama, she is pretty sure she could get more through a seemingly gridlocked political system than the US president has done. And when she feels the CIA overstep the mark in spying on her, she does not hesitate to expel their Berlin station head, forcing a bigger power to face up to principles she appears to believe in more strongly.

Merkel, then, gives the lie to the generally accepted assumption that great leaders have to be clearly extrovert or compellingly charismatic. This fits with Jim Collins's view of leadership in business.

In *Great by Choice*, the renowned author on management describes as 'an entrenched myth' the idea that successful leaders are always risk-seeking visionaries. 'Actually the best leaders we studied did not have a visionary ability to predict the future. They observed what worked, figured out why it worked, and built upon proven foundations.' You only need to see the way Merkel behaved during the eurozone crisis, putting the long term ahead of the short term, whatever the criticism and unpopularity this approach provoked, to appreciate the thoughtful concentration that goes into her decision-making. Here, even allies like David Cameron and Barack Obama were urging her to speed up, think bigger, be bolder – classic leadership responses. Tony Blair and Gordon Brown would have done the same. But she would not be rushed; nor would she lose sight of her own, and Germany's, character and strategic priorities. If the price was deep unpopularity in some of the poorer countries of Europe, not to mention headlines, even in serious UK publications, denouncing her as 'a threat to the world', she would rather have the short-term opprobrium than live with – or let others live with – the long-term consequences of failing to do what she considered to be the right thing. She gives the impression of someone who is not going to be rushed. Whereas in Britain a coalition government was formed in five frantic days after the 2010 election, after the German elections of 2013 Merkel took a calm and orderly two months to form her 'grand coalition' with the SPD. Coalition government is, of course, a way of life in modern Germany and not in the UK, but that considered approach is telling. In this ever more frenetic world she sees the role of leadership as calming things down, focusing on the big things, taking the time needed to see them through, and – this part is not to be underestimated – to get her way.

Historian turned Labour MP Tristram Hunt says: 'There is little doubt that this period of European history will become known as the Age of Merkel. There is a dignity to her. She regards the role as significant and gives it stature; she is capable of ruthless political management to public finances and strategy but she is also there at the World Cup Final and she knows how to mix it, the dignity and the person. There is nobody else quite like her. She has elevated herself beyond others. That is quite an achievement, as is her power, considering she actually runs a coalition government.'

There have, of course, been plenty of leaders from the charisma/ visionary camp who have won, from Gandhi to Clinton, but the fact that an Angela Merkel can be so successful – or for that matter, a geeky Bill Gates or a chilled Joachim Löw – shows that something else is at work in a successful leader that is more profound. Yes, they may well have that indefinable air of authority, or immense private charm, or even a slightly controlling manner that compels attention, but that's not what sets them apart. What makes them remarkable is that they possess the ability to focus ferociously on the things that matter. Or as the American economist J. K. Galbraith put it: 'All of the great leaders have had one characteristic in common: it was the willingness to confront unequivocally the major anxiety of their people in their time. This, and not much else, is the essence of leadership.'

The depressing fact is that there are very few political leaders who meet this exacting standard. All too often, they prove to be poor strategists, who allow themselves to be buffeted about by events, rather than people with vision who have a goal to achieve. I'm often struck when talking, say, to businessmen and women, how negative a view they tend to have of today's political leaders. Former BP chief executive John Browne, for example, argues that politicians talk a good deal about 'delivery', but are not driven by it. The key to great leadership, which, as he puts it, is 'focusing relentlessly on meeting your strategic objectives via measurable results', is often sadly lacking. He believes business does it better 'because we have to'.

THE SINGLE-MINDED LEADER

Winston Churchill is perhaps the person who best illustrates the J. K. Galbraith requirements of a first-rate leader. That most dynamic and charismatic of statesmen, with a quick mind and quicker wit, proved himself ferociously ambitious and fearless when it came to grabbing opportunities to fulfil that ambition. When he failed to win the Oldham by-election in 1899, for example, at the age of just twenty-four, he made a tactical switch and set off for South Africa – where the Second Boer War had just broken out – to make his name through military glory. He then returned to England, became an MP and was First Lord of the Admiralty before he was thirty.

The point to appreciate here, though, is where that huge, complicated and idiosyncratic personality *didn't* get him. Able and forceful Churchill may have been, but a career assessment before the Second World War would hardly have judged him an unqualified success. The botched Gallipoli campaign in the First World War cost him his job. As Chancellor of the Exchequer in the 1920s he masterminded Britain's disastrous return to the gold standard. By the 1930s he was out in the wilderness, seemingly a spent force. Had he died in 1939, most of us would never have heard of him, let alone queued to name him as the greatest ever British leader. And though an enormous figure of global history now, many of his contemporaries were less than admiring. E. D. Morel, who defeated him for the Dundee seat at the 1922 general election, said: 'I look upon Churchill as such a personal force for evil that I would take up the fight against him with a whole heart.' When Churchill became prime minister in 1940, Sir Henry Channon, the Chamberlainite MP, noted in his diary that this was 'perhaps the darkest day in English history'. Those who worked with him were frequently critical, too. The Chief of the Imperial Staff, Field Marshal Sir John Dill, said ministers wasted a great amount of time having to deal with 'silly minutes from the PM'. Churchill may have had natural ability, but – certainly before 1939 (by which time, remember, he was in his sixties) – few apart from Churchill himself would ever have imagined that he was heading for a very short list of universally acknowledged great leaders.

What transformed him, and history's perception of him, was his ability in the 1930s to identify correctly the major anxiety of the time, to use Galbraith's phrase, namely the threat that Nazi Germany posed and then, after 1940, to focus single-mindedly on defeating Hitler's regime. His stance wasn't a foregone conclusion – he was a staunch anti-Communist and had previously expressed sympathy for Fascist Italy. He also had past form when it came to misreading situations and getting things badly wrong. But on this one crucial issue he read the signs and arrived at a simple truth: that Nazi Germany had to be defeated, and his and the country's energies directed towards that. All his ambition and undoubted flair had previously got him just so far. It was only when native ability was harnessed to an acute moment of insight and a dogged determination to act on it that he took the steps to becoming a great leader.

In more recent times, a political leader who, I believe, fits the Galbraith view of leadership is Mikhail Gorbachev. We spoke at the same conference in Sharjah, UAE, in 2014 and I was able to talk to him. The anxiety of his time was that the world might destroy itself through nuclear war. That was, as anxieties go, big. As Soviet president, he was one of the key architects of the end of the Cold War and is defined by that major act of leadership, his place in history secure, his reputation in most parts of the world strong, though perhaps not as strong as he would like in his homeland, where much of his legacy is being reversed by those who believe he went too far in ceding power.

He and US President Ronald Reagan, as he explained, started out from mutual suspicion, but made judgements of character and intent such that they could, to misquote Margaret Thatcher, do business with each other. Together, they took huge steps in the arena of nuclear disarmament. It was great to hear the two defining words of the Gorbachev strategy that became known worldwide, *glasnost* and *perestroika*, from his lips. It was great to hear that he was still on message – I admire a politician who sticks to his message – when saying what the world needs now is 'global glasnost and global perestroika'. This was more than an old man reliving past triumphs, because he applied those principles to the modern age. He said that governments were failing because they pretended to agree with underlying principles of openness and reform, but did not practise them. We spoke on the day Ukraine President Viktor Yanukovich fled his country. 'They talk democracy but are not democratic. They talk dialogue but it is not real. They talk engagement but they don't engage. And people won't put up with it, the corruption, the greed, the contempt for the citizens.' One sensed he had Putin in mind as much as Yanukovich.

That winning blend of vision and focus that Churchill and Gorbachev displayed is nicely summarised in the following observation.

> I would say a person who is a good leader is a person who has ideas and has a vision of the world. To have a vision of the world, you have to have a philosophy of the world and values that are important for you. So I must say the first work a leader has to do is analyse what he wants, what is important to him, and the second step is to make that real. Our job I find very interesting because it's more than being an intellectual.

The speaker here is again our more than intellectual friend Arsène Wenger, and it's interesting to note that an insight that applies so well to great political leadership should come from someone who occupies a completely different sphere. But then Wenger has thought very deeply about the nature of leadership, and the importance of focus and a driving idea. 'An intellectual,' he says, 'is a guy who lives for his ideas; a football manager is a guy who needs to have ideas as well, but then he has to show that these ideas work and to transform it into a practical aspect.'

Having a strong overall vision, and the will to see it brought into reality, has two important corollaries. The first is the very obvious one that a leader has to make and take responsibility for the really big decisions. You can have all the Cabinets, kitchen cabinets, back-room staff, friends and family, but ultimately the big decisions on the big issues – making them, taking them, seeing them through, explaining them and trying to make them work – are what leadership is all about, whether it's deciding if troops should be deployed, or if a particular company takeover is desirable, or which members of the squad should be selected for a Cup Final, or who is best fitted to be appointed the deputy head of a school. There simply is no escape from this – and every leader should have tattooed on the inside of their eyelids the words 'leaders make decisions' so that they see them when they wake each morning. As John Browne says: 'It is not quite as fast as a tennis player in a grand slam final, but the decisions come at you all the time, and you have to make those decisions, knowing you cannot always predict the outcome with absolute confidence. Leaders are the ones who can handle that, handle all those decisions coming at them from all angles.'

> 'I believe as well a leader can be a fantastic person who can influence other people's lives in a positive way.
> Therefore he has a great responsibility.'
> **ARSÈNE WENGER**

And naturally not all decisions, or the people who make them, are going to be welcomed with open arms. Big decisions are likely to be controversial. All leaders go through periods of being popular and unpopular. History takes its time to make a settled judgement. Leaders therefore have to try to handle the bad times – and there will definitely be bad times – in the same way they handle the good. Churchill, having led Britain successfully through the Second World War, had to cope with crushing election defeat in 1945, when the electorate (correctly) assessed that he was not the man to take the country into peacetime. But his resilience showed in his humorous rejection of the Order of the Garter that was offered to him: 'Why should I accept the Order of the Garter when the British people have just given me the Order of the Boot?' And, of course, he then went on to regain power six years later.

Resilience implies a thick skin, and given what is constantly chucked at people who put their heads above the parapet, this is an essential quality. The fact is that the person at the top is going to be criticised, whether fairly or unfairly. I have worked with leaders in politics, business and sport, and the one thing they have in common is the belief that they don't get a fair press. To help them keep some sense of proportion, I often bring out a file of remarks made about Lincoln, Churchill and Mandela to show today's leaders that figures greater than them had far worse to deal with 'in the good old days', and that their legend survived it all because they delivered on their major objectives. Abraham Lincoln, for example, was described by Wilbur F. Storey's *Chicago Times* as 'a lank, nerveless, almost brainless, and vacillating old man' whose 'judgment (always weak) was paralyzed'. Elsewhere he was variously described as 'a thing, mean, brutal, unprincipled, vulgar, a blunderer, a charlatan, a temporizer, a crude, illiterate, bar-room witling'; 'fungus from the corrupt womb of bigotry and fanaticism . . . a worse tyrant and more inhuman butcher than has existed since the days of Nero'. His enemies were exhorted by newspapers to consider killing him 'for the public good'. As for Mandela, it's worth recalling William F. Buckley's assessment of him in a 1985 edition of *National Review*: 'Where Mandela belongs, in his current frame of mind, is precisely where he is: in jail.'

Obviously, no skin should be so thick that you become impervious to critics who may have a point. But it does need to be thick enough to live with the hurt that criticism and attack may inflict. And thick enough to withstand criticisms that are just part and parcel of being a leader in any situation where others are entitled to express a view. Let them. But don't let them stop you taking decisions that have to be taken. And don't let second-guessing of what they might say guide the decision-making process.

THE DISTRACTED LEADER

If a great leader is by their very nature focused, it follows that the leader who lacks clear goals or is too easily distracted is rarely successful, however charming or dynamic he or she may be. This is perhaps why we are frequently disappointed with so many of our political leaders. Too obsessed with day-to-day coverage, too easily blown off track by day-to-day events, they have a tendency to flit from issue to issue, rarely engaging with them fully and rarely joining up their various responses into a considered overall approach.

It's hard to know whether this is because politics in the era of twenty-four-hour news and the Internet has got harder or whether politicians have got weaker – or both. Wherever the balance of blame may lie, it's deeply worrying. If you can't focus or prioritise, and really give the time and effort to the most entrenched challenges, how can situations be improved? And if you're always turning your attention to what is newsworthy rather than what is important (and the two are usually not the same thing) how do you create or stick to a long-term strategy? Bill Clinton, when I interviewed him after he left office, said: 'Too many decision-makers define their reality according to that day's media. It is almost always a mistake.' He is right.

What this means is that politicians all too often change strategy and message, and do not focus on a set of priorities and keep taking them forward. They get bored and distracted before the public is even aware of what it is that bores them. Remember the golden rule from the strategy chapter that 'just when the communicator is getting bored with saying something, that is when there is an outside chance of it reaching the outer radar of public opinion'. Less effective leaders lack true discipline, and, as Jim Collins writes, 'discipline is consistency of action'. He goes on to elaborate what this means in practice:

> Discipline is not the same as regimentation. Discipline is not the same as measurement. Discipline is not the same as hierarchical obedience or adherence to bureaucratic rules. True discipline requires the independence of mind to reject pressures to conform in ways incompatible with values, performance standards, and long term aspirations.

It's a world view constantly endorsed by such figures from the world of sport as Brailsford, Woodward, Mourinho. Sadly, it's less common among the political class.

Tony Blair understood this need for discipline and focus on key strategic priorities of domestic policy better at the end of his leadership than at the beginning, when he could be fretful, focus on too many things at once and worry overly what the media said about him. He says that he started out very popular, but not so effective, and by the time he was much better at the job, he had become less popular, largely because of the Iraq war. Yet many of New Labour's most telling reforms in areas such as health and education – both in terms of investment and the structural changes (academies, treatment centres, patient choice, foundation hospitals) – came towards the end of our time in office, rather than at the beginning.

VISION VS REALITY CHECKS

In my dealings with Rupert Murdoch's senior executives, I was always struck by how much he figured in their thoughts and actions, all the time. 'What would Rupert think?' was constantly on their minds. At one level this was impressive. It showed how Murdoch was absolutely at the centre of his organisation, a strong and strategic leader. People around him were anxious to anticipate what it was he wanted. At another level, though, such a mindset on the part of News International staff was indicative of a cultural problem. It suggested that a certain climate of fear operated. When people are endlessly second-guessing what their boss wants, the result is unlikely to be a happy one. They will stop thinking for themselves and they will start making mistakes. It's hard not to think that Murdoch's iron grip of his empire helped to create that fear, and that is in part what led to the cultural and moral malaise which then hit some of his papers, and has damaged his reputation.

There's a further danger with this approach: it can totally cut the leader off from a sense of reality. There is a well-trodden path among rock stars and film stars which sees them going from being normal but talented people to abnormal, unreasonable, irrational people, destructive of themselves and of others. Top-level sports people, particularly with the fortunes they can earn today, can experience a similar disconnect. This is often to do with the fact that the bigger a star gets, the more the people around them cease to act as voices of reason. Instead of protecting them from the abnormality, they play to it and make it worse. Abnormality becomes the norm, and people lose sense of the real world, become obsessed with their own, out of touch. Fame does it, wealth does it, power can do it.

> 'Keep your eyes on the stars, and your feet on the ground.'
>
> **THEODORE ROOSEVELT**

Tony Blair once said to me that the life of a prime minister was 'a conspiracy against normality'. Abnormally long hours. Abnormally big decisions. Every aspect of what you say and do subject to 24/7 analysis and commentary. Round-the-clock security. It was essential for him, therefore, to be surrounded by people who made sure that he remained as normal as possible, given the abnormal circumstances, and that his entourage similarly tried to live normal lives in far from normal jobs. To achieve this required the principle I mentioned earlier of 'maximum openness for maximum trust'. Of course some things had to stay secret. But in my experience openness in a team, wherever possible, works best.

In New Labour we encouraged a culture in which nobody had to be afraid to say what they thought, and everyone understood their role in making sure the 'conspiracy against normality' did not damage Tony as a leader or as a human being. Other world leaders were sometimes shocked at the interplay between Tony and his staff, Jonathan Powell and me especially – we both used gentle mockery to keep his feet on the ground – but nine times out of ten he welcomed it, partly because he has a sense of humour, partly because he had enough awareness of self and of history to realise power can do funny things to people's minds. I'm not sure Putin has anyone in his entourage who dares to suggest he is overdoing the macho image and should stop riding horses bareback, and bare-chested.

Once, Tony was due to make a speech almost immediately after we landed in the US. It was an important one. On this occasion it fell to my PA, Alison Blackshaw, to make sense of the scribbled changes on old drafts we were working on. Usually she would ask me to read over the new draft to ensure changes had gone in correctly. However, I was now briefing the press at the back of the plane, and Tony was agitating for the speech. She hovered by him as he read it, and after a while plucked up the courage to say: 'Prime Minister, I know you are the prime minister and I am only a PA, but I think you had it a lot clearer in the first draft you wrote at Chequers last weekend.' Tony asked to see the first draft again, read it and said, 'Yes, you're right, take those top three paragraphs and delete the first four pages of what we've just done.' It might not have been a hugely significant moment in itself, but it was symptomatic of the culture. Alison knew that if he had disagreed there would have been no blame attached to her or unpleasant consequences. Quite simply, Tony was not a big blamer.

Of course, while those around a leader have a responsibility to keep the leader's feet on the ground, only the leader can create the culture that ensures this. George Bush Jr always impressed me with the way he behaved towards his staff. He seemed to be familiar with all sorts of details about the lives of drivers, bodyguards, waiters, secretaries. Jacques Chirac and Vladimir Putin, by contrast, always struck me as imperious with staff, which made them nervous – and not in a productive way.

With some leaders, there's also the danger that their outlook changes over time: getting better in some ways, worse in others, and generally less popular with time, is a fairly common path. Looking at former German Chancellor Helmut Kohl, for example, I can't help wondering if the Kohl of the early years would have succumbed – or been allowed to succumb – to the lax approach to political fund-raising which saw his reputation as a Titan of post-war European politics crash when he preferred resignation as his party's honorary chairman to naming controversial donors whose funds he had channelled the CDU's way. For some leaders, their strengths become their weaknesses: Kohl was brilliant at reading people, and getting his way with them, even if it meant sometimes playing fast and loose with the rules. It served him well in good times, and when you are rebuilding Germany as a real power, unifying East and West, leading the process to a historic European monetary union, you are being marked out as a great historic figure doing great and historic things. But if you stop listening to others who may be warning of the dangers of something seemingly trivial alongside these important issues of state, or if one generation of advisers is replaced by another, and the second generation lacks the experience or confidence to speak truth unto power, the little things can bring you down. Leaders have to have a sense of their own agenda, they have to have confidence in their own strengths and abilities. But the longer they are in power, the less reliable their own political warning signals may be, and that is when they need to be open to the warning signs from others. All three major European leaders of that era – Kohl, Thatcher, François Mitterrand – were accused of losing touch by the end of their time in power.

There's no doubt that the media plays a part in this creation of unreality. During the Thatcher era, it changed fundamentally, becoming in some ways more demanding for leaders. Alex Ferguson cites TV as the single biggest change factor in football over his career, and it exerts a powerful influence on all areas of life – business, for example, has a global TV industry all of its own. The issue is not just the distorting mirror it holds up to what is really going on. It's that it drives leaders to believe their own propaganda when it appears to be working, and dismiss sometimes legitimate criticism when it's not, and to court popularity for its own sake, losing sight of what really matters.

Here, I have to confess, I may have sometimes gone too far during Labour's time in office. Allowing Tony to appear in a Russian soap opera for the BBC World Service. Inserting him into a storyline in *Coronation Street* (I still wince at that one). Letting him feature –

and record his own voice – in *The Simpsons* in the run-up to the Iraq war (a framed cartoon of his performance is on his office toilet wall). Saying 'Yes' when asked if I thought he should do a Comic Relief charity TV sketch with comedy actress Catherine Tate. These were all responses to the changing media landscape. They all generated very good coverage. They can all be argued for. But I wonder if we did not accelerate a trend to celebretise politics at a time when what it needed was something that played more to Tony's other strengths – strategy, seriousness, big challenges and working towards them. The symbol of this shift became the Downing Street reception at which stars like Noel Gallagher of Oasis and American actor Kevin Spacey were photographed with Tony and a headline from the time –'Cool Britannia' – stuck, and was pinned on us as something we were actively and strategically pursuing, as though the importance of modernisation lay in the lives of celebrities rather than what celebrities tend to call 'real people'. Angela Merkel's example shows that leaders – however much they may be in the media spotlight – don't have to play the media game. She went into the dressing room to celebrate Germany's World Cup win because she loves football, not to get photographed. It was the players who wanted pictures with her and tweeted them to their followers. But, seeing the speed with which politicians tweet their views about anything and anyone who happens to be in the news, or how celebrities are brought in to advise on important policy issues because of their celebrity rather than their knowledge, I fear she may be fighting a lonely battle for the political tribe as a whole.

CREATING THE INNER CIRCLE

This need for constant reality checks and sage advice from others is part of the importance of teamship which I examine in the next chapter. All leaders need a team around them. And they need to know how to work with that team, how to inspire them and gain inspiration in return. In this respect it's interesting to note that while Churchill was clearly infuriating to work for in many ways – remember Field Marshal

Dill's complaints about 'silly minutes' – according to Sir George Mallaby, Undersecretary at the Cabinet Office: 'Anybody who served anywhere near him was devoted to him . . . He continually exhibited all the characteristics which one usually deplores and abominates in the boss. Not only did he get away with it but nobody really wanted it otherwise.' Leaders must inspire through their ideas, but also through their language and their conduct.

People usually talk about 'the leader' and 'the team' but I would suggest there is also a power group between them, the 'inner circle', for want of a better term. It might be just one person, or it might be a small group of trusted lieutenants. These are not yes-men and women but the people you go to for honest views and honest disagreements. Of course, there's always a danger with certain larger-than-life leaders that they only hire people who agree with them, but great leaders are not afraid to get the best people they can. As Jack Welch, the former CEO of General Electric, puts it: 'You've got to be very comfortable with the brightest people alive being on your team. Always get the best people because if you haven't you're short-changing yourself.' Welch was big on empowering people. He urged his staff to have ideas, make sure the idea was good, the analysis was thorough and then impose it on him, the leader. Richard Branson is similarly obsessed with finding the right talent – he even goes so far as to give people new challenges in areas outside their expertise so they can 'reinvent themselves'. Warren Buffett only sets the salary of the top people in any of his businesses. After that he trusts them to decide what others are worth, and meanwhile focuses on doing the things he feels he is uniquely qualified to do, like capital allocation, pricing and analysing the numbers sent to him day after day. He demands all the data, but he lets his leaders lead.

As for Bill Gates, when he was asked at a university Q&A what his greatest decisions were, he did not mention technology or money, but said:

My best business decisions have had to do with picking people. Deciding to go into business with Paul Allen is

probably top of the list, and subsequently, hiring a friend
– Steve Ballmer – who has been my primary business
partner ever since. It's important to have someone you
totally trust, who is totally committed, who shares your
vision, and yet who has a different set of skills and who
also acts as something of a check on you. The benefit of
sparking off somebody who's got that kind of brilliance is
that it not only makes business more fun, but it really leads
to a lot of success.

The importance of key hires is often dramatically demonstrated in
American politics where the president's (or presidential hopeful's)
choice of a vice president says a lot about the political platform
being created. When a US presidential candidate selects his 'veep
running mate', it is one of the biggest media events of a campaign.
Read any presidential memoir and you will see the extraordinary
effort that goes into the research, trying to get the right person.

The media tends to focus on the
complementary skills the running
mate will bring. So Mitt Romney, the
last Republican nominee in the US,
went for Paul Ryan. Young – forty-
two – to Romney's early sixties. More
cerebral, to balance Romney's
tendency to shoot from the lip. Less
conservative than Romney on social
issues. More clearly a public service
man than a money man – they knew the Obama camp was going
to go after Romney on his wealth and how he made it. In choosing
Joe Biden as his number two, Obama was doing something similar.
Biden was older and more experienced, a six-term senator. He had
a track record on foreign policy, having been chair of the Senate
foreign relations committee. He was more street-smart, more a man
of the people.

'You've got to be
very comfortable
with the brightest
people alive being on
your team.'
JACK WELCH

When the pick goes wrong, the results can be corrosive at best and disastrous at worst. When John F. Kennedy picked Lyndon Johnson, despite the tensions between them, it was partly because of LBJ's brute political force, something JFK sometimes lacked. It was also because he did not really see him as presidential material; he thought he would be a good number two, never a number one. But the lack of sympathy between the two men and, in particular, the mutual loathing of LBJ and Robert Kennedy, caused persistent problems. It's impossible to know how this might have played out had Kennedy survived to a second term, but it would surely have had an increasingly negative impact.

Far worse – catastrophic for John McCain in fact – was the decision made by Obama's opponent in 2008 to choose Sarah Palin as his running mate. I shake my head in bemused wonder every time I think of it. McCain had attributes that Obama lacked, above all vast experience, of the world and of Washington. McCain was already in his early seventies, but he had energy and was a good campaigner. However, his 'base' of activists was anxious, and pressing for a game-changing move to counter the appeal of the charismatic Senator Obama. So he appointed Palin. Young to his old. A woman to his man. Attractive to his bald and, well, Washington-man look. Someone able to connect with 'ordinary' Americans in a way that McCain believed Obama could not. 'It was definitely a worrying moment,' recalls Obama's campaign manager David Plouffe. 'It fired up the media and the Republicans, and it certainly made the weather.'

But here's the thing. Plouffe and I agree that tactically, it was brilliant. Strategically, however, it was disastrous, and destroyed what chance McCain had of overhauling Obama's lead. To anyone with an OST approach to life, it was obvious.

McCain's objective: win the election.
McCain's strategy: experience, and differentiation from Bush.

The Palin appointment took a gun and blew a hole through both planks of the strategy. The main attack on Obama was inexperience, and he was placing at 'one heartbeat from the presidency' someone who described her experience of foreign policy as being able to see Russia from Alaska. Her interview with broadcaster Katie Couric on the subject is the most toe-curlingly embarrassing political interview I have ever seen, and I have seen plenty. Suddenly, McCain's history of heart problems became a live issue. As for the 'I'm not Bush' part of his strategy, in which he had tried to be strong on military and foreign policy, loyal to Bush but distancing himself from perceived failings over Iraq, he was elevating someone who made Bush look like a lily-livered liberal. McCain undermined his own strategy in pursuit of tactical gain, and so cut across his own objective. As such it was a disastrous failure of leadership. He was rushed by his own team into making a decision that surely, deep down – he is not an unintelligent man, and his continuing contributions to foreign policy debates show that – he must have known was a mistake. He created a global political celebrity in Palin, and a strategic calamity for himself. 'Within a few days, we knew it was definitely a mistake, which came as a big relief,' says Plouffe, 'and what McCain saw as a big moment for him became a huge moment for us. The media played along with the idea she was good for him, but the public were ahead of them.'

You find a need for the same kind of duality in football, between manager and captain. As Arsène Wenger says in *The Manager*:

> When a relationship between a captain and a manager is strong, it makes the team stronger and it makes the manager stronger. When that relationship splits, the club is in trouble because there is nothing worse for the team than to get two different messages from two different leaders.

Wenger goes on to explain how the dynamic works:

> We speak about what he thinks the team needs, and about any special difficulties inside the dressing room. He mustn't tell you everything, and usually they don't – there are

WINNERS   64

normally some things they don't want to tell you that
belong specifically to the dressing room and I respect that.
However, there needs to be trust and that trust is built by
going through a season together. That relationship is the
difference between losing six games on the trot and only
losing two or three. Through that solidarity, they get
together to turn it around.

The point Wenger makes here needs to be emphasised. He's not
suggesting for a moment that the captain should be some kind of
echo. As in American politics, the manager is looking for a complementary force. But whatever disagreements might occur in the
manager's office or the corridors of power – and disagreements can
be healthy – that inner circle needs to present a united front in
public. Most of the time I was in Downing Street, Tony and I got
on really well, despite all the pressures. The times it got difficult
was when he worried that I was allowing my mood about him, if
we'd disagreed about something, to impact negatively on the building
and the people around me. He would say: 'I need you to be totally
honest with me in here, but when you go out there, you mustn't
let people think we're on different pages, because they'll get
confused.'

To complicate matters, the dynamics within that inner circle
are likely to change over time. The longer a leader leads, the more
colleagues he or she will probably have to disappoint by not giving
them a promotion they want, or appointing someone else over their
heads. However close members of the inner circle are, this is not a
group of friends. If a leader allows personal preference to dictate
strategy, or avoids a difficult decision in order not to upset a close
lieutenant, then he is not leading. 'All things to all men' is best
taken as an insult. Difficult conversations have to be had. The best
a leader can achieve in such circumstances is openness and total
honesty. Beyond that inner circle, there are other stakeholders to
consider. A business leader, says John Browne, must, while taking
account of outside investors, directors and shareholders, take greatest

care over those who report to him directly. A sports leader has various audiences, and has to learn to manage upwards (boardroom), downwards (players and staff), laterally (fans, media, sponsors, other stakeholders). How he decides to prioritise those relationships will depend to some extent on personality, but will also dictate success or failure. Alex Ferguson, once success started to come, had a good grip on all those key relationships: a supportive board, inspired players, adoring fans, cowed media; he became untouchable, so long as the success continued, and having those relationships sorted helped ensure that it did.

Another good example of a great upward manager is Arsène Wenger, who even survived many trophyless years without being seriously under threat of dismissal. His understanding of economics and his ability to place himself at the centre of commercial and business decisions have gone down well with successive owners and boards, including the frugal American majority shareholder Stan Kroenke. Wenger won considerable silverware in his early years. But securing Champions League football for seventeen successive seasons, when constrained by a budget directed towards building a new stadium, and long-term stability is arguably as big a success, and certainly the reason he survived a period of relative failure. Wenger is a strategic leader on and off the pitch, and his real legacy might best be judged long after he has gone.

EGO VS TEAM

When management expert Jim Collins analysed how world-class companies went from 'good to great', for his book of that name, he noticed a trait in the leaders of those companies: they talked less about themselves than about the team. Collins calls them Level 5 leaders; not without ego, or self-interest, but they channel their ego needs into the larger goal of building a great organisation. 'Level 5 leaders look out the window to attribute success to factors other than themselves. When things go poorly, however, they look in the mirror and blame themselves, taking full responsibility.' Leaders of lesser, merely 'good' companies did the opposite. 'They looked in the mirror to take credit for success, but out the window to assign blame for disappointing results.'

If the leader thinks 'it is all about me', then he will not be a good leader. Even in the harsh media environments of advanced democracies, leaders tend to have people fawning upon them, making them feel more important than they are, and it can be seductive; it can make leaders feel that they, rather than the interests of the people they are serving in their leadership, are what matter most. When that happens, they've had it. Level 5 becomes Level 0. Leaders must always have a strategy. And they must always appreciate the team.

One of Alex Ferguson's biggest influences was Jock Stein, who led Celtic to become the first British club to win the European Cup, in 1967, and who had Ferguson as his assistant when he was manager of Scotland, including on the night he died after having a heart attack. Ferguson noted that both in public and private, whenever asked what made him successful, 'he always talked about the players, Jimmy Johnstone this, Bertie Auld that, never about himself'.

Great leaders, though they have to be ruthless at times, should strive to be as loyal to their team as they expect their team to be to them. Sport, business and politics have traditionally been considered macho worlds and therefore concepts such as 'giving the players a bollocking', 'hairdryer treatment' and 'taking people down a peg' have become associated with management and leadership in these worlds. But look at the great leaders, and that rarely happens. Arsène Wenger is almost comic in the way he claims in interviews not to have seen incidents in which his players misbehaved. It is his way of sticking to a principle that he doesn't criticise the players in public. Look at how Alex Ferguson stood by Eric Cantona when the Frenchman momentarily took leave of his senses and launched himself into the crowd to kick a jeering Crystal Palace supporter as he was walking to the dressing room after being sent off. Ferguson's famous 'hairdryer' did indeed come out from time to time, but far less frequently than the reputation suggests. 'If you do it every match, the effect becomes negligible. You have to know when to go over the top to get a reaction, and when to be calm to get a reaction. That is about knowing your players.'

Joe Torre, who played and managed at the top level, including winning four World Series with the New York Yankees, sounds almost fatherly as he talks about the players he managed. 'As a player you think about yourself, as a manager you have to think about all twenty-five players,' he tells me. 'You have to be able to read them. Some players say they are desperate to play but they might not be feeling that good. Some players say they don't want to play but they are just hiding their nerves that way. I felt as a kid, all the games you play, whether it is a ball game or dice or whatever, you are learning how to deal with people. As a manager you are dealing with lots of different people, lots of different characters, getting the best out of them you can, but also looking to the next team, moving people in, moving people out. As a manager I would say to the players, you just get the best out of every day, focus on your game, don't worry about the things that you don't need to worry about, leave that to me. They have to know you are their leader, looking after them as well as pushing them hard.'

The two key themes of his leadership style were 'trust and commitment'. 'You have to earn their trust, you cannot take it for granted. If you earn their trust you will get their commitment.' He says he had players who had real natural talent, but who were not winners, and some who lacked natural talent, but were. 'It's not just about skill. It's about your

> 'You have to know when to go over the top to get a reaction, and when to be calm to get a reaction.'
> **ALEX FERGUSON**

effort, and the job of the manager is to help them be the best they can be. It's like with kids in school: if a kid should get all grade As and doesn't, that's disappointing. If a kid is expected to get Bs and Cs, really does his best, tries his hardest, gets those grades, you've got to make him proud of that. In our country, I think it's a bit of a problem the idea that the only winner is the one left standing at the end. But if you do the very best you can do, use your talent and grind it out, that is a win in its own way.'

He had plenty of rules to his leadership but one was sacred. 'If it was bad news, they got it from me. If I wasn't picking a player who was expecting to be picked, if there was a player I had to trade, no matter how uncomfortable it was, I would tell them and I would try to tell them why. Sometimes they would be sad, hurt, upset, I sometimes found it very difficult, but in those circumstances I think it's better to be honest, even if it's uncomfortable, than talk to them like you're a robot. And players have to be able to deal with tough times – that is about character.'

Leaders also have to know when to say nothing. My own club's manager at Burnley, Sean Dyche, was a rough, tough defender as a player; has a rough, tough look about him – he is often compared with Stone Cold Steve Austin, the American wrestler – and a rough, tough, gravelly voice. 'You would not mess with him' has become a commentator cliché about Dyche, who has done a brilliant job at Burnley with very limited resources. Yet he genuinely stunned me when he said he never criticised the players after a match. I asked him what he had said to Scott Arfield, one of our best players, who had given the ball away against Blackburn Rovers, our closest and most hated rivals, a team we had not beaten for thirty-three years, and his mistake led to the game ending in a draw. 'I said nothing,' he said. 'What do you mean nothing?' 'I mean nothing. I just gave him a pat on the back, and said nothing. Do you not think he knows he fucked up? Do you not think he will go home and lie there and just wonder why he fucked up, and how he let everyone down? Course he knows that. So what good is there in me charging in and making it worse? We had a calm chat about it the following week, but at that point I said nothing. You have to be careful, because some players will take a bollocking OK, and it will improve them. Others it makes them worse.'

Perhaps I shouldn't have been so surprised, because whenever I have led teams, I have sought to take that approach too. It's fair to say that of all the issues that have given me political and media grief – and still do – the so-called 'dodgy dossier', a paper on Iraq under Saddam Hussein (not the one Tony presented to Parliament by the way, though that distinction has long been forgotten thanks to repeated – dare I say strategic – media misrepresentation), is close to the top of the list. I have never named the person who was responsible for taking material from the Internet without attribution, without telling me or other members of my team, because ultimately he was a member of my team, and so I was responsible. Tony was my leader, and I sought to be loyal to him, and honest with him, at all times. I led my own team and I sought to be loyal to them, and honest with them too. And I expected – and generally got – the same from them.

THE NEED FOR AUTHENTICITY

If all this implies that there is some ideal, photofit leader, then nothing could be further from the truth. There is no single style that works. Think of the world of football. Wenger is different to Ferguson who is different to Mourinho and it is hard to imagine a manager less like Mourinho than Sir Alf Ramsey. Dour, taciturn, suspicious of the media, but who would ever dare say Ramsey was not effective when he remains the only man who has ever delivered a football World Cup for England, a situation unlikely to change in my lifetime? Mourinho believes players can be personal friends of the manager. Ramsey did not. To listen to Bobby Charlton talk of what Ramsey was like to work for – it sounded terrifying at times, but he certainly got the best out of his players – is to understand that the personality of a leader, and the emotions he inspires in the team, is an essential ingredient in the team's performance. Charlton once gave me a wonderful description of mealtimes in the England camp, the players seated at round tables together, chatting quietly, Ramsey on his own in the corner, sometimes with his coach Harold Shepherdson. 'Once we had been on a fantastic overseas tour, he had organised it all, and the players press-ganged me into thanking him on their behalf. I was terrified going over to talk to him, he just had that way, but I went over and I said, "The players want me to thank you for the trip and for everything being so well organised," and he nodded, said thanks and that was it, then he went back to his dinner. So I said, "Don't know about you but now I'm looking forward to getting back to see the wife and kids." He looked up at me and said something like "If I had known that was your attitude, Bobby, I'd have left you at home!" He was impossible in some ways, but you just wanted to do well for him.'

Compare that approach with that of Vince Lombardi, perhaps the most successful and revered sports coach of all time, who led the Green Bay Packers to five NFL Championships in the 1960s. The Super Bowl trophy is named after him, such is his legend in the sport. There are so many qualities peers, players, friends and commentators recall – his analytical mind, his powerful personality, his thorough playbook, his repetitive coaching style, his fanatical love of American football – that his genuine rapport and the teamship he built with his players is often overlooked. In an interview with *Sports Illustrated* after leaving his position as head coach of the Packers to move to the front office, he demonstrated quite how seriously he took the principle of teamship and having a personal as well as professional relationship with his players.

> There's a great closeness to a football team, you know – a rapport between the men and the coach that's like no other in sport. It's a binding together, a knitting together. For me, it's like father and sons, and that's what I missed. I missed players coming up to me and saying, 'Coach, I need some help because my baby's sick,' or, 'Mr Lombardi, I want to talk to you about trouble I'm having with my wife.' That's what I miss most. The closeness.

Great leaders, then, may be warm and approachable or cool and aloof. That comes down to personality and management style.

What they do have in common, though, is that they are respected. Take Clive Woodward, for example. I would suggest that his personality is a mix of shy and extrovert, obsessive but also able to relax and laugh at himself, capable of harsh and even ruthless decisions, but also compassion. In terms of the impression he wanted from his players, though, if he had to choose between being respected or liked by them, 'I would go for respect every time.'

For all the negative media a manager may attract, the phrase he dreads hearing most of all is 'he's lost the dressing room'. It means respect has gone. When Woodward asked me to work as his communications adviser for the British and Irish Lions tour of New Zealand in 2005, one of the first things I did was get his autobiography, *Winning!* In the chapter titled 'My first day with the team', he recounts his speech to the England rugby squad the first time he met them in 1998.

> We are going to throw away all that we've ever done before
> as an international team, and we're going to rebuild it all
> from the ground with a new way of thinking . . . Whatever
> greatness you think we may have achieved in the past
> means nothing, because I don't think England has ever
> produced a great side capable of dominating the world.

It was a rather more polite version of Brian Clough's first team talk on day one of his disastrous forty-four-day tenure as Leeds United manager, when he told them they could throw all their medals in the bin, because they hadn't won them fairly.

Woodward's opening gambit was a bold move. It was ambitious. It could have been taken the wrong way, as Clough's certainly was. We discussed it in one of our pre-tour meetings. 'Some of them looked at each other, and I could see them thinking "he's talking big, isn't he?" and also maybe thinking I was criticising them for the past. But what I was doing was getting that message out, that I wasn't interested in coming second, and that to come first we were going to have to change.' At the same time he recognised one key factor in leadership: that speech was merely sowing seeds; he knew that he needed to win the trust and respect of his players, and that would be a gradual process, related to the actions inherent in the plan he had. 'It was actually something I relished. Because I had confidence in my ideas and I felt there were enough guys there who shared the real desire to win, to be better, to get the best out of themselves and out of each other, which in the end is what a team is about. I also knew there would be some who wouldn't get it, and they would be moved on and others brought in to freshen things up, give you the chance to develop a new approach, a new culture.' He had complete faith in his ability to gain the respect of his players in this way. 'The one thing I am really clear about is that leaders don't get respect by default of their position. You get it through the quality of what you do. Detail in every aspect was fundamental to my strategy and I always felt that if the players recognised that my attention to detail was second to none, on a practical, personal and professional level, then I would gain their trust.'

He also wanted his players not just to follow the leader but to be leaders themselves. Woodward views leadership as more than just giving Churchillian speeches in the dressing room. It is about educating the team on the fundamentals needed to win. 'What, why, how are my three favourite words. To achieve real excellence and get into the real detail of what you are doing to win, you have to be able to answer those three questions about everything you are doing, at all times. What are you doing? Why? How?'

Sport needs on-field leaders as well as off-field leaders. Brian O'Driscoll, the most capped rugby union player in history, who played 141 test matches, 83 as captain, tells me: 'I was twenty-three when I was made captain of Ireland. I was scared to be honest. I had never seen myself as a leader, I had only ever captained my college team twice, at under 20s. I was leapfrogging senior players and it was hard. I really had to work at making sure I said the right thing, at the right time, in the right way. But the most important

thing was always playing well, leading by example on the field. I
found that bit easier than the leadership off the field.'

ARROGANT HUMILITY

The steely resolve and sense of purpose that defines a great leader,
then, can come in many forms. It may well be wrapped up in a
larger-than-life figure; but it may just as easily be personified in
someone who, on the surface, seems self-effacing, possibly even a
little anonymous. These are the Jim Collins's Level 5 leaders like
Darwin E. Smith, a 'seemingly ordinary' man who in the 1970s and
80s transformed an unexciting paper company, Kimberly-Clark, into
a major player.

IBM founding father Thomas J. Watson Sr, and his son of the
same name who took over as chief executive, are examples of leaders
who could drive employees hard, but in the context of genuine
motivation and support, and a belief in the basic good qualities of
their workforce. Watson Sr, in carrying out an 'open-door policy',
had an unfailing weakness for the worker; his managers rarely won
when a worker complaint surfaced. On the other hand, he and his
son were tough to the point of ruthlessness when their core values
of service to the customer and unstinting quality were violated. They
saw themselves almost as parents, expecting a lot from their staff,
but caring about them too.

Ray Kroc at McDonald's is another example, a pathbreaker in
treating people as adults, in encouraging staff at all levels to make
their opinions known and to innovate, in providing training and
development opportunities for all, viewing everyone as 'members of
the family'. I was very sceptical about the McDonald's 'Academy',
until I went there and saw the buzz among young people for whom
this was their first experience of work, and they clearly felt they were
part of something bigger than themselves.

And here's the thing: leadership is not just about the man or
woman at the top. Leaders operate at every level. A winning team
is full of good leaders. You meet them behind shop counters, you

meet them behind reception desks in hotels, you speak to them in call centres – you meet plenty of their opposites too; but when you meet a real leader at any level in an organisation, you have a fair idea it is well led from the top. Go to a school, a hospital, a department store, a bank, a training ground, a campaign HQ: the first person you meet, whether a doorman, a receptionist or a PA, is the person that will guide you, they become your leader. How they do their job will tell you something about the quality of the leadership from the top. Leaders must trust their teams, but above all themselves. The best team leaders are the best team players.

3
TEAMSHIP

'If we are together nothing is impossible. If we are divided
all will fail.'

WINSTON CHURCHILL

SEEING THE BIGGER PICTURE

One of the highlights of my time with the British and Irish Lions in
2005 was an exercise overseen by Humphrey Walters, a 'leadership
and winning consultant' who has helped the England rugby squad
and Chelsea FC among others, when we were given the task of
painting 'The Big Picture'. The overall objective was to create 'a
vision of what the organisation was going to aspire to in the form of
a picture encompassing elements of what was necessary to get there',
the kind of blah-babble likely to irritate a group of elite sportsmen.

The first step was to split people into small teams. England
hooker Steve Thompson was on mine and immediately muttered
'Whose crazy idea was this?' as we were told to put on white police
forensics overalls. Each team was then given three canvases which
would form different parts of the final painting. On one canvas we
had a pencil outline of what we had to paint. The second canvas
had a partial outline and the third canvas was blank. In total, there
were sixty-four canvases to be completed.

To get our hands on brushes and paints, we had to pass a
difficult general knowledge test. The test could only be passed with
a 100 per cent score, so it became obvious that only by cooperating
with other teams would we get all the answers.

Each canvas had a grid reference number on the back. To complete the outline drawing so that the lines joined up across the panels, you had to find the team with the abutting canvas and work with them both on the outline and the colours. There was a deadline, so being able to work under pressure and in the right sequence was critical. Once the deadline was reached, Humphrey Walters took the canvases and fitted them together on a huge frame.

We had a break and came back for Walters to reveal the finished image, which included an enormous representation of the Lions logo. Huge rugby players, Steve Thompson among them, looked open-mouthed at what they had done. We were amazed at how good the end result was, given that we had had no idea of what the finished painting was supposed to look like when we were doing it. As a bonding exercise, it was impressive, and we all gathered to get a team photo with the painting, literally a symbol of what well-organised teams can achieve.

So teamship: without a great team, you cannot achieve great things. To that extent, good strategy, while vitally important, is simply the first step on the way. Strategy without a team to deliver it will be stillborn.

LEADERS, WARRIORS AND TALENT

When former Barclays and RBS executive Craig Donaldson was building Metro Bank, the first brand-new British bank in more than a century, he turned to Humphrey Walters to help shape his leadership team. 'We started out really small, four of us in a rented office,' Donaldson recalls, 'then as we grew and became successful, we suddenly had hundreds of people, stores opening all over the country, customers going into the hundreds of thousands, so leadership roles had to become more clearly defined.'

Donaldson was particularly struck by a story Walters told about England captain Martin Johnson hauling Jonny Wilkinson out of a ruck and telling him to get to his position at fly half. 'He said there were three types in a team – leaders, warriors and talent. Leaders set the direction. Warriors make the trains run on time. Talent makes the difference. Wilkinson was talent and so had to be where his talent could best be used. That insight was really important, made me realise we were all still trying to do everything, because that was the way we thought we helped each other. But actually we needed to be much clearer about who did what, and those three roles – leader, warrior, talent – helped me fashion the team for the next steps forward.'

This leader/warrior/talent distinction is a reminder that not every team player has to be a 'star', in the usually accepted sense of the word. I have been lucky enough to spend time on the road with top cycling teams, Team Sky and Garmin among them. In 2013, I had a great day out as a guest of cyclist David Millar and his Garmin team in the Dauphiné Libéré, one of the big events leading up to the Tour de France. Coaches, masseurs, *soigneurs*, mechanics, chefs, drivers, admin support – all had big roles within the team. On the road, Millar was team captain but Irishman Dan Martin was the man the nine riders were trying to support, all of them dedicated to making sure he did the best he could. Behind me in the team car sat Canadian head mechanic Geoff Brown, whose job was to ensure the riders' food stayed fresh and drinks stayed cold, and more importantly to be ready at a moment's notice to grab a spare wheel from the roof and get out and change it if a rider had a puncture. Some days, he has little to do. Some days, he saves the team. As if to symbolise the very essence of teamship, driving us all day behind the peloton was Charly Wegelius, the *directeur sportif*, directing race tactics over the radio from the car. He was a professional rider for more than a decade, and never won a single race, because that was not his job. A warrior, now a leader, directing the talent from the car.

> 'Individual commitment to a group effort – that is what makes a team work, a company work, a society work, a civilisation work.'
> **VINCE LOMBARDI**

The need for a great team to deliver a great strategy is true in every walk of life. Even golfers, boxers, tennis stars and Formula One drivers, who might look as though they do it all on their own, don't. There's always a team behind them – in the case of F1 a vast army, led by literally hundreds of engineers. When I first met Lance Armstrong, before his fall from grace, and asked him to name his greatest sportsman of the age, he said Michael Schumacher – 'no question'. Why? 'Because as well as being a great driver, what raises him above the rest is his skill as a leader. He drives that whole team. He is the difference.'

The leader/warrior/talent trilogy, and that need for different people with different strengths, is nowhere more apparent than in Schumacher's world, the world of Formula One. While races go on for over an hour and a half, round and round a three- or four-mile track, races can be decided by the few seconds a car spends stationary in the pit lane.

The pit-stop team has to carry out a pre-rehearsed tyre-changing routine, sometimes with other mechanical adjustments, every nano-second counting, every move filmed for analysis, in the full knowledge that any mistakes could cost them the race. All team members have clearly defined roles. All must be aware of these roles. All must have the trust of each other, and of the driver so he can sit stoically for those few seconds before going back onto the track for the intense physical and mental demands of driving at over 200mph with just seconds separating the cars.

As the car enters the pit lane, the number of staff waiting in the bay can vary. At McLaren, for example, it will be twenty-one, but if mechanical adjustments are required, it can be as many as twenty-six. There are three 'managerial' positions. The car-release man at the front is primarily responsible for checking that work on the front axle of the car is being completed correctly. This includes any adjustments to the front wing or brake pads. The second manager is in a similar position at the back of the car to see work on the rear axle. The third is the 'pit-lane clear indicator', who has an unobstructed view of the entire pit lane to check the safety of the car's entry and exit.

As the car stops, the front jack operator will lift the front, then swivel the jack and his body out of the car's exit path so it is ready to leave. At the same time the rear jack operator will lift the rear of the car, having prepared the jack as the slowing car enters the box. These two have the job of keeping the car elevated while the mechanics carry out their necessary duties.

Each wheel has three men responsible for the changeover. The wheel gunner loosens the nut before the wheel release man removes the wheel and clears it from the surrounding area. Then the 'wheel on man' must fit the new wheel before crouching to clear visibility so the wheel gunner can come back in to tighten the nut on the new wheel.

Meanwhile, another two members of the team – one each side – have the specific task of holding the car to ensure symmetry and to avoid a tipping motion.

Amid all this activity – the basics – there may be the need for extra mechanics as ordered by race engineering, a whole other team of people analysing data from over two hundred sensors trackside; if a steering wheel change is required, for example, the driver will remove the steering wheel and pass it out of the right side and the steering wheel changer will lean into the cockpit from the left-hand side, fit the steering wheel and immediately step away from the car. Also on standby will be two radiator duct clearers who in the event of adverse weather or debris will deal with any extra requirements.

And yes, this all has to happen in a few seconds – the fastest ever was 1.9 seconds – every moment filmed from every angle so that afterwards the management can go back and make sure nobody slipped up even by a millisecond. It's about the most perfect example there is of the power of the supremely well-organised team.

WARRIORS: DON'T FORGET THE BUS DRIVER

There's a tendency in many organisations to underplay the role of the warrior: the person who has a crucial job to do but is not necessarily one of the obvious 'stars'. In an election, a perfect example of the warrior – and proof of the need for a great warrior – is the bus driver.

The lead-up to a general election is an exciting time. The preparation work is sometimes tense and absorbing, but often dull and grinding: you have to get the logistical nuts and bolts into place, and you spend hours poring over papers and maps and diaries. Then the date is announced and amid an intense, volatile atmosphere, that preparation starts to take the shape of a real campaign, the outcome of which has the potential to be life-changing for millions of people.

During the New Labour years I would give little pep talks to party staff. It was an opportunity to make sure they understood objectives and strategy. And though we were all there for Tony, I always reminded people: 'We don't have a campaign unless and until the bus drivers are happy.' Why? Because the bus drivers were crucial to success. Let's say we had scheduled a 6.30 a.m. start but then had to bring our plans forward in the light of new data about constituencies, or to respond to something our opponents had done. That might mean the buses having to leave earlier. If the bus drivers weren't onside for that and didn't feel part of the team, as they were woken early and told that plans had changed, the campaign as a whole would suffer.

I would tell the team the famous story of an encounter President John F. Kennedy is said to have had when visiting NASA HQ. He had been talking to scientists, astronauts, the experts charged with putting together the plan to deliver on his bold objective that America should be first nation to land a man on the moon. As he left, he saw a cleaner, with a mop, and asked him – though it must have seemed pretty obvious – what he did. The reply came: 'Sir, I am here to help put a man on the moon.' I love that story. The cleaner would not know how to assemble a spacecraft, could no more fly to the moon than . . . fly to the moon, but he knew that his leader – the president – had set the objective, and he had a sense of the strategy, because it was being taken forward all around him. Most importantly, he knew that for it to be successful, the people heading moonwards needed to work in a spotless, efficient environment, and his job was to be part of the cleaning team that created it. My message to the election team was: 'Whatever your job title, whatever your role, you are here to make Tony Blair prime minister.'

James MacGregor Burns, who won a Pulitzer Prize for his biography of Roosevelt, said that transforming leadership occurs 'when one or more persons engage with others in such a way that leaders and followers raise one another to higher levels of motivation and morality'. The cleaner's response demonstrated that the team

> We achieve more together than we do alone.
> **LABOUR'S NEW CLAUSE 4**

leaders had successfully implemented two aspects of team-building: universal awareness of objective and strategy, and real motivation throughout the organisation. In goal celebrations, often the first person Alex Ferguson hugged was the kit man Albert Morgan. That sent a powerful motivating message all around the ground, the club, and to their following. In many elections campaigns, HQs will have a 'staffer of the day', and campaign managers who know how to build a team will make sure it is usually a warrior rather than a talent.

Most days in Downing Street, because I was in early, police officers, doormen and cleaners were the first people I saw. All had a crucial, specific role within the organisation. But they also had a wider role: they influenced how everyone operated. The messenger knowing you are a tea-aholic, and making sure there is a tea on your desk as you come out of the shower. The duty clerk who knows where the prime minister is, and whether he can be interrupted. The security guy who has seen you have been getting an almighty kicking, and just says 'What a load of rubbish those papers write, give 'em hell' as you walk towards the press briefing room. These people matter so much to your mood, your morale and therefore your performance. They don't just do their jobs; they make the team tick.

They also serve as a reminder that to make a team great, you don't need – indeed, you don't want – a whole group of people whose ambition is to achieve the number-one slot. Nor should it be held against them that they might not be suitable for it in any case. History is littered with people who were perfect in the number-two slot. Brian Kidd failed as a manager with Blackburn Rovers, but has been a successful first-team coach at both Manchester United and City. Al Gore very narrowly and controversially lost an election against George Bush that Bill Clinton would probably have won comfortably, but in his time he was a good vice president.

Great warriors know their worth and are happy with the role they play. I, for example, as a political editor with the *Daily Mirror*, then at the Labour Party, later in Downing Street and now in my part-time role with Portland PR company, have worked for almost thirty years with David Bradshaw, a brilliant wordsmith who can turn out words in anyone's name on any subject in a matter of minutes. So prolific was he for Tony that the prime minister was once 'honoured' (irony alert) with the 'Freelance Journalist of the Year' title at the UK press awards. I often wanted to promote Bradshaw, but he wasn't interested. He knew what he was good at, and just wanted to do it. Warrior, and talent, but preferring to be seen more as a warrior than as talent or leader, with the extra responsibilities they bring.

FINDING THE TALENT

Insecure leaders only want warriors who will obey orders, yes-men. Great leaders want talent who will challenge too. This may well involve bringing in people who are cleverer, more able or knowledge-able about certain things. It may involve bringing in people who are tricky to handle. But for a great leader the advantages outweigh the disadvantages.

Abraham Lincoln, in this as in so much else, is the model here. Doris Kearns Goodwin's book about him, *Team of Rivals: The Political Genius of Abraham Lincoln*, happens to be President Obama's favourite book, along with (they all have to say this) the Bible. I sent it to Alex Ferguson when I first came across it, and he said afterwards that though it was ostensibly about politics in a different era, it was actually about leadership and team-building, and it made him think differently about both.

Team of Rivals is essentially Lincoln's story, but it is also the story of the three people who were his rivals for the presidential nomination, William H. Seward, Salmon P. Chase and Edward Bates, plus a fifth main character, Edwin M. Stanton. Stanton had absolute contempt for Lincoln, as, at various stages, did the others.

Like Obama with Hillary Clinton (a defeated opponent he made Secretary of State), Lincoln built his team from his fiercest rivals, and somehow got them working together to manage crisis and achieve enormous change across America. His first priority was to make Seward Secretary of State. There was a fair amount of cajoling, flattery and manoeuvring before he got his man, then a little outma-noeuvring as Seward sought to press for even greater influence. In persuading Bates to be Attorney General, Lincoln seems to have left him with the impression that he was at the front of the queue for top jobs, a piece of dissembling that is not unique to politics. As for Chase, Lincoln managed to secure his service as Secretary of the Treasury.

Ultimately Lincoln had to get rid of Chase, who threatened resignation once too often, but the others came to adore him. All said by the end that Lincoln was the nearest thing to perfection in a human being that they had ever encountered. He was a great leader, in part because he was a great team-builder, one able to take talent wherever he found it, regardless of what they thought or said of him in the past. But this was also an act of strategy, summed up in his own, as ever, pithy words: 'I destroy my enemies when I make them my friends.' Perhaps he had Stanton in mind – in his kinder moments he used to call Lincoln 'a long-armed ape' – when he made him Secretary of War. Lincoln's political genius was holding all these factions together, and getting them to work as a genuine team in a remarkably difficult set of circumstances. He also knew he needed exceptionally talented people, and to achieve that he had to put to one side whatever bad feelings or thoughts he might have had, or whatever hurt he had suffered at their hands. That is real leadership, the ability to bring together people of huge ego and huge talents, and make them gel as a team.

We saw the same spirit of forgiveness alongside hard-headed reconciliation in the relationship between Nelson Mandela and President F. W. de Klerk, whose insight about the political realities, the needs of South Africa, and the character of Mandela, was so important to the final stages of ending apartheid as a governing system. They were a modern team of rivals. There were members of Mandela's team, fellow sufferers in the long struggle, who were fearful of compromise: they opposed his decision to talk to the government, and to negotiate rather than simply demand what they all – correctly of course – believed to be their right. As the leader, Mandela had to make the difficult decision to go ahead, and eventually, because his tactics worked, they would all agree that he made the right move, and pursued the right strategy. Mandela listened to the team, but ultimately had to rely on his own judgement to lead it.

> 'Coming together is a beginning; keeping together is progress; working together is success.'
>
> **HENRY FORD**

Lincoln and Mandela are likely to be linked forever as leaders who played major roles, at different points in history, in the pursuit of a world free of racial inequality. They both had remarkable conventional political abilities. But they had something else too – the ability to build and lead a team of all the talents they could find, and the ability to forgive those who had punished or sought to damage them, and include them as key players in the team. We took some of those lessons and insight into the Northern Ireland peace process. One of the reasons it worked as well as it did was that fate and chance had conspired to have a large number of exceptional people in the right place at the right time. Tony and Bertie Ahern leading their countries. Clinton as US president, fascinated by the issue and dedicated to doing what he could. Sinn Fein leaders Gerry Adams and Martin McGuinness deciding to take a different course when they did, and able to take most of the Republican movement with them. John Hume and Seamus Mallon in the SDLP. And for all that they could be infuriating – as exceptional talent often is – both David Trimble and Ian Paisley at different stages played fundamental leadership roles in making change happen. There was a lot of luck involved. But there was a lot of talent around too, and it made the difference; and at various points there was a willingness to forgive, even if they will never forget the atrocities or injustices of the past.

A willingness to utilise the abilities of very diverse, sometimes combative people is common to most successful organisations. When I consider Tony Blair's first election team built in 1994 – built with our objective (winning) and strategy (modernisation) in mind – I see a leader determined to get the people he wanted, and I see a large collection of people of enormous diversity. We had people like Jonathan Powell, chief of staff, who had a brilliant diplomat's mind but could be naive when it came to everyday politics. (That could also be a strength – inexperienced in the ways of the Labour Party, he would often say 'Isn't this a bit silly?' and so challenge conventional wisdoms.) We had arch-modernisers like Peter Mandelson, close lifelong friends like Charlie Falconer and Anji Hunter, traditional policy wonks like David Miliband. We had people who were conciliatory and others who were challenging, and some, like Philip Gould, with his insightful strategy papers and brutally frank focus group reports, who could be both: my favourite of his thousands of memos memorably began: 'From PG to TB, cc AC/JoP – Basically, the public think you are losing the plot, and if you don't get a grip soon, you're on your way.'

THE ROLE OF THE INSIDE OUTSIDER

If it's vital to make sure you have strong talent within the team, it is also important to have 'team members' who actually stand outside

it. In political campaigns, for example, I have found Alex Ferguson
a great provider of support and advice to me, particularly on dealing
with pressure. When Dave Brailsford was worried about anger towards
Victoria Pendleton, who had become romantically involved with coach
Scott Gardner in clear breach of a team rule, he decided to think
right outside the box: he came to talk to me about Northern Ireland,
and how the process of reconciliation had been managed. It wasn't
a crazy idea. So much of what we did in Northern Ireland involved
trying to get through emotional and historical barriers to focus on the
here and now in a way that benefited the process going forward. That
was what Brailsford was trying to do with Pendleton. Some of the
same principles applied – focus on where we are trying to get to,
repair relations which are fractured, in a way that respects all sides
in terms of understanding how the problem arose. Then talk, trust
and negotiate. Pendleton and Gardner had clearly gone against the
team rules and culture, but ultimately Brailsford did not want to lose
a great talent. Gardner was obliged to leave the team, but eventually
Brailsford decided the only way to resolve the situation was to accept
what had happened and give Pendleton the support *she* wanted, which
included being allowed to have Gardner both as her partner and as
part of her coaching team. She won a gold and a silver medal at the
2012 Olympics, and married a year later.

The point about 'inside outsiders' is not just that they can bring
a fresh perspective to what may seem an intractable issue, but that,
because they are not an integral part of the team, they are free from
the prejudices and emotions that inevitably shape life on the inside.
Political leaders, indeed all who are in a high-profile position, are
wise to hold on to school friends, university friends, former colleagues
from different walks of life, experts met along the way, to perform
that role.

MANAGING THE TALENT

'There are two types of player,' says Roy Hodgson, who has managed
sixteen football teams in eight countries. 'The players who bring

what they have to the team and make the team good, and players who use the team to make themselves look good.'

A remark like that immediately brings to mind the prima donnas of life – self-obsessed, difficult and wayward. But it's interesting to note that Hodgson acknowledges how many great talents are also great team players. It's a view shared by one of baseball's greatest names, Joe Torre. 'As a player,' he tells me, 'I always had the team thing, if I could help the guy to the next base, and there is nobody out, great, it is not just about hitting a home run.' And it was a mindset he took with him when he moved from being a player to becoming a manager. He went out of his way to make sure that great individuals appreciated their role in a wider group. 'The atmosphere you build within a team is so important. I would rather a team where everyone made a contribution than a team where we are looking to one or two guys to do everything. What I would always try to convey to my players is that if we can get that team atmosphere, special things can happen.'

He tells me the story of an important Yankees play-off game in 1996, when he had to make a selection choice between two players, Darryl Strawberry and Cecil Fielder. 'Both had talent, both had different qualities. They both wanted to play but Darryl said to me, "I think you should play Cecil because he will take it worse than I will if you don't." This was not about Darryl lacking the will to win, or the will to play, he had both of those, and he was a great player. This was him understanding the team dynamic, and not just thinking of himself. You need grown-ups like that in a team. That is what I mean by special things happening.'

In this context I'm reminded of a story that cricketer Brian Lara told me about a conversation he had, as a young player trying to get into the West Indian team, with the legendary Vivian Richards. 'Viv said I just needed to go out and score hundreds. This is Viv Richards talking so you listen. But for the next period I could hardly hit it off the square. And I worked out it was because I was just thinking of me, my score, my game. I had taken the team element out of the equation and it wasn't right for me.' Richards batted

often at number 3 and while he didn't want Gordon Greenidge and
Desmond Haynes to lose their wicket, 'he couldn't wait to get out
there. He just wanted to bat.' But as Lara graphically points out:
'The thing is you have to be open to all options. If you're sitting
there as a number 4 or 5 batsman and you're hoping the openers
stay in for a couple of hours, take the shine off the ball, tire out the
bowlers, so you can go in and do your stuff, in other words only
thinking of your own situation and your own score, you might not
be in the right mindset when the wickets fall and you find you're
out there early with the ball still shiny and the bowlers pumped up
and on top.' It's not just common sense that should make a talented
person a team player, but a degree of self-interest too.

It is when you get to the crease, says Indian great Sachin
Tendulkar, that you must focus more clearly on yourself. 'The
essence of cricket is batsman versus bowler, one against one, every
ball a duel. You know always you are playing for a team but when
you are out there it is you against him. Everyone else is there as
support,' he told me.

Of course, there still remain the great stars who are not natural
team players. Interestingly, I can think of comparatively few in the
world of business because I think that even the greatest entrepreneurs
very quickly realise that they need good people around them. But
sport inevitably abounds with them. And they can – of course – be
tricky to manage. Think of the early Cristiano Ronaldo – a truly brilliant footballer who had a tendency to separate himself from teammates when celebrating, pointing to his name on the back of the shirt,
then beckoning colleagues to salute him; or, according to coach René
Meulensteen, sometimes playing the blame game when things didn't
go so well. Ferguson's attitude to him is a revealing one. Famed for
his insistence on the wider interests of the team, he nevertheless made
huge efforts to keep Ronaldo happy. 'When managing exceptional
talent,' he says, 'you have to make sure you are creating an environment that makes them feel they can become the best in the world
because that is how high players like Ronaldo are always aiming.' He
even went so far as to design new changes to the training ground

'because Cristiano will appreciate it'. Pep Guardiola would name Lionel Messi as his most special talent at Barcelona, and in 2008 gave a very good illustration of how to handle such talent. Messi was sulking because the club was refusing to let him represent Argentina in the Beijing Olympics, which clashed with the Champions League qualifiers. He even took the case to a tribunal, which ruled against him, and in favour of the club. Guardiola saw an opportunity and persuaded club president Joan Laporta that short-term loss would be outweighed by the long-term gain of making Messi feel valued. 'Leo, I'm going to let you go because I have been an Olympic champion and I want you to be one too,' he said. 'But you owe me one.' Messi was thrilled, helped Argentina to Olympic Gold, and thereafter played his heart out for Guardiola.

It's a delicate balancing act, which can very easily tip if not carefully managed – alienating other members of the team who may feel under-appreciated. At the very least, you need an astonishingly strong team spirit to cope with the large ego. Ben Ainslie, the world's most decorated Olympic sailor, and leader of the most remarkable team comeback of modern times, when he turned an America's Cup 8–1 deficit into a 9–8 victory, is adamant that in any team you look not just for the most talented but also for the right mix of person-alities to cope with what can otherwise become an unstable group dynamic. 'I could see some members of the team weren't being used properly. It just needed someone with a fresh perspective to come in and say, "We can still do this but you guys all need to do more." My role was a mix of sailing and leadership. You need more than one leader in a team but they can't be all leaders,' he says, a remark that reminded me of Clive Woodward's observation: 'You need more than one obsessive in a team but they can't all be obsessives or the whole thing would go haywire.'

Ainslie explains that during the race, the whole team is wired up to be able to communicate constantly, but only the helmsman and the tactician speak. 'The key to teamship is everyone having clearly defined roles and carrying them out, being aware of the roles of others but giving them the responsibility to get on with it, and also understanding that mistakes get made, and when they do, you just get on with it. Teammates don't have to be best friends, but there has to be respect.'

> 'You need more than one leader in a team but they can't be all leaders.'
>
> **BEN AINSLIE**

Dave Brailsford says: 'The main job of a coach is compliance. Once you understand the optimal training programme to achieve your goals, it is about finding the way to get the team member on board with that training programme. It doesn't work if they only do 80 per cent of what they need to do. Everyone has to be integrated and everyone has to be working at their best for the team to be at its best. They can't all be the same, but they can all be the best they can be.'

I ask Mercedes team boss Paddy Lowe about the difficulties, well documented, of managing both Lewis Hamilton and Nico Rosberg, part of the same team, but both desperate to win. What would he do if he felt one of the drivers was doing something to damage the prospects of the other? 'There have been a few instances of that,' he smiles.

'They're not teammates at all, are they?' I suggest.

'That's a good point. No, they're not really. One of my biggest headaches has been about trying to create fairness between two drivers who both want to win.'

'Do they try and psyche each other out?'

'Yes, probably.'

'Is that a good thing?'

'Yes, I think so. In the end they are sportsmen and if you remove from them a sense of competition they're going to start underperforming.'

'But you're like the manager of two sportsmen competing against each other in the same team.'

'I suppose so. On race day I sit bang in the middle of the pit wall. The thing is they both want to win, and that's good. We want them both to do well and we support them in that. They do have to respect each other, and for sure they do.'

I should say here we met before the infamous incident at the Belgian Grand Prix when Rosberg clipped Hamilton's car and ended up facing what Mercedes called 'suitable disciplinary measures', believed to be a large fine. Relations with Hamilton, which were already strained, were inevitably stretched further by this unfortunate collision. At the time, Rosberg was ahead in the overall championship standings, but the incident served merely to fire up Hamilton even more, and he went on to beat his 'teammate' to the world title.

WHEN TALENT HAS TO WALK

Obama campaign manager David Plouffe says they 'learned from the infighting of the Clinton machine', adding: 'We were a very cohesive unit around him, and that sense permeated throughout the whole campaign, right down to precinct level. If campaigners feel the team at the top is not united, they are likely to reflect that. If the people around the leader show clear unity, that too becomes habit-forming for the team. People don't have to want to spend every minute of every day together, but they definitely have to have a sense of working for each other. If the leader of the team signals that he is a team player, that has a real force in a campaign, in terms of organisation, motivation, the energy people are prepared to put in. And the fact that when things go wrong he will maybe just give you a bit of a beady look, but there are no recriminations and no shouting because frankly there isn't time, the challenge goes on, you pick up where you left off and you go back to work for the team.'

When Gordon Brown and Peter Mandelson, back in Opposition, were refusing/failing to work together, we got chief whip Donald Dewar, respected by both, to manage a reconciliation of sorts. The relationship between Gordon and Tony in government, though, proved more problematic – and at times more toxic. And this raises the question whether, however talented Gordon undoubtedly was, it would have been better for the team as a whole had Tony sacked him. As Tony says in his memoir, the problem with Gordon was that he was both brilliant and impossible.

The tragedy of the New Labour years is that Tony and Gordon started out as friends and colleagues, and achieved great things together, but ended as rivals – the opposite journey to that taken by Lincoln and his team, or Obama and Hillary Clinton. Tony certainly thought about sacking Gordon often enough, and was close to it once or twice. I felt at times he should, at others he shouldn't. When I interviewed Scotland's First Minister Alex Salmond for *GQ* magazine prior to the Scottish independence referendum of September 2014, he said that if your gut instinct says you should make a big call, it is best to make it early, adding that he was in no doubt Tony should have sacked Gordon. I am still unsure. When it came to the 2005 election, I felt our only chance of a clear win rested in a strategy focused on the economy, which meant bringing Gordon back to centre-stage, with an understanding that he would eventually take over. We won the election, but given all that has happened since, inevitably people still wonder whether it was the right course to take. Talking to some of the Lions players – I was preparing for their tour of New Zealand at the same time as trying to direct the 2005 election campaign, and like everyone they were reading media reports of difficulties between Tony and Gordon – they were very much in the 'get rid of him' camp, coming as they did from a world where even the best were dropped from time to time. One or two of them suggested we tried 'marriage guidance' or 'therapy sessions'! When I told Tony sometime after I had left Downing Street that I was seeing a psychiatrist regularly for my depression and addiction issues, and that it might be an idea to get him in to have a session with Tony and Gordon, he laughed. 'I am prepared to think out of the box,' he said, 'but not that far.'

In politics, of course, you don't always have carte blanche when it comes to selecting people to serve on your team. Coalitions might be forced upon you. Diplomacy requires you to work with other leaders you may detest. You may find yourself having to accommodate particular interest groups, or take account of people's health or personal scandals which lose you members of your team and force you to rebuild. But the question still arises: at what point does a talented person become more trouble than they are worth?

For me, the classic case is President Truman's dismissal of war hero General Douglas MacArthur, who had been Supreme Commander, Southwest Pacific Area, in the Second World War. He had defended and later retaken the Philippines, accepted the Japanese surrender and overseen the occupation of Japan between 1945 and 1951. Unlike Truman, who wanted to limit military intervention in Korea, MacArthur wanted to invade China and smash communism, if necessary using nuclear bombs. Truman ordered him to stop promoting ideas that directly contradicted government policy. He didn't, and on 9 April 1951 the president removed MacArthur from his command.

A year after Truman's death in 1972, broadcaster Merle Miller published a fascinating oral biography, including an interview in which he said:

I fired him because he wouldn't respect the authority of the President. I didn't fire him because he was a dumb son of a bitch, although he was, but that's not against the laws for generals. If it was, half to three-quarters of them would be in jail . . . I'm afraid he wasn't right in the head. And there never was anyone around him to keep him in line. He didn't have anyone on his staff who wasn't an ass kisser . . .The only thing I learned out of the whole MacArthur deal is that when you feel there's something you have to do and you know in your gut you have to do it, the sooner you get it over with, the better off everybody is.

The candour in that statement is remarkable, way beyond what he said at the time, but all true, and driven by the threat MacArthur was posing to teamship, and so to the execution of government strategy.

As a Sunderland FC supporter, Metro Bank CEO Craig

Donaldson says he learned from their one-time manager Martin O'Neill, who told him some of his squad were 'fantastic players but not nice people, not team players', and that he was moving them out. Donaldson now operates a FIFO – 'fit in or fuck off' – approach to recruitment and personnel development. 'If people support the team culture, there will be a role. If they are cynical about what we are trying to do, there won't.'

DEALING WITH THE ENERGY SAPPERS

If highly talented people can sometimes cause disruption to a team, so can their opposites: the people in every organisation who are jobsworth, negative or disenchanted. There are always some, which partly explains why Jack Welch had his rule that the worst performing 10 per cent of staff had to go every year. Funding Circle, the innovative peer-to-peer lending firm, follows a similar course.

When I was flitting back and forth between the Lions' preparations in Wales, and the Labour 2005 campaign in London, I became acutely aware of the 'sappers' element at Labour HQ. We won that campaign, but we could have won more conclusively had we all managed to pull in the same direction without the energies of some being sapped by the negative energies of others. I'm reminded of the quote board on the wall as you enter the training ground of my football team, Burnley: *'Only the person who isn't rowing has time to rock the boat.'*

I have lost count of the number of sports coaches who tell me they have visited, or would like to visit, the SAS headquarters in Hereford. You can certainly learn a lot about teamship and the winning mindset there. There is a very simple reason why they are called special forces: they are very special. One of the most impressive groups of people I ever met in my life was a special forces team working in Afghanistan, who oozed not just physical and mental strength and courage, but camaraderie and mutual respect. Clive Woodward is a fan of the military too, and it was after a team visit to the Royal Marines in 1999 that he made some important judgements about which of his

England rugby players were energy sappers and which were energisers – 'they're the two main types in a team'. He wanted a squad full of the latter, with no place for the former. He saw energy sappers as the main obstacle to success and was determined either to change the character of the players in question – not easy – or to remove them from the team. After some of the exercises with the marines had been completed, the brigadier overseeing the England team's visit, unprompted, gave Woodward a list of players who 'would never make the marines' because of their general attitude. It matched Woodward's own list of doubtfuls and energy sappers, and they were moved out and replaced.

Dave Brailsford nicely sums up the kind of people he wants on the team and the culture they need to feed. 'I want a culture that is hungry and ambitious, doesn't see barriers, constantly creating, but organised and disciplined, otherwise change can spiral out of control.' As we chat, he sketches out the 'Energy

> 'Only the person who isn't rowing has time to rock the boat.'
> **SIGN AT**
> **BURNLEY FC**

Investment Model' by Donald Tosti, whose work became prominent in the 1960s. It has energy along the x axis and attitude along the y. High energy + positive attitude creates a team player. Low energy + negative attitude creates a drag on the team. In the other two quadrants are 'positive attitude + low energy = spectator' and 'negative attitude + low energy = cynic'. There is not much to do with the people in the bottom left-hand quadrant. The other two groups can be guided and coached into the top right-hand box; and if they can't, it's FIFO time. 'When I'm implementing change we want all people involved in the process to be players, with positive attitude and high energy. Spectators won't have ideas on implementing change and cynics will only see the barriers in implementing change.'

More often than not, he says, he prefers the cynic to the spectator. 'If someone is in a cynical mood towards change we can have a discussion and if the leadership is good you can win them round.

Spectators are more difficult. They are the guys who don't give you an opinion on what you're doing and just say "yeah, I like that". It goes without saying you have to just get rid of all staff in the low-attitude, low-energy section.'

For his part Jack Welch calls them 'resisters', adding: 'These people usually have to go . . . They are change killers: cut them off early.'

BUILDING THE TEAM

One of my favourite theories of team-building is the so-called Tuckman Theory, named after an American professor in educational psychology and group dynamics, Bruce Tuckman. It is a four-phase approach: forming, storming, norming and performing (FSNP). The six young Manchester United youth players – David Beckham, Nicky Butt, Ryan Giggs, Gary and Phil Neville, Paul Scholes – the class of '92, who became the nucleus of one of the club's best ever teams, are a great sporting example of it. In the forming phase, team members are cautious and uncertain. Think that 'first day in a new job' feeling, or the suspicions the five Northerners had of 'cockney boy' Beckham. As people begin to settle in under pressure, with conflicting perspectives and opinions, team members jockey for influence and battle to be close to the leader, in Manchester the youth team coach Eric Harrison. Patient and impatient people clash in this storming phase, trust becomes important and if there is no clarity around goals and roles, confusion and division surface. A leader has to make sure that he marries the right people to the right roles and has the right people working together in order to negate the potential impacts of the storming phase, when the team comes together, and starts to gel, hopefully in a creative and energetic environment. That certainly happened with the Manchester United youth team. It happened too with current World Champions Germany, whose players grew up together under a modernised system. Their final against Argentina was a classic encounter, with the best player in the world, Messi, against the best team. The team won.

The norming phase of FSNP comes when people get to know and accept each other and develop the 'norms' that make up the formal and informal operating systems. Partly as a result of a mistake in the forming phase of New Labour when, stupidly, John Prescott was excluded from some important strategy meetings, we set up a new structure. In advance of shadow Cabinet meetings, there was a gathering of the 'big guns' – Tony, John, Gordon and Robin Cook, with me and sometimes Jonathan Powell as the only non-politicians. It was often a very difficult forum, but we tried to ensure it was the place where strategic and policy arguments were confronted rather than avoided so that these four were broadly on the same page before taking issues to the shadow Cabinet. The final stage, performing, takes place when understanding and experience within the organisation is used to produce results for the team and for one another. The quicker a team can shift through the gears from forming to performing the better. That is when teamship develops. The team behind the London 2012 Olympics showed this kind of process being put into place again and again.

FROM TEAM-BUILDING TO TEAMSHIP

Effective team-building recognises the core principle that it is not possible to separate the performance of the individual from the performances of other members of the team. Like another quote from the board hanging on the wall at Burnley FC's training ground dressing room: *'In a real team, the instinct for individual self-promotion is realised through the pursuit of the team goal.'*

The effective team has good leadership, a strong and shared sense of strategy and objectives, the resources to deliver them, and clarity as to individual roles. That is the essence of *team-building*. Slightly separate from this is *teamship*, which is more like the glue that holds the team together: a sense of openness and creativity, a resistance to the blame game when things go wrong, and a culture that encourages development, adaptability and endless renewal. Another way of looking at this is to distinguish between differentiation and integration. *Differentiation* is the process by which organisations allocate people and resources to tasks and establish relationships in order to achieve goals, dividing things up to give the team the best chance of success. *Integration* is the process of coordinating tasks, people and functions to achieve unity of effort – getting everyone to 'pull in the same direction' or 'be on the same page'. Effective leadership in implementing these two elements together is the key to team-building.

> 'In a real team, the instinct for individual self-promotion is realised through the pursuit of the team goal.'
>
> **SIGN AT BURNLEY FC**

In New Labour, we did team-building well, teamship less well, differentiation OK, integration less so. Compare and contrast the ups and downs, the fallouts of the New Labour years with Warren Buffett, in his eighties, and still able to boast that no CEO of his companies has ever walked; or the 'band of brothers', as Gary Neville calls the class of '92, or the similar story at FC Barcelona. Xavi, a double European Cup winner and a true one-club man, says Barcelona's La Masia academy develops players and human beings: 'The majority of us are from "this house" – not just the players, the coaches too, the doctors, the physios, the handymen. We're all Barca fans, we're all a family, we're all united, we all go out of our way to make things work.'

So once you've built a team, how do you engender teamship? Ensuring people are properly motivated is at least part of the answer. In psychology, motivation is defined as the process that initiates, guides and maintains goal-orientated behaviours. It is what causes us to act, whether it is getting a glass of water to reduce thirst, or delivering a speech to make a point central to a campaign. It involves the biological, emotional, social and cognitive forces that activate behaviour. In everyday usage, however, the term *motivation* is frequently used to describe *why* we do something. In order to build a successful team and give your team the best chance of achieving your objective, having every member of the team motivated to achieve the same objective is essential. This is why the first three chapters of this book are so inextricably linked. OST is imperative because you can't have everyone motivated to achieve the main goal unless the objective, strategy and tactics to get there are coherently communicated to all staff. And the principles of teamship and leadership are what provide the framework for motivation. Yet again, the Brailsford cycling revolution is a good example. Tim Kerrison, his head of performance support at Team Sky, says that the 'culture of excellence' and the 'passion for continuous improvement' operate at every level. In the retail sector, John Lewis is regularly cited as being among the most efficient, most popular and most admired companies. Its ownership model, in which 70,000 employees are partners with a genuine stake, puts teamship right at the heart of the company philosophy. Some of the best corporate videos I have ever seen have been from John Lewis where staff talk about the company, and the sense of genuine belonging comes through. And when managing director Andy Street talks of 'the happiness of our partners' as being the firm's 'ultimate higher purpose', on paper the words can look sickly, but heard amid the culture of the company, alongside people who work there, they feel totally authentic.

Just as important as understanding what creates teamship and motivates individuals to become team players is realising what does not. Money would be high on my list. People want their skills and talents properly recognised, and that is partly done through wages, but we also need a sense of purpose and dynamism – something to get us out of bed in the morning with real desire and expectation.

Purely financial reward is rarely, if ever, going to provide that – and if a team member thinks it is all that matters, then alarm bells should ring. It's interesting to note how rarely successful people cite money as the single driving factor (though I suppose a cynic would argue that that's because usually they have it).

The Internet era has led to the creation of some of the richest – and youngest – billionaires of all time, yet one Internet star who stands out from that is Wikipedia founder Jimmy Wales. He is far from poor, has always run a for-profit business alongside the Wikipedia charity, and makes good money delivering speeches around the world. But perhaps the question he gets asked more than any other, given Wikipedia is up there with Google and Facebook as part of Web history, is whether he resents not being in the billionaire class with their founders? He gives a convincing sense that the answer is no. 'I honestly never thought about it in terms of money,' he tells me. 'I just had the idea of an online encyclopedia, it took us a while to work it out and when we did I just wanted to make it work. I am not sure it would have been so good if we had thought about it as a moneymaking venture. Sure if you have 550 million people using it that is a big advertising opportunity but I never wanted advertising on there . . . I think for something that is about trying to help the world have all human knowledge for free, that doesn't work.'

He also defends those who have become billionaires, saying they have rarely had wealth as their main motivation. He recalls a 'geeky lunch' in Davos, attended by the founders of Facebook and Google, super-rich hedge fund managers, and a US senator or two. 'I was sitting next to Mark Zuckerberg and some of these finance guys started talking about what kind of private jet they had, and I said to Mark "Have you got a private jet?" and he said "What would I do with a private jet?" I think when he talks about connecting up the world and making it a more peaceful place, that is the motivation. Sure, it is commercial and they make a lot of money but I don't think that is the driving thing. I don't even think about not being a billionaire except when people ask me. I don't envy those guys, I feel we did something very different, very good for the world, very good in terms of spreading knowledge, something that will last. That means more to me than not being a billionaire.'

Certainly, in my view, when it's just money that counts, the results are seldom happy, and don't make for contented, well-motivated teams. I was asked to address a hedge fund and investment bank conference, with the specific brief to advise them – frankly and, yes, lucratively – on how to deal with the 'opprobrium' (their word) they felt. I said maybe they had a bad reputation because they deserved one, not least because they never put their heads above the parapet to explain what they did, appeared to be motivated by money alone, and felt the inequality which most people dislike was actually OK. They knew intellectually that they ought to do something about it, but didn't know how. One of them told me that if he chatted to a stranger on a plane or at a reception, he said he was an engineer. I thought that was sad. At one level – measured in purely financial terms, the size of their homes, cars, boats and bank balances – these were highly successful people. But the teams of which they were part were producing dysfunctional results – think of all the banking scandals there have been, and the loathing of the bonus culture by those outside it – precisely because they were being motivated by the wrong things, self and profit, not team and mutual advance. I have done some work with Berenberg Bank, whose former UK chairman Andrew McNally is arguing publicly now for a new approach to capitalism, based on equity not debt, and underpinned by greater social purpose. He says: 'The financial world is full of very wealthy, very unhappy people who fail to see there might be a link.' He is wealthy by most standards, but says he is more motivated by his approach to the need for a new set of dominant values and debates about a different post-crash capitalism. And while there is plenty of evidence to show that as a person moves from poor to comfortable, their happiness grows too, there is no such correlation in the move from wealthy to very wealthy.

Twitter co-founder Biz Stone, who has gone from an upbringing on welfare to a life of exorbitant wealth, has an interesting take on this, saying in his autobiography that having a lot of money 'amplifies who you are. If you're a nice person, and then you get money, you become a wonderful philanthropist. But if you're an asshole, with lots of money you can afford to be *more* of an asshole; "why isn't my soda at sixty-eight degrees Fahrenheit?"'

Arsène Wenger says in *The Manager* that the hardest but most important element in recruitment is establishing what intrinsically motivates players. He looks for the answer to these questions: 'does he have a willingness to learn, a hunger to improve? Is there an inherent competitiveness, and a desire to win, that underlines everything they do? Players are made very rich very quickly, so if he has the money and is only motivated by the money, where does he go? We manage to keep traditional values at the foundation of all we do; respect for people, solidarity when people are in trouble, supporting players' families, keeping our word. Basically old-fashioned qualities are still respected here and maybe that is why people have fond memories of our club.' Solidarity, support, values – these concepts are fundamental to good teamship.

He can get quite emotional when talking about the power of a team culture. 'Solidarity is very important. You can see this when individual sports are turned into team sports occasionally – like the Ryder Cup in golf. It becomes a different sport. It adds something by being together, the emotions, going for something together, and suddenly the interest becomes bigger, suddenly it is about "us" not "me". Human beings subconsciously understand that alone I am nothing, but in a team I can achieve great things.'

Indeed, the first evidence of sports psychology as a science is thought to be the work of Norman Triplett of Indiana, who discovered in the 1890s that people rode their bikes faster if they were with others.

One of the most stunning examples of this phenomenon, and the power of a team, is the race that led to Michael Phelps breaking the Mark Spitz record with his eighth gold medal in Beijing. It was the 4 x 100-metre freestyle relay, and the medal was brought home not by Phelps, but teammate Jason Lezak, who overhauled French world record-holder Alain Bernard on the final leg. At the changeover, Bernard was a body length ahead but Lezak, at thirty-two the oldest male swimmer at the Games, delivered a world record split time, 46.06 seconds, to help the US win by eight hundredths of a second, the closest race in history, both the US and France almost four seconds inside the previous world record. So Lezak, swimming for a team of four, and knowing a place in history for someone else was at stake, swam faster than he had ever swum for himself, by a margin of almost two seconds.

Sadly, there are still plenty of instances of great teams who achieved great things but who never quite achieved great teamship. Fulwell, the independent film-makers who made the *Class of '92* documentary – essentially the story of six players forging friendship through teamship – wanted to put together a similar film on the key architects of New Labour. The idea was to take Tony, Gordon, Peter

> 'Human beings subconsciously understand that alone I am nothing, but in a team I can achieve great things.'
> **ARSÈNE WENGER**

Mandelson and me, and film us talking about the old days, and then meeting all the other key people like John Prescott, Bill Clinton, other politicians and team members. I mentioned it to Tony, who laughed even louder than when I suggested he and Gordon have a joint shrink session. So I told Fulwell: 'Sorry, no chance.' It is sad, really sad, considering the success we had together. In sport, the concept of teamship is bolted into the core of everything. Some are better team players than the others, but they do at least understand the value of the team. Politicians seem more suspicious of the concept of the team. There is a reluctance to have a shared agenda, they constantly want to marry it to their own. In a democracy, winning is about the only way of addressing it within a party, and even that is not totally guaranteed, as Thatcher and Blair both learned. Or Clinton or Bush, both of whom had to deal with warring factions in their administrations. But note how often the absence of teamship ultimately ends in tears.

I recall being with Australian PM Julia Gillard in Canberra on the day former leader Kevin Rudd made his move against her. It was brutal stuff. She knew she had lost control, that the enmities against her from Rudd were now unmanageable. She was putting on a brave face, knew that the coup was coming; and as I talked to people that day I remembered a phone call I received from my friend and fellow diarist, Tory MP Alan Clark, in the run-up to our second election landslide win in 2001. 'We are totally fucked,' he said. 'Glad to hear it,' I replied, 'but why?' 'Because we now hate each other more than we hate you.'

If the world of politics has anything to tell us about teamship, then, it is about the dangers of not having it. On this topic few are more qualified to speak than Ric Charlesworth, a first-class cricketer for Western Australia, an Olympic medal-winning hockey player and a successful coach, but also a medical doctor and for ten years a Labor MP. He contrasts the team ethic that he finds in an operating theatre or in sport with the naked and often self-serving ambition he noted in politics. 'I saw the worst of it,' he says, 'a lot of self-interested people, people passing questions to the opposition to ask their own minister to embarrass him.' And it's interesting to note in this context how different the route through politics is from that you find in other walks of life. Here there's virtually no training or talent management; assessment, recruitment and promotion systems are haphazard and rarely explained, so that 'who's up, who's down?' is as much about gossip and often wrong conventional wisdoms as about hard analysis. Difficulties that a business leader or sports manager would eradicate are tolerated because 'politics is different'. The system of 'candid, consistent feedback' that Jack Welch feels to be so vital in business is lacking.

Peter Hyman, a colleague of mine in Opposition and government who has since gone on to found and head one of the first free schools, judged 'outstanding in all areas' by Ofsted inspectors, says he took lessons good and bad from politics. Good was resilience, the importance of vision and narrative; bad, the lack of proper systems to manage and develop the team. 'I think politics is uniquely bad at certain things, there are no proper management structures, and that goes for the Civil Service as well as the ministers and the special advisers. We managed to get a lot done and more or less make things work because there were always a lot of big brains in the room, enough people with nous and energy, but it really was no way to run an organisation as important as a government.' He was critical of the

culture in political circles, where the tendency leans towards demoli-
tion of arguments rather than construction of ideas.

I wonder if this natural tendency to look for differences with
colleagues in politics, rather than forge teams, stems from the fact
that to become a politician, you must first make that very individual
decision to go for it. Talented athletes discover their talent young
and so perhaps they are more willing to look to older people, parents,
coaches, agents, to guide and nurture, even when they are supremely
famous and wealthy young men and women. People building a
business rarely do so on their own. They have an idea and then
they need to find the money and the people to help develop it, and
if it works, and they grow, they have to build a bigger team.

For a politician, though they might be inspired by a party, and
share its values and policies, it is nonetheless a hugely personal and
life-changing decision to stand for election. You know the team
matters, but it is not essential to some of the early steps you take
on the political ladder. I think a lot of people in politics underplay
the influence those around them and those players of the same
'team' can have on their success. It is certainly a lot easier to ignore
them than in a football match, a rugby match or on the roads of
the Tour de France.

CREATING A TEAM CULTURE

When Tom Peters and Robert Waterman in their renowned business
book, *In Search of Excellence*, conducted a survey of 2,000 male
adults working in business, they discovered that '70% of the sample
placed themselves in the top quartile for leadership qualities, 60%
rated themselves in the top 10% of the population when it came to
getting along with others'. Yet they also discovered that most bosses,
alongside a positive assessment of themselves, take a negative view
of their team. So, for example, whereas at high-performing IBM
they discovered that goals and targets were managed so that 70–80
per cent of employees met them, at another company only 40 per
cent did so. In other words, although most people start off with a

positive view of themselves, those who lead them often undermine this fatally when they are putting a team together. 'Label a man a loser and he'll start acting like one.'

Peters and Waterman discovered that 'most managers know very little about the value of positive reinforcement. Many appear either not to value it at all, or consider it beneath them, undignified, and not very macho.' However, their evidence showed that excellent companies not only recognise its significance but know how to manage it well. That includes, of course, not overdoing it: praising every single action loses its impact.

If giving praise where praise is due is one essential attribute of a successful team, not taking credit for someone else's achievement is a natural corollary. Harry Truman was right: the team will achieve more if nobody cares who gets the credit. It must have been tough for designer Jony Ive to hear Steve Jobs take public credit for work and ideas that came from him and others within Apple. But if Jobs can perhaps be forgiven on the grounds that in aligning himself with all the great ideas and innovations he thought he was serving the brand's broader strategic goals, Ive can be praised for never ceasing to regard himself as part of a team. It is enormously to his credit that his colleagues tell how 'he always says "we" rather than "I" when talking about new products or new designs – even when we know it was really all down to him'. Another Jonny, Wilkinson, who has probably done more Man of the Match interviews than anyone else, always made me smile when he was speaking on TV: even if he had scored every point, he would always first talk up the team, never his own role.

What neither Jobs nor Ive can be denied is the passion they put into their work, and how that passion has communicated itself throughout the organisation, and ultimately to customers as well. A culture is built on the values and beliefs of a company, and the intensity with which they are understood and communicated.

Management guru Jim Collins, author of *Good to Great*, writes: 'The good to great companies did not say, "Okay, folks, let's get passionate about what we do." Sensibly, they went the other way

entirely: We should only do things that we can get passionate about.'
He cited interviews with board members at Nucor, pioneers in mini-
mill steel manufacturing and one of his good to great companies.
Only one out of seven picked technology as the number one factor
in the shift, and most focused on work ethic, simple structures,
resistance to bureaucracy and imaginative recruitment. These are
cultural drivers around which a team can be built.

Some view culture as something an organisation 'is' (my view)
and others as something an organisation 'has'. However, successful
leaders must believe that a new team culture *can* be created. There
are quite specific symbolic things that can be done to create a sense
of shared culture: the colours that sports teams wear, a company
uniform, a flag or logo, the physical environment and equipment in
which people operate, the norms and patterns of their lives together.
Every school you walk into feels slightly different; that is because
of its culture, which penetrates walls and stairs and ceilings. Culture
transcends individuals within the team and so upholds the values.

As important as building shared
goals is removing obstacles to shared
goals. At Barcelona, Pep Guardiola
insisted on Castilian and Catalan as
the only languages spoken, and
arranged seating plans at mealtimes
to encourage the players to avoid
cliques. His rules and fines system
were not about control but, rather, to encourage solidarity and
responsibility. He hated that the first team trained with journalists
and fans watching, so pushed through the development of a
'fortress' where the players could practise, relax, eat, rest and
recover in seclusion and as normal human beings while retaining
the feeling of an elite environment.

> 'Label a man a loser
> and he'll start acting
> like one.'
> **PETERS
> AND WATERMAN**

Some of the most exciting and dramatic stories of teamship
come in the music world, where bands form and, as often as not,
bands fall apart. Bono has described to me the feelings he has for
his U2 bandmates. He says they all have big egos, there can be

friction between them, and sometimes the other three might resent his special fame as lead singer and global campaigner, but they are a real team and when they take to the stage, 'There's a really powerful chemistry there. We feel it, and the fans feel that we feel it and that becomes part of the whole show. It's a wonderful feeling.'

No team-building experience is better and more direct than the one where each individual thinks they can learn from, rely on and trust the person sitting next to them in the war room, or playing alongside them on the stage or on the pitch. When that happens, not only is it a great feeling, which builds strength and confidence for any future challenge; it also means that a 'culture' has taken hold. It is not dissimilar to an army, where soldiers know they can trust each other, both their ability and their character.

These exact same words and concepts – trust, mutual respect and clarity of role – came up when I interviewed Bear Grylls, now a worldwide TV star with his survival and adventure programmes, an accidental career he embraced after being invalided out of the SAS with a broken back, and then being noticed for an extraordinary book he wrote about climbing Everest. 'The SAS is a team of individuals. It is the ultimate meritocracy, it doesn't matter how you speak, if you have earned that beret on your head that's it. Once I joined, I felt so proud to be part of this family that I would do anything for them, never let them down.'

That is what Clive Woodward told me he wanted in his dressing rooms – 'a player looking right or left, and whoever is there, he knows he can trust him'. Aussie Rules coach Leigh Matthews goes further: 'I'm convinced that a successful footy team needs the same fabric of trust, respect and role-playing discipline as an army would going into battle.' It's the same in political campaigns. Unfortunately, it doesn't happen as regularly as it does in sport. Indeed, there is one glaring omission from this chapter, the New Zealand rugby team which, despite Woodward's preparations, tore the Lions apart. There is a whole book on how the All Blacks became the best sports team in the world. Given the painful memories, I am not the person to write it.

4

THE STRATEGIST: JOSÉ MOURINHO

'Winning is not the only thing that matters. But it is certainly the most important.'

JOSÉ MOURINHO

José Mourinho is without doubt a successful leader, a renowned team-builder and motivator, and by my definition someone possessed of a good strategic mind. Looking at Mourinho through my OST prism, I see someone whose objective is always to win (be that a match, a tournament, the race to sign a player, a fight with the media, a mind game, or a battle to secure his reputation); whose strategy is rooted in building the teams that suit the style of play he wants to impose on his own players and then his opponents; and whose tactics are endlessly, pragmatically adaptable according to who those opponents are.

As a strategist and a massive football fan, I thought all this with absolute conviction – until I sat down and discussed Mourinho and his beliefs at length with the man himself. Then I found myself and my own long-held views, not just about Mourinho and football but about strategy more generally, being challenged. And who am I to argue with Mourinho, who has delivered success in four countries, and has become a byword for charismatic, innovative leadership in the world's most watched and most important sport?

His first managerial job at Benfica in 2000, after coaching roles at Sporting Lisbon, Porto and Barcelona, was brief but successful.

He then took over at lowly União de Leiria in 2001, leading them to their highest ever league finish. Success at Porto brought him to much wider attention. After his appointment in 2002 he won the Portuguese League and Cup double and the UEFA Cup in his first season, before stunning the football world by winning the UEFA Champions League in 2004. Between then and 2013 he managed Chelsea, Inter Milan and Real Madrid and won trophies in every single year, becoming only the fourth manager to win league titles in four different countries. So the record is pretty clear. But how? And why did we disagree on strategy when I have always tended to the same views on the subject as one of his greatest rivals, and a manager he admires, namely Alex Ferguson?

The key to understanding him, I think, is that in addition to being a leader, team-builder and strategist, he is a disruptor. He has certain fundamental footballing principles, but he loves to surprise, and to upset the equilibrium.

It is when I ask him what strategy and tactics mean in a footballing sense that the disruption begins. He takes quite a while to answer, in between giving me the shrug and the curved bottom lip pout which are known to millions around the world who follow the Premier League and enjoy his colourful, cocky, never dull match day interviews.

'In the end I don't think there is a big difference between strategy and tactics. Not in the names.' This is not the answer I want, or expect, and he can see that from the puzzled expression on my face. 'For me in football the difference is that the strategy is directed to a certain moment or a certain game. The tactic is something you develop over time, all the principles of the game you train day by day by day.'

'In my world,' I say, 'it's the other way round. The strategy is your driving plan. The tactics are directed to a certain moment.'

'Not for me,' he shoots back. 'The tactics are the model, the principles. So let's say, day one, I come in, I want Chelsea to be a team that is always pressing, high up the field, high pressing, blocking, that is what I want. The basic tactics are made up of, say, twenty items. So, when the keeper has the ball, does he go short or long? That is a tactic. When the other team has the ball in midfield, where do our players go, what do they do, what is their aim at that moment? When a striker moves into this area, that area, what is he looking for, what is he trying to do, how do the other players react, when he moves there, where do they go, what are they looking for, what are they trying to do to the opposing defenders? These are parts of a tactical model, they are like the DNA of the team, the tactics that say what kind of team we are.' These are ingrained in the players through hours and hours, day upon day, of training habits and decisions to make sure the tactical plan is understood and executed.

'Strategy – being strategic – this is when you do something for a certain moment or a certain game. Every game, we analyse opponents, real depth, real detail, and then we try to predict how they play and we say "so today we add a particular strategy to our tactical system". If we play Liverpool at Liverpool we add this to the way we play. Then maybe the next game is Hull City here [we met at Stamford Bridge, Chelsea's stadium] and we play a different way, we make this strategic plan, we add it to the tactical model, the basic tactical model is the same, the strategy depends on the moment, depends on the context.'

I think I can see what he is saying. In his case – and perhaps this applies more generally in sport where tactical considerations are so often the difference between winning and losing – his objective is winning; his strategy

> 'The tactics are the model, the principles.'
> **JOSÉ MOURINHO**

is tactical supremacy; and his tactics are strategic adaptation. Now maybe I am trying too hard to fit his own views to mine, but I ask him if I am on the right track.

'Yes, exactly,' he says, then he reflects, tries to think of an example I might understand. The night before, Uruguay had beaten England 2–1 in the World Cup. Mourinho was clearly unimpressed by England's response after Uruguay's first goal. 'So they are losing, and if they lose, they are out of the tournament, so they have to score. They made two changes at 1–0 down in the game. But when [England manager] Roy Hodgson made these changes, Sterling out, Barkley in, then Lallana in for Welbeck, I couldn't see a change in the game. Same tactical model, same system. No strategic change. It was like he had taken this [picks up the glass of water in front of him] and replaced it with this [puts my glass where his had been]. The same against Italy, glass for glass, glass for glass. Only late against Uruguay when it was 2–1 and a few minutes left, Lambert on, midfielder off, did he change glass for bottle.'

Mourinho is less jovial than I expect him to be, but much more open and also much more thoughtful. Before answering directly my next question – what should Hodgson have done? – he says something which makes me wonder if he isn't reflecting on our differing definitions of strategy and tactics. 'I am glad you bring up this point, about the strategic side of the game. Strategy is needed more and more, because as the game has grown and developed, so has the technology that is used, it has all changed, and it means everybody knows everything about everybody.' As a result, he says, 'it is more difficult to make a surprise'.

I bring him back to the point under discussion. 'What about Uruguay and England?'

'Yesterday Uruguay was playing with Suarez and Cavani up front, two up front. England have four at the back – Johnson, Cahill, Jagielka and Baines. You are losing 1–0, you need to get a draw at least, so I say take one defender off and play three at the back, put an extra man to midfield/attack. You still have three v two at the back. With four v two you never get a man anyway, the strikers move around, they pull you apart, break you up, three v two you can go man to man and one gives cover and sweep. So maybe take off Baines and play Cahill sweeper, Johnson and Jagielka marking one each, an extra man to midfield or attack, and then Uruguay has to adapt too.'

You can see differences in the way teams play the game that flow from the personality of the coaches, he says. As an example he points to Argentina coach Alejandro Sabella. He considered him to have been 'more strategic' in the game against Bosnia-Herzegovina than Hodgson had been, or Spanish coach Vicente del Bosque, whose period of extraordinary success in recent years ended in abject failure in Brazil 2014, the first team to exit the tournament, with England not far behind. Argentina were expected to win against Bosnia, they were leading 1–0 at half-time, but playing badly. 'Their tactical model was not delivering as expected, so Sabella changed it. They started three central defenders plus the guy from Man City, Zabaleta, on the right, and Rojo on the left, so five defenders. But he was not happy, so he took one defender out and brought in an extra striker, Higuaín.' The smile indicates Mourinho's approval. 'That was good strategy. He was already winning. Normally when someone reacts to the strategy point of view it is because there is risk, things going wrong. He did that and he was winning.' Hodgson and del Bosque, he says, are 'more traditional, more calm, with less intervention, but Spain, they played two matches and did exactly what I am saying to you.

> 'Strategy is needed more and more, because as the game has grown and developed, so has the technology that is used, it has all changed . . . everybody knows everything about everybody.'
>
> **JOSÉ MOURINHO**

Glass for glass. They are losing – so Diego Costa out, Fernando Torres in. Why? Play them together. You need to change. They will say, ah, but Spain has its own system, its own philosophy – hell, if it is not working, you change.'

I hope Mourinho won't object when I say that, looking to political parallels, he reminds me of Ho Chi Minh, the revolutionary leader who went on to become prime minister and president of Vietnam. Ho Chi Minh did some seriously bad things in his time – no real comparison there then – but in terms of using the right tactics, analysing the external environment and his opponents to win in conflict, he was brilliant. He was pragmatic to the last, both in the international diplomatic arena and on the war fields of Indochina. The fact that there still remains a debate about whether he was a Communist or a Nationalist demonstrates his chameleon-like ability to adjust strategy and tactics dependent on external conditions. Is Mourinho an exponent of the beautiful game, or someone happy to grind out 1–0 wins? He is both, but because he has success and charisma, we tend to think more of the beauty. Perhaps it is this pragmatism that makes him see strategy and tactics not so much as separate parts of the operation, but integrated and interchangeable.

It was hard not to laugh when Mourinho criticised Sam Allardyce in post-match interviews for playing 'nineteenth-century football' when he sent out an ultra-defensive West Ham side to win a point at Chelsea; because if there was ever a game that Mourinho could only win by playing prehistoric football, he would.

'Surely Allardyce was right to play the way he did,' I say, 'if he decided that was the only hope of getting a point, stopping you from playing, going for a nil-nil draw.'

'Of course he was right.'

It's interesting that Mourinho singles out Liverpool when giving his general answer about adapting a tactical model with a specific strategy, for it was he who put a stop to Liverpool's Premier League title hopes in 2014, with a 2–0 win at Anfield, despite a truly paltry 27 per cent possession during the game. Liverpool manager Brendan Rodgers complained afterwards that Chelsea 'parked two double-decker buses' in front of a goal (the cliché for a defensive set-up is usually one bus). Just how much his players sign up to the Mourinho mindset, however, was clear from the comments of André Schürrle afterwards: 'The purpose of the match was to win. We won. That is all. People who criticise us are jealous, pure and simple, because we won.' Schürrle is now a World Cup winner with Germany too.

Mourinho is one of a growing number of managers who did not play to a high level. He insists this has never been a problem with players, and I sense here, too, it is because he has taken a very strategic – my meaning not his – approach to his own career.

Recognising he wasn't going to make it as a player, he turned his mind to being a manager at a very young age, though he was in no rush to get there because he knew he had a lot to learn, and set about learning it with the same methodological approach he brings to opposition analysis. He studied sports science at university in Lisbon, an education that would allow him to implement innovative ideas on the approach to fitness specific for football. At the same time he took all the necessary coaching courses in Scotland. He also worked as a PE teacher – according to colleagues applying the same level of detail he applies to management today – and coached at youth levels in Portugal. However, it was when Bobby Robson became manager of Sporting Lisbon that Mourinho gained his real opportunity for on-the-job learning from a master. Fluent in five languages, he was appointed as an interpreter for Robson who had no knowledge of Portuguese. Mourinho impressed Robson not just with his translation skills but his ability to impart football knowledge to the players, both in training and during games. Over time Robson began to give him more responsibility on the coaching side. He then took him as a coach, translator and eventually assistant manager when he moved to Porto and then to Barcelona. After Robson left Barcelona it was expected that Mourinho would leave with him but new coach Louis van Gaal was also impressed with the abilities of the young Portuguese and kept him on as his assistant.

While Mourinho comes across as someone who always wanted to be a manager, always knew he would be a manager, and a good one at that, he says this long learning process he went through was the most important part. 'When I took the decision to be a manager and stopped being assistant, it was when I felt I was completely prepared from the technical point of view. That academic part or the formation part is the most important part.' When he was mocked by fellow manager Carlo Ancelotti before a Champions League game in 2010 for having no

> 'The purpose of the match was to win. We won. That is all.'
> **ANDRÉ SCHÜRRLE**

experience as a player, Mourinho retorted with the fact that he spent the time Ancelotti was a player learning how to be a manager.

If any players were tempted not to take seriously someone who had no senior playing experience, he quickly blew them away both with his motivational skills and above all his attention to detail. Not quite Ho Chi Minh here, who spent two years preparing and planning for the single battle of Dien Bien Phu in 1954. But talk to anyone who has ever played for Mourinho, and before long 'his attention to detail' comes up as one of his key leadership strengths. This is shown in all the key areas of management that players perhaps notice most – training, recruitment and opposition analysis. Mourinho is fascinating on all three.

He is a moderniser when it comes to training, a product of that very early decision to do a degree in sports science. He understands the value of the information the science geeks give him and knows how to apply it to training. He is well known for introducing football-based fitness sessions, seeing very little value in old-style long runs or sprint sessions without a ball. His fitness coach, Rui Faria, is heavily involved in the planning of all sessions and has more input than most fitness coaches at leading football clubs.

We met just after the fixtures for season 2014/15 were announced, and Chelsea's first game was away at Burnley, my team, so I took the opportunity to ask him how he went about analysis of the opposition. He said that as soon as Burnley were promoted, his backroom team would have begun some analysis. Once he knew it was the opening game, he would watch a couple of videos of an entire Burnley match from last season himself, and expect his analysts to watch a lot more. But he was also making his own analysis of the bigger picture. 'They keep the same manager, so even though a top team in the Championship has to prepare differently to a team in the Premier League that will be one of the weakest, their basic approach will be similar to last year. They are not a rich club so they are unlikely to bring in six, seven new players. We will be looking at basically the same team, and at a minimum I must get to know their players. We will be finding out where they are training pre-season, what friendlies they have, and we will send people to watch. If they are in Austria say, maybe one of the TV channels there will cover it, we get the video, I watch it maybe. I have to prepare the team properly every game, but I don't like to play Burnley first. They are feeling like winners, they are new, the fans are excited, it is like a Cup tie. So the analysis will be deep, to try to find their weaknesses.'

When the game came around, I was in my usual seat at Burnley a few rows behind the away-team dugout. Having talked to him, it was fascinating to watch him. I could see from his reaction when a Chelsea player did something that did not fit the tactical model. Virtually every time a player played the ball backwards, he would stamp, pout, wave his arms, turn to his assistants and express his displeasure. When Burnley took the lead, his face became a picture of grim determination. When Chelsea equalised, he celebrated for a few seconds, then found one or two things to criticise about the goal they had conceded three minutes earlier. When they scored a beautiful second goal, following what seemed like dozens of passes, including one that was sublime from new signing Cesc Fàbregas, he celebrated with a lot more gusto, and evident pride. And when they scored a third, before half-time, he ran all the way down the bench, fist-bumping or hugging all the substitutes. Yet for me the most impressive moments came as the final whistle neared, with the points pretty well wrapped up, when first John Terry made a slip, and then Gary Cahill passed the ball backwards when Mourinho wanted it passed forwards, and he was still stamping his feet and demanding to know why the tactical model was not being followed.

At half-time and full-time, I chatted with Chelsea technical director Michael Emenalo, who is responsible for recruitment, liaison with the board, and advising on all football issues. He was happy, not least because Fàbregas had played and fitted in so well. But when I mentioned Mourinho shouting at Cahill towards the end, he said: 'Ah, yes, José always wants more, that's how he is.'

On recruitment, Mourinho says: 'Scouting is difficult for me, because I cannot travel so much. During the season I don't have so much time but also if I go to watch a game it is immediately a big noise, who is he watching, who is he trying to buy? So others have to watch, we have recruitment people everywhere. But when I feel comfortable to tell my club "this is the guy", it is usually when the players are playing in the same league where I am or where I have been. So Fàbregas, I know a lot about him. He played in my league four years, two here and two in Spain, he is a player I have seen many times, playing against my teams, I learn a lot, also I watch him every week on TV. Let's say there is a good player at CSKA Moscow, he is recommended, I watch videos, I like him, maybe I travel to see him play once but I don't know enough so it is a gamble. Can I trust him? Can I trust his people? Will he fit with the others? The scouting department are good at always trying to give you the best information but it might not be enough.'

'Ah, yes, José always wants more, that's how he is.'

MICHAEL EMENALO

Just as he is not quite sold on my concept of strategy, he takes something of a different view of leadership too. In managing footballers, it is less about vision than knowledge, he says. 'I think the thing that I have that has helped me be successful in my career is the way I am prepared for my job, the knowledge I have about my job. People used to think that it is about personality, the way you lead people, this kind of thing. These can be a plus but the basic thing of success is the way you are prepared to do the job. With my personality, principles, my leadership, these are all things that are complementary to what I do.' Surprisingly perhaps, given rugby is not a huge game in his native Portugal, he is a big fan of the game, but he says there is no way he could transfer his skills to that very different sport, much as he likes it. 'If I was to be a rugby coach I would not be successful, I cannot read the game, cannot feel it, smell it, don't know how to organise a training session, develop players. I know football. I would fail at rugby.' Modesty Mourinho-style.

Mourinho is acutely aware of the need to stay ahead of others when it comes to analysing developing trends of change. Football is a very fluid industry. All of Mourinho's top players are internationals, so they mix with players from other clubs, they work for different coaches, they talk, they swap notes in the everyday run of things. They also get transferred, and what manager would not want to pick the brains of a player who had come from a top rival club working under a top rival manager? Mourinho has another example. 'Assistants become managers,' as he did. 'So my assistant becomes a manager somewhere else. He takes with him everything we have done, everything we do, all the knowledge. New ideas spread quickly. So keep having more new ones.'

He points to the decline of Spain at the 2014 World Cup, and alongside it Barcelona's poor season by their standards, to show what happens when a team excels and, bit by bit, other people catch up unless the team manages to think about the next thing and the next and the next. 'The teams that do well, everyone looks at them closely. You see that another team stopped them from scoring. Get me the video, how did they play, how did they do that? What were the tactics? You also look at the team itself and you see how they play, and you can take things from that too. You have to keep trying to improve. Even if I win a title, I am never happy.' This restless desire always to improve requires the kind of devotion and dedication that means holidays are short and interrupted, and there is little time for other interests. He says he will be a football manager 'for as long as I can – what else am I going to do if I don't have football?' The only time he seems to struggle in our interview is when I ask about outside influences, role models, people in different walks of life who have inspired him or made him think about things differently. He says he occasionally saw a motivational quote that said something about a situation he was in, but that was about it. 'Sure, you might look at something a Bill Gates or someone said, but football is so specific, so intense, it is every day. Three matches a week means six press conferences, so we play, we train, we analyse opponents, we do media, we work hard. Maybe others do it but I find I do not look outside the game.' I don't detect much sentimentality in there either. Does he miss Fergie? He shrugs. 'Life goes on.' Did he feel sorry for David Moyes when he lost his job at Manchester United? 'I feel sorry for anyone who loses their job.' Was it an impossible job? 'Why impossible?'

> 'You have to keep trying to improve. Even if I win a title, I am never happy.'
>
> **JOSÉ MOURINHO**

Mourinho has never been out of work since he became a manager, and you sense he would find life difficult if he was not involved in running a football club at the highest level. 'I could never be an international manager. Not enough games, not enough time with the players, not enough training, not enough intensity – that is not a life for me.'

He says change in management has been dramatic since he worked for Bobby Robson at Barcelona in 1996. 'Everything has changed. Before, football was made by managers and players, nobody else. In this moment it is the players, the entourage, families, agent, the father, the uncle, the social media, it is a totally new world.'

It is what the players have become in terms of their celebrity that has driven a lot of the change, he says. 'I find the direct relationship with players OK. If you are a real leader and experienced and strong and they feel that, it is not a problem. The problem is all the things they bring together with being a player these days. I can say to the team, "So tomorrow we have a game, so no commercial work today. But an agent – someone who is also making money out of the player – he may already have organised it, a player is booked to do something to promote a product, a commercial thing, and he has already told the press, fixed an interview. So you are permanently in these situations where you have to fight, you have to confront all the problems. This is the change. And you must select which are big problems and which not, which fights to pick.'

He says that when the social media revolution was beginning, the reaction of most clubs and most managers was that players should be banned from using it. 'It was a big drama, what if they leak information, what if they show pictures from the dressing room, the dressing room is sacred. But you couldn't stop it, and you were crazy to try. These days, they tweet in the hotel, on the bus, in the dressing room, before the game, after the game, sometimes a picture hugging an opponent!' The grimace suggests he does not approve but he says: 'If you cannot stop something, you must adapt. If I stopped a player, he would just tell the agent, the brother, the girl-friend, and they do it for him.'

I don't think he is asking for sympathy. In addition to being among the best-paid managers in the world, he has his own big commercial deals – the huge Hublot on his wrist presumably part of the reward for his 'ambassadorship' for the watch company, one of several such lucrative endorsements. But the fact that players are now so wealthy, and so famous, means many have become brands themselves, and that development has not necessarily made team-building easier. Mourinho does not believe that most top players are primarily motivated by money, however. 'Once they have the contract, the money is in the pocket, they are all wealthy, they are all millionaires. I think the motivation still comes from wanting to win, wanting to be good.'

Yet the night before, immediately after England's woeful perfor-mance against Uruguay, the first commercial on ITV was goalkeeper Joe Hart advertising shampoo, then striker Daniel Sturridge asking us to believe he likes nothing better than to gulp down a Subway sandwich, then Hart again, this time for Doritos. Thousands of disappointed England fans took to social media to make clear the view that perhaps if they concentrated more on football, they would perform better. Who knows?

'Again, it is something you cannot fight,' Mourinho says. 'They make their money that way. Yesterday I found something ridiculous about the Portugal team [at the World Cup in Brazil]. They play every three or four days, travel in between, so they have one or two sessions together maybe. Yesterday Portugal had 12,000 people watching the open training session. It was live on TV in Portugal, 12,000 people, shouting and so on. You cannot possibly prepare properly for the match like that. In the end I realised because the session was open the federation sold it to two companies, so it is more important to make money than have a proper training session. If I am the manager of Portugal, maybe I fight this but maybe they say to me, I pay you your salary, do it. This is where a lot of football has changed.'

This upward management is something Mourinho has also had to learn, what with an all-powerful owner in Russian oligarch Roman Abramovich, alongside the downward management of players and staff for whom he is ultimately accountable, and more lateral relationships with sponsors, fans, media. In terms of the impact of the media on a match, he says ultimately it is irrelevant. But talking to the media has become a big part of the job, a leadership skill without which a Premier League manager at the top level cannot really perform to full advantage. 'The two things you cannot avoid are playing matches and doing press conferences before and after. Everything else you can choose – but playing and media, you have to do them.' He says he doesn't read much of the press, and is pretty scornful of pundits. 'The technical comment that says he should do this, do that, I don't read or watch and I don't care. I care more when it is something organised against the club, when something looks like they have an agenda, then it is difficult not to react.'

He is widely seen as a good media performer, but he sees that relationship as being there merely to serve more important relationships, especially with the club hierarchy, the players, opponents and fans. He was one of the first to realise the impact that the media explosion around football would have, and took a deliberate decision to put himself centre stage, partly because that is his character, but also to take pressure very deliberately from players. Calling himself a 'Special One' at the start of his first spell with Chelsea may have sounded arrogant, but he was also setting himself as the main media focus for that purpose. The media may be irrelevant to the outcome of the match, but he is very skilled at using it to inspire and motivate his own side, players and fans and hierarchy alike, undermine and intimidate opponents, and above all emphasise the importance of winning and teamship. Similarly, when he threw his Premier League winner's medal into the crowd in 2006 – later auctioned off for £21,600 – he was signalling that though he is the 'Special One', the players are the performers who deliver on the field, and the fans are part of the team too. That was an act of leadership as much as showmanship. I noticed at Burnley that whenever the Chelsea fans sang his name during the match, he pointed towards the pitch and urged them to direct their support at the players.

'What do you like the players to think of you?'

'I want them to feel I am very good at my job.'

'So respect?'

'Respected for the way I do my job.'

'Fear?'

'No. Maybe sometimes you have to shout in the face of someone, but fear is not good.'

'Do you like them to like you?'

'If possible. But I want them to think I am good at my job. That is the most important thing.'

On several occasions, when the team has been flying to an away match, and there has been a mix of business-class and economy seats on the charter, he says that he has given up his business-class seat for a player. He brings to mind Sun Tzu's *The Art of War* (essential reading for anyone interested in winning).

Regard your soldiers as your children, and they will follow you into the deepest valleys; look on them as your own beloved sons, and they will stand by you even unto death.

There is the story of the famous general and philosopher Wu Ch'i.

He wore the same clothes and ate the same food as the meanest of his soldiers, refused to have either a horse to ride or a mat to sleep on, carried his own surplus rations wrapped in a parcel, and shared every hardship with his men. One of his soldiers was suffering from an abscess, and Wu Ch'i himself sucked out the virus.

Perhaps even Mourinho would baulk at that, but he does say that 'the players' bodies are the most important bodies in the club. If I arrive at a match with back pain, so what? If a player has back pain, it can be a problem, so better he is comfortable and takes my seat.'

He has a reputation for being a great motivator, but plays down his skills in that area. The reason? 'You cannot change the nature of people, only maybe a bit at the margins,' he says, so the more important thing is making sure you get the right people in the first place.

A few days after our meeting, Luis Suárez provoked worldwide condemnation for biting an opponent – the third time he had done so in his professional career – in the match between Uruguay and Italy. Mourinho was not to know that was going to happen. But interestingly, when we talked about the nature of players, he had singled out Suárez – who had scored twice to dispatch England the night before – as an example of a winning mindset he admired. He loved the fact that Suárez, substituted late on, cried with joy as he sat with teammates and reflected on what he had achieved. 'Suárez will die to win, and kill to win.' Again, the approval is clear.

I ask who he had that had that same will to win as Suárez. 'So many,' he says, but the first he names is Didier Drogba. 'He looks a polite guy. Didier could not bite [maybe he did know what was coming in Uruguay's next match] or elbow or get a red card like that, but when he is going out on the pitch, he is going there with only one purpose. He is going there to win the game.'

Here we come to the crux of the Mourinho personality. 'Sometimes I say to the players, "Enjoy the game." They know what I mean. I mean that if they lose, they won't enjoy it. If they win, they will. That's it.'

5

THE LEADER:
ANNA WINTOUR

'Leadership is coming up with an idea and executing it.
Ideas are a dime a dozen.'

ANNA WINTOUR

I have to confess that as the possessor of just three pairs of work
shoes – black, brown, casual – I know nothing about the world of
fashion, but even I have long been aware of the name Anna Wintour.
The interest in her crosses generations, my young fashion-designer
next-door neighbour telling me Wintour is 'the most important
woman in the world'; and women of my age repeatedly using the
phrase 'fashion and cultural icon' to describe her influence. The
interest also spans the Atlantic (fitting, considering her father was
British and her mother American), London society seeing her as
one of theirs, the States feeling that her twenty-six-year editorship
of *American Vogue*, and her broader contributions to the country's
life, arts and politics, make her one of theirs. So major a figure is
she that her fame transcends her industry.

Before I actually met her, I sounded out various opinions and
established something which was clearly known to other people
without me ever having given it a thought, namely that she is one
of those rare people whose very name has become something of a
brand, certainly something much bigger than a job title, even the
title of 'editor of *American Vogue* and [since 2013] artistic director
of Condé Nast', could ever convey. It was remarkable the extent to

which the same words were trotted out – icon, trendsetter, scary, powerful, tiny, elegant, 'the look' – suggesting that whether people liked or disliked, admired or disrespected, they all had the same basic sense of her. Yet I suspect part of her appeal is that people are not really sure. Winning enigmas are particularly interesting. This is especially so in the era of social media, where people put out so much information about themselves voluntarily that there is little left to know or imagine. She is the Banksy of the fashion world – we see a lot of the job, but less of the character, and that works to her benefit, just as an even more extreme approach works to the benefit of the graffiti artist.

I was speaking at a sports conference in New York on the same day that I met Wintour in her twelfth-floor Condé Nast office in Times Square, and by the time I got to the conference, word of the meeting was out. I was genuinely taken aback by the interest that seemed to generate, among men and women alike: 'I hear you met Anna Wintour. What is she really like?' The 'really' in that query is significant. It indicates that the questioner has a sense of the persona, but a lack of certainty about the real person. That's what happens when a mythology forms around someone, and they go from interesting to icon.

Other research had suggested she had a reputation for being quite cold, and a bit intimidating. I found her neither. Reserved in certain ways, certainly, but definitely not lacking in humour or warmth. She didn't strike me as someone who likes to blow her own trumpet, which of course merely fuels the mythology. Perhaps because the interview came shortly after the end of the rugby season, she reminded me of Jonny Wilkinson in the way she turned any question aimed at getting her to set out her own strengths to words of praise for her team. It sat oddly with the reputation for being a scary, ferocious, even bullying boss. She says she liked *The September Issue*, the documentary on *Vogue*'s biggest ever issue, for the fact that it was 'good for Grace'. Grace as in Coddington, who has been at Wintour's side as creative director throughout. 'I have always known she is a creative genius but it was great that everyone else

could see that too,' she says of her 73-year-old colleague. Seventy-
three! It's quite remarkable that the two women driving so much of
modern fashion, and with such influence on young people, are both
of pensionable age. Karl Lagerfeld, the creative director of Chanel
and Wintour's choice of number one in fashion, is even older. 'You
talk about longevity,' says Wintour. 'Here is a man in his eighties,
running a multi-billion-dollar company, constantly innovating. It
was struggling when he took it over and he has reinvented it over
and over again. He is brilliantly creative, interested in everything,
multilingual, a painter, a writer, an illustrator, a designer, a film-
maker, definitely a leader . . . in my world, definitely a leader.'

Having met her, and spoken to people who know and work for
her, that phrase 'definitely a leader' – something she was clearly
reluctant to say about herself – is what has made her such a success
over such a long time. I had imagined that the theme of innovation
– fashion being all about the new – would be the most fruitful area
for our discussion. But the more we spoke, the more I developed a
sense of being in the presence of someone whose real strength was
'show not tell' leadership, all the more impressive because of her
size – she is indeed quite small – and her occasionally rather shy
manner.

I re-watched *The September Issue* the night before I went to see
her. I read the comments of its director R. J. Cutler: 'You can make
a film in Hollywood without Steven Spielberg's blessing, and you
can publish software in Silicon Valley without Bill Gates's blessing,
but it's pretty clear to me you can't succeed in the fashion industry
without Anna Wintour's blessing.' That is a powerful leadership
position to be in. The question then is, how do you use it? And
how do you sustain it in a world that is all about change and churn?

One overriding impression the film left upon me was how the
very mention of her name – the Anna factor – seemed to act as a
galvanising force upon people inside and outside the magazine.
This is not to be underestimated, and is indicative of the power
of reputation. Think of Wilkinson again: even All Black Dan Carter,
perhaps the best fly half of his time, said that any player who saw

Jonny Wilkinson's name on the opposing team sheet was at an immediate disadvantage. Think of the players who saw Alex Ferguson stepping out to the technical area with ten minutes left; the governments and businesses who heard George Soros was taking an interest in their affairs; or look what happened when Ben Ainslie joined up late in the day to try to rescue a losing America's Cup campaign – it was partly his presence that turned things around in one of the greatest comebacks of all time. Reputation is a particularly powerful winning currency. Wintour has a lot of it in the bank.

Another impression she made in the documentary was of someone who reacted quickly and instinctively, based upon having very strong views of what she liked and what she didn't; and yet beneath the decisiveness there was probably more than a hint of vulnerability. The quick, instinctive side means that she can indeed come over as stern and snappy. Partly that is her character, but it is also the product of a lesson she learned from working, early in her career, for a weak boss with a very different leadership style. She won't say who the boss was, but she saw how not to do things. 'She was incredibly indecisive, she would take so long to make up her mind and then days or weeks later she would change it. I learned from that that the most important thing is to be decisive and sure and impart that to the people working for you. It's like parents with their kids: when parents are waffling then the kids get insecure – so be clear, be sure. Even if you aren't sure of yourself, pretend that you are, because it makes it clearer for everyone else. Most people prevaricate. I decide fast. I think it's helpful to people who work for you. The world we are in is about instinct and being fast and responding.'

The closest I can get to drawing her into admitting that her strengths are of leadership is when she says: 'I am very organised and I am a very good delegator. People work better when they have responsibility. We talk about what needs to be done, and then I assume it is done. I like to know what's going on but I'm not double-checking and triple-checking.' She says that beneath her in the organisation

are 'really smart people who can do things I can't do. I am not creative at all.' I sense a bit of false modesty with that one, insist that she
cannot possibly claim to lack creativity when for two decades and
more, she has produced a magazine that has helped to define the age.
But she is adamant. 'I can't make anything. I don't know how to
make a dress. I couldn't go on a shoot and create an image. I can't
write a script. I have so much admiration for people who can do these
things, because I would have no idea where to start. I am always
responding to other people's talents. I am not the talent.'

'But you have a vision for the
magazine, surely that is a big part of
the creative process here?'

'Even if you aren't
sure of yourself,
pretend that you are,
because it makes it
clearer for everyone
else.'

ANNA WINTOUR

'That is a totally different ability
to someone who can make things. I
have a feel, I know what I want for
the magazine, and I try to make decisions which I think are best for the
magazine, but I couldn't do all the
things required to make it happen.'

Much as she values the team,
though, she embraces the idea that leadership must carry with it
a sense of loneliness at times. I ask her if she has anyone in the
team with whom she can really unburden herself, admit the private
doubts and insecurities that she won't reveal when wearing her
decisive-leader face. I have in mind the fact that Tony Blair would
occasionally display a very different, anxious sense of himself to a
small number of his team. Again her reaction is instant. 'No, I
don't do that. I don't feel that is their responsibility. It's mine. I
will discuss things with lots of people but I don't like to put that
burden on them, it's not their job; it is my job to figure things
out.'

'So does that mean you're putting on a front a lot of the time?'

'I don't think so. I just think we know each other so well, we
have been working together such a long time, so we don't play
games. Before you arrived, Grace was in here and the September

issue was turned upside down for various reasons, and we were laughing about it. What can you do? I mean, take a Valium!'

It is partly her longevity that has made her such a force in her own world, but within the team there is another factor at play – *their* longevity. On the day I visited *Vogue*, my partner Fiona was seeing an old friend who used to work for Wintour, and who said that her staff tended to be incredibly loyal, which is why they stayed so long. It all jars with the media stories of harshness with underlings, the 'Nuclear Wintour' or the 'Wintour of our discontent' sobriquets, or her being the basis of the Meryl Streep character in *The Devil Wears Prada*. To play up to the image, she wore Prada to a screening of the film, and told a press conference: 'I beat all my assistants, lock them in a cupboard and don't pay them.' Since interviewing her, I have met all manner of people who have worked with or for

> 'I am always responding to other people's talents. I am not the talent.'
>
> **ANNA WINTOUR**

her. Some say she is inspiring, kind, a great boss, who expects more of herself than anyone else. Some, however, could barely conceal their hatred, one in particular saying she felt belittled and scared the whole time she was there. 'She once ended a conversation on the phone and just dropped the phone in my lap, as if to say "I am too important to hang up my own phone calls".' Majority opinion, however, contrary to the *Devil Wears Prada* image, was in the former not the latter camp.

Existing staff, who number former Obama fund-raiser Hildy Kuryk among them as *Vogue*'s communications director, certainly suggest the loyalty works both ways. But the desire to build a team around a mix of experienced old hands and young talent – the well-known 'youth and experience' combination favoured by sports managers – is not about sentimentality. Another hard-headed leadership point comes out when Wintour says: 'If someone leaves for another job, on a personal level I might be sad, but I always see it as an opportunity, to find someone new with something different to offer, someone who might be able to teach me new things too. I have certain key people here, they do tend to stay a long time, the managing editor was here fifteen or sixteen years, she retired, and it was the opportunity to bring in a wonderful man from *New York* magazine. I am always looking for new talent.'

This attitude of never looking back is essential when leading teams in need of renewal, as political leaders and sports managers know. Wintour applies it to her editorship more broadly. She recalls a conversation with Bea Miller, her predecessor as editor of *British Vogue*, where she was in charge for two years before the move to New York. 'She said something that has always stuck in my mind. She had just closed an issue and I said, "How was it?" and she said, "Anna, it is always about the next one." I have followed that approach. We never have post-mortems. We move straight on. I don't need people to tell me if it was a good issue or a bad issue; we know, so we just move forward.' That same approach applies to the use of data, for example the market research about who and where readers are, what they like, which faces on the cover sell best. 'It is helpful, but in the end I do rely much more on instinct. I look at the pictures from a shoot or I read an article that comes in, and I react quickly, this is great, this isn't, use that, don't use that, redo this one. I make the decision that I think is right for the magazine. I feel I know what the reader wants.'

If that last sentence is delivered with particular emphasis, it is perhaps because of the circumstances of the one time she was sacked, as a junior fashion editor on *Harper's Bazaar* in the mid-seventies, and told by her boss, 'we just don't think you will ever understand the American woman'. There is no apparent rancour – 'it was their magazine, they were entitled to their decision' – but it was clearly a major motivating event in her life. 'I think everyone should get sacked at least once. It forces you to look at yourself. It didn't feel it at the time, but it was definitely a good thing for what it taught me. It is important to have setbacks because that is the reality of life. Perfection doesn't exist.'

This is another important aspect of leadership, the belief that setbacks are opportunities to learn, and it is always possible to improve. 'Did you watch the Tonys?' she asks. I didn't. 'Well, they were presented by Hugh Jackman, who is a friend of mine and I emailed him congratulating him on how he did it, but he got a couple of reviews that were not so favourable and I said "it was unfair" and he said "no, it's great to get that because it makes you think and you try to see if you could have done better". Actually, I feel the same way, I always think "how can I be better, how can I change things?" That's why this is the perfect place for me, because fashion is all about change, moving forward, never thinking about the past, always the next thing.'

> 'It is important to have setbacks because that is the reality of life. Perfection doesn't exist.'
>
> **ANNA WINTOUR**

As to whether she thinks she does understand the American woman, she says: 'I certainly feel I understand our reader.' There too is an interesting insight – 'reader', singular not plural; in other words a sense, a vision in her mind, of who and what the *Vogue* reader is, and what she as editor can do to connect with that person. 'For *Vogue* it is a very fine line. We need to be part of the conversation but we cannot be too far ahead or too far behind, just in it. If you get too edgy and too distant you disconnect from the reader, and if you are too boring you disconnect in other ways. I remember Ralph Lauren always said to me, "I don't want to be too hot or too cold, I just want to be a brand like Coca-Cola or Nike." I feel the same about *Vogue*.'

What comes through is a genuine passion for the magazine, as a brand, and as a platform. 'I get up every day at 5 a.m. – I have always been an early riser – and I always look forward to coming in to the office. The best thing being editor of *Vogue* is being able to work with and celebrate amazing creative people. This is not a job you do only at a desk. I really think you have to go out and see things, screenings, theatre, exhibitions, I travel a lot. Every time you go out, even a walk in the street, you have an idea. You come back and you say "I saw this and we should maybe cover it and what do you think of this?" and I throw it to the team. It is very important to listen but ultimately as editor you have to decide.'

She is clearly proud of her own longevity, effusive about the way Condé Nast chairman, S. I. Newhouse, 'lets me get on with it, believes in the responsibility going to editors, gives you all the support and the resources you need, gives you the canvas and then you decide how you are going to fill it'. Not once has she had the temptation Alex Ferguson had, a decade before he finally stepped down as Manchester United manager, to leave it all behind. 'It is just an incredibly exciting place to be, just when you think you might have seen it all, something new and invigorating comes along. So the Web has changed how we operate. Me personally, I have taken on a role now working with the editors of other magazines, which gives me another dimension. I work with the Metropolitan Museum of Art and hope I can bring something different to that. I worked on the two Obama campaigns [fund-raising] and that was new and exciting.' One of Obama's campaign team told me: 'Anna worked her butt off. What I saw was someone who takes any challenge really seriously. She was superb for us. I saw the leadership skills in her so clearly. Sometimes people come into campaigns and it is about them not the campaign, and I'll be honest, I thought that was what we would get. But she came in and was determined to make a difference, and she did.'

Her father once told her he called it a day as editor of the *Evening Standard* when he started to get too angry. 'I don't feel angry. I am very happy with what I do.' She also clearly prefers what she sees as a more classless society in America to what she grew up with in Britain. 'I feel a bit homeless actually. I felt quite isolated growing up in England, not because of family but with it being such a class-driven culture, and one of the things I like here is that it is not all about class and where you went to school and what your parents do, and everyone in New York is from somewhere else, and that creates a very positive force. I love it here.'

The one time she takes a while to answer a question is when I ask if she sees herself as a journalist. She grew up surrounded by newspaper journalism and says she regrets never having worked for a newspaper. 'I don't write, I am not a writer, I see myself as someone who responds to the times and the culture, to a moment; is that a journalist, I don't know.'

Part of that skill, and what has perhaps set her apart among her fashion media peers and put her in this extraordinary leadership role for an entire industry, is seeing where the culture is heading. Grace Coddington credits Wintour with having foreseen the scale of modern celebrity culture. 'I don't know if I was the first, but you could see it coming. Partly it was to do with the way the models were changing. They were getting enormous attention, becoming huge celebrities in their own right. They loved being celebrities, and it made the traditional celebrities want to be models. Before that happened, actresses wanted to be taken seriously so it was all dirty sneakers and blue jeans for them and they saw the attention these girls got and it flipped.'

'Was that an innovation?'

'Yes. We started it slowly. We decided to put a celebrity on the cover, and that was really controversial. I think Madonna was the first one and it was not universally popular. I remember one guy said to me, "When I think of *Vogue*, I think of Katharine Hepburn, not this!"' Which confirmed her view that the change was justified. So Winona Ryder and Sharon Stone in 1993, Julia Roberts the following year, Demi Moore the one after that, then by 1998, Sandra Bullock, Claire Danes, Renée Zellweger, Liz Hurley, Oprah Winfrey (having agreed with Wintour she should lose a bit of weight first), Hillary Clinton and – one she seems to think may have been a step too far – the Spice Girls.

'Is the celebrity culture a force for good?'

'It's unavoidable, it just is, there's nowhere to hide. I don't know if it's good or bad, but you can't deny it.'

'Do you see yourself as a celebrity?'

'I don't think about it, I honestly don't.'

'But when you arrive at a show and the photographers are shouting your name?'

'It's part of the job.'

'Do you like "being Anna Wintour"?'

'I don't think about that, I really don't. Ask my brother [*Guardian* political journalist Patrick Wintour]. I don't have a high-powered life out of work, I like to go to the country for the weekend with the kids and the dog and play tennis. I am very good at turning off. I don't like the city at weekends, I have a garden I adore, a life that is very private and the polar opposite of all of this.'

She names another female media leader, former *Washington Post* owner Kay Graham, as a role model; and as to whether she is aware of being a role model herself, which can go with the turf of leadership, she says she is aware of it when she does a graduation and girls ask her how she got to where she is, 'but I don't think about it otherwise. I don't get out of bed and think "right, I must do something to be a role model". I live life the best I can, try to make the right decisions for the magazine and the company and at a personal level the family. It is not a conscious thing.'

The spin detector in me could say that the focus on team, the playing down of her own qualities, ambition and reputation are part of the creation of the image that has served her well, made her a major force in US life, culture – the Metropolitan Museum of Art renamed its halls of fashion 'The Anna Wintour Costume Center' – and, thanks to the fund-raising for Obama, politics too. But having spent time with her, and spoken to people who have worked with her past and present, I do sense that her winning streaks are an instinctive understanding of the importance of clear leadership, and her devotion to the job and the opportunities it gives her. It all reminds me of the Navratilova remark quoted earlier: 'Do what you love and love what you do, and everything else is detail.' That certainly seems to be Wintour's way. She was still at school when she was filling in a form about her ambitions and her father suggested she put 'editor of *Vogue*' as that was so clearly what she wanted to be. She didn't even hide it in her first interview at *Vogue* in 1982.

Then editor Grace Mirabella asked Wintour what her dream job would be and was unsurprisingly taken aback by the reply: 'Your job.' Mirabella did her best to make sure it never happened. But six years later, Wintour was in the chair. Ambitious? Certainly. Ruthless at times? Without a doubt. Possessed of real steel when she needs to be? That too. They are all, like it or not, qualities required of leaders.

Her office feels less like an 'office office' than a rather beautiful working space someone might create in their own very luxurious home. The photos tend to be of others. And the reason the Navratilova quote seems so apt is that she positively sparkles with excitement when she is talking about someone she clearly sees not just as a role model but a real hero, namely Roger Federer, who has become a close friend. 'Roger is a god,' she says. But is he? I ask. Is he really so much more special than other tennis players? 'He is *so* elegant,' she sighs. 'But what I really love about him is that when he was at the height of his powers, he was always clear that he could improve, he could get even better at what he did. I really admire people who do things exceptionally well. I think Roger really cares about the sport. He cares about it the way I care about my world, it is not just about him, he is a student of tennis history, involved in the future of tennis, and I admire him so much. When I watch tennis, I see gladiators, I love the sport, the ebb and the flow, seeing how they size each other up, the psychological side, like how Rafael Nadal gets inside Novak Djokovic's head [we spoke just after the two had met in Paris]. That psychological side of life is fascinating, and Roger is supreme at that, always calm, always elegant. That's one of the reasons I love *Vogue* so much, because it gives you the ability to recognise all this talent, whether that is a designer, or an actor, or a tennis player.'

In so far as she sees herself as a leader, it is not just of *Vogue* but as a representative of the fashion industry itself, and it is in this that her fame and reach lie. 'I do see *Vogue* as being for and about the fashion community. That explains some of the causes we have taken up, and when we take something up, we really do it. I want

Vogue to be seen as more than a magazine. It is a force, a force to help people, particularly people in the fashion community. If you look at the young designers who have come out of the fashion fund we set up after 9/11, they won't mean anything to you but they are the key names in American fashion today and out of that terrible time something really great and important happened for all of us, so that has been an extraordinary initiative that we started here. Or HIV: the fashion community was one of those most devastated by HIV and way back in the nineties the community got together and that was spearheaded by *Vogue* and we raised money for awareness and education – we couldn't do the research but we had an important message to get across to everybody. People forget how scared everyone was, and we took a leadership role – that was important to me, important to people who work here. I don't want to sound like a crusader, but we felt a responsibility to help and we did that. It might seem like it's all glamour and fantasy – and we can all subscribe to a bit of that – but it's hard work, and everyone here is committed to working hard because we believe in what we do.'

Virtually every part of the conversation comes back to leadership and teamship, and I ask her for a definition of leadership. 'It is coming up with an idea and executing it. Ideas are a dime a dozen – it is how it is carried out. If we are working with something for the museum, or a big HIV event, we are very selective about what we do, and we really do it, make sure we make a difference.'

'So leadership is about prioritising?'

'Yes, and about making a difference. It is very easy to put your name on something but you really have to do things properly.'

Here is where it is important to understand she has economic influence too. Just as she led a call to arms for the fashion industry over HIV, or post 9/11, so in 2009, when fashion was being hit hard by the effects of the global financial crisis, she persuaded New York Mayor Michael Bloomberg – 'She's not a person you want to say no to,' he said – to get the city to sign up to a late-night shopping party. Some of the big stores, including Macy's and Bloomingdale's, were initially wary, conscious that customers were going through hard times. But she wouldn't take no for an answer, called in favours from celebrity friends to visit the stores which got involved. 'Fashion's Night Out' became what one commentator called 'a Mardi Gras moment in the middle of Lent'. Macy's sales rose considerably. So did the sales of other stores large and small. But more than that, she felt she had had an idea, executed it well and properly, helped her industry, and helped economic morale too. The following year she took the idea to more than a hundred US cities and sixteen other countries. She has taken the same approach, and raised tens of millions with it, in the pursuit of the charitable causes she decides she and the magazine should promote.

But if this suggests a touchy-feely side that is all about getting pats on the back for worthy deeds for the great and the good, she is not someone afraid of controversy, another trait required of strong leaders. Her support for fur in fashion has made her an obvious target of animal rights organisations, and she has had physical, verbal and symbolic attacks as a result. Journalist Peter Braunstein, later jailed for a sexual assault on another woman which sparked a multi-state manhunt, said that Wintour would go to a hell guarded by large rats, where it would be so warm she wouldn't need to wear fur. A very different kind of US female icon, Pamela Anderson, named Wintour as the living person she most despised, 'because she bullies young designers and models to use and wear fur'. Equally, she regularly gets attacked for being elitist. If any of it upsets her, it is not very apparent. She may be thin, but her skin is not.

On the surface, and the public profile, her qualities are all about fashion. But what comes through much more strongly is the sense of a decisive leader with a clear overall vision, and a determination to communicate certainty even where there is doubt. One other important leadership quality she has is the ability to stay focused, even in a crisis. 'The worst time was '97, because of the economic situation, but we just got on with it. There is such strength and stability here. There have been down times and will be in the future, but you just deal with it. I don't feel we have had a real crisis. The history of *Vogue* is extraordinary and you have to be respectful of that. When I first came, I was creative director working with Alex Liberman and he made the magazine what it is today and I was so lucky to have that time. He bridged a period when fashion was a vision of loveliness and he could bring it to the street. I spent a lot of time with him when I was first here and he was the most important teacher for me.'

Further unexpected evidence of the ability to stay focused on the important and the long term, not a passing problem, came when I asked her if she had ever lacked confidence about her own abilities? Did she, for example, on day one in 1988, walk in and really feel that she had what it took to do the job? I was now unknowingly intruding on private grief. 'Day one was awful, a total nightmare, because a gossip columnist had done a full page saying I only got the job because I was having an affair with the boss. It was totally untrue, but that kind of cast a shadow on the first day. I was just trying to hold up my head and get through it.'

But having landed the job she always wanted, she was determined to make changes, both to staff and to the style of the magazine. That much was clear from her very first cover, November 1988, of a model wearing a pair of cheap faded jeans with a $10,000 Christian Lacroix jacket. By her own admission, 'it broke all the rules' of previous *Vogue* covers. The model, Michaela Bercu, wasn't even looking at the camera, and her hair was blowing across her face. Now that Wintour is the fashion force she has become, all manner of theories and analyses have been made of why she chose that cover. So far as Wintour is concerned, there is nothing terribly complicated about it. She sensed 'the winds of change' blowing through fashion. The photo she chose had not been planned as the cover. The printers even called to make sure the picture really was meant to be the cover. But her instincts told her it was a better cover than the one that had been lined up. It worked.

As for the story about the affair that allegedly got her the job, she ignored it, as she has many other stories since. I ask, for example, about her widely reported wild week with Bob Marley. 'I never met Bob Marley, not once.' But it's on Wikipedia. 'I have no idea where that came from.' It is what happens when people become enigmas and, if they stay around long enough, myths.

Anna Wintour's name is now part of fashion legend. But as I headed off to my conference at Yankee Stadium to be assailed with questions about her, the impression she left on me had nothing to do with clothes, and everything to do with being a very special kind of leader. That impression followed me all the way home. Even Lindsay Nicholson, one of my closest friends, and herself a hugely successful magazine editor in the UK (most recently with *Good Housekeeping*) was jealous of the time I had spent with Wintour. She explains the fascination: 'She has defined a management style for the magazine industry, and she has defined a leadership style for women more broadly. Our industry has more women in senior positions than most and a lot of that is down to her.'

'So do magazine editors like you want to be like Anna Wintour?' I asked. 'In my world,' she replied, 'everyone wants to be like Anna Wintour.'

6

THE TEAM PLAYER: EDI RAMA

'I learned so much from sport that I try to apply in politics now.'

EDI RAMA

Edi Rama stands out in two respects. At 1 metre 98 centimetres (almost 6′ 6″), he is, I believe, the tallest current world leader; he is also the only prime minister who has represented his country at sport. The two facts are related, in that the sport was basketball, where short men tend not to prosper. The country is Albania, a Communist dictatorship when he played for the national team, and now a fully-fledged democracy in which his Socialist Party coalition won a landslide election victory in 2013.

I know Rama well, having worked with him as an adviser for several years, first in Opposition, now in government. As with Tony Blair, he has that winner's determination to build the team he thinks he needs to secure his objectives. When I first met him, I knew him only vaguely as the artist who had become Mayor of Tirana and who had used public-space art to try to brighten up a city still emerging from the dead hand of Enver Hoxha's forty-four-year rule. I was aware too of his voluble complaints that the ruling Democratic Party had stolen the election when he sought another term as mayor. As with Tony, at first I said no to his approaches, because I had many other things going on. Plus, though I got to know, and became sympathetic to, Albania during the Kosovo conflict, it did not arouse

my passions, obviously, in the way that trying to help change the
government of the UK had done. However, again as with Tony, I
was won over by the zeal and hunger he showed for victory, also
by his positive vision not just for his country but the whole Balkan
region, and finally, because I found him and his key advisers so
likeable. It helped that he loves sport as much as I do. He even
knew – a little – about Burnley, and didn't object when we proposed
changing the party's official colour from scarlet red to claret, my
team's colour.

He is a huge admirer of Tony, something of a hero in Albania
because of the leadership role he played over Kosovo; also, he says,
because 'New Labour and Tony's Third Way were the models for
us'. We worked on a rebranding of the party, under the banner of
'Renaissance', and a policy and communications strategy closely
modelled on the New Labour, New Britain campaigns of 1997 and
2001 in particular.

For the purpose of this book, however, the interest is less how
he won, and more what he learned from his career in sport that
helped him to win, and helped to prepare him for a life in politics.
And actually, we must indeed start with his height, and the advantage to which he puts it. 'Having a large presence was an asset in
basketball,' he tells me over lunch at a restaurant near his Tirana
office, 'and it's sometimes an asset in politics too.' He says that the
very first time he entered parliament he was struck by what he calls
'the physical aspect' of political debate. 'Following politics on TV
has something of the feel of following football by watching training
sessions on TV. It's difficult to get very excited about it, or even to
understand what's going on. Watching parliament on TV, you never
get that strong sense of the physical aspect, of people's shape and
stature, and how you can tell through the groupings and the body
language who is up and down, who is confident, who is winning an
argument.'

Of course this is not just about height, and there have been
many successful short leaders. Napoleon was 1 metre 68, just over
5′5″. Vladimir Putin is not much taller at 1 metre 70, though he has

eight centimetres on his colleague Dmitry Medvedev. But academic research carried out at Texas Tech University found that when people were asked to draw an image of leaders, they mainly drew tall and broad, not short and slight. I think it's fair to say that Charles de Gaulle, at 1 metre 96, is viewed rather more favourably than Putin-sized François Hollande, though admittedly height is far from being the main factor. And at least Hollande can look down a few centimetres on his predecessor as French president, Nicolas Sarkozy.

But Rama does feel that the ability to command space and attention are important sporting and political assets. 'When you get onto a basketball court, all your teammates beside you, pumped up and ready to go, you form impressions of the other side, their strength and unity, their mood and body language. Of course the physicality element is stronger in sport, but something similar happens in politics, where you can read the mood of one side or the other simply by looking at them, sitting there all together.' Having so often entered a sporting arena for high-level competition helped prepare him for leadership, he believes. 'I think I have a much stronger understanding of the dynamics of a team because of my experience in sport.'

Describing his first entry into the sessions hall of the Albanian parliament, he says: 'For me it was like entering the basketball arena. You feel immediately, and you feel it physically, which side you are on, and which side your opponents are on. You feel that before a word has been spoken. It is about where you take your place, what kind of people you are with, the looks you give to each

'I have a much stronger understanding of the dynamics of a team because of my experience in sport.'
EDI RAMA

other. The feelings you are trying to engender that "we are all on the same side". This is very similar to sport. You feel the team, and you feel the shared importance of trying to make it work. You feel the need to join with your teammates, to help your side feel and look confident and, in my case as a leader, to lead it through the debates.'

Sport, of course, gave him several years to be a part of teams good and bad, and to learn from both, not just the sporting technicalities, but lessons in the three interrelated areas examined so far – strategy, leadership and, especially, teamship. On the last of these, he says that though he learned from his own teams, he learned even more from the teams he lost to. Like so many sportsmen and women, he says defeat is often a better teacher than victory.

'I played for Dinamo, a good side in Albania, but we kept being beaten by Partizani, a team that I called "the eternal champions". I'm afraid I called my own team the losers, because though we beat many teams, this one team always seemed to get the better of us. They were the eternal champions and we were the eternal runners-up. It was like the story of Mourinho's Chelsea and Wenger's Arsenal. They are so close in terms of quality, yet Mourinho always seems to win when they meet. We were not a bad team, but we couldn't seem to beat Partizani.'

Over time, he worked out why, and his explanation today underlines just how important it is to understand the closeness of strategy, leadership and teamship within any winning organisation. 'The eternal champions squad had a game strategy and stuck with it,' he says. 'And they were able to stick to their strategy because they had leaders in the team who felt secure in their positions, including when they were under pressure – in fact *especially* when they were under pressure. That security in their own abilities, their own position, the support of their teammates and coaches, this is what gave them a strength we didn't have.'

It wasn't that Dinamo didn't have a strategy, he says, just that they were less effective in implementing it. 'We would agree a game strategy, we would hopefully all understand it, but we had difficulties in sticking with it. And the reason for that was that our leaders did not relate to each other properly, they did not hang together, and that meant there was no security for their teammates.' The other team, he says, had a 'superior' culture, less focused on individual talent, more on team strength. 'Culture comes from values and from leadership. To the eternal champions the victory was everything and they were ready to accept any part they had to for the sake of winning; victory was naturally very important to us also, but less important than the performance of each individual. And that meant we were not a team. So we lost. The other team won. Because they were a team. Simple.'

He then goes into comical descriptions of the post-match post-mortems, which sound like the more fractious meetings of political teams trying to work out why they have lost a campaign. 'We would have agreed a plan but then individual players would do their own thing, and the plan fell apart, but just as nobody would take responsibility for sticking to the plan, nobody would take responsibility for why it went wrong. One guy would say "Why did you do that?" and another would say "Hold on, first you did this" and it just went round and round and round, and we had nobody – I was too young for it, I guess – standing up and saying "Hang on, this is why we're losing".'

Though Partizani probably did have better players technically, he says it was not ability but failure to stay on strategic course that meant Dinamo were always second best. And this was down to the personalities of the people involved, more individualistic, less willing to subjugate ego to a team effort, more, dare I say it, like a political team than a sporting team. 'Maybe we had too many intellectuals,' he smiles.

This importance of having a strategy binding the team, and making sure they stick to it, is now a fundamental part of his approach in government. Rama is drawn to strategic minds. He it was who introduced me to Garry Kasparov, after the chess maestro visited Albania as part of his unsuccessful campaign to become president of the game's governing body, FIDE. He described Kasparov as 'one of the cleverest people I have ever met', and especially with regard to his views of strategy outlined earlier. 'He has a genius view of some of the problems we are wrestling with.' Rama echoes Kasparov in saying, 'you should only change the strategy if you really have to, because the situation has changed so much'.

When playing for Dinamo, the strategy was changing not because it had to, not because the fundamentals had changed, but because too many players were thinking of their own role, not the objectives of the team, or changing tack purely because they were losing early on.

Rama has sought to apply to political team-building what he learned from what his basketball team did well, what they did badly, what Partizani did well, and above all what he learned when he was called up for the national side.

Just as José Mourinho and Anna Wintour learned from great bosses, so too, when he was selected for Albania, did Rama learn from the example of his captain and leader, Agim Fagu, especially with regard to how he brought on and developed younger talent. Rama, I should add, has a young team of ministers by most governmental standards. 'Obviously when you are selected for your national team, that is a great moment for any sportsman, and also you would not be human if you were not a little more anxious and nervous than usual, and how the team leader deals with that, how he helps you deal with it, that is so important. Agim was particularly good with the younger players; he was always trying to get the older ones to help the youngsters score; he liked teaching them tricks; he wanted to bring them into his confidence and make them feel important.' Fagu would later become Albanian ambassador to the UK, taking his sporting skills into diplomacy, and often went back to help the younger players train.

'Sport at a senior level also taught me the different roles that people can play at different ages and different stages of their career. Talent is limited in any sphere so it's important to get the best of what talent is available. Take an older player in the final stages of his career – I think of someone like Ryan Giggs in my favourite English team, Manchester United; or of Andrea Pirlo in the team I was cheering at the World Cup, Italy – a player but also a teacher and leader, experience being put to greater benefit than merely the passing of the ball. Partizani had Gazmend Çaçi who was a fantastic player but also a great teacher and leader in the field. So when we played together in the national side, I learned a lot, first and fore-most the joy of playing alongside a big and generous star who found immense pleasure in winning, not just in shining for himself.'

This approach, focused on trying to build a team with the right blend of youth and wisdom, is something else he says he has tried to take directly into political leadership. 'In sport, managers and coaches often talk of the dream teams being a mix of energetic younger and wiser older players, and the same goes for politics. You need experienced people around you. But you also need innovators, people with ideas and energy, huge enthusiasm and the beliefs of idealism. The old must support and inspire the young, but they must also let the young express themselves. Basketball also taught me that the more secure you are, the more comfortable inside yourself and the more confident in your own skills, the more you can become a leader, free from the fear that you are fighting to stay and enjoying the lights of the scene as you enter the arena; once that feeling comes, the more you are able to empower the others and share your winning ways with them.'

This too came from his role model, Gazmend Çaçi, confident enough within his own skin to focus on the performance of the whole squad, each and every player, and worry less about any threat, perceived or real, to his own position. 'He was a real force of nature, really in a different league, and if Albania had

'Talent is limited in any sphere so it's important to get the best of what talent is available.' **EDI RAMA**

not been a Communist dictatorship at the time, and he had been free to travel, he would have easily been a star in any major European team. When playing for Albania, I often heard the story of how Çaçi was in conflict with another key player and they didn't even talk to each other. And yet when they played, he assisted the guy to score more points than ever. They hated each other off the court, but on it shared a deep desire to win. That was impressive.'

Rama is anxious to achieve such team-building in politics – no mean ambition given that, even by the standards of UK parliamentary debate, Albania's political discourse is a rough battleground. Indeed, animosities between government and Opposition have often been cited by the European Commission as a reason for holding up progress towards EU candidate status, now secured. This is a place where former prime minister Sali Berisha tried to persuade the public that Rama suffered from schizophrenia, and demanded on national TV that Rama's mother admit this, an attack that led to Mrs Rama taking legal action. And when one of Rama's youngest and smartest ministers, Erion Veliaj, was about to get married, Berisha stood up in parliament and said his wife-to-be was a whore. Veliaj took no action other than to say that Berisha, whose rants were protected by parliamentary privilege, was a tired and silly old man. It is not pretty, and Rama has to know how to handle himself, without ever getting down that low.

That said, he is very aware that in politics teammates can sometimes be forced upon you, and that leaders have to deal with people they would not always choose as teammates. Rama says this is particularly important for smaller countries like his, because so much of what they hope to achieve is dependent on building alliances with other countries, whether trying to repair damaged relations within the previously war-torn Balkan regions, or trying to persuade the EU to let Albania become a member, or in trying to get the richer countries of the world to invest in a country whose image he knows has to improve. It is not easy. As I have learned when telling people in Britain I have worked there, they are as likely to mention gangsters, prostitution and the film *Taken* as they are any noble attempts at change. But Rama believes the change can come by altering the reality on the ground, and by forging the new alliances, be it with encouraging and supportive leaders like German Chancellor Angela Merkel, or some of the detractors he still has in the region.

'You often have to work with people you might not like, welcoming them into your home, or taking them to a basketball match. But part of the art of leadership is getting rid of any personal anger and mobilising for the sake of success even those you would rather never see.' He wouldn't thank me for naming the ones he would put into that category, having made these improved international relations a strategic priority when he was first elected.

This desire for team-building was very apparent when it came to the pre-election wrangling between parties. Again, despite the political risks of bringing perceived enemies into the team, he entered into a coalition with a former Socialist prime minister, Ilir Meta, who had set up his own party, LSI. Their coming together notwithstanding past difficulties helped guarantee the landslide that followed, and their relationship has been an important part of the success of the government. It also chimed nicely with his broader message that renaissance had to involve the overcoming of bitter divisions of the past, home and abroad. So teamship can be built by reaching out to other teams, and by knowing that teammates are always going to be a mix of different talents, different skills and personalities. The job of leadership is to bring out the best in them.

Having the core team signed up to an overall strategy is particularly crucial when the strategy comes under pressure. If the team is not aware of the overall goals, and understanding the need for pursuing them, they are likely to break up when events conspire against them. Here Rama knows the importance of honest assessment of a given situation, frank discussion about options, but always with a mind on the overall strategy.

Just how hard it can be to stick to that strategy, and keep the team focused upon it, was illustrated by a bizarre and unwelcome mingling of sport and politics during a football match between Serbia and Albania, a European qualifier, in Belgrade in 2014. After decades of mutual hatred, not least because of the ethnic cleansing of Kosovar Albanians under Serb leader Slobodan Milošević, Rama was pursuing improved relations, and the Serbs appeared to be responding. Angela Merkel was taking the lead in actively encouraging greater cooperation between Balkan nations, and she had also become a strong supporter of Albania's campaign for EU candidate status. A date was then fixed for a meeting in Belgrade with Rama's

Serbian opposite number, Aleksandar Vučić, which would be the
first between the two countries' leaders for sixty-eight years. Then,
days before, disaster at the Partizan Stadium. Though Albanian fans,
other than a few FA officials and VIPs, were banned from attending
the match, and though there was a massive security presence inside
and outside, someone managed to fly a drone inside the stadium
carrying a 'Greater Albania' flag. Its landing on the pitch, and the
Serb players' attempts to remove it, provoked a huge brawl between
the two sides, which in turn provoked physical attacks by Serb
spectators on Albania's players, and the match had to be abandoned.
More damaging for Rama, Serb media immediately began to claim
– totally falsely according to the Albanians – that the drone was
operated by his brother, Olsi. The story went round the world. 'It
was a storm, for sure, and although I was saying publicly that sport
and politics should be kept apart, it was very hard, because an
incident like this was going to get global attention, and with the
planned meeting between us days away, and with a century of wars,
conflicts and paranoia to be left behind, the timing could not have
been worse.'

In the following days, the Serbs accused the Albanian government of organising an act of provocation, which Rama strongly
denied. Meanwhile, Albanian people took to the streets to 'celebrate'
and hail Olsi Rama a hero for something he hadn't done. The
celebrations spread to Albanians in Priština and Skopje, the capitals
of Kosovo and Macedonia, driving the Serbs to even greater anger
and paranoia that the drone incident had been a deliberate message
from so-called Greater Albania. Yet Rama did not waver in his
determination to make sure the meeting with Vučić went ahead,
even though Vučić was under pressure domestically to call it off.

'It was vital that we try as best we could to stick to the strategy,
no matter how much noise was going on outside.' Of the drone
incident, he says: 'It didn't change the objective of pursuing better
relations with Serbia, for our two countries and for the region, so
it was important to keep going in trying to do that. Kasparov said
that thing about chess being like trying to paint a masterpiece while

someone is tugging at your sleeve. Well, this was a very big tug at our sleeve, but we could not let them tear the sleeve away. The bigger picture had to be painted; the strategy could not be changed.'

Something else Rama and I discussed with Garry Kasparov was the importance of an 'optimal, maximalist' approach to strategy, so that the instinct of a team, instead of playing safe when things were going well, was to understand the need to drive on, seize even more advantage. This is all about what I call 'the killer instinct', what Rama calls 'making the most of every situation', and what Kasparov calls 'poetic licence for maximalism'.

Kasparov's favourite business example is the iPod. 'Steve Jobs was an optimiser. Despite the world literally lining up to buy each new iPod version, Apple released the iPod Mini, basically competing with its own dominant product. Vendors were shocked, consumers a little confused. The iPod was great, so why clog up supply lines and marketing campaigns with a new one? Because Jobs was a killer. Even if the Mini competed with the iPod, it squeezed his competitors' market share even more. It showed everyone how far ahead of them Apple was and consolidated Apple as a brand of the new and cool. That was more important to his strategy of staying on top than a few margin points and a stock backlog.'

My favourite Rama example of killer instinct came some months before the 2013 election. He was already well ahead in the polls, and some of his team were advising that we play safe, avoid risks leading to mistakes. But we came up with a political equivalent of this maximalist approach. We were in a meeting at the Socialist Party's HQ, running through the most negative comments that voters and media were saying about him. It is not nice for politicians to have to hear a stream of abusive remarks, but Rama's background as an artist and sportsman gives him a desire for creativity and boldness often lacking in politics and campaigns. In addition to having had his work widely exhibited, he has published a book of the doodles he does on his agenda every day using felt-tip pens from the vast pots in front of him. His office wallpaper is made up of his own drawings and paintings.

More seriously, his creative instinct shone through when we were discussing his 'negatives', and I made a suggestion most politicians would reject out of hand, but which he agreed to immediately. It was to base an entire speech to his own party convention around a series of clips beamed into the hall, recorded by people saying not why they *would* vote for him, but why they *wouldn't*. So we sent a film crew around the streets asking Albanians to deliver a direct message to camera, telling us why they hated Edi Rama. 'You are just as corrupt as the other guy,' says one. 'Your sums don't add up,' says another. 'I wouldn't trust you to run anything.' 'I just don't like you, you're so arrogant,' says a third. Once the party delegates got over the shock of seeing their flag-waving, rah-rah convention being intruded upon by opponents and haters, Rama explained that these people had to be persuaded if the party was to win. Then he dealt with their criticisms and complaints one by one. It was a turning point in the campaign, when the momentum in his favour started to become unstoppable. Later, some of the critics backed him publicly, gaining another burst of positive coverage for Rama. He had seen the potential of doing something that, from the perspective of actually very good ratings, he hadn't needed to do, but he did it. 'Poetic licence for maximalism.'

There is something else Rama has in common with Tony Blair. They watch a lot of football on TV, and they like to see the different strategies and personalities emerging from interviews with managers, now a major part of the spectacle that is modern football. 'These guys are never off the media,' Rama says, 'and they are global, and you can see so much of the character of a team in studying the character of the team leader. With Ferguson, he always had that control and authority, but also a real passion and positivity. Guardiola is like a bag of energy, you can see his mind fizzing the whole time. Mourinho is just brilliant, that confidence, I sometimes watch him and imagine the effect that must have in private on his players.'

I was in Albania during part of the 2014 World Cup and watched matches with Rama, including England's exit. 'What was fascinating was how you could see so clearly which of the teams were real teams, and they didn't always have the best players. Colombia, Chile, Costa Rica – most of their players wouldn't get in the big clubs who make up the teams of countries like Spain, Italy or England. But they were better teams. Germany was the one big footballing power whose collective strength was even greater than the sum of its considerable parts. Germany has become something like that as a country too under Angela Merkel's leadership, which partly explains why she and her country are so dominant within the EU.'

He shares my view that Merkel is a very special kind of modern leader, aware of her own power, but also conscious of the need to make sure people understand properly what she is trying to do with it. 'It comes back to my theory about leadership not being singular; in the end, to succeed you need your people to own

> 'In the end, to succeed you need your people to own the strategy.'
> **EDI RAMA**

the strategy, to feel the burden of the responsibility and not to feel alienated as can happen if they are simply told what they have to do, without sharing the understanding as to why. Ego might come into play, but ensuring the egos benefit rather than damage the team is essential. Merkel is the most powerful figure in Europe, but she doesn't feel any need to say it, or act like it. She is great at building alliances and winning arguments, and even greater through being the calmest driving force imaginable.'

There is one final point of connection between sport and politics that he is keen to make. 'In politics, as in basketball, the results depend so much on the preparation you make to meet a challenge, and from basketball I have learned that the preparation will depend very much on the spirit you build as you are developing your strategy. Taking the strategy forward, you are dependent on many other factors and people, some helping, some – like your opponents – entitled not to help, and so you must adjust your leadership based on who those people are and how they relate to what you are trying to do. We are never working in a vacuum. We are always working with a complicated mix of factors swirling around us. Some we can control. Some we think we can control. Some we can't control at all. Try to control what you can, and adapt to the factors you can't, and the more you can do that within your strategy, the greater chance you have of success, knowing that nothing is guaranteed.'

Having now become prime minister, he accepts that his political career has been more successful than his basketball career, but he adds: 'My time in basketball can take some of the thanks for that, both what I learned from winning and what I learned from losing to others. I use and adapt a lot from that old life. There are many differences, of course, but there are parallels. I enjoyed playing sport to a good level, but more than that, it has been good for what I do now.'

PART 2

IT'S ALL IN THE MIND

7

THE RIGHT MINDSET

'The most important muscle is the one between your ears.'

IRONMAN WORLD CHAMPION GUY LEECH

'WHO WANTS IT MORE?'

So all great organisations need the basic building blocks that will help them succeed: a strategic grasp, leadership to hold things together and drive them forward, and a team to put plans into action. But those building blocks in themselves, while essential, are not all there is to it. What ultimately separates those who succeed from the rest is what goes on between their ears and in their hearts and souls. It's how they feel and think, and how they turn those feelings and thoughts into action in pursuit of their objectives. You can have the greatest strategy going, with a perfectly capable leader and team, but without the right mindset these are nothing.

And it's important to understand that 'the right mindset' is not about possessing a particular skill or level of intelligence. It's about the attitude you take to a challenge, and how you use and develop the qualities you have to maximum effect in meeting that challenge. Technical skills take you so far. Mindset is what comes into play through other qualities required of a winner: mental strength, determination, resilience, the ability to respond in the right way to failure, the ability to handle pressure. People are often very dismissive of the supposedly 'great' football player who can't articulate a sentence in post-match interviews without an 'erm', a 'you know' or a 'like

I said'. 'Why are so many professional sportsmen so thick?' they ask. But this is to confuse a great intellect with a winning mindset: the reason that a football player is described as a 'genius' when he's clearly no Einstein is because he has phenomenal technical skill – as do many footballers – but more than that, he knows how to create the right mindset to change the course of a game, make the decisive pass, score the deciding goal, and do it on a sustained basis. Indeed, one of the reasons this chapter is heavily sports-orientated is that sport is where I have most often felt in the presence of winning mindsets in what seems like the purest form.

Baseball's Joe Torre says: 'Just because players have great ability it doesn't automatically mean they're winners. I came across plenty of players who had ability but they were happy to settle for mediocrity, that was good enough. Derek Jeter [in 2014 aged forty, playing his last season after twenty years with the Yankees] was not the most talented player in the world but when it came to will to win, and the will to lead, he was something else. That is an intangible, you cannot put a number on it. The mental side is what makes the difference; attitude and mindset. What made Derek special was something pretty simple: he turned out for work every day and was just determined to do his very best, every single day.'

This is where the question 'Who wants it more?' comes in. Like Jeter, Gary Neville would accept he was not the most talented player in the world, indeed he says he was not even the most talented in his house, giving that accolade to his brother Phil. One of Neville's pre-match rituals was to retreat to a dressing-room toilet cubicle, reflect on his direct opponent for the match and ask, 'Will he want it as much as me? Will he run as far as me?' Or, as Jose Mourinho says of the players he admires most: 'Will he die to win, kill to win?'

In January 2014 Australian cricket captain Michael Clarke stood at the back of the room where his England counterpart Alastair Cook was cutting a forlorn and beaten figure, admitting he was considering his position after eight successive defeats to Australia. As Clarke began his own press conference, he was asked if he felt any sympathy for Cook. He paused, a clear battle going on inside him between the compassionate human and the competitive leader. The competitive mindset won. 'I don't think feeling sorry for an England captain is the right thing to feel.'

'Who wants it more?' suggests something else about a winning mindset, too. It's tempting to view success in the abstract – we all want to do well in a generalised kind of way – but to win we have to pitch ourselves against something or someone else. Olympic swimmer Michael Phelps, who has won twice as many Olympic gold medals – eighteen – as anyone else in history, once told me that it was 'winning

> 'You need fear and doubt to drive you on. Without it, you end up living in the past and being happy with what you achieved.'
>
> **A.P. McCOY**

nothing in Sydney' (he was just fifteen at the time, for heaven's sake) that made him do everything to ensure he won four years later in Beijing. 'Going there, fit, and losing. That really hurt.' Few things motivated Phelps more than the fear of losing. This put him in a certain elite category of athletes, according to Eddie Reese, US swimming team coach at the 2004 and 2008 Olympics. 'Eighty per cent of swimmers like to win and 20 per cent hate to lose and 95 per cent of the Olympic team are from the hate to lose group.'

Four years earlier, in Atlanta, a teenage Ben Ainslie had a similar experience. 'I only won silver,' he recalls, 'and I was totally devastated. I was thinking this might be my only Olympics, because sailing in Britain is so competitive.' Instead, he went away, learned the lessons and resolved to turn it around four years later. He did so in spectacular, brutal fashion, displaying the killer instinct for which he is renowned. He was even criticised by Sir Roger Bannister no less for just how far he was prepared to go, but Ainslie insists: 'If it is within the rules, and helps you win, you do it.' He has won gold in every Olympics since. Ainslie, who attributes his winning mindset and loathing of defeat to having been bullied at school, looks for mindset advantages everywhere. He said that as his career progressed, he used his reputation as a weapon that affected his opponents even before the race began. 'If you keep beating them, eventually they think they're racing for second place and that gives you a good start before you're out there.'

This hatred of defeat comes up again and again among winners. 'I didn't really enjoy success at the time because I was on to worrying about the next race' is how Paralympian athlete Tanni Grey-Thompson puts it. Or, the great words of two-times Olympic decathlon champion Daley Thompson: 'When I lost my decathlon World Record, I took it like a man. I only cried for ten hours.'

Mental skills coach Andy McCann, who was named by Welsh Six Nations Grand Slam-winning rugby captain Sam Warburton as one of the reasons for his and the team's success, puts it this way: 'Those that get to the top have one of two mindsets. A *go to* mindset, which is where your central motivation is the desire to win. And a *move from* mindset where your big driver is fear of failure. Neither is right or wrong. They just are.'

Michael Jordan is one outstanding sportsman who clearly has a 'move from' mindset. It's interesting to note that when he was inducted into the Basketball Hall of Fame, many of the people he thanked were not the ones who had helped him to win but those who had made him confront, or worry about, losing. He thanked Leroy Smith, who was picked ahead of him on a varsity team, 'because when he made the team and I didn't, I wanted to prove not just to Leroy Smith, not just to myself, but to the coach that picked Leroy over me, I wanted to make sure he understood – you made a mistake, dude'. He thanked his room-mate Buzz Peterson, not for being a great room-mate but for winning a 'Player of the Year' award ahead of Jordan. 'Buzz was a great person, it wasn't a fault of his. It was just my competitive nature – I didn't think he could beat me, or that he was better than me as a basketball player.' He thanked players who were deemed to be better than him, and bigger names, because he said they drove him to prove he was at least on their level. He thanked journalists who had doubted and criticised him, and who 'put so much wool on the fire that it kept me, each and every day, trying to get better as a basketball player'. And if anything sums up why Jordan is among the greatest winning mindsets ever, it is his final comment that 'limits, like fears, are often just an illusion'.

This is what distinguishes the will to win from wanting to win. Everyone *wants* to win, or they say they do. But are they prepared to do what it takes to be in a position to win? My mother loved to win at bridge, and she bid and played a grand slam two days before she died, having said it was one of her last wishes many times. But she was just as happy when she lost, provided 'I did my best and enjoyed it'.

> 'When I lost my decathlon World Record, I took it like a man. I only cried for ten hours.'
>
> **DALEY THOMPSON**

That is not, as I often told her, and for which I was often told off, a winning mindset. A winning mindset is better expressed by Pakistani fast bowler Wasim Akram who says: 'Will to win is not about wanting to win: it is about *needing* to win, and then doing what you need to do to be a winner.'

The same principles hold true in other walks of life. I've been struck, for example, by just how competitive great entrepreneurs are, how much they hate to admit defeat and, simultaneously, how they often look to, and study, rivals to create that vital competitive edge in their psyche. Richard Branson, for example, pitches himself against British Airways, whom historically he has loathed (mutually). Charles Dunstone of TalkTalk makes no bones about it. 'It's good to hate your rivals. We hate BT.' It ensures an edge to the conduct of business.

MANAGING THE COMFORT ZONE

It's very hard to excel if your mind is in the comfort zone. Take contemporary British politics, for example. Can the Cabinet or shadow Cabinet, for example, really say that they are waking up every day, asking themselves the 'who wants it more?' question, and then putting in the work and effort needed to show that the answer is them? If it's possible for a team to win an election, then a second, then a third, by taking a relaxed and chilled approach to its work, I have yet to meet that team. None of the UK main parties communicate that sense of absolute focus and determination to do all the things you need to do, in terms of policy and personnel, campaigning and organisation, to get over the line. Compare that mood of coasting with Narendra Modi's stunning win in India. Of course he was helped by the sense that the Congress Party had had its day, but that cannot explain the scale of his victory: he won in part because he wanted it more, campaigned harder, built a better infrastructure, took the decisions that needed to be taken and never stopped working at it.

Pressure is a word usually heard negatively. Managers who lose games are 'under pressure'. Politicians whose poll ratings dip or who are attacked from within are 'under pressure'. CEOs with a falling share price are 'under pressure'. But they are always under pressure. The issue is not how to avoid pressure altogether, but how to handle it constructively, because pressure can be a phenomenal ally in the winning business. It can create physical, emotional and psychological change which can help focus and sharpen the mind, give greater energy to the body, and improve performance. Pressure is good. As Andy McCann puts it: 'Pressure is an opportunity. It is there because "this matters".'

Conversely, the dangers of avoiding pressure are there for anyone to see: complacency and stagnation. Garry Kasparov, the world's greatest chess player, came crashing down when he lost his world title to Vladimir Kramnik in London in 2000. As he explained to me: 'I was at a very high peak and felt invincible. Not only did this make me complacent, but it also meant I had ceased to grow in areas that I did not require to win. I was crushing the competition, so why worry?' Yet it was precisely because he was winning, he says, that he should have kept the pressure up. 'This is why you must always challenge yourself with doing new things, leaving your comfort zone.' In Kasparov's case, the comfort of previous victory proved toxic. Leigh Matthews says that after he finally coached Collingwood to their first Aussie Rules premiership title following a thirty-two-year drought in 1990, the next season 'we went soft, complacent, just going through the motions'. Or as the Uruguay football coach Óscar Tabárez put it in a not dissimilar context: 'Victory is the sweet that can rot the teeth.'

Romanian gymnast Nadia Comaneci knew not only victory but perfection in the eyes of others, when she became the first to be awarded 'the perfect ten' at the Montreal Olympics in 1976. So where do you go after that? Where is the room for improvement when the sport's experts have decreed that you could do no better? The answer is that you soak up the applause, enjoy having gold placed around your neck, but you do not accept it *is* perfection. When I interviewed her back in 2003, she told me: 'You know, I did not think it was perfection. I felt I had done better in training but sometimes you don't see yourself as clearly as others do. I don't think I was perfect, but the judges did and that's what counts. The funny thing is that the scoreboards were not equipped for a ten. They had room for three digits with a decimal point after the first one, so it could go up to 9.99. So when the score came up, it was 1.00, which is not exactly a big score. But of course everyone knew.' Seven perfect tens delivered four gold medals, but it was her own belief that there is always room for improvement – whatever the judges say – that drove her on to more Olympic gold four years later.

All this echoes a conversation I once had with one of Manchester United's back-room team when watching a training session at a time when both Wayne Rooney and Cristiano Ronaldo were playing for the club. Both were stars. Both were adored by fans. I was saying how special they looked, even training. But the coach said to me: 'Ronaldo could become the best player in the world; Rooney couldn't.' He said that Ronaldo never ever stopped believing he could improve, whereas Rooney 'thinks he's made it'. He had indeed 'made it', by most people's definition, in that he was a talisman player for England, hugely wealthy, successful, but the coach said: 'He wouldn't get in any international coach's world eleven. Ronaldo would get in them all.'

> 'Victory is the sweet that can rot the teeth.'
>
> **ÓSCAR TABÁREZ**

Few people ever reach the Kasparov or Rooney level, but many of us have experienced our own version of this. Once something becomes too familiar or easy, mediocre routine can all too easily settle in. I've found this for myself in the arena of public speaking, which is one of my main activities. Now public speaking is actually one of the most common phobias known to man, up there with snakes and spiders. Lance Armstrong told me that the first time he did a big speech – to a Nike conference – it was one of the most terrifying moments of his life, worse than anything he had ever encountered in a bike race. It's something I have got very used to, but a few years ago, on a day-to-day basis I started to reach a point where I felt complacent. My speaking had reached a plateau – it wasn't bad, the speaking agencies were getting good feedback, local Labour parties and mental health campaign groups were asking for more, but I was going through the motions. I was in the comfort zone. My way of putting an edge back into it was to stop delivering prepared remarks, and ask the audience to submit written questions as I arrived so that I would have to build a speech around them there and then. The element of the unknown ensured that I was kept on my toes a bit more, was more aware of my audience, and therefore better able to talk about the things that mattered to them. It also meant I started to enjoy it again.

It was fear of the comfort zone that drove England rugby coach Stuart Lancaster to hire Matt Parker from British Cycling. As Parker puts it: 'I've never come across anyone in the top 2 per cent in the world at elite sport who operates in the comfort zone. Dave [Brailsford] never allowed the comfort zone to settle at cycling, and in rugby I think we have an environment in which the players have to be looked after, but they understand the premise that top athletes don't get anywhere by operating in the comfort zone. Pursuit of excellence has to be relentless; people underplay the amount of time and effort it takes to be the best in the world at anything. It should not, and it cannot, ever be comfortable, because the moment you feel comfortable you stop challenging yourself, so you stop improving.'

A degree of pressure may also be what spurs people to initial greatness: think of all those winning sportsmen and women who have come from backgrounds that are far from comfortable and who decided early on to submit to a gruelling training regime that would transform their lives. The history of boxing is made of such people. Or take Haile Gebrselassie, Paul Tergat, Hicham El Guerrouj – three great African runners I have interviewed, all of whom stressed their background as a prime motivator. (The reason, incidentally, why Gebrselassie's arms and hands do not operate with the evenness normally associated with elite long-distance running is because he used to run ten kilometres to school and ten back, carrying his books in the same hand.) Or what about Dunga, the Brazilian captain and manager who told me he learned to play football by rolling socks into a ball and practising all day with it; or his compatriot Dani Alves, who from an early age had to pick melons from 5 a.m. to help out the family; or his teammate Dante who learned his skills playing in the car park of the supermarket where his mother was a cashier, and who had to sell his possessions to raise the money for a train ticket when offered a trial by a club two hundred kilometres away? Many successful people who have come from more fortunate backgrounds have similarly put themselves under – or been submitted to – early pressure. Richard Branson had parents who encouraged him to take risks from an early age, and supported him if the consequences were not perfect, including when he landed up in trouble with the police for publishing adverts for cures for venereal disease, or breaking the customs and excise laws in getting Virgin Records off the ground. 'When I was little,' he tells me, 'we would go out for a drive and when we were a few miles from home my mum would drop me off and say, "OK, find your way home." It was about teaching us to be independent and resilient.'

PRESSURE GOOD, STRESS BAD

What I'm talking about here, though, is pressure not stress. Pressure can be a force for good, driving you to excel. Stress, as former England striker turned BBC broadcaster Gary Lineker says when talking about the way youngsters are coached in England, is hugely negative. Far from prompting achievement, it makes it seem unattainable. Lineker thinks it partly explains the failings of the national team. 'Kids have to be taught to love the game, and love the ball. People don't set out to teach fear but that's the result of the way they're coached, the way parents scream at their little kids to "get stuck in, take him down", all this nonsense. Putting pressure on kids at that age is ridiculous. All you should say to a little kid playing football is "enjoy it, and work hard if you have a talent". Winning comes from a lack of fear, from confidence, from having a strength and presence of mind to enjoy being able to handle pressure – at the top level of anything, sport, media, business, whatever, you have to savour it, love it.' In other words, it's wrong to be made to feel that you have to feel scared in order to succeed. You do, however, need to learn to live with, and if possible enjoy, pressure, because it's part of what's needed to thrive at the top level.

'The interesting thing about coaching is that you have to trouble the comfortable, and comfort the troubled.'
RIC CHARLESWORTH

Feeling pressure is inevitable in any activity where you are seeking to excel, and it can yield physiological benefits, producing adrenalin which helps you focus and provides added energy. Stress is counterproductive. As Andy McCann puts it: 'The sense of nervousness becomes overwhelming, the heart rate soars, the pulse races, you get short of breath, you might shake or get chest pains. You worry you're losing control.'

Former England cricketer Jeremy Snape gives a classic description of what happens when stress strikes as he recalls for me events in Calcutta in 2002, with 120,000 people in the crowd, and England on track, chasing down a big Indian score. Then disaster, when Snape made a mistake which led to star player Freddie Flintoff being run out. As the Indian crowd went into delirium, Snape had to stand there alone as Flintoff trudged off and the next player came out. 'I had three minutes to fill. I could have thought about recalibrating our run chase and reflected we could still be on course, or I could have worried about how my teammates were reacting to the mistake I made, what the fans and the media were saying. I lost the battle. My next shot was played not by me but by these negative voices in my head. I was stumped by almost two metres, and as I walked off I had to confront the fact that I had choked under pressure because I lost my focus and I lost all sense of perspective.'

An instance of an unusual form of stress came when Leigh Matthews was playing his last Grand Final for Hawthorn against Essendon in front of 100,000 people in Melbourne. Just as he was completing his preparations, he was interrupted by the club's reserve team, who were euphoric at having won the curtain-raiser. 'I knew it was going to be my final game before retirement,' he recalls, 'so already that's quite emotional. When they came in, they meant well, but it tipped me over the edge. Crying after a game is fine, let the emotions out, but not before! It meant I wasted a lot of emotional energy that should have come out on the field. That experience stuck with me and it's something I took with me into coaching, that at the really big games the challenge for the coach is to keep the players calm. The hype and the excitement and the atmosphere, you'd have to be made of wood not to feel the importance of the occasion, but you have to be careful not to let the motivation tip into arousal that's dangerous. It's what happened to me that time and we lost the game. Motivation is "I want to be here, because I know I'm going to feel good and make others feel good if I win". "Arousal" is where the adrenalin that can help with maximum athletic performance goes too far and you lose control, you lose energy and you lose concentration. Getting that balance right between the pressure of the moment being good and the arousal becoming too intense, that's the challenge on the day of a Grand Final. I coached in five Grand Finals and that experience with the reserves definitely helped me.' They lost the match heavily, and he was in tears again as despite the defeat his teammates carried him off shoulder-high in recognition of his remarkable career.

> 'You can't be a dickhead all week and play good on Sunday.'
>
> **JACK GIBSON**

So it's a delicate balancing act. You need the pressure, but you can't afford to be hamstrung by the stress that pressure can create. What is certain, though, is that the pressure does need to be there. I for one don't believe that success can be achieved effortlessly – the idea of the carefree genius is a myth. Even those who may come across as relaxed rarely are when you drill down. Lineker is a case in point. He was one of the first top sportsmen I met – though at the time I didn't know just how top he would become – as we went to the same senior school in Leicester. He was not the most naturally talented footballer of his era (he is just a month younger than Diego Maradona, for starters) and his laid-back manner suggested he might not have the mental toughness required either. But he had a mindset composed of two driving thoughts: 'I want to be the best at what I do; to be that, I have to be more determined and cleverer than others who might have more natural ability.' He applied that in football, and so reached a level of achievement that put him second only to Bobby Charlton in England's all-time goal-scorer list; he is also the only Englishman to have won the 'Golden Boot', awarded to the player who scores the most goals in a World Cup. 'I might not have looked it but I was unbelievably driven,' he recalls. 'I remember once scoring two goals in a game we won and I came off and the other players could tell I wasn't happy and it was because I really wanted to get a hat-trick that day and I should have done, but I missed an easy chance. From very early in my life, I wanted to be the leading goalscorer, first at school, then with every team I played for, then with England, I wanted to be the best.

Getting the Golden Boot was amazing for me because even as a kid the thing that drove me was this idea I had that if I worked hard I could be the best goalscorer in the world. Believe me, I worked. I didn't enjoy training, but I did it, I worked hard, thousands and thousands of hours, when my mates would be out having fun.'

The question, then, is not how to ignore pressure, but how to handle it, and avoid falling into what ex-England football manager Glenn Hoddle once described as 'the terror zone'. This is something most of us have experienced: it's the place where pressure becomes so intense that you feel ill, panic-stricken and unable to cope, and where, if you're not able to check your feeling, you lose strength and confidence and start to make the wrong calls. Plenty of students will testify to that when approaching exams. It's what led me to fail my driving test five times despite my instructor telling me I was a good driver. For politicians or business people, it comes when you are hit by the seemingly unanswerable question – think of Home Secretary Michael Howard being well and truly skewered by *Newsnight*'s Jeremy Paxman simply asking the same question again and again – or it's the car-crash moment: I can still see the expression on Gordon Brown's face when radio presenter Jeremy Vine played him the tape of the prime minister calling a woman voter a 'bigot' without realising his microphone was still on. And remember the look on the faces of the journalists hearing BP boss Tony Hayward dig himself deeper and deeper into a hole virtually every time he spoke when handling the Deepwater crisis. For footballers, it can come when the dreaded penalty shoot-out is needed to settle matches. Some of the most dramatic moments of failure have come when players who would normally score with ease suddenly blast the ball over the bar or tap it lamely into the arms of the goalkeeper.

Glenn Hoddle gave a fascinating insight, in Mike Carson's book *The Manager*, into how he coped with the build-up to the World Cup in France in 1998. 'I probably had more pressure than the Prime Minister – because even he was putting pressure on me to win!' He talked of a squad visit to see a West End show when word got out and huge crowds appeared. 'The weight that I felt was enormous – and we were just going to the theatre!' But he then came up with an answer that worked for him. 'I learned then that if I could approach pressure with real gratitude, the pressure would actually shift before my eyes. It's an amazing thing, and I wish I'd known it when I was twenty. But if you can take a really pressurised situation and be grateful for this pressure – suddenly you diffuse it, it disappears . . . If you don't, the pressure builds up, and can quickly take you to your terror zone.'

Gary Lineker recalls the time England were losing 2–1 to Cameroon in the 1990 World Cup Finals, and were awarded a penalty. 'As I prepared to take it, I thought, "I am now in a position millions of mere mortals would love to be in, so I am not going to be scared, I am going to enjoy it. I can make a mark here."' In other words, he didn't feel fear. He felt pressure, and loved it. He says he felt 'special and proud' that he was the one lining up to take it, and that gave him the confidence to do what he had done so many times in training – blast it home. He did the same in the shoot-out at the end of extra time, which England won. 'It's a wonderful feeling,' he says, adding swiftly: 'But if all you feel is fear, you have no chance.' He said the commentator cliché that shoot-outs are a lottery is nonsense. 'I love penalties. I loved taking them. I love watching them. They are the ultimate test of a player's technique under pressure.' Ben Ainslie says: 'You must learn to love the pressure.'

The temptation here is to respond: 'Easier said than done.' The Lineker–Ainslie approach, after all, suggests a fundamental inner confidence that many of us might not feel in high-pressure moments. But there are strategies that can be called on to achieve that necessary moment of, if not calm, avoidance of panic. This is something that Clive Woodward learned from his visits to the Royal Marines in the late nineties. Three young marines were introduced to Woodward's England squad by their brigadier with the simple words: 'these men should be dead'. The marines then gave a graphic description of how, despite relatively little combat experience, they fought their way out of a deadly skirmish. 'We were all sitting there thinking, "How the hell did you get out of it?"' recalls Woodward. 'And they told us it was a situation they had gone over in the class-room, and in training, again and again. Even though it was happening for real, the training kicked in, and they somehow got through it.' For Woodward it was an important moment. 'We took that thinking away, and started applying it to prepare for pressure moments in rugby. The best way to deal with pressure is trying to predict what might happen, practise, and then when you've predicted it you are in a better place to handle it.'

He then describes 'the scariest thing I have ever done in my life': a simulated helicopter ditching exercise on that four-day visit. 'They start off by showing you a video from the eighties of pulling a helicopter out – everyone inside is dead but they are all strapped in. So they create this exercise where you have to get out of a heli-copter when it ditches and you are strapped in. They had a huge swimming pool and above it is a big square box that simulates a helicopter. It's all about how you're going to get out of this box when you're dropped into the water. How are you going to get out of the one small hole? How are you going to communicate as a team so you all get out? There is in fact absolutely no danger – the back is completely open so if you panic you can just unbolt and swim out. But the pressure we felt was incredible, the heartbeat racing, and the fear of what was going to happen was huge. When they drop you in, they turn the box upside down a few times to disorientate you, and it is pitch black and you mustn't panic. And the biggest fear by the way is letting your teammates down and bottling it by swimming out. You hit the water and you've got to go out one by one, and if you're eighteenth out, you've got to wait for ninety seconds underwater and not panic. Also, they're filming everything and everyone so if you bottle it you know it's going to be shown to all your teammates in the meeting that night. It was great fun but Jeez it was scary.' An extreme situation, then. But, through practice, it was one that could be overcome. It was partly through this experience that T-CUP (Think Correctly Under

Pressure) became one of Woodward's mantras. And Woodward applies a similar approach to dealing with the media or other potentially stressful situations. 'If you imagine the worst thing that can happen, first it forces you to think through how to deal with it, and then nine times out of ten the worst doesn't happen.'

Endless practice and preparation, then, not only improve your skills but help you cope with the pressure of a difficult situation. The last time I was genuinely nervous before speaking in public was at the Chilcot Inquiry into the Iraq war, though less on the day itself than in the preceding weeks. I knew it really mattered. Once I received the email telling me when I was due to give evidence, I therefore threw most things out of the diary for some time beforehand, to devote myself to preparing for it, with the dictum from Benjamin Franklin on a Post-it on my computer, 'By failing to prepare, you are preparing to fail.' I knew the media attention would be big and largely hostile, I knew the potential consequences were serious, so I spent hours reading and rereading all the relevant documents. I worked through all the difficult questions that I might expect from the Inquiry panel and made sure I had the answers. Thinking in ink, I wrote everything down, again and again, until I had it all locked away inside my head. I got together friends with forensic minds and asked them to think of the toughest questions, and then grill me. I imagined the worst. I put myself in the position of aggressive journalists determined to knock me off my stride as I went in, and worked out how to deal with that. As it was a cold, snowy day, with ice on the ground, I wore old shoes with rough soles less likely to slip when I arrived at the QEII Conference Centre, a huge media pack outside. I imagined being stormed by protesters during the hearing; it didn't happen, but it has happened at other events, and the prior visualisation has helped me to stay calm, not overreact, trust others to move in and sort it out. I imagined a situation where one of the panel wouldn't let me finish a point I was making, and thought through how best to handle that. I tried to be rested but wanted to feel stretched as well. I also had a session with Andy McCann to 'get my head in the right place'.

We can all develop our own coping strategies when we feel pressure reaching stressful levels. I used to hold a paper clip and press it into my palm. That was taught to me by a lawyer in a libel case when he said the other side's only hope was to get me to lose my temper. He said it was a simple diversion strategy, moving irritation caused by someone else to pain caused by myself. Another one, taught to me by McCann, is just to rub both thumbs and forefingers together, and smile. This works because we are taking control of something we can control – those little actions – and enjoying the fact that only we know we're doing it.

Of course, being prepared doesn't necessarily remove the unpleasant side effects that go with feeling nervous. Tanni Grey-Thompson, one of the best Paralympian athletes of all time, used to be sick before any big event. She designed her diet around it, not eating toast for example, 'because toast is horrible to throw up'. England rugby star Jonny Wilkinson first experienced pre-match nausea at the age of seven, and before virtually every game thereafter. It's a horrible feeling. But in both their cases preparation and prior experience helped make it manageable, and the pressure of which it was a manifestation helped them perform.

THE POWER OF FOCUS

So far I have talked about preparation and focus in a rather negative way – as a means of staving off the problems that pressure can give rise to. But it's also important to acknowledge the absolutely central place that both play in the positive aspects of a winning mindset.

Talent without focus doesn't succeed. You hear this time and again from the people who reach the top. Former Manchester United youth team coach Eric Harrison, for example, talks of a player from the Beckham–Giggs era who personifies this – Raphael Burke, an immensely talented player whom few now will remember. 'I still feel disappointed to this day,' says Harrison. 'He was such a talent, but didn't make the most of it.' Burke himself says, 'I was talented, but I didn't sacrifice like the others did.' His talent, in other words, only took him so far. Mindset let him down. The right stuff in so many ways, but the wrong attitude. By contrast, Gary Neville, a member of the same class of '92, concentrated ferociously on the game. Like Lineker before him, he took a conscious decision to tell his friends he wouldn't be able to go out with them in the way that most friends do, because his focus was football. He established a routine – bed by 9.15 every Thursday and Friday night for a Saturday match, girlfriendless aged sixteen to twenty – and went on to become United captain, a treble winner, an England regular, now an England coach and respected TV commentator. His attitude reminds me of the great Muhammad Ali quote (one of many): 'I hated every minute of training, but I said: "Don't quit. Suffer now and live the rest of your life as a champion."'

> 'Mental toughness is doing things you don't want to do.'
> **CRAIG BELLAMY**

Focus is not some abstract desirable quality: you have to focus *on* something – whether it's an immediate hurdle or an ultimate goal. I always remember when rock-star campaigners Bono and Bob Geldof were lobbying Tony Blair before a G8 summit in Germany, and Tony was warning them that for various political reasons he was not going to be able to deliver all they wanted regarding the writing off of Third World debt. Geldof went into one of his customary effing and blinding rages. Tony tried to calm him down, by saying we would get there but because of all the different agendas of the G8 countries, it felt like we were looking at Everest; to which Bono replied: 'When you see Everest, Tony, you don't look at it, you fucking climb it.' It was a brilliant encapsulation of a mindset Bono told me years later he learned from Geldof: 'I have never known anyone quite like Bob. He just does not understand the word "no".'

Perhaps the best way to appreciate what focus can look like is to consider a sportsman who is the extreme embodiment of it: Tiger Woods. Woods' former coach, Hank Haney, has written a fascinating account of his time with him, *The Big Miss*, in which he describes how Woods practised. He would take small breaks, during which he stood or sat in silence taking in the previous twenty or so shots. When Haney asked him what he was doing, Woods replied, 'I'm just thinking about what we did.' This would usually occur when they were working on something uncomfortable for Woods and it represented his willingness to concentrate on weaknesses: he didn't just want to play better than everyone else, he wanted to practise better too. 'It was like his Church,' says Haney. This illustrates something we should all do well to consider: the difference between simplicity and ease. Woods makes things look simple. But what he does is not easy. It is the result of natural talent, certainly, but allied to phenomenal hard work, training and focus.

Such focus can be extraordinary in its intensity. A player on the PGA tour, Grant Waite, once asked Woods, busy practising on the range, if he wanted to meet motocross world champion James Stewart. Initially Woods had no idea who the man was, but once Waite had explained that he was the first African American to make it big in the sport, the golfer became more interested, thinking he could learn something about Stewart's approach to competition and his mindset under pressure. Waite introduced them. After a while Woods asked him what he ate pre-competition. 'Oh, nothing special, just a Coke and a Snickers.' The answer told Woods that Stewart wasn't in his league as an athlete or a winner. He just turned away and went back to hitting balls.

Rude? Probably. Tunnel-visioned? Certainly. Socially a bit weird? Yes. But this gives you an idea of what focus entails. When I ask Andy McCann, one of the most selfless and giving people I have ever met, to list the components of a winning sports mindset, he puts 'selfishness' first. 'They have to be totally focused and determined to get what they can out of this phase of their life, and then they're more likely to do the things and make the sacrifices needed to win.' I once followed Woods for a few holes at a tournament. The crowds were huge and, as he walked from green to tee, very close to him. Fans were cheering and hollering, urging him on. I could sense the ones closest longed for him to look at them, just one little piece of eye contact, acknowledgement of their support. But apart from the occasional tip of his baseball cap after a successful putt, there was nothing. Eyes fixed ahead, it was as though nobody on the course existed but him and his caddie.

Haney views Woods' mental strength and ability to execute great shots under intense pressure as unrivalled, something he credits to his mother Kultida – of Thai Buddhist descent – who is often unheralded compared with his father Earl. 'These qualities, foremost among them an extraordinary ability to focus and stay calm under stress, also included selfishness, obsessiveness, stubbornness, coldness, ruthlessness, pettiness, and cheapness.' Put those qualities together and you perhaps see an utterly focused, totally self-obsessed, not very nice human being, but Haney says: 'When they were all at work in the competitive arena they helped him win.' And that, of course, is all Woods really cares about. His father Earl was proud of the way he 'trained' Woods in the art of concentration.

> I pulled every nasty, dirty, obnoxious trick on my son every week. I dropped a bag of bricks at the impact of his swing. I imitated a crow while he was stroking a putt. When he was ready to hit a shot, I'd toss a ball in front of him; I would stand in front of him and move as he was about to hit the ball. Sometimes he got so angry he would stop his club on the downward swing and glare at me. Then, one day, instead of glaring, he smiled. I knew then he had learned and he would be a great, mentally strong golfer.

Haney's descriptions of Woods' focus reminded me of the special forces soldier in Kosovo who told me that one of his superiors used to address the team with a porn film playing just behind him and warn the soldiers there would be trouble if they allowed their eyes – their focus – to wander towards it. He wanted them looking at him, and listening.

I've seen this kind of focus, in a less extreme form, among many people I admire. Politicians, such as Tony and Bill Clinton, facing a difficult interview or debate, would sometimes fall silent, retreat into themselves and think things through repeatedly and remorselessly. Ian Botham has admitted to me that he could be selfish in pursuit of his goals, putting daily concerns to one side, including family, to concentrate on the particular sporting challenge ahead. Sebastian Coe and Brendan Foster similarly confess that often friends and family would be invisible as they went into the mindset needed pre-race. And Nick Faldo tells me that while he sometimes experienced a charge from the support of a crowd, more often, like Woods, he just blocked it out of his mind.

Ben Ainslie says 'emotionlessness' is an important asset under pressure, and names Woods and Roger Federer as the masters. 'I think emotion comes into the performance when things are going well, and you can be confident, which is good, or cocky, which is bad. Then when your emotions are down, you feel a lack of confidence, and that can hurt performance. So actually just focusing on the process, whatever else is going on, it is so important. Woods in his pomp was unbelievable. He expected to win. Schumacher was the same.'

Michael Phelps' coach Bob Bowman taught the swimmer numerous acronyms, one of which was WIN: what's important now? Bowman says, in Phelps' autobiography *No Limits*: 'One thing that separates Michael from other swimmers is that if they don't feel good they don't swim good. That's not the way it is for Michael. Michael performs no matter how he's feeling. He has practised it a long time. He knows exactly what he wants to get done, and he's able to compartmentalize what's important.' This too is hard, but vital, and again something we can all relate to. You are about to go

> 'I am in the zone when my positive thoughts are beating the negative and the conscious and subconscious are in harmony. Then I am operating by instinct and that is a wonderful feeling.'
> **SACHIN TENDULKAR**

to an important meeting. On the way you get a call with some bad news, or a worry about one of your children. It is almost impossible to put it out of your mind. But emphasise the 'almost'. During that meeting you have to put it out of your mind, or else you won't get the best out of yourself. Not easy, but there are techniques that can help. If ever you see a New Zealand All Black running his hand over his brow, he might well be wiping away the sweat. But it's also one of their 'centring techniques', as is raising their head to look at the stadium roof; it gets them back focused on what they are meant to be doing at that moment. On the golf course, Nick Faldo found that talking to himself would help. 'Sometimes the conversation with myself comes out and I'll literally be saying "Right" – I say "right" a lot – "Right, come on, get the fuck on with it, concentrate, you dick. Rotate, turn, hit."'

Faldo, who won six majors, says that his all-time hero is not a golfer, but Björn Borg. 'I modelled myself on him. I learned later that when he played a bad shot, or suffered a bad line call, he just stood still and twiddled his racket twice, flick, flick, like that, and that reset himself. Technique was vital, of course, but his temperament was the key. I liked the way he just got on with it, whatever was going on around him, staying focused and disciplined.'

Andy McCann explains to me why golfers take practice swings. 'It's partly to practise the shot, obviously, but it is also to centre themselves and slow themselves down. Adrenalin makes us do things faster than we normally would. If they swing too fast they hit a bad shot, so they centre and slow. The other thing is they're trying to put all thought out of their mind apart from the shot. At that moment they don't want any thought, positive or negative. They want the process, not what they're feeling.'

Now here's what can happen when you lose that crucial focus. In the Sydney Olympics, American Olympic shooter Matthew Emmons was heading for gold, with one round left. He took his final shot and then realised to his horror he had aimed at the wrong target, and so scored zero. He explained later that in his mind he was already on the podium, celebrating his win. He didn't win. On another occasion, also heading for a win, he did the same thing again, the memory triggering the action.

It is that kind of spectacular failure that requires resilience in the aftermath. It is to the League Managers Association's credit that in the macho world of football management they have compiled a guide to psychological well-being, a lot of it based on the work of Stanford professor Carol Dweck and the perpetual face-off between 'the growth mindset' and the 'fixed mindset'. Many politicians could take a leaf out of the same book.

The fixed mindset avoids challenge, gives up, ignores criticism, feels threatened by others' success, fails to fulfil potential. The growth mindset embraces challenge, seeks out obstacles, learns from criticism and failure and other people's success, and is always looking for more achievement.

FROM FOCUS TO OBSESSION

It's not hard to extrapolate from the way successful people operate that there's more than a degree of obsession involved. When I asked Clive Woodward to name his single most important quality, he did not hesitate. 'I am an obsessive.' When I've talked to any of the many athletes who have gone through the guiding hands of a Woodward or a Brailsford, or a Wenger, Ferguson, Mourinho or Guardiola, the same words and phrases keep coming up: obsessive, obsessed, driven, attention to detail, never accepting second best, hate losing at anything. They have big-picture leadership skills, the ability to inspire with a vision of success, but it is the obsessive focus and attention to detail alongside that vision that puts them into the super-elite league. If you want to win any major contest, you have to be obsessed with winning, and obsessive about doing what is required to win. Obsessed with the objective; obsessive in implementing the strategy and tactics.

Of course 'obsessive' is not always seen as a compliment, but Clive Woodward says that in the land of the winners, it must be a positive. 'I like the word obsessive,' he says. 'I like it because so many other people don't like it. It sets you apart. If someone calls you an obsessive person, they think there's something wrong with you, but I pride myself on it. My definition of obsession is a single thought or action occupying someone's mind. I regard myself as an obsessive person in the sense that once I set out to do something, I want to win –whatever it is. It's a good trait. It's not something you should be worried about. You can live a perfectly normal life with that mindset. Obsession is not about sending emails after midnight and trying to prove how hard you work; obsession is just obsession for the detail of the what, the how and the why you've got to do all the things you need to do to win.' One of the real pleasures of working with Woodward in 2005 was seeing up close Jonny Wilkinson, and his phenomenal attitude to training and prep-aration. I ask Woodward what set Wilkinson apart. 'He was always first at training and the last to leave. No matter how well he played he had an ability to criticise himself.' Wilkinson told me that after a match he would focus internally on his own game, things he should have done differently, run it round in his head, again and again, 'always finding things I could have improved on'.

Teams are inevitably a mix of different sorts of people. Sports psychology is in part about getting the best out of each individual for the benefit of the team. When performance psychologist Dr Phil Jauncey was working with the Brisbane Lions Aussie Rules team, he made players and coaches complete a questionnaire, from which he analysed their personalities according to four types: mozzies who prefer instinct to thinking; enforcers who like control and who tend towards anger and denial; thinkers who worry and need clear instruc-tions; feelers who need constant reassurance. Everyone is a mix of those four, and his questions were designed to get the balance right, and help coaches deal with the individuals. Head coach Leigh Matthews turned out as 35 per cent enforcer, 27.5 per cent thinker, 20 per cent mozzie, 17.5 per cent feeler. That self-knowledge, he says, helped him understand his own decisions better. Also, though he insists he did not pick or drop players according to these profiles, it did make him think about the psychological balance of the team as a whole. And here's an interesting one in today's world where WAGs are sometimes as famous as their husbands or boyfriends: 'We even did a profiling evening with the wives and girlfriends one time. This enabled everyone to understand each other a little better and, to be football selfish, how to assist their playing partners to be better footballers.' Now that is paying attention to the detail of what has an impact upon the individuals who make up a team: real mindset professionalism.

8

THE EXTREME MIND

'There is definitely a link between hyper achievement, and being a slightly or even seriously unbalanced personality.'

DAVE BRAILSFORD

THE DANGERS OF OBSESSION

I once spent a night in Dublin with footballer Roy Keane when we were both appearing on a new TV chat show there, and while he was fantastic company – funny, straight-talking, full of great anecdotes and strong opinions – I felt that he was just a moment or two from explosion. His now famous enmity with Alex Ferguson, who he knew to be a friend of mine, was clearly in development, and amid the laughter and joking – Bob Geldof was there too, geeing things along – I sensed a simmering anger that could erupt at any time. And I reminded myself that here was a great footballer who, in the course of his career, had received thirteen red cards. Arsenal's Patrick Vieira – Keane's great rival – is in my experience laid-back, relaxed, charming, clever. But in his time, his obsessive competitiveness meant that he tied with Duncan Ferguson as the most red-carded player in Premier League history. I vividly recall a programme Keane and Vieira once did together when the Irishman said, rather chillingly, 'My job was to hurt people.' He certainly did hurt them, not least with his assault on Alf-Inge Haaland in a Manchester derby in 2001, launching a leg-breaking, knee-high tackle on Haaland and then continuing to berate him as he lay on the floor over an incident some years before when Haaland had accused him of faking an injury. That was not his 'job'. His job was to drive his team's midfield. The obsessive desire to win, in other words, can reach a tipping point beyond which it becomes counter-productive – and, indeed, dangerous for both oppressor and victim.

The most dramatic and famous modern global example of a winning mindset becoming so obsessed, so obsessive, so unwilling even to brook the possibility of defeat that too many lines got crossed comes in the form of Lance Armstrong. When I left Downing Street in 2003, one of the first projects I took on was a series on great sportsmen and women for *The Times*. The Texan cyclist and cancer survivor was my top target for an interview, and I was thrilled when he said yes. I freely confess that I fell totally for the Armstrong legend, finding him personable, intelligent, funny, warm, charismatic. I believed his protestations that he was the most drugs-tested athlete on the planet, had never tested positive, and it was time his critics let go. And I loved his mindset, summed up in what was without doubt the best single quote of the series of interviews running over several months.

> When I was sick, I didn't want to die. When I race, I don't
> want to lose. Dying and losing – it's the same thing.

As we sat drinking coffee in the Girona apartment he was then sharing with singer Sheryl Crow, and I heard those words leave his lips, perhaps the former journalist in me should have been more alert to the logic. I did ask him if he really meant it, that the fear of death when being treated for cancer was on a par with the fear that he might lose a bike race to Jan Ullrich. He said he did, and I believed him. Knowing what has been confirmed since, a confession of doping finally dragged from him, the logic is obvious: if you equate losing a race with losing your life, then just as most people would do anything to stay alive, so in his case he would do anything to win.

There was another moment too, which in retrospect should have alerted me. I asked him who, if anyone, he hated. He asked me to turn the tape off – the only time he did so. He said he hated David Walsh, the *Sunday Times* journalist who was pursuing him relentlessly. He picked my brains on what I knew about him – not that much – and made clear he was determined to get revenge on him for 'this fucking assassination of my character'. Again, a hint that the mindset had gone beyond that of a mere sporting winner – which he certainly was – to something more extreme and dangerous. Today, I can only cringe when I read his quote that his cancer 'caused me to be a brutally open and honest person'. I cringe even more at how I faithfully recorded – and believed – his statement that 'I'm not the first and I won't be the last [to face allegations] but I know the truth and that's what matters to me. People want to know that the guy who worked the hardest and fought the hardest and got the best coaches and the best teammates went out and won fair and square, and that's what I've been doing.' His is a story of what can happen when the desire to win goes beyond any legal or moral limit, either through greed or more likely simply because winning becomes an obsession – and a need – of the same significance as staying alive.

'Dying and losing – they're the same thing.' That may be a sociopathic mindset, I don't know. But it is an ultra-winning mindset, for sure. How many coaches tell their charges to 'fight as though your life depends on it'? How many businesses tell their staff they are in a life-and-death struggle for survival? Plenty. How often did Tony Blair say to me, or I say to him, 'If we don't sort this, we're dead'? Often enough. Armstrong, though, really meant it.

How to know whether you are going too far, how to know if you are losing perspective, how to know whether the desire to win is blinding you to other important realities – family, friends, mental stability, moral compass – these are issues likely to face all who operate in high-pressure, high-stakes situations at times. Once it happens – and there are those who say it happened to me, not least my partner Fiona – then bosses, colleagues and above all the family and friends you are neglecting become vital to ensuring the mindset does not stray into the danger zone. It is why, once again, it's so important that people don't surround themselves with yes-men, scared to challenge or confront.

I emailed Armstrong when I began writing this book and asked if I could see him again. 'Sounds good to me,' he replied immediately. 'You would want to do this in person?' I said yes, and we then began to discuss logistics, and agreed Austin, Texas, was the place to meet. Then he went quiet, so it hasn't yet happened. But it looks like it's on again, hopefully in time for the paperback, and he knows I might push him a little harder.

There is still a part of me that wants to admire Armstrong. Standing on the barren roadside high up Mont Ventoux, and seeing him lead the field in blistering heat, sweat falling from his chin in an incessant trickle, his heart rate sustained at levels most people could not endure for one yard let alone mile after mile of mountain climb, his sinewy legs pumping at a pace that had his bike and body seeming to defy gravity, there was something almost spell-binding about his athleticism. But it's a reminder that an obsessive mindset that has to win at all costs can contain the seeds of its own destruction. Armstrong won for years, but has ultimately lost so much. In the now much-derided world of banking, Fred Goodwin and Bob Diamond felt like winners, and were treated like winners, for most of their lives. No more. Rupert Murdoch's papers got a lot of the best stories over time, and he built up considerable power and influence, but his reputation, and that of many of his journalists, has been battered.

We see it elsewhere too: football clubs which win for a season but end up bankrupt; schools which focus on easier subjects to get exam grades up, rather than investing in teaching, having great results for a couple of years but being found out in the end; businesses which pursue short-term profit over developing quality products and motivated staff not growing in the same way as those who think long-term; politicians who take short-term choices ahead of long-term strategy losing over time and so being judged harshly by history.

HARNESSING THE EXTREME MIND

But just because obsessiveness can become destructive doesn't mean that anyone with what I suppose one could term an 'extreme' mind should automatically be regarded with suspicion. In fact, the opposite is often true.

One of the most telling things I have heard about the mindset of winners is a remark made to me by Billy Beane, the man who transformed Oakland A's baseball team with data-driven analysis which became famed throughout sport and beyond as *Moneyball*, first the best-selling book, then the Brad Pitt movie. 'The reason all really successful people have to be slightly mad,' he said, 'is because people like that are not capable of living in the comfort zone. It is a state of mind that makes sure you never rest on your laurels, always focus on the next thing, never ever let yourself slide into that comfort zone.'

Now 'mad' is not a term that should be readily bandied about, but I do think Beane is on to something here. The fact is that people who want to succeed, to push things that bit further, tend to have characteristics that place them beyond what is generally defined as 'normal'. Nassir Ghaemi, the Iranian-born professor of psychiatry and pharmacology at Tufts Medical Center in Boston, and a renowned expert on bipolar disorder, says that 'normal' people are naturally conformist. They go through education and career paths in which the goal is often to be liked and to achieve according to the norms of a previous generation, parents who want to keep them safe and secure, teachers who want to get them through standard exams. Ghaemi believes this 'normality' obsession discourages the development of skills needed to win. Great achievement therefore requires something beyond normal.

My point here is not that 'normal' is somehow wrong or unproductive. But neither is that true of the converse. I used to think I was something of a lone voice whenever – with my mental health campaigner hat on – I would talk about the benefits as well as the problems associated with mental turbulence: the fact that I can look

back at a nervous breakdown in 1986 as the best thing that ever
happened to me, because it forced me to turn my life around; the
fact that the mental torture of depression allows you to appreciate
good times more; and that the mania that sometimes comes before
and after a depressive episode can produce great bursts of activity
and creativity. I am not recommending the psychotic attacks which
led to my breakdown and hospitalisation. Nor am I willing the horror
of depression upon anyone. But I am saying that characteristics we
would associate with mental health 'problems' might also be the
engines that help one to overcome, to succeed, to win.

Professor Ghaemi, for example, with whom I shared a platform on 'power and madness' before a performance of *King Lear* at the National Theatre in London, argues that innovation and creativity are 'explicitly a reflection of mania'. He suggests there are four main features of mania: increased rapid thought, increased physical and mental activity, increased likelihood of taking risk, increased confidence and self-esteem. When

> 'The reason all really successful people have to be slightly mad is because people like that are not capable of living in the comfort zone.'
> **BILLY BEANE**

taken to excess, as I know, those characteristics can be dangerous,
potentially deathly. But, as I also know – from both before my
breakdown when I was a young journalist, and after I had recovered
when I took on new and bigger challenges – there can be enormous
advantages in those characteristics when the mania is more or less
under control. As Philip Gould pointed out, I came up with some
of the most important lines for Tony Blair when going through a
manic phase, and others when in the throes of what he called 'the
glums'. I wrote the first draft of my third novel, about a teenage
alcoholic girl, after cogitating and getting writer's block over a year
or so, in nine days. One of them was Christmas Day. I couldn't
stop once the creative dam broke. That was mild mania making me
more creative than usual. By definition, increased rapid thought and

increased physical and mental activity enable you to work harder, get more done, so provided the work is good and the decisions being made are the right ones, this should in theory lead to more success and achievement. Additionally, no innovation happens without a degree of jeopardy. As Voltaire said, there is no greater pain than the birth of a new idea and part of the pain is the anxiety that it could go wrong.

When I ask Dave Brailsford which other walk of life he has learned most from, he doesn't hesitate in his answer. 'Psychiatry – no doubt about it.' He describes his hiring of psychiatrist Dr Steve Peters as 'maybe my most important single act of innovation – definitely innovation, not marginal gains; Steve was much bigger than a marginal gain'.

Elite cycling is about engineering, aerodynamics, fitness, endurance, teamwork, tactics, planning, diet, a mass of interlinking technical, logistical and human issues and characteristics. But to Brailsford, the mindset of the athletes is more important than any of those. 'Most teams will get to the same place in time, in terms of logistics and engineering, so it will be the performance of the athletes that makes the difference, and getting them in the best mental and physical shape is what coaching and leadership are about.'

When Brailsford came across him, Peters was dealing with psychopathic personalities at Rampton high-security psychiatric hospital. 'I realised that a lot of the things he knew applied to our riders. I'm not saying they're psychopaths, but what makes them special is that their minds don't work in the same way as most people's. They are extreme. Extreme ambition. Extreme talent. Extreme drive and ego. But there are risks with that too, risks to them as individuals, and risks to the team. They can be strong but they are also vulnerable, and Steve was brilliant at making the strong side stronger and the vulnerable side less vulnerable.'

I sat through a Peters presentation to Team Sky's sponsors, at the heart of which was the insight that we have a rational part to our brain – the human – and a more emotional and less controllable part – the chimp, and these are in perpetual struggle. Controlling or at least managing the chimp so it does no damage, or can actually be made to do some good, is essentially what Peters' work with sports stars is about. This understanding of how your brain works, and how you can exercise more control over it, has given Peters a list of testimonials from top sports stars, thanking him for the role he played in their success, footballer Steven Gerrard and cyclists Sir Chris Hoy and Victoria Pendleton among them. Troubled snooker star Ronnie O'Sullivan, with his history of depression and addiction, also credits Peters with helping him turn around his career.

Peters' insights show that our minds are not in a constant state of equilibrium – nor are they programmed to be. We should not therefore be afraid or regard it as a problem that great achievements may involve a degree of mania. Some of the finest names in history faced real mental health turmoil at times.

A few years ago I co-wrote a booklet with historian Nigel Jones for the mental health campaign Time to Change, in which we set out the mental health stories of five of the greatest figures in history: Winston Churchill, Abraham Lincoln, Charles Darwin, Florence Nightingale and Marie Curie. All had what doctors today would define as some form of mental illness. The booklet was called 'A World Without' and asked people to imagine a world in which those five had never been able to fulfil their potential because their mental frailties had been viewed as overwhelming obstacles. It would be a very different place. They were all major change-makers, their influence still with us today. Florence Nightingale, for example, single-handedly reinvented the basic concept of health care as well as challenging the idea that women could not be medical professionals. She badgered bureaucrats, chivvied male chauvinists, and relentlessly pressured authority with the awesome power of her character, becoming an adept politician along the way. But she had a personality that today would be described as bipolar. For their part, Churchill and Lincoln were both depressives – in Churchill's case, of the manic variety.

How can this lack of 'normality' be turned to advantage? Often,

I think, because there is a compensating benefit. Ghaemi believes there is a strong link between depression and realism, which can contribute to leadership skills required in times of challenge and difficulty. This may in part be because depressives have experienced such lows that they can envisage many different – often bad – outcomes and this ability perhaps allows them to lead well in a crisis, or to have better strategies for avoiding it. 'The thing about crisis is that the depressive imagines the worst and works to avoid it,' he says. 'The optimist believes they can handle the crisis and that everything will turn out fine.' When Prime Minister Neville Chamberlain was pursuing a policy of appeasement, Churchill was constantly warning him about the danger of Hitler and the need for a stronger riposte. Indeed, his first public warning about the possible threat posed by German rearmament was in 1930, when Ramsay MacDonald was prime minister. Then in March 1934 he told Parliament: 'Germany is arming fast, and no one is going to stop her. I dread the day when the means of threatening the heart of the British Empire should pass into the hands of the present rulers of Germany . . . I dread that day, but it is not, perhaps, far distant.' It was a steady message through the premierships of MacDonald, Stanley Baldwin and Chamberlain. Were his depressive instincts making him more realistic about the threat that Germany posed, and Chamberlain's optimism blinding him to reality? Ghaemi, for one, believes so.

Ghaemi thinks depressives tend to be more resilient too. 'Melancholy seemed to drip from him as he walked,' observed Lincoln's law partner William Herndon of the US president. But he said Lincoln had an inner strength, 'as tough and gnarled as seasoned hickory wood, and the increasing hostility that his outspoken politics provoked as the country drifted into war, seemed to bounce off him like peas from a peashooter against a wall'.

Ghaemi also argues that there are major potential benefits in having people in organisations who might be characterised as having 'manic' minds. Their self-esteem tends to be high, so they will be convinced they can overcome failures on the road to innovation and their performance will stay high despite setbacks. As we saw in the teamship section, they may not always be easy to manage, but their contribution will be invaluable. If it is the leader who has elements of a manic personality, he or she needs to have enough self-awareness to select a strong but more 'normal' deputy and support team. Many such pairings come to mind: Margaret Thatcher and Willie Whitelaw, for example (maybe that's what Thatcher meant when she said of her deputy, seemingly oblivious to the double entendre, 'everyone needs a Willie', someone who is not manic, does not have ambitions beyond the position they hold, is just solid and sound in their advice and nature). Aware of my own mental tendencies, I was always very careful in the choice of my deputies, like Godric Smith in Number 10, and wanted caution as well as creativity to be high on their list of attributes.

While mania and depression are often just lumped together as 'mental illness', Ghaemi is clear about the differences between them. People diagnosed with 'mania' tend to be ultra-innovative, highly nonconformist and prefer working alone, whereas depressives have a lot of characteristics that enable them to be good team leaders. 'With mania you don't feel empathy whereas depressives feel great empathy and that tends to be born out of their own experiences.' Martin Luther King was a manic-depressive (both Ghaemi and I prefer it as a descriptor to 'bipolar disorder'), and was notable for his energy and high self-esteem, which contributed to his charisma – important in any campaign leader – and forward-thinking – important in strategy. Ghaemi believes, though, that his depressive side outweighed his manic side and that the qualities associated with depression – particularly understanding of human emotional pain – allowed him to be an exceptional and empathetic team leader. He had to manage enormous egos from rival factions of the civil rights movement, many of whom thought that a violent struggle would be a better way to achieve their goals, and he did this through what Ghaemi describes as 'possessing huge empathy for everyone'. He did not try to dominate or overwhelm the powerful personalities who made up the somewhat uncoordinated team. Currently writing a book about Martin Luther King's manic depression, Ghaemi says he managed them through empathy.

Other forms of extreme behaviour can be beneficial too. For example, it's not unusual for anxiety to go hand in hand with creativity. Charles Darwin, one of the members of our 'World Without' hypothesis, had chronic panic attacks and mental torment that often left him in floods of tears. In stressful situations he'd experience palpitations, skin inflammation, agoraphobia, blinding headaches and agonising stomach cramps. Over twenty-five years he consulted more than twenty doctors in a vain bid to find a cure. He visited spas such as Malvern and Ilkley, subjecting himself to 'water cures' and the treatment of quack physicians. Darwin's illnesses, however, accompanied a restless intellect that couldn't accept the status quo and that was constantly asking 'what if'.

Overall, one needs to think of the benefits and pitfalls of mania as a bell curve, with performance on the y axis and mania on the x axis. If we are prone to extreme mania we need to train (or medicate) ourselves to control it. If, by contrast, we do not regard ourselves as having any of the features of a manic personality, but would like to be more productive, we should try to emulate some of the positive aspects of mania. Andy McCann taught me that you can do this by focusing on a familiar thought or reaction that comes into your mind, and then saying: 'Now I intend to change the way I'm thinking.' You may reject the new thought, but at least you're forcing yourself to challenge your conventional thinking.

One drawback of having a personality that displays signs of mania is that success doesn't always or automatically bring happiness. Dave Brailsford's team has criticised him for not allowing proper celebrations after a great win. Layne Beachley was the same when she won her first surfing world championship. 'I felt relief, not joy. The only title I enjoyed was the last one.' Tanni Grey-Thompson says she was always straight onto the next challenge. In all these cases, because of the personality types involved, the tendency was to look ahead rather than to enjoy the present. It's certainly true of me, and I will always regret – resent, even – failing to enjoy three election wins at the time. Grey-Thompson accepts this is 'not normal', adding: 'I'm not balanced at all, though I'm better now I'm not competing, but obsessive, fiery temper, bordering on manic, all of those things. When I had Carys [her daughter], I took a week off training and she came to training aged two and a half weeks. I'm not sure that's very normal behaviour.'

The reason it's important to understand all this is that a lot of stigma is still attached to anything that smacks of 'abnormal' mental activity. And that means that many organisations are missing out on having more potential winners in their midst. I had to pick up Tony Blair (Mr Normal – and I certainly never saw signs of what my psychiatrist would define as mental illness, whatever the Blair haters may say) after he published his memoir in 2010. In it, he wrote: 'in my experience there are two types of crazy people: those who are just crazy, and who are therefore dangerous; and those whose craziness lends them creativity, strength, ingenuity and verve. Alastair was of the latter sort . . . ' A few hundred pages later he said that if I had still been around in his final days as PM, when the media were even more ludicrous than at the time of my departure, I would have rampaged around like 'a mad axeman'. Pressed by my fellow mental health campaigners, I took to my blog with a rare criticism of Tony, pointing out that he was playing into stereotypes we had been working hard to break down.

I find it sad, and hugely limiting, that while people in sport have recognised the importance of psychology in achieving success, and openly employ psychiatrists and psychologists such as Steve Peters or Andy McCann, in other walks of life the idea that you need to engage with the ways in which people's minds work, and accept that many different types of mind have a contribution to make, is regarded not as a common-sense opportunity, but as a potential embarrassment.

A few years ago, for example, I went cycling with Graeme Obree near his home in Irvine, Scotland. Obree's life was dedicated to beating the world record for the distance covered in one hour on a bike, and this was made into a film, *The Flying Scotsman*. Obree has a history of mental health problems, severe depression, several suicide attempts, struggles with sexuality. He told me: 'I have no doubt that to get to the top you have to be obsessive, obsessively focused and driven. I was obsessively focused and driven. You either are or you aren't. I was.'

When he finally set the record, it was in front of a tiny crowd, because he had failed a day earlier and just decided he was going to do it again the next morning. 'It was death or glory, it really was. I didn't notice anything around me, no crowd, no media, nothing, all I saw was the black line on the track. It was obsessive. And I was like that, probably, because I was ill. And now I'm not so ill, and it means I'm not so obsessive, and I can't do it like I did. That is the truth. There you are.'

The understanding that the state of the athlete's mind is at least as important as the state of the body – and indeed that the two are inseparable – has gained broad acceptance across all sports. As Sebastian Coe puts it: 'I know there are some athletes who think they get mental strength by lying down by the track with headphones and calming music, but supreme physical conditioning is what will give you mental strength.' Brian O'Driscoll tells me: 'You will not have mental strength without physical strength. If the body has no more to give, there is next to nothing the mind can do about it. And if the mind has no more to give, there is not much the body can do about it.' Clearly the demands in sport are predominantly physical, and yet it is now seen as routine to have proper psychological and psychiatric support. In politics and business, by contrast, where the challenges are more mental than physical, no such attitude change has taken place. It's a huge mistake, born of the fact that people all too easily feel threatened by those who are different, either in terms of background, or of views, agenda or ambition. And it's considered to be an admission of weakness ever to suggest that you yourself are suffering any kind of mental strain.

Yet the stress under which political and business leaders work – the hours, the sheer volume and nature of issues they are having to deal with, the shocks and setbacks that come with the turf, the time spent separated from family – are all likely to have a negative psychological impact. It would be far better to acknowledge this and work with it, but most leaders just plough on. 'It really surprises me,' says Andy McCann, 'that maybe 90–95 per cent of top athletes will have proper psychological support, but politicians who are operating under massive pressure think they can do without it.'

Perhaps I should leave the last word on this to Sebastian Coe, someone who knows sport, politics and business from the inside. At the Moscow Olympics, a sports psychologist was advising him on how to create a 'normal' environment as he prepared to go for gold. The usually mild-mannered athlete was having none of it. 'Do you think I'm normal? Do you think what I do is normal? Do you think running three times a day, a hundred miles a week, is normal? I don't. Don't tell me I'm normal. I'm not normal. There's not a single person in this team who's normal. We're all fucking mad.'

> 'You will not have mental strength without physical strength. If the body has no more to give, there is next to nothing the mind can do about it.'
> **BRIAN O'DRISCOLL**

9

THE POWER OF VISUALISATION

'We think in pictures way more than we think in words.'

NICK FALDO

VISUALISING SUCCESS

Actor and comedian Jim Carrey was so confident that one day he would make it big that in 1983 he wrote himself a post-dated cheque for $10 million, which he intended to cash in 1993. At the time he was a struggling comic, whose appearances in films and on TV amounted to zero. Not long after, he started to land a few small roles, then bigger ones, and before long he was turning roles down because he was too busy. His father died in 1994, by which time Carrey was worth much more than $10 million. His cheque went with his dad to his grave.

And that, in essence, is how visualisation works: imagining what winning looks and feels like, and then going for it. It may sound absurdly simple, but it's extraordinary just what a powerful tool it can be.

My conversion to the power of visualisation came in what may sound the unlikely context of a charity football match. It was, however, a pro-am match played in front of 72,000 people at Old Trafford, and one that involved a range of stellar football names, including the greatest player of all time, Diego Maradona. One of my current life rules is to mention that 'I played with Maradona' to someone every day.

I suspect it was my controversial profile as much as my passion for football that led the organisers of the first UNICEF Soccer Aid match to ask me to join an event that also involved pop stars such as Robbie Williams and Nicky Byrne, film stars like Damian Lewis and Alessandro Nivolo, and celebrity chefs like Gordon Ramsay. We spent a week training, eating, drinking, playing and bantering together. And then the night before the match, coach Ruud Gullit and his assistant Gus Poyet told me that, at the grand old age of forty-nine, I had done enough to merit inclusion in the starting line-up, and that they wanted me to play left wing back, alongside World Cup winners Marcel Desailly and Lothar Matthäus as centre backs, with Maradona, another World Cup winner, ahead of me as a central midfielder.

On the morning of the match I was so excited that I gave up trying to sleep at around five, and went for a walk along the canal, as far as the stadium, where the only sign of life was litter blowing in the wind and seagulls hovering. I then went back to the hotel, where I bumped into Maradona's jet-lagged friend, Boca Juniors vice president Richard Willmott. We had breakfast, chatted, and after a while I asked what Diego was planning to do before the evening kick-off. 'He can't sleep either,' he replied. 'Just texted me to say he was thinking of going up to the stadium for a kickabout. Do you fancy coming?' It was like asking a teenage boy if he fancied a night out with Jessica Alba.

So I fetch my kit, we pile into a van and off we go to a silent, near-deserted stadium. By the time we've changed, there are perhaps fifty people to watch us. We have a problem, though. The pitch hasn't been mown and the groundsman doesn't want it damaged. So after a bit of argument, I hear one of the most remarkable sentences I have ever heard in my life. 'OK, but only Maradona and Alastair allowed on the pitch. Everyone else stays here.' Maradona walks on, slowly, and I follow. He breathes in, fills his lungs and then lets out a noise that I can only describe as a cross between a war cry and a child's exclamation of glee. 'Whooooooooaaaaaareeeee-yaaaaaa.' Then he laughs, turns to me, and says: 'I am imagining the game, visualising how it will be, imagining how I will play.' He's speaking in Spanish, but I understand enough as he tells me how much he loves football, like a man loves a woman or a child loves a parent. It makes him happy because he knows he can make other people happy. We walk the length of the pitch, and he is very deliberately looking all around him, at every part of the turf and of the stands. He asks me how many people are coming tonight. 'Seventy thousand,' I say, and his eyes light up. Then he points around the ground, and says: 'Full, full, full, people, people, people.' I start to copy his lung-filling breathing exercises, and he nods in approval.

By now, a few balls have been rolled onto the pitch, and we jog slowly towards them. His knee is playing up, he has an impressive array of scars on both legs, and he moves gingerly at first, but as I pass a ball to him, he becomes a different person; the rather rickety frame turns into an athlete-cum-ballet dancer. He lets the ball hit the side of his boot; it rolls up his leg, over the tattoo of his friend and hero Fidel Castro, up to his thigh, then he flicks it away, turns his body almost to a right angle and volleys the ball goalwards. I pass another ball, this time too softly, but he runs for it, flicks it up and then heads it in the air, again and again and again, running as he goes, before bringing the ball to a stop, on his neck. It sits there for a few seconds, then he lets it roll down his back, over his thigh, down to his foot, holds it still for a second or two, flicks it up in the air and crosses it back to me, inch-perfect from forty yards.

After a few minutes of this, he wants to do some shooting practice. We have four balls and he signals that I should roll them to him one by one. He hits the first into the corner of the net from twenty yards, then runs off in celebration. I mean celebration. Not like a child pretending he is Lionel Messi scoring in a park kickabout. I mean like Diego Maradona when he was winning World Cup Finals. He runs, thumps his chest, shouts and screams at imaginary people. The 'crowd' – now up to around seventy-five – watches on with a mix of amusement and awe. Then he's back, wants to try some more, deliberately aiming to hit the crossbar. Miss. Miss. Hit. Miss. Hit. Hit. He wants a harder challenge now, says he will hit the angle of the post and the bar. Bullseye first time. Off for another celebration, and the spectators are already so used to it they are cheering him on. He looks happy now.

As we walk off, he is surrounded and does what he has done every day of his adult life – signs autographs, poses for pictures, works at being Diego Maradona, legend. Back in the changing room, he showers, gets dressed again, says: 'It is going to be great. Tonight will be great.'

We now have Richard back with us, so I ask him to interpret, and ask Maradona what he was doing when he was celebrating goals scored into an empty net. Back comes the answer: 'You must visualise the victory.'

Mental skills coach Andy McCann says there's a lot of method in the seeming Maradona madness. 'When you visualise, yes you compete only in your mind, but it can have such a powerful effect that your entire body feels as if you're competing physically. The brain can't really distinguish between a visualised and an actual experience. To the brain a neural pattern is a neural pattern. MRI scans have shown that blood moves around the brain even if you're only visualising. And the more you get used to what to expect, the better you'll cope.'

Shortly after our interview, he sent me the latest edition of the journal *Scientific American Mind*, which reported a study from Oslo University proving that visualisation affects the body at a cellular level as well as just blood flow in the brain. It showed that visualising rooms getting dark affected the dilation of the pupil (measured by lasers) in the same way as when the light was actually adjusted. It's scarcely surprising, then, that nearly all the sports stars interviewed for this book have used some form of visualisation, and regard it, as Maradona did, even for a charity match, as an important feature of the winning mindset.

Just visualising what success looks like can have an astonishingly powerful psychological effect. Jürgen Klopp, the charismatic German coach who built Borussia Dortmund into one of the world's best club sides on much smaller budgets than his rivals, says that he gets as much value from showing his players videos of their own goal celebrations as of scarily good examples of their opponents' brilliance. Both Sachin Tendulkar and Brian Lara, the two finest batsmen of their generation, tell me that when they reviewed an innings they focused more on their good shots than their bad ones, to reinforce the positive thoughts they'd had when playing them.

> 'The brain can't really distinguish between a visualised and an actual experience.'
> **ANDY McCANN**

Similarly, Nick Faldo tells me how he used previous success to drive future hopes. Of course he loved winning majors, but he says that his 'single greatest moment of golfing joy' came in May 1975 when he won the Berkshire Trophy, an amateur competition. 'I have never been so happy. I won a trophy as big as a vase and on the way home I wound the windows down and I was so happy I was screaming, I mean screaming, all the way home. Then after that, I was on the rampage, it seemed like I was winning everything.' That feeling of winning stayed with him, and he used to recall it in motivation for the rest of his career. Now he advises young golfers: 'You'll blow some tournaments before you win. Get mad, analyse, learn. The trick is to use the good stuff and bin the bad stuff. Don't go recalling crap all the time. Remember the good moments, and use them when you face a challenge you've faced before.'

Visualising success can also work when it involves not looking back to past success but forward to the success you hope will come. When coaching surfer Layne Beachley, Rob Rowland-Smith would make her sprint to the place where the medals would be handed out in a tournament. 'Righto, Layne,' he'd say, 'I want you to see yourself as the winner of this event. I want you to see yourself as a world champion. I want you to lie in bed and look at the ceiling and see yourself surfing to the best of your potential and being the best you can be, standing on the podium holding that trophy above your head.' He says his work on her mental side was every bit as important as the physical training. 'So many of our athletes today underachieve because they don't work the most important muscle in the body – the six inches between the ears.'

Visualisation can also be used to slow things down and calm people down. Aussie Rules coach David Parkin sometimes got his entire team, minutes before a big match, to lie down on the dressing-room floor, close their eyes and visualise what they had to do in the match to come. But it was as much about calming them down as firing them up for the challenge ahead.

And you don't need to be a sportsman to learn how to visualise. Richard Branson says his creation of Virgin Airlines, of which we will hear much more in the next section, was built on an image. 'The picture I had in my mind was of people getting on a flight, being met by smart, smiling cabin crew, taken to a comfortable seat, having good food and entertainment, enjoying the flight. I visualised how good a flight could be, and I could feel and visualise how successful an airline dedicated to that kind of flying could be.' Similarly, Metro Bank CEO Craig Donaldson says he carries a vision in his mind of his young son several years hence, studying at university, drawing money from a Metro Bank cashpoint, and his best friend saying 'I bank with them too, they're brilliant', and his son responding 'My dad built them'. 'When I'm really feeling a bit pressured, and not sure why I'm doing all this, that image pops in my mind, and I keep going.'

Visualisation is also about how you see the arc of your life. Nick Faldo and Ian Botham both recall being told by careers officers that they should look for 'a proper job' rather than pursue their sporting ambitions. Faldo says that aged fifteen he was told: 'We reckon you're very good with your hands so we'll get you onto a production line.' Faldo's vision, though, was rather different: 'I said, "My production line will be hitting golf balls, mate, because I'm going to be a professional golfer."' That image in his mind gave him clarity about an ultimate goal, ensuring that he didn't become distracted by an alternative path or a dissenting voice.

I experienced this power of the visual for myself when, back in 1994, I was agonising over whether to accept Tony Blair's invitation to work for him. Three images kept coming into my head. In one, I was still a journalist and watching John Major return to Number Ten after the next election, and thinking 'maybe I could have helped stop that from happening'. In the second, Tony was walking into Number Ten, I was in the press pen, thinking 'I could have been part of that', and in the third, I was walking behind Tony as he stepped into Number Ten. It was that image that came to dominate and helped me make what, before then, had seemed a very difficult decision.

I've also found over the years that I've been able to draw on visualisation to help me through difficult situations or to put them into context, getting a sense of perspective by conjuring up images of events that will help restore a sense of proportion. When I was preparing for my appearances before the Chilcot and Hutton Inquiries, I would remind myself of challenges overcome in the past – large and small, from election wins, nervous breakdowns, deaths of friends and family to trips to the dentist even, taking my mind forward to that feeling of being able to enjoy the first food and hot drink when the effect of the treatment wore off.

I find myself approaching the very different challenge of writing a book in the same way. I visualise the final result: a printed book with a cover. I visualise the book's structure and all the potential problems that come between embarking on it and completing it. And if I reach moments when I ask myself, 'Why did I bother with this? Who cares?' I visualise what I have gone through with other books I've written, and recall that positive feeling when the book was completed, the cover design agreed, and then the finished product arrived. Above all I visualise people reading it – at home, on a train, in bed. It's not only a way to keep myself going but a way of thinking ahead about challenges to be conquered.

Perhaps Biz Stone, co-founder of Twitter, and one of the live-liest, quirkiest minds I have come across, has the answer as to why this should be so.

Visualise what you want to see happen for yourself in the next two years . . . The goal isn't to solve anything. If you take an idea and just hold it in your head, you uncon-sciously start to do the things that advance you toward that goal. It kinda works. It did for me.

VISUALISING CHALLENGES

Michael Phelps would spend hours visualising a race before he got in the pool – he even trained himself to dream about swimming. He would visualise everything going well, every stroke perfect, every turn at the end of each length perfect, every kick perfect, all ending with another win. But he would also visualise things going wrong. His goggles filling with water so he couldn't see. A competitor doing better than expected. Losing his momentum on a turn. Losing count of his strokes. And as he visualised, he worked out what he would do, how he would get through the bad moments that might come. He was training himself to think correctly under pressure.

This approach paid dividends in the final of the 200 metres butterfly at the Beijing Olympics, when, with over a length to go, his goggles did indeed fill with water and he couldn't see anything. But because it was a scenario he had visualised often before, having anticipated the crisis at the start of the third of four lengths, he began to count the strokes. He timed the turn perfectly, completed the last 50-metre length in twenty strokes as planned, broke the world record and picked up his fourth gold medal of the Games.

Phelps' approach shows that visualisation often goes beyond a single-stage ambition or goal. When visualising a competition, he was thinking through all the processes involved from start to finish, along with all the potential problems that might arise. Golfers, too, will think not just of playing a single shot but how they will tackle a particular course, hole by hole. And from my conversations with Sebastian Coe and Brendan Foster when I decided to run a marathon, I know that visualising each day's training was an essential part of preparation. I would wake up in the morning, and the very first thing that came into my mind was the training run I would do that day: the distance, the route. I would run it in my head before getting out of bed, and then get up and run it. Some days, my mind would tell my body that a particular route wouldn't work – too long, too short, too hilly, too flat – and I would visualise another one. Other days, my body would tell my mind that it was thinking of doing too much, and I might cut down on the route that popped into my head on waking.

Nick Faldo talks in terms of putting challenges and problems into a 'mental bin'. 'I've always been brutally honest with myself about my game. I may play a good round but I'll get in and say to myself, "That was a crap shot at the seventh. The pin was left and you went far right, sucker. Now next time, don't do it." Then put it in the mental bin. Sometimes if I'm under real pressure, I'll tell myself I'm not in a tournament, I'm on the practice range, and I just relax a little. You can do that with your mind, train yourself to feel different, use nerves to drive performance, but if it's getting a bit much, you wind down the dial.' So visualisation works alongside self-talk.

If this all sounds suspiciously vague and unprovable, there is ample research to back up the power of visualisation in improving performance. If the Oslo University study showed that visualisation can affect the body's responses, another study, involving an American basketball team, actually showed players getting better. Here, during pre-season training, the team was split into three groups. One group practised throwing hoops for an hour a day for the next thirty days. The second group was given time off, but asked to lie down in a quiet place, and simply visualise: imagine repeatedly the act of preparing to throw, then throwing the basketball through the hoop. The third group was told they could go off and do whatever they liked – effectively stay on holiday. When the experiment period was over, all the players were brought back to throw hoops and measured against their previous stats. Group 3 showed no improvement at all. Group 1, as one might expect, showed a 24 per cent improvement. And group 2, the visualisers, showed a 23 per cent improvement. In other words, simply by visualising, the second group improved their skills almost as much as those who had practised hard.

As well as enhancing performance, visualisation can also help deflect negativity. McCann, for example, employed it to help a rugby player under pressure, Rhys Priestland, who was getting hammered on social media after a poor performance. 'Social media is a menace. Athletes have a lot of time resting and hanging around and can spend too much time on Twitter,' he says. 'Rhys was taking it so hard and very personally. I talked to him as Rhys, not as a rugby player. I said, "Rugby is what you do, not who you are. You are not as good as your last game but your next game." I also showed him video of his great moments, and actually what emerged was that he felt he had been indecisive on the field and we had to work on that. So he did.'

But they also did visualisation work on what sort of person was sending the abuse. 'You see the words and they all seem to carry the same weight, but if you have in your mind a picture of some guy who couldn't hold let alone kick a ball, looks bitter and nasty, probably living on his own in a horrible dingy bedroom, and then why are you worrying? Judge your game by your criteria and the coaches' criteria, not his.'

The next day after seeing McCann, coincidentally, I was meeting Dave Brailsford and Chris Froome, who were preparing for the 2014 Tour de France Grand Départ in Yorkshire. Froome mentioned he was getting a fair bit of abuse on social media. I took what McCann had told me and also explained that if Twitter were a newspaper, the volume of tweets attacking him would fill half a line on page 55, and the people writing it couldn't get on a bike, never mind ride it up a mountain.

Negative thoughts come from inside, but in any high-profile walk of life they come from outside too, not least via the media. Cricket in particular has a galaxy of former players as pundits who can be the most effective at undermining their successors. Wasim Akram, himself a media commentator now, has very clear and very good advice for players: 'Ignore the negative comments. Ignore all the criticism.' What if they are right, though? I ask. 'You'll know anyway, so will your coach and your team mates and you can work on it. But don't listen to the negativity. You have to be positive to get the best out of yourself and the people around you and you won't be positive if you're carrying all these negative comments and opinions around in your head.'

A VISUALISATION CASE STUDY: WALES RUGBY STARS AT WORK

To get a real sense of how a prolonged visualisation session works, I ask Andy McCann to talk me through his preparation with Wales rugby stars Sam Warburton and Leigh Halfpenny on the morning of a game.

First he tells athletes to stand and centre themselves through breath control. 'You can see the transformation in that there is a clear sense that in their mind they are playing or competing,' he says. Even though there is no ball, no crowd, nobody else in the room, these sessions are extraordinary for their tension.

When visualising goal-kicking, McCann asks Halfpenny to step slightly to the left and simply imagine a past kick that gave him particular satisfaction. 'He often picks a difficult kick he took success-fully,' says McCann. This cements the memory. McCann then asks him to step back, recentre himself through breathing, and then take the same kick again but by fully engaging his body even though there is no ball. He goes through every single motion that he would for a real kick, almost a minute of mental and physical preparation, stepping, deep breathing, a series of deliberate body movements; in his head this is clearly for real. He steps up and kicks the imaginary ball. McCann just asks, 'Successful?' If it is, then the process is immediately repeated, only this time visualising a kick that may come in the game later that day.

'I never talk about his kicking technique,' says McCann, 'only about his mind.' He adds that the length of time Halfpenny prepared for a kick alone in his hotel room was just three seconds short of the time he took for a late successful kick in front of 60,000 fans later the same day.

Halfpenny always wants to rehearse in his mind a kick to win the match in the last minute. This is partly because in a World Cup semi-final against France, with Wales down to fourteen men, he had the chance to win the match with a last-minute penalty, and missed it. 'To be fair to him, it was out of his usual range. But he was totally gutted, and I said to him in the dressing room, "OK, you feel ghastly now, but if that situation arises again, do you want to take it?" Yes, no doubt, he said. "OK, keep that thought."' 2012, Dublin, Ireland vs Wales, thirty seconds left on the clock, Wales are down 20–21, Halfpenny gets a tough kick for the match, he does it.

At the heart of McCann's work with athletes is a personal identity statement, a short sentence that says who you are when you take the field. 'I like it to be selfish, about them. I like there to be a bit of arrogance in there. I like it to be in the first-person singular and in the present tense. "I am a good athlete." That is meaningless. "I am the best athlete on this pitch." OK, great, but is it true? You have to relate it to performance markers. So when I started with Sam Warburton, it evolved. He wanted to be the best on the field, but did we have the evidence? So we started with "I am an athletic number 7 and I will show it by making x carries, y tackles", whatever.

'Ignore the negative comments. Ignore all the criticism.'
WASIM AKRAM

'Over time it changed and developed to "I am a world-class number 7". Taking that thought into a match can give you confidence and positivity. We prepare for this in words and pictures that they can access any time on their iPad or phone. So the day before a match they might want to look at pictures of friends and family, people they want to do well for. But on game day, I just want them thinking of themselves and the match. The last thing I will say to them before they go out is something like "look me in the eye and say to me that there is no place in the world I would rather be than here, and now".'

For his part, Warburton, who became Welsh captain aged just twenty-two, and has since captained the British and Irish Lions too, names McCann as one of his most important influences. 'When you think how much effort we put into making our bodies stronger, it makes obvious sense to me to make the mind as strong as possible too. Whether it's relaxation when stress levels are too high, visualisation when I can think through preparation in a way that's very different to training on the field, or it's just having someone who knows me and the way my mind works, and who knows when my confidence is a problem, he has been a huge part of any success I've had.'

When Warburton was told he was Lions captain, seen as one of the greatest accolades in the game, McCann was among the first people he called. 'It was a big step up, so I knew I would need his help. He took it to the next level. We already had the personal identity statement but now we worked on what he called a leadership compass, where you take on a quality for north, south, east and west, and you have them in mind, and draw strength from them. So mine were professional attitude, positive attitude, developing relationships with the players, and most importantly leading by example on and off the field. Whatever I did, I wanted it to be reflecting one or more of these four things.' They turned it into a real compass which he saved on his iPhone and looked at as often as most sportsmen look at their Twitter feeds. They also worked on a manual together, 'Warby's Winning Ways'.

For McCann's part, he says the player has to want to engage in these techniques for them to work, and top professionals like Warburton want to engage with anything that will improve their performance. One of his proudest moments, he says, was when Warburton was named 'Man of the Match' in a Six Nations game against Scotland in 2013, days before being named Lions captain.

'He had been struggling all week, feeling a lot of pressure, and his confidence was low.' Warburton recalls: 'My confidence was shot to pieces, it was like I was a different person to the one that had had this great run of form. Andy was the man I turned to and we just talked and he slowly got my mind to a better place. We won 28–18 and when I came off and went into the dressing room Andy was the first person I looked out, to give him a big hug and just say thanks.'

THERE IS NOTHING YOU CANNOT VISUALISE

So far I have focused on sport because those involved at a very high level have been particularly open to the power of visualisation. But I would argue that there is scarcely a challenge in any sphere of life that cannot be more easily overcome by prior visualisation. Take the unpleasant but sometimes necessary task of firing someone, for example. Jack Welch is just one person I can think of who would have the likely conversation with that someone in his own mind first – in other words, he would visualise the way things might go. This wouldn't distract him from what he knew would have to be done (Jim McCann, founder and CEO of 1-800-Flowers Inc., recalls Welch grabbing him by the lapels and giving him an important piece of advice: 'Jim, have you ever heard someone say: "I wish we'd waited six more months to fire that bastard"?'), but by visualising it first he could be reasonably confident that when he had the real conversation, he wouldn't inflict unnecessary pain in an already difficult situation. Sometimes he would even go beyond visualising to acting it out, with his brother Chris playing the part of the 'victim'. Former England manager Glenn Hoddle did something similar when telling footballers they weren't being selected. He would get a coaching colleague to play the part of the player, and ask him to go through all the possible responses – hurt, anger, silence. Usually, though not always, these rehearsals accurately predicted the way the final conversation would go.

Making a speech involves much the same approach. Visualisation followed by rehearsal can help calm nerves, pre-empt the unexpected and improve performance. A famous concert pianist developed chronic stage fright. A sports psychologist suggested to him that when he played at home, he did so dressed in his tails and with a powerful spotlight shining on him. The panic subsided in weeks.

Top-flight politicians and business people make hundreds of speeches, but just a handful each year that really matter. Then it's important to put in extra effort, including visualisation of the mood in the room – if, for example, there is sullenness (Tony Blair at the TUC comes to mind), you'll need a different style to that for an audience filled with excited anticipation. Visualise the reaction to difficult points, know when you want and need applause to emphasise a point or break the rhythm of a speech. The best speeches are masterpieces of visualisation, of course. Bill Clinton would evoke images of the future, new jobs, new alliances, old challenges met in new ways. Fleetwood Mac's 'Don't Stop (thinking about tomorrow)' was his campaign song. For similar reasons, and the need to focus on a vision for the future in inspiring support for change, New Labour chose D:Ream's 'Things Can Only Get Better' as our song for the 1997 campaign. It proved a powerful choice.

THE POWER OF REVERSE VISUALISATION

If visualisation helps you to improve your own performance, it works in reverse as well, when you work out how others visualise you, and use that against them. Maradona's virtual single-handed win against England for Argentina in the 1986 World Cup quarter-finals is remembered most for his 'Hand of God' goal (one of his favourites of all time, he told me). But his other goal in the match was a masterpiece, as a string of defenders struggled and fell in his wake. It's worth a trip to YouTube to see how Maradona essentially moves in a straight line, because he knows the defenders are expecting him to dribble in various directions to get round them. They have visualised based on how he plays. He reacts based on how they have visualised. Peter Reid, one of the England players beaten by him that day, admitted to me that 'his reputation beat us in a way'. Cricketer Sachin Tendulkar said that once he had established a strong reputation as one of the best batsmen in the world, he could sometimes feel that the other team and especially the bowler in action at the time were worried as he went out to bat. They were visualising being hammered by him, and that helped him.

In this context, it's also worth pointing out just how damaging negative visualisation can be. In a long interview Tanni Grey-Thompson makes several mentions of 'my worst ever race', the 800-metre final at the Athens Paralympic Games, when she got stuck behind the slowest girl in the race and never retrieved the situation. As we relive the race together, it becomes clear that in the immediate build-up to the race, she had started to feel less confident than usual. 'I had started to visualise things going wrong rather than things going well. And guess what? They did. I lost confidence. Normally as I got closer and closer to the start, my mind would empty, but I was having these thoughts, what if this, what if that, what if I am too slow at the start, and yep, I was too slow at the start. My mindset failed me. It was really the only time it happened as bad as that. I was tired, tired of the politics, tired of the training, just had a child, so tired as a mum, but it was definitely the mindset that failed me.'

All of this underlines how much of sporting, or indeed any other, battle is won and lost in the mind. I recall the one period of William Hague's spell as Opposition leader when we were a bit worried about him. It was because he was regularly drawing or winning in the battles with Tony at Prime Minister's Questions, and the key to his success was his genuine wit. He was developing a more confident demeanour every time he delivered a good line, of which there were many. We had to stop it. So we worked out very deliberately a line that we felt would undermine the way he was performing. Over several weeks Tony hit home the line, that Hague was 'all jokes, no judgement', with the Jack Welch-style discipline of someone who knows the importance of the message in getting into someone's head. It had two effects. It highlighted the extent to which he was making the wrong policy decisions because of lack of judgement. And he became defensive, and stopped being so funny. Then his confidence dropped again.

FROM VISUALISATION TO ACTION PLAN

I've talked about visualisation as a mental exercise, but as with strategy, where Marilyn Monroe's 'think in ink' maxim applies, it's worth giving the visual a physical reality. The value of this can be seen in the results of an experiment done at the Dominican University of California when 150 adults of all ages were split into five groups and asked to think about business objectives they would like to meet in the coming month. The first group was asked to think about the objectives but not do anything further once they had. The second group had to go one step further and write down their objectives. The third group had to write down the objectives, and explain what they intended to do to meet them. The fourth group had to do the same as the third group, but also share their objectives and plans with a friend. The fifth group had to do the same, but in addition write a weekly progress report to the friend.

At the end of the experiment, group 1 had achieved 43 per cent of its objectives, group 2 61 per cent, group 3 51 per cent, group 4 64 per cent and group 5 76 per cent. Writing it all down, communicating it to others and tracking the progress in the written word had been a huge help to group 5, who achieved far more than the others.

In other words, there comes a point when visualisation has to reconnect with all the other attitudes, values and techniques that create a winning mindset. In visualisation, as in all else, being strategic about it will give it added value.

10

THE MINDSET OF AN UNBEATEN WINNER: FLOYD MAYWEATHER

'I don't even think about losing.'

FLOYD MAYWEATHER

Amid the sporting winners and high achievers I have been lucky enough to talk to, Floyd Mayweather is unique among them all: in his chosen career, professional boxing, he has never known what it is like to lose. Even Muhammad Ali, seen by most as 'The Greatest', lost five of his sixty-one pro fights. Mayweather's record is forty-seven fights, forty-seven wins, twenty-six of them by knock-outs, ten world titles in five divisions, and still going strong aged thirty-eight. Also, with his own boxing promotion company, and a greater hold on TV income from his own performances than anyone else in sport, it has all turned him into the richest athlete on the planet, which means the richest of all time. His most recent fights worked out at almost $1 million for every minute in the ring. In Las Vegas, where he lives, some of the locals claim a big Mayweather fight can bring close to a billion dollars to the economy, and he gets a large slice of it.

So which winning box does he tick? Is he a strategist? You don't get to be as good as he is, and put together the deals he has done, without knowing what you want to achieve, and how. Is he a team player? Boxing is perhaps the ultimate individual sport, fighter against fighter; yet Mayweather has built a good team around him – 'The

Money Team', as he calls it (Mayweather loves to talk about money, and how much of it he makes) – so is it his skill as a team builder and leader that sets him apart? He wouldn't be out of place as an innovator either. From early in his career, he described himself as an 'entertainer', whose mission was 'to sell tickets'. But it annoyed him how much others took from the sale. His split from promoter Bob Arum led Mayweather to take control of his own fights, and his marketing and communications skills revolutionised boxing promotion. Or, given what he openly acknowledges as an upbringing most would have found difficult to the point of overwhelming, should he praised for a quality such as resilience?

To those new to the Mayweather phenomenon (I will come on to why he is not as well known globally as Ali), for now just be aware of a few facts that might suggest so: mother Deborah a drug addict when he was a child; his mother's sister, also a drug addict, dead from Aids; father Floyd Senior a former pro boxer, who had fought the great Sugar Ray Leonard and who coached Floyd Junior either side of a three-and-a-half-year spell in prison for cocaine trafficking, which he was still serving when his son fought his first pro fight.

So Mayweather saw an awful lot growing up, like needles in his backyard and his mother's single-room apartment, his father selling drugs to his mother, and Floyd Junior being all too often on the wrong end of Floyd Senior's beatings. He also got caught up in his dad's drug-dealing life: the only one of my questions he opted not to answer was when I asked him to tell me how he felt that, as a baby, he was held as a human shield by his father, under attack from a gunman known as 'Baboon' – who also happened to be his mother's brother – after the two men fell out over 'business'. In an interview with the *Los Angeles Times*, Mayweather Senior admitted holding his son by the ankles and hanging him upside down in front of him to cover as much of his own body as a one-year-old's frame could. 'If you're going to kill me, you're going to kill the baby too,' he told Baboon, aka Tony Sinclair. Floyd Junior's mother was screaming: 'Give me the baby,' but his father refused. 'She was pulling the baby out of my arms so her brother could shoot me. But I wasn't going to put that baby down. I didn't want to die. It wasn't about putting my son in the line of fire. I knew [Sinclair] wouldn't shoot the baby. So he took the gun off my face, lowered it to my leg and bam!' The shot tore apart his calf and his boxing career never really recovered from the injuries.

Floyd Junior has had plenty of public wars of words with his father through what is clearly a troubled, sometimes close, often angry relationship, though given some have been for fight-promoting reality TV shows, it's not easy to work out what are genuine feelings and what are being emphasised for the cameras. Some of the 'scenes' between them are truly vicious, and seem real enough, as when Floyd Senior goes to Floyd Junior's gym, and tries to portray himself, rather than his brother Roger, as the true author of his son's success. Son insults Father over his lack of fighting success; reminds him of the beatings he used to give him. 'We don't need you here,' says Son, then turns to the Money Team and shouts: 'Get that mother-fucker out of my motherfucking gym,' insisting 'there are only two motherfucking Mayweathers that count. Roger made the name and I took it to the next level.'

Floyd Senior believes that he deserves more credit for his son's success, having coached him in the early days before he was jailed, at which point his brother Roger took over. He feels, too, that despite his life as a drug dealer he did the best he could for his son – indeed, that in part he was dealing in drugs to ensure his family had 'food on the table and clothes on their backs'. Mayweather himself says that his father helped him learn to fight. That was about it. Yet today, though he is on record as saying he basically raised himself, with help from his grandmother – 'no her and I wouldn't be here' – and that he only went to his mother's when 'my grandmother was mad at me' he seems to want to be as positive as he can about the life his parents gave him. 'Most important to me, more than my success or my wealth or my reputation, is family. My father and mother, my four children and even my TMT [The Money Team] family. I care most about having healthy, supportive relationships, being there for each other, securing their futures, providing for them on a daily basis and making them comfortable and happy. My children have a whole different life than I had because I want them to. They mean everything to me and it's why I work so hard for my success.' Homes, cars, holidays, clothes, he seems to take care of a lot of people, not just direct family. He is rarely without a huge wad of dollar bills and regularly dispenses cash to people, not always small sums either. At weekends, the Mayweather home is filled with family, the Money Team and others from his circle enjoying his hospitality. He likes going out with big groups of friends, and though he doesn't drink will lay on as much drink as others want. He can sometimes tend to the macho boxing stereotype, making sure there are plenty of women there 'to balance up the fact most of TMT are men', and is on record as saying that 'females' are a bit like cars: 'If you can have twenty rather than one, why wouldn't you?'

Yet as he tries to give his own children a life he never had, and indeed that few children anywhere have – not many young kids have Canadian singer Justin Bieber turn up at their birthday party, or hang out with rapper Drake – he is determined, whatever the bitter rows of the past, to say nothing that could be deemed as hostile to his parents. His mother hasn't touched drugs in years and is now much closer to him, and an important behind-the-scenes figure. 'We had turmoil and hardship in my family and there were many rough years. That story has been well documented. But I can look back and say that although they weren't the best of conditions and my parents had their own problems, I always felt love from somewhere. Sometimes and early in my life it was my dad, sometimes my mom. But the person I believe who helped mould me and keep me on the straight path was my grandmother Bernice. She stepped in and raised me and early on taught me right from wrong. That was a big influence on me and helped me believe that I could do anything I wanted to do. I always knew I was going to be successful but having someone like my grandmother tell me so made a huge difference.'

His grandmother, mother to Floyd Senior, Roger and Jeff, all three of them boxers, was the one who kept telling him he was going to make something of himself, and she knew what it was – fighting. She was the one who, when he was worrying that maybe he should look for some kind of trade to learn, told him no, no, no, you're a fighter and you're going to be the best. With his father inside, Mayweather dropped out of high school to focus exclusively on his boxing, knowing there was money to be made, and early on seeing himself as the head of the household, the one his mother and others in the family would look to for support.

Mayweather too has seen the inside of a jail – another popular boxing culture caricature – aged thirty-five, convicted of domestic violence against Jodie Harris, the mother of three of his four children. He continues to protest his innocence, insisting he did a plea bargain to avoid his children having to endure a bitter trial involving their estranged parents. He served two months of an eighty-seven-day sentence, most of it in solitary confinement, and also did a hundred days' community service. He believes being 'black, rich and outspoken' were the three main reasons the system decided he had to be punished.

Rich and outspoken he certainly is, and he hides neither. Not long after our interview, he posted photos on Twitter of two cheques he had just cashed, for $70 million. That he did build himself up from what by any standards was a difficult background and upbringing in Grand Rapids, Michigan, is beyond doubt. But though his sport is renowned for stories of boxers fighting their way from the ghetto to greatness, it's not how Mayweather sees himself. He believes he was destined for greatness all along.

OK, so far so arrogant. But he is quick to add that for all the natural talent he had, what he has achieved would never have been possible without his work ethic, and a mindset that, once he turned professional in 1996, never ever considered the possibility of losing.

This refusal even to countenance defeat is why in the end, despite his other qualities, it is Mayweather's extreme but positive mindset that particularly fascinates me. He is unique not just in never having lost a professional fight but unique among all my interviewees in this mindset that sees fear of defeat not as something to drive him, which, as we have seen, is what many top performers do, but as something that must not be allowed to exist. Basketball star Kobe Bryant, a friend, has talked of Mayweather's 'almost maniacal drive' being the single most important ingredient of his success.

'I do believe God has given me a special gift and being a great fighter was my destiny,' Mayweather tells me, thanking the Almighty, as so many American athletes do, for his talent. 'But trust me, if I hadn't committed to the years, months, days and hours I have spent developing my destiny I would never have gotten as far as I have in the sport.' He sees life as a mix of what we are born with, what happens to us regardless, and what we make happen to ourselves; he calls it a mix of 'fate and free', fate deciding where we start out in life – our family, our background, our natural character, talents and genetic make-up – yet all of us free to make choices about how we use those talents and how we face up to the difficult questions and situations life poses. 'Fate and free will go hand in hand, and I have used both to my advantage and their full potential.' Even his spell in jail, he says, was 'a negative I turned into a positive'. He made a documentary about the build-up to going to jail, making mental comparisons with previous bad times in his life as an aid to get through it; he got angry in there, for sure, but he stayed focused on what he would do when he came out, and on doing so announced plans for a fight that gave him what at the time was the biggest ever guaranteed purse for a boxer, $32 million, itself less than a third of what he would earn from later fights. 'Tough times don't last,' he says. 'Tough people do.'

The more you delve, the more you realise that he just was not, and is not, prepared to accept that the childhood and the youth he had should somehow define who he is now, and how he got to the place he's at. He got there by talent, hard work, support from the right people at the right time, and an unshakeable belief in his abilities and his sense of destiny. Now, I can see how the idea that if you believe you are the best, and if you work hard enough you will be, can sound totally removed from the lives and life chances of most people – that there is nothing in Floyd Mayweather's winning ways that relates to anyone but Floyd Mayweather. However, if you bring it down a level, as Mayweather does at times, and see it in terms of 'being the best you can be at what it is that you do', then it's not out of reach at all, but something most people will strive towards at some point in their lives, even if the last time is a school exam or a driving test, or making an impression at a job interview.

Like many people at the very top in a chosen field, Mayweather attracts both adulation from his fans and hatred from his detractors, not least on social media, which he uses regularly to make major announcements, take views from fans about who he should fight, and where he posts pictures of himself which at times seem designed to provoke the haters, like the ones boasting how much he earns. 'There is too much hate in the world,' he says. 'I am a positive person looking for only positive feedback. If you ain't got that, you can't be around me.'

> 'Tough times don't last. Tough people do.'
> **FLOYD MAYWEATHER**

Yet Leonard Ellerbe, chief executive of Mayweather Promotions, suggests there is a deliberate strategy to the fighter's often controversial public image. 'Bob Arum had Floyd very much as second to Oscar De La Hoya. When Floyd branched out on his own, and found new ways to promote fights, he was happy for people to see him as the villain.' Mayweather himself says that if people pay to see him fight because they want him to lose, or because they want him to win, he is happy either way. 'I like to give people what they want, and they want me to be extravagant.' His fight with De La Hoya was the first to be promoted via the medium of in-house-produced reality TV, breaking new records for money made for both fighters, the take totalling $120 million with 2.4 million buying the fight on pay-per-view. De La Hoya has said he is proud to have been part of a fight that changed boxing forever, and which made him vast sums of money, but he told a US documentary-maker: 'It was the biggest event in boxing history in some ways, but ultimately I lost, and I have to live with that for the rest of my life.'

Oscar De La Hoya was a great boxer, so what does it say about Mayweather's mindset, and his ability to play mind games, that he 'got inside my head', as De La Hoya has admitted. It says that although the 'rags to riches, ghetto to greatness' story fits with the image and history of boxing, it is far removed from how he sees himself and his success, which he puts down to this supremely positive mindset and everything that goes with it – focus, concentration, dedication, determination, resilience, confidence, psychological strength. All this has put him in the Ray Robinson, Muhammad Ali, Sugar Ray Leonard class of fighter, and then in a class above, that unique winner in never having known defeat, but unique perhaps too in never allowing himself to contemplate it.

'The key quality for a winning mindset,' he says during a break in preparations for his fight against Marcos Maidana in September 2014, 'is believing in your ability to win. From a young professional in boxing I believed that I would end up being a great fighter and throughout the years I have done everything necessary to get there. If you believe you can do it, then everything else falls into place.' When he talks about doing 'everything necessary', he is talking about a training regime and a dedication that few can match. He is talking about a level of preparation for a fight in which he is looking to do things slightly differently, slightly better – not just better than his opponents but better than his last fight.

So when I ask him the question I have asked so many sportsmen and women – 'What drives you more: love of winning, or fear and hatred of defeat?' – he alone says simply: 'I don't think about losing.' And then, as though there is something frankly a bit stupid about the question, he adds: 'Who would do that really?' The logical answer to that question is 'just about everyone', including people he would also acknowledge as winners, but he seems genuinely to feel that the belief that you can win is what will drive you to do the things necessary to win, and worrying about the possibility that you might not win would simply get in the way of that.

'I don't have a fear of defeat and it is certainly not what drives me either. My legacy is what drives me. I put great time, energy and preparation into my career and that is what I hope people will remember about my success when it's over. I care more about being a complete fighter and practising my craft to the best of my ability which means success.' He even suggests – admittedly from the rare vantage point of never having lost, reminding me of the billionaires who say they never cared about becoming rich – that he wouldn't have minded if there had been a defeat or two along the way. 'I don't have a loss in my professional career, but it's not always about winning and losing anyway. It's knowing that you have done everything you can to be great at what you do.' Of course, in his case, it is the doing 'everything you can to be great at what you do' that has ensured he has never lost.

For a man of many words (watch the reality TV films on YouTube if you want to see a man who knows how to talk), his shortest answer is to this three-part question, the second and third parts of which are rendered immediately superfluous and irrelevant by the one-word response to the first.

'If you believe you can do it, then everything else falls into place.'

FLOYD MAYWEATHER

'When you get into the ring, have you ever thought you might lose? If so, how did you get through that? If not, what was the closest?'

'Never.' And that is that.

I remind him of something Sugar Ray Leonard said recently: 'I always felt I would give Mayweather a hell of a fight but now I am not so sure since my brother who is my biggest fan says I wouldn't stand a chance.'

'What do you say to that?' I ask.

'Ray and I would have had a hell of a fight together but you know who would have won – TBE [The Best Ever]!'

Part of his appeal is a flamboyance and a wit often lacking in

professional sportsmen, for example in one fight leaning over the
ropes to correct something he heard a ringside TV commentator
saying about him using a new style. 'That's the second time he's
done that,' said the commentator. 'It's the third time,' Mayweather
shouted over to him between punches. And when Nelson Mandela,
no less, said that the whole of South Africa was supporting unbeaten
Philip N'dou – he had won all of his thirty-one fights by knockouts
– and the former South African president gave the fighter advice on
how to beat Mayweather, he responded: 'Nelson Mandela's a great
man, he's big in America, but Mandela can't get in there and fight
for him.' Mayweather knocked out N'dou.

Mayweather talks a lot about being 'relevant' and it's something
his influential PR adviser Kelly Swanson, often referred to as 'the
most powerful woman in boxing', ruminated on when I met her in
New York before she fixed the interview. 'When you've done something for so long, and you've done it so well, how do you fill that
gap? What do you do with your life, when that part of your life
comes to an end which, even if you are as good as he is, you know
it will?' In the coming years, we'll find out the answer to that question, most likely with documentary crews tracking every step. But
I would lay a bet that Mayweather and his team will work it out,
that he'll stay pretty, keep ensuring 'Money' is the most suitable
middle name, and make sure his legacy as a fighter is protected
once he stops.

When you look at the pictures of Mayweather as a child, you
see a good-looking young boy, but nothing to suggest he would one
day be what Floyd Mayweather Jr has today become, living the
remarkable life he leads, with the private jet, the beautiful homes,
the buzz that surrounds him wherever he goes. But he says none of
it feels abnormal to him. 'It feels normal to drive in a white Rolls-
Royce or a Bentley. It feels normal to be making the kind of money
I do, and enjoying the reputation I do. I always thought this would
happen.' He puts it down to three very different parts of the body
– 'brain, chin and heart'. Most of us don't need our chin in the
same way boxers do, but the brain and the heart are where the

mindset is made, and Mayweather's combination of the three has served him every bit as well as the combinations that have seen forty-six fighters leave the ring dreaming of what might have been. 'Maybe,' he says, 'they had thought about losing before they got there, in which case they had lost already.'

Boxing is a sport that has always required colourful characters, and armies of hype merchants, to maintain public interest. So having a smart, charismatic, clever, controversial, good-looking and supremely talented boxer like Mayweather constantly reminding us how good-looking he is, how none of his opponents has ever managed to destroy those looks, and telling us he is TBE, is all of a part with the history and legend of the sport. Yet that TBE label seems to be forgotten when he is in more reflective mode, suggesting that being the world's richest athlete does not lead him to claim he is better than a Tiger Woods or a Roger Federer, or some of the big stars of basketball who are personal friends. 'I don't compare myself to other people. I think that's a complete waste of time. I have so many friends from other sports, particularly in the NBA – Kobe Bryant, Paul George, LeBron James – that are the best in their sports too. It is a mutual respect that we have for each other, I believe, because we are dedicated to being and proving we are the best. I can't name everyone I respect and admire, but I give the greatest praise to others who reach their potential the hard way – not cutting corners, cheating or relying on others to succeed. There are so many great athletes, actors, doctors, lawyers, writers, other people who are great in their own right. Sure I call myself and believe I am "TBE" but that is my own belief and I am comfortable believing in it too.'

And yet he also says he is 'absolutely not' annoyed that Muhammad Ali cornered 'The Greatest' title, though there might be a subtle boast in his use of tenses. 'Ali *was* the greatest and an amazing fighter. Oh – and his legacy is something to be recognised and celebrated too. I have the most respect for Ali and looked up to him when I was a young fighter. I respect all of the giants of the sport of boxing as there are so many to recognise for their contribution to the sport.'

Ali set the gold standard for sportsmen as entertainer, with his quips, his charisma, his poems, his boasts, his one-liners, and with his looks closer to that of a Hollywood actor or pop star than a prizefighter. As with Mayweather, though, it was all rooted in raw talent, and hard work to make the most of it.

The big difference between them is that Mayweather chose very deliberately to focus on just one part of the American dream as he fought from one win to the next: money. Ali was conscious early on of his own political potency and symbolism. His legacy is as much about race and equal rights, his refusal to fight in Vietnam, his conversion to Islam. Mayweather does not see himself as a world-changer in the same way. He is a fighter pure and simple, and in the US there are only two ways to measure whether you are the best or not: your win/loss ratio (as I've said, 100 per cent in his case), and your wealth (beyond anyone else's in sporting history). Mayweather long ago had enough money to keep himself, his family and his friends in style for the rest of their lives, but he needs to keep on winning, and keep on showing he is a winner.

Perhaps Ali and Mayweather, both the greatest of their generation in their chosen sport, represent two different generations more broadly: Ali's more radical, more politically engaged, more determined to right wrongs; Mayweather's more materialistic, more focused on wealth and celebrity and pure entertainment.

Ali's name and legend are known to virtually everyone on the planet, and when he dies, the reactions around America and the world will not be far off those which greet the death of a global leader. Mayweather is known to anyone who has an interest in sport, yet I have been surprised to discover quite a few people barely aware of his existence. But as a sporting mindset needed to deliver a sporting OST, and as an unbeaten champion, Mayweather is out there on his own. The chances are, too, that because of the way he fights, and the way he looks after himself, he may be able to avoid the kind of illnesses which have reduced Ali's quality of life over many years. That is a win of sorts as well.

PART 3

STANDING OUT FROM THE CROWD

11

BOLDNESS

'It is only by being bold that you get anywhere.'

RICHARD BRANSON

Sir Richard Branson is nothing if not bold. The founder of a student paper aged seventeen, he moved into selling records when he was twenty-one, before starting his own recording business. His Virgin brand is one of the best known, and most popular, in the world, with cruises and hotels the latest additions to the portfolio.

So much is in a name, and I ask him why he decided to call his record business Virgin. In point of fact, he says, it wasn't his idea: he'd suggested Slipped Disc Records (admitting that Slipped Disc as the umbrella label wouldn't have been ideal when he moved into aviation and space travel). But then one of his young female colleagues said, 'How about Virgin? Because we are all such virgins at business?' Everyone in the room loved it. Virgin was born.

'Why didn't you name her in any of your books?' I ask.

'Because I can't remember her name.'

Shocking, I suggest, given her role in his success.

'Can you remember who you slept with at that age, let alone who you worked with?' he shoots back. 'You know, the authorities wouldn't let me register the name for three years because they thought it was rude. I had to write saying the *Oxford Dictionary* meaning of the word virgin is "pure, untouched, unblemished" and asking which parts of that are rude. Finally they relented.'

The Virgin label certainly sums up the confident 'newcomer' image, something Branson has managed to retain despite reaching pensionable age. His has always been a challenger brand, a series of iconoclastic ventures in which he was never going to let lack of experience stand in the way of entrepreneurship. And it was a remarkable display of self-confidence that took Branson into perhaps his bravest venture: Virgin Airways. Here was a sector of which he had little knowledge, which was famously competitive, and dominated by a handful of very powerful players. 'My colleagues and friends basically thought I had gone mad.'

So what prompted such a complete departure from what Virgin had done before? 'One word: frustration.' Being bold, he argues, means identifying a change you want to occur in the world, and having the drive to bring it about. This is what separates out spectators and players: if we see things we don't like, we can either moan about them, or 'do something'. Branson is in the second camp. Virgin record stores were born of his frustration at the dullness and sameness of what the market had to offer. The record company was founded because he found it infuriating that there was so much musical talent around but so few outlets for it.

Virgin Airlines was established on another frustrated impulse. Branson was trying to fly from Puerto Rico to the Virgin Islands. 'We got bumped,' he explains. 'So I hired a plane and sold the spare seats on it. Not difficult.' A subsequent, even stronger influence was his realisation that existing airlines just didn't offer a very enjoyable experience. 'The airlines in those days were awful, generally state-run, and for most people, it was a crap experience. I had a sense of what could be achieved, and I didn't see it as a barrier that I had no background in the industry. In fact, as the airlines were so dire, I thought it was probably an advantage. I thought, "Why can't we create an airline that gives a good flying experience?" Most of my bold moves come out of that kind of personal frustration.'

Branson tells a wonderful story which demonstrates the essence of his commercial courage, showing how a small tactical idea can create a huge strategic opportunity, provided you are bold enough to seize it. It was the height of the 1992 recession, and the airline industry had been badly hit by a decline in trade. In spite of the difficult times, though, Virgin was trying to raise £10 million to implement a new innovation: seat-back video screens. I'm sure most young people assume planes have always featured such entertainment systems – but like many bold ideas, it didn't seem so obvious at the time. In fact, it was considered such an odd concept that, astonishingly, Virgin couldn't raise the funds to back it. Branson was close to dropping the idea when he had the brainwave of incorporating this tactic into the broader strategy of the business at the time – expansion during a time of recession; 'being greedy when others are fearful', as Warren Buffett puts it.

Branson called Boeing CEO Phil Condit. He said he would buy ten new Boeing 747-400s, if Condit would throw in the new seat-back screens for free. Condit, stunned that anyone would want to buy new planes during such a severe recession, promptly agreed. Branson then took the idea to Airbus, and bought eight more planes. 'It was easier to get £4 billion credit to buy eighteen new aircraft than £10 million for the seat-back video sets,' he says. So, while working within the objective of challenging the established airlines and expanding during a recession, Branson was able to circumvent obstacles and secure an important tactical advantage.

THE ESSENCE OF BOLDNESS: CLARITY, TIMING, LUCK

It's tempting to assume that boldness defines Branson, but it's a little more complicated than that. In the first place, he is far too savvy to embark on a new venture without doing his homework. For example, having been attracted by the idea of starting his own airline, he compiled a list of the things he needed to find out about aircraft leasing; he rang the only airline at that time offering cheap fares across the Atlantic, People Express, to get a sense of how they operated (and was encouraged to find that their line seemed to be permanently engaged – clearly room for another player, he decided); he spoke to Freddie Laker, who had tried and failed to sustain his own airline, to find out what mistakes he thought he had made and what opportunities were there.

Though Branson is second to none in having big, bold ideas, he is the first to admit that he needs others to turn them into reality. 'I have always been careful to get people who really know how to make things happen in practical terms,' he says. 'I left school early, started the magazine, and I felt like I was being thrown out there to learn the art of survival, and I realised it was possible to achieve more than people expected and when you have done it once you can be cheeky, you do it again and again and the challenges get bigger and bolder as you go on. I am dyslexic, which is limiting, and I knew I needed people better than myself, so I was not always trying to impose my own ideas but be a good listener and get the best from people. That has been the pattern – have the idea, get people to help me make it happen, then have another idea, set another challenge, hopefully bigger than the last one.'

So his boldness in aviation came not at the beginning but at the end of a mental process. He had an intuitive idea. Then he sought to find the data that would allow him to form an impression of the way things were, pose any relevant questions, and then begin to imagine how things might be done better – how he might innovate, and build the team to do it. It was at this point that boldness entered the equation.

Actor Kevin Spacey tells me a similar story of how personal frustration – a businessman hacked off at having to pay a fine for the late return of a videotape – led to innovation bordering on revolution in how we consume entertainment. 'The guy was Reed Hastings and he is CEO of Netflix. The idea came from him thinking "Why can't I pay a reasonable rate to watch this video as often as I like, and keep it for as long as I like, so long as I pay the subscription?"' The same bold mindset came into play when Spacey and director David Fincher were hawking hit series *House of Cards* around the TV companies. 'They all wanted a pilot. We didn't want to do one because pilots are so limiting. Netflix bought two series before we had shot a single scene, based on two scripts and a narrative arc. That was bold, unheard of, and it has paid off. *House of Cards* has been their biggest success in every country where they exist.' It paid off not least because of another bold move, the decision to put out all episodes at the same time, so that viewers could choose when to watch, rather than the content producer deciding. 'We learned the lesson the music industry failed to learn,' Spacey says, 'namely that if you provide the content when people want it at a reasonable price, they will pay not steal.'

I think one can see the same Branson-style processes at work in New Labour's finest achievements which, whatever the Blair haters say, were numerous. No one, I think, supporters and detractors alike, would

> 'Caution won't win elections, boldness will.' **TONY BLAIR**

dispute that Tony Blair was bold (one of his finest speeches said of New Labour that we were 'at our best when at our boldest'). He demonstrated this quality from the very beginning when he decided to abolish Clause 4 of the Labour Party constitution – a rallying point for traditional socialists committed to nationalised industries and utilities. Socialist ideologues argued it should not be tampered with. Pragmatists felt that it did not need to be tampered with – it could simply be ignored. Tony, by contrast, felt that to abolish it, and debate its replacement in a high-profile way, would send a powerful message about the modernising tendencies of New Labour, thus cementing the core strategy in the public mind. He was certainly taking a risk, knowing as he did that it would spark divisive debate and that the public tend not to trust divided parties. But it was also a calculated risk decided upon after much thought and reflection, based on the insight that if people hadn't wanted to see a change to the party outlook they wouldn't have elected him so convincingly as leader.

His interventions in Northern Ireland and Kosovo were, to my mind, even bolder, but again these were calculated risks. With regards to the Kosovo conflict, the Supreme Allied Commander in Europe, US General Wes Clark, warned me that Tony was putting himself out on a limb in advocating not only continuing air strikes but the threat of ground troops, with the preparedness to see the threat through. Tony's approach led to considerable tensions in his relationship with Bill Clinton, among others, yet it is now generally accepted that this was morally, and strategically, the right course of action. He had used the available information to make a judgement about the situation, and to determine whether the level of risk involved was acceptable. This was always rooted in a strong sense of what he needed to achieve.

It is not hard to find further examples of this kind of Branson–Blair style boldness at work. Amazon founder Jeff Bezos has his idea for 'the everything store', and sees that the Internet makes it possible. A massive thought, born of a bold imagination. It has changed the way we live. Similarly, Elon Musk not only founds PayPal, SpaceX and SolarCity Corp but decides his real goal in life is to get the world to shift from oil-fuelled cars to electric ones. Hence Tesla Motors, which within years has gone from zero to a capital market valuation well on its way to matching traditional car giants, and which has also put all its patents out there, available to anyone, so that others can join in the race he is trying to win. To dismiss patents as 'a lottery ticket to a lawsuit' is a pretty bold approach in itself!

In the sports arena, Dave Brailsford has helped spearhead the rise and rise of British cycling. Asked what one word sums up his modus operandi, Brailsford says: 'Ambition. Big, bold ambition.' There are echoes of Branson when he adds: 'What excites me is a big bold thought like: "No Briton has ever won the Tour de France, why can't we win the Tour de France?" I don't see complications very easily. I don't see the obstacles, until you drill down. I sometimes get manic moments where I decide there's nothing we can't do here; get the right people and there's no limit to what we can achieve. So let's go for something really exciting. Then I get home and I think "Fuck, I can't believe I've just done that". So you go from setting an overly ambitious target because it is exciting and then worrying about failing. It's kind of a cycle. We haven't thought through every step at the start. Stating the ambition is the first big step, then we work it out.'

For all these people, therefore, there is restlessness and frustration, then a moment of clear perception, followed by a determination to act upon it. Yet there are always factors in play over which
the entrepreneurial individual has less control. Timing is certainly
one. Freddie Laker's early venture with Skytrain had struggled in
the mid-1970s, in part because conflict in the Middle East had driven
up the price of oil. At the end of the 1970s and into the early 1980s
he arguably expanded too quickly, but he was also hit by Britain's
economic downturn and by the devaluation of sterling which made
his debts more expensive to service. Branson, by contrast, started
his airline when the worst of the recession was over and built it
during the boom times of the later 1980s.

Luck plays a part, too. Freddie Laker was talented but often
unlucky. Branson is highly skilled, but also, on occasion, very lucky.
Take the test flight of his first plane, *Maiden Voyager*, when some
birds were sucked into one of the engines, causing it to explode. It
was something that could happen to any plane, but in such a safety-
conscious industry a problem with a new company's very first flight
could cause it to be its last. Fortunately for Branson, though, the
one press photographer around on that day worked for the *Financial
Times* and decided not to run the picture ('We're not that kind of
paper,' he said). Looking back some years later, Branson concluded:
'If that photograph had appeared in the press, it would have been
the end of Virgin Atlantic before we'd even begun.'

That said, Branson has also had his share of setbacks and bad
luck. Not long after our interview came the test flight crash of his
Virgin Galactic spacecraft, killing one of the pilots, and further setting
back his latest ambitious project.

When I ask him, 'So what about big bold ideas that haven't
worked?' he instantly replies, 'Virgin Cola,' a rather pained grimace
crossing his face. 'It did fine in the UK, then we arrived in New
York in a Sherman tank, and said we were taking on Coca-Cola.
At first they ignored us, but then realised maybe they couldn't, and
they basically decided to throw at us all the resources needed to
wipe us out. They succeeded.' Fortunately, for Branson, his successes

have outnumbered his failures. But boldness generally needs an element of luck – as well as very good timing – to succeed.

The point to make here, though, is that throughout our lives we all experience measures of good and bad luck. Few people are so fortunate or unfortunate as to enjoy or suffer only one. Indeed, in his book *Great by Choice*, Jim Collins demonstrates very scientifically that successful and unsuccessful companies have invariably experienced similar doses of good and bad fortune. It's what you do in the circumstances that matters. Bold visionaries make the most of good luck, and look for the positive rather than the negative when bad luck strikes. 'I think the fact some of our exploits failed spectacularly and often was a good thing, because people love a comeback story,' says Branson. 'Even when we failed there was the sunken boat with the word "Virgin" sticking out of the water, same with the balloons. When we finally did the boat Atlantic record, they even interrupted coverage of the football World Cup. Money can't buy that kind of publicity.'

Branson's Twitter biography encapsulates this personality nicely: 'tie-loathing adventurer and thrill-seeker, who believes in turning ideas into reality. Otherwise known as Dr Yes.'

> 'Physically I'm a chicken, mentally I'm bold.'
>
> **JEFF BEZOS**

This is a mindset lacking in too many organisations – and certainly in modern politics – where the tendency is often to look for the negative first. Throughout my professional life there is a phrase I have sought to ban from discussions: 'The problem is . . .' This is not because I think you should live in denial of problems, but in my experience, 'the problem is . . .' usually conceals an excuse or an inability or unwillingness to think through the issue. It creates a brick wall. It prevents bold or imaginative thinking. Famously, Margaret Thatcher said that the reason she liked Lord Young was that he brought 'solutions not problems' to the Cabinet table. The fact that he continues to be cited as the best example of this approach perhaps emphasises the relative rarity of such people. Both Justin King and Peter Hyman, in retail and education respectively, have told me that in meetings they insist on positive points being made before any negative reaction to any proposal or observation.

So an upbeat attitude helps fuel the ambitions of the Bransons of this world, makes them prepared to leave the comfort zone, venture that extra mile that will make the difference, eager to win but prepared to accept setbacks. The bold mindset also understands that possible failure comes with the package. Elon Musk says that when he started Tesla, he put their odds of success at 'less than 50 per cent'. For her part Internet entrepreneur Martha Lane Fox says: 'You have to be prepared to fail if you want to succeed.' She goes on to elaborate. 'I have always tried to have completely preposterous ambitions that are totally unrealistic, and then I end up somewhere short, but doing OK.' When she and Brent Hoberman founded lastminute.com in 1998, their ambition was to become 'the biggest UK commerce site, and then the biggest in the world, across all sectors'.

'So you wanted to be Amazon?' I ask.

'Something like that. We succeeded though, did well. Just not as well as those original ambitions. I'm a generally optimistic person. I get motivated and excited by a challenge and go for it. If you're not bold why should you expect anyone else to be bold for you? It's like Goethe said: "Boldness has power, genius and magic in it." I judge the success of my boldness by the impact and scale of change in the world. I want to change hundreds of thousands of minds.'

It's also worth pointing out the effect that boldness can have on the wider team or organisation: quite simply, it has a halo effect. People see positive action being taken and feel inspired by it – it injects a sense of energy and enthusiasm. That is what Charles Dunstone of TalkTalk means when he says that the style and approach of Branson and Blair was what he sought to emulate in his own business, both in terms of innovation and boldness. 'I liked the optimism they brought to everything they did, the informality, the sense that anything was possible. They were a breath of fresh air, really bold, no challenge too big, and the atmosphere they helped create was great for people like me.'

BOLDNESS VS RECKLESSNESS

Boldness, then, is an essential attribute, but at what point does it run the risk of becoming recklessness? The honest answer – or cynical, depending on your viewpoint – is that it all depends whether the gamble comes off or not. The decision taken by Holland's manager Louis van Gaal to substitute his goalkeeper as a World Cup quarter-final penalty shootout began might have gone down in the annals of sport as a supreme example of recklessness – had it not paid off. Had former RBS chief Fred Goodwin completed his purchase of the Dutch giant ABN Amro in more stable financial times, rather than become the symbol of banker greed in the crash, he might still be acclaimed something of a banking genius today. Any medal-winning drug cheat in sport who has never been exposed – and who knows how many of those there are – will think they did get away with it.

A more considered answer, though, takes into account the nature of the risk involved. In itself, taking a bold decision that doesn't come off is not the unforgivable act of an irresponsible person. 'In sport, boldness is not about doing ridiculous things, it is about backing your belief in yourself,' says Brian O'Driscoll, 'taking a risk in the moment in the knowledge that because of your experience and your mindset, it is more likely to work than not; and knowing that if it doesn't, it won't put you off being bold again next time. Matches turn on moments and you have to grab them when they come. High risk, high reward, that was always in my mind.' Branson's Virgin Cola venture was, in business terms, a mistake since it failed. But Branson took important lessons from the episode, and lessons well learned, when your mindset is as positive as his, can render a mistake one worth making, whatever the pain at the time. The first lesson was the importance of differentiation when challenging an established brand. 'We had a good product with

Virgin Cola but ultimately what we were delivering was no different to Coke, it wasn't distinguishable enough, and with their size and brand recognition they were able to blow us out the water. It is very different with the airlines. We have continually produced something better than the rest, so even when BA threw everything at us, we could still thrive.' The second lesson he took was about the calibration of risk: the demise of Virgin Cola did not mean the demise of Virgin itself. The company was much bigger than the risk it took, which meant he was not going to let that setback stop him and the company being bold in the future.

A telltale sign of recklessness is that it involves an unhealthy element of ego. A sense of self-worth is, of course, central to successful people; but the key issue is the service to which it is put. I worked for several years for publisher Robert Maxwell. He was someone possessed of a bold mindset, for sure. But he had megalomaniac tendencies which meant he couldn't take advice or criticism, couldn't see beyond his own role, and so made many mistakes, and was eventually driven to suicide, I believe, by the scale of his errors.

Maxwell was a shameless self-promoter, another symptom of an overinflated ego. Some might argue that Branson is too. But there is a difference: he puts his public image at the service of his business. To say that he 'loves publicity', and to intend this as a criticism, is to misunderstand his purpose. He took a deliberate decision to make his own image and profile part of the Virgin brand; getting himself noticed is part of the wider goal of raising brand awareness. His ballooning exploits – bold to the point of genuinely life-threatening – were partly about generating brand profile for a tiny airline unable to match the big boys in advertising and marketing spend. The same can be said of his Blue Riband crossing of the Atlantic. And nobody could disagree that it was bold of him to fly a Virgin plane into Baghdad, and leave with the prime minister, Edward Heath, and hostages who had been held by Saddam Hussein. Indeed, that was the move which made BA chairman Lord King realise Branson was a threat, not just an irritant. As a result BA launched the so-called 'dirty tricks' campaign against Virgin. That led to another bold decision from Branson – to sue. He won, and so, far from destroying him, the campaign made both him and his airline more popular, and more established as a challenger. Branson's boldness has become part of his public persona, and that has reflected onto the brand. Consider Virgin Galactic, Branson's new space programme: a massive project and yet it seems like a natural next step for Virgin, and the fact that it does tells you a lot about the way Branson is, and the way he is perceived – a man who is constantly pushing the boundaries. And though the crash in November 2014 was clearly a setback, amid the sympathy for the lost pilot was an expression of Branson's determination to press on.

Branson says he has never fully overcome childhood shyness, and for a great communicator he can be strangely mumbling and inarticulate at times. But he was one of the first business leaders to understand instinctively what strategic communication means in the modern media age: that everything you do, and everything you say about yourself, must hang together as a coherent whole so that key messages and values are consistently communicated over time.

That boldness is a fundamental part of his mindset is clear in everything he discusses. He is highly critical, for example, about British governments' failure to cater for aviation expansion. 'It means Britain is going to get left behind. We last had a new runway in 1945 and still they prevaricate. The lack of bravery by the government has resulted in us being kept in a little box. We have 3 per cent of the slots at Heathrow. After just fifteen years in Australia we have 40 per cent of the market because they built runways and we have no restraint re slots. We compete properly there, and in America, but not here and sure it is frustrating but as a British person I just find it so sad.' One might expect that of someone so closely involved in aviation, but his open thinking extends to topics such as drugs, where he argues that for too long people have been trapped by preconceptions and rhetoric. 'We should see it as a health issue, not a crime issue,' Branson suggests. But to do that would mean a radical reframing of an issue demonised in the public debate for decades. A politician who wanted to take on that challenge would have to be prepared for the inevitable flak and it's a risk that nobody in a really prominent role has been willing to take – so far. However, Branson says: 'I just do not believe that boldness is a vote loser if you are actually doing the right thing, based on the facts, reality and a country's needs.' These are brave words, but they're not reckless ones.

Of course in the political sphere, one man's 'right thing based on the facts, reality and a country's needs' is another's half-baked nonsense or unpardonable folly. Tony Blair's handling of Iraq is a case in point. His judgement was in my view perfectly understandable: he believed that Saddam Hussein had an active weapons of mass destruction programme (as did not just US and UK intelligence services, but the French and German intelligence services too); he felt the risk of Saddam using them, or them falling into the hands of terror groups who had shown themselves capable of an act of violence as grotesque as the attack on New York's Twin Towers, was real. Richard Branson, by contrast, thought, like many others, that joining the Americans in toppling Saddam was a mistake, that even if the threat was there, it did not merit war and all it entailed. And of course, part of the case for war having been intelligence pointing to the reality of a WMD programme, when it became clear the weapons were not there, critics felt not only vindicated, but betrayed. I know many people share those views. I meet such people regularly. Arguably, one could say that Branson's 'reality' was out there, and some argue that it was the success of Tony's bold moves prior to Iraq, not least in Kosovo and Sierra Leone, that blinded him to the dangers. I believe he went in with his eyes open, making, of the two bold choices he faced, the one he believed to be right for the country, based upon the facts as he

> 'I just do not believe that boldness is a vote loser if you are actually doing the right thing.'
> **RICHARD BRANSON**

understood them. Ultimately, it was a judgement call. The tough ones always are.

THE DANGER OF INACTION

The risks inherent in acting boldly are obvious enough. What is frequently forgotten, though, is that acting hesitantly or doing nothing can be equally risky. This is demonstrably the case in the political sphere. Here, looking as though events are controlling you rather than the other way round immediately suggests weakness. And failing to act implies a lack of vision or determination. Look at the political pain Barack Obama suffered when, asked what his strategy for IS was, he said: 'We don't have a strategy.'

It was one specific act of indecision that may have fatally undermined Gordon Brown as prime minister. He had shown his capacity for boldness many times, not least with a whole raft of economic reforms as chancellor, like the first major decision of the Blair government, Bank of England independence, which helped secure a key part of our economic strategy for more than a decade. And he showed his bold side again towards the end of his time as PM, in his impressive handling of the global financial crisis. But before that, not long after he took over from Tony, the boldness gene deserted him with regard to the idea of a snap election after an impressive start in office. Both on and off the record, people close to him ramped up the idea that he was considering going to the polls. The Labour Party was put on alert, and battle plans prepared. David Cameron publicly urged Brown to 'bring it on', while privately telling colleagues they weren't ready.

But Gordon agonised, before going on to say it wasn't happening. The master of financial action now became the victim of political inaction. A debate which should have stayed internal damaged him when it got out. My assessment is that the discussions were dominated by 'the problem is . . .' people giving reasons one way and the other, and only seeing the downside of both, so that eventually doing nothing won. I am not sure Gordon's standing

among the political classes ever recovered from that. And it undermined the public perception of him.

As for doing nothing, this only works in a world where no one
else is doing anything either. Business history is littered with the
corpses of organisations that thought the status quo was good enough.
Kodak is a well-known example from recent years: a global giant that
thought it could ignore digital photography when it should have been
embracing it. It filed for bankruptcy protection in 2012. In politics,
I look at the Green Party which grew along with growing concerns
about the environment, but failed to see perhaps that harsher economic
times would see the issue slip down the agenda, and the nationalist
anger, which usually accompanies economic difficulty, create space
for a party like UKIP as the small party that people wanted to hear
from. They didn't adapt to that change. As a result, although the
Green Party rose in late 2014, the environment has sadly slipped even
further down the agenda, alarming considering the future of the planet
might be at stake. In sport, look at the decline of Spain at the last
World Cup, or the West Indies in cricket, to see what happens if you
fight the next campaign with the tactics of the last one.

It's a salutary thought that since he started Virgin Airlines, all
eighteen of the airlines Branson saw as rivals have gone, with the
sole exception of British Airways. No doubt back in the 1980s they
all saw Virgin as a flash-in-the-pan upstart. They all had their
business model. They proposed to stick to it. The result: complacency, inability to adapt, failure to keep improving. Branson takes
a very critical view of their inaction. 'The ones that failed,' he says,
'did not give their teams the tools required to do their job, whether
in providing better entertainment, food, comfort, service or staff
motivation – all the things that go into making flying a positive
rather than a negative experience.' I interviewed him the day after
a party at Gatwick airport to celebrate the airline's thirtieth anniversary. 'We outlived a lot of those other airlines not by being the
biggest but simply by making sure we gave people an enjoyable
experience. Thirty years ago, with one plane, the *joie de vivre* of
the staff was tremendous and I wondered "will it be like that in

thirty years?" and I think it is, and that's with over three hundred planes now.'

The reason Branson is such a role model for entrepreneurs is that he is someone who says all the time 'it doesn't have to be like this'. 'There is a feeling of freedom to what he does,' says Charles Dunstone. 'The world has changed so much in the last thirty years, and his style, more informality, more excitement, has been great. There's been a decline in respect for brands whether it's government, the Church or supermarket brands, and that's opened up all sorts of possibilities for challenger brands to come in and disrupt and that's what Branson does so well.'

12

INNOVATION

'We are what we repeatedly do. Excellence, then, is not an act, but a habit.'

ARISTOTLE

FINDING THE RIGHT WORD

It was 2000 and Clive Woodward faced a real problem. The England rugby team was going into matches well, but for some reason, when it came to the beginning of the second half, they always seemed to start sluggishly. The coach turned to Humphrey Walters, who knew next to nothing about international rugby, but a lot about solving problems. He asked a question. 'What do they do at half-time?' Woodward talked him through the process. Walters asked another question. 'Why don't they put on new shirts? It might help get them back into the same mindset as before the game.' The players were sceptical. Woodward insisted. It worked. It is now standard practice in most professional sports to start a second half with new, clean, dry kit. Obvious, once it was done.

All too often when people talk about innovation, they assume it means inventing something completely new and totally ground-breaking. Innovation and invention, though, are not the same thing. Inventors create something virtually from scratch. Innovators take a product or a process and improve it to their advantage. Occasionally, of course, the two things come together. Tim Berners-Lee, for example, seen as the creator of the World Wide Web, is one of those rare people who can be seen as both inventor and innovator. But to innovate successfully you don't need to have an inventor's mentality.

'We didn't invent anything,' says Billy Beane, one of the great innovators in sport, whose recruitment processes were used to revolutionise first Oakland A's, then baseball as other teams grudgingly admired and soon copied, then other sports and indeed businesses, as they adapted his methods to their own world. The innovation was the use of sabermetric, evidence-based analytics to find undervalued players in an inefficient market. By doing this, Beane was able to offset the financial restraints to which the club had to work against some brilliant hirings, enabling the team to make the playoffs in both 2002 and 2003.

Put like this, it sounds very simple. But various factors came together to create this breakthrough. First was the initial perception which actually came from – as Beane puts it – 'clever guys who had come from outside the sport'. Then Beane's profound understanding of the sport encouraged him to do something with this perception. 'It needed someone who understood the changes that needed to be made but who was in some way already accepted by the game.' And finally, as with so many innovatory moves, boldness was required to see it through: Beane had to take on the institutionalised scouts who had previously been so closely involved in hirings and make it happen. 'My status as an ex-player was essential. Players might take things from outsiders today. Not then.'

Getting really smart people to work together in a culture of innovation is what has made Apple one of the most successful companies of our lifetime. Yet they too are less inventors than innovators – their success built on taking products that already existed, rethinking them and doing them better. And for all that Apple has become the latest global symbol of free-market enterprise America, it's worth noting that their innovations were often of inventions developed by the big hand of the state, the US government: the early Internet, GPS, touch-screen display, Siri. It's what Apple did with them that counts. When Garry Kasparov was talking to me about Steve Jobs's killer instinct, back in the chapter on strategy, he said: 'Remember the Rio MP3 Player? Nobody else does either.' His point is that Apple innovates to beat rivals, a process that sees them taking on outsiders, and their own processes, with equal vigour. How did the development of the iPod as a series of world-beating products come about? Through a culture within a company that demanded innovation, invested massively in R&D, and threw minds together likely to deliver magical and groundbreaking innovations. They didn't set out with a plan for the iPod. It emerged from the innovation culture, nicely summed up by their brilliant chief designer Jony Ive: 'In a company born to innovate, the risk is not innovating. The real risk is to think it is safe to play safe.'

In fact some would even question whether 'innovation' describes accurately what is required when people need to up their game or make changes. I see Dave Brailsford as one of the great innovators in sport, as do his peers, but as happens when we meet up, saying so can lead to an argument about the meaning of words. 'For me I don't think innovation is the right word because innovation implies major step change but that isn't really what elite sport is about. It's semantics, I guess, but the whole point of what we do is continuous improvement. That's what elite sport is about and if you're not thinking about continuous improvement all day every day you won't be competitive.' Outsiders look at what Brailsford has overseen with regard to processes, training methods, planning and equipment – not to mention results – and cannot fail to see an innovative mind and team at work. But he insists: 'When you figure out that continuous improvement is going to be at the heart of everything you do, then your mindset is centred around that, full stop.'

Bill Endicott, a former White House Director of Research and Analysis, coach of fifty-seven medal-winning Olympic, World Cup and World Champion canoeists, and servant of the US Marine Corps Reserve, believes success comes through 'a fascination for the process'. 'During the course of my life,' he says, 'I've been around top performers – Harvard professors, congressmen, the US president, Marine Corp generals, World and Olympic champions. They all have something in common that we don't pay enough attention to.

All of them are fascinated by all the little details of what they do, they inevitably do them more than anybody else and in so doing they reach levels of understanding that most of us don't even realise exist. A great coach can demonstrate this fascination for the process for his sport and then teach it to his athletes.'

> 'Marginal gains means looking at all the things we do, and never assuming we couldn't do them better.'
>
> **DAVE BRAILSFORD**

A key factor here is adaptability. To innovate you are always adapting to new ideas, new ways to use resources, new ways to interpret data or information. However, where innovation goes beyond merely adapting is when a process is improved to your competitive advantage. Adaptability on its own is exploiting the sunshine or the rain; innovation is making the weather. Innovation changes conditions; adaptation responds. Innovation is changing the competitive conditions to your own advantage; adaptability is adapting successfully to changed competitive conditions set by others. Both are vital components of winning. However, the most successful businesses, sports teams or politicians are those who adapt through innovating, rather than those who innovate through adapting.

If all this sounds like playing with words, it is important to an understanding of what most successful innovation really involves. It doesn't have to be about flashes of genius or 'thinking the unthinkable', though there may be moments of that. For the most part it's about that 'continuous improvement' that Brailsford demands; it's about constantly questioning what you're doing and wondering whether there's a better way to do it, as Billy Beane did; it's also about doing something before your competitors, rather than reacting to what they have just done. It's what Brailsford has made famous in sport by calling it 'marginal gains', an approach adopted by Metro Bank CEO Craig Donaldson, who not only names Brailsford, a man he has never met, as a big influence, but hired Humphrey Walters as part of his leadership coaching team. In fact, I hear bits of both of them as we sit in his Holborn office and he tells me: 'The marginal gains philosophy sees innovation not as giant steps but a focus on continuous improvement.' Couched in these terms it's less intimidating – and more achievable – than the word 'innovation', baldly stated, might imply. Think dry shirts at half-time, rather than discovering penicillin or inventing the telephone, and everyone can be an innovator. And, to my mind, there are four types of innovation.

TYPE 1 INNOVATION: SEEING A NEW OPPORTUNITY

Some of the best ideas come from a single insight, and these are often the ones that turn out to be game-changers. We saw in the previous chapter how some of Richard Branson's best innovations came out of moments of personal frustration, for example 'flying is such a crap experience' leading to Virgin Airlines. And what of the man who hero-worships Branson, Sir Charles Dunstone, one of Britain's most successful innovators? When mobile phones were first invented – yes, invented, albeit as an innovation developed from the basic telephone – his job was selling them for NEC to BT and Vodafone, who in turn were selling them on to big business customers. Then came a moment of very clear perception. 'It is the only decent strategic thought I've ever had in my entire life,' he recalls. 'It was to see that if there was one group of people mobile phones were going to help more than big business, it was the self-employed, plumbers and roofers who would be out working, and if they had a phone with them they could take more bookings. That was the insight, I guess, and that was what we had in mind.' At the time mobile phones were largely associated with 'yuppies and big business'. Dunstone saw a much wider opportunity and seized it. 'We started off sharing a flat with a music publisher. We called it Carphone Warehouse because most of the market was carphones, and warehouse because we didn't want people to think our entire operation was in half a flat. We almost called it Professional Cellular Services, but as we were putting an ad in the *Evening Standard*, I thought that's not a good name, and came up with Carphone Warehouse.'

If that sounds like the small garage where Jeff Bezos started to build the online bookstore that has grown into one of the giants of the World Wide Web age – Amazon – that's because all ideas start small. They start as ideas. It is the ambitions that are large, though even in his garage, Bezos had no idea quite how big Amazon would become.

In some cases, type 1 innovation may well involve taking an idea that has worked elsewhere, perhaps in a different context, and adapting it successfully. There were actually Internet bookstores before Bezos came along. He just did it better. Entrepreneur Martha Lane Fox talks about innovation as 'adapting something already existing and spotting a gap in the market'. That she has the innovative mindset is clear from her latest UK business, a string of karaoke bars called Lucky Voice. Where did the idea come from? From her being in Japan, getting taken to a karaoke bar, seeing the huge fun people had, and thinking, 'Why wouldn't this work at home, especially as so many of the great songs people love to sing are ours?' 'We have ten up and running now,' she says, 'and my plan is to develop them so they become better than the Japanese ones and then I'll take the innovations we make back into the Japanese market.'

TYPE 2 INNOVATION: ADDRESSING A PROBLEM

Dunstone's and Lane Fox's 'Aha' moments came with the sharply focused perception of an *opportunity*. For others it comes with the sharply focused understanding of a *problem*. Type 2. Take Twenty20 cricket. It was the brainchild of Stuart Robertson of Hampshire, worried that the numbers attending county cricket matches were falling because many cricket enthusiasts no longer had the time to devote a whole day to watching a sometimes sleepy encounter between two county sides. His solution? If people don't have time for traditional cricket, establish a shorter form of the game, with each side limited to a single innings of twenty overs, so that those with busy lives will be able to find time for the sport, which in turn is more exciting for the media companies whose finances keep professional sports afloat. As innovations invariably do, in a sport as conservative as cricket, in a country as conservative as England, his scheme attracted opposition, and was only passed by county cricket chairmen by a narrow margin: eleven votes to seven. But Robertson's innovation quickly served its purpose in terms of energising interest in cricket, among both the public and the media, and it then spread to the rest of the cricketing world. Within four years, Twenty20 cricket had its own World Cup; an innovation designed to revive the sport in one country ended up transforming the sport globally, culminating in the creation of the new Indian Premier League six years ago, now the most watched and commercially successful cricket league in the world, with a brand value over $3 billion. Manoj Badale, owner of IPL team Rajasthan Royals, suggests Twenty20 and the IPL is 'up there with the UEFA Champions League as the greatest sporting innovation of our time'.

In a very different sphere, I would suggest that Ireland becoming the first country in the world to ban smoking in the workplace, in 2004, is an example of type 2 innovation: a problem was identified (despite government campaigns, tobacco-related illnesses and the enormous cost of dealing with them remained a constant), and a solution enacted (ban smoking in social environments such as pubs and clubs, shops and factories, in order to lessen its appeal and acceptability). Once Ireland led, we followed, and so have many other countries around the world. A similar claim of advance through type 2 innovation, in the area of public policy, could be made for city bike schemes, which target problems as varied as congestion, environmental degradation and obesity, and which have spread around the world, doubling from 236,000 bikes in use in 375 cities in May 2011, to 517,000 bikes in 535 cities two years later. True, the first such scheme (in Amsterdam in 1965) failed because of thefts, but by the mid-1970s a model had been established that has proved remarkably robust. Today, the two biggest schemes in the world are both in China, with 90,000 bikes in Wuhan and 60,000 in Hangzhou.

TYPE 3 INNOVATION: EXPLOITING THE PROBLEMS OF OTHERS

Type 3 innovation arises from looking at what others are doing, establishing what they're doing wrong, or what they're doing right that could be done better, and then formulating a plan accordingly. This tends to involve a range of approaches and solutions. The impetus for Craig Donaldson's Metro Bank was not one single idea about how banking should be in the twenty-first century, but an understanding of people's dissatisfaction with the existing banks. In other words, it involved – and here too Donaldson was learning from the approach of Brailsford, Beane, Woodward and other innovators in sport – 'asking the right questions'. 'Why is my bank only open when I'm at work? What about weekends and evenings? Why does it take so long to get a new card? Why is my mortgage looked after by one part of the bank and my current account by another? Why can't I speak to a human being when I phone?' Metro Bank took the ten top criticisms of other banks and built their own bank by providing alternative answers to them, and then pursued a policy of continuous innovation to stay ahead.

In the same sector, Funding Circle has also become a successful innovation by examining the processes of others, notably the banks. An online marketplace which allows savers and investors to lend money directly to small- and medium-sized businesses, it was the first site to use peer-to-peer lending for business funding in the UK and has now taken the model to the US. Their business activity has trebled every year since they started in August 2010. Co-founder Samir Desai says Funding Circle emerged from inefficiencies in the financial sector, in particular the costs and the time it took for small businesses to get loans. 'What sense does it make, in an era when everything is moving online, that to get a loan you make an appointment to see a bank manager and then sit around pushing paper at each other? The banks could behave as they did because only they could facilitate the transfer of money around the world but now with the World Wide Web and the development of our own trusted platform we could bring together people who wanted to invest money, and businesses which needed the investment.' His definition of innovation is 'looking at an already established process of doing things, recognising weaknesses and inefficiencies, and then adapting that process to your own advantage'. Billy Beane couldn't have put it better.

The online news service the Huffington Post, founded in 2005 by the writer and journalist Arianna Huffington, is another great type 3 innovation: an idea emerging from a profound understanding of the limitations of existing organisations and their approaches in dealing with powerful waves of change. I have to confess that when she asked me to speak at the launch of the UK version of the Huffington Post I was sceptical, despite the success she was having in the US, of Arianna's bold ambitions for the first global online 'paper'. But she had grasped that while many media outlets back in 2005 had an online presence, it tended to be tacked onto everything else they were doing rather than being thought through in the context of how the Internet actually operates. 'The gap I saw,' she says, 'was the fact that you had the online world developing and you had the papers and TV not sure how to adapt and react, and the new idea was that it was possible to be both the platform and the journalist. The journalism had to be good, but the platform, the fact there were no deadlines, limitless space, this was where the innovation at the basic level could come from. Anyone who had an idea, anyone who had something interesting to say, they could say it. One of our early taglines was "The world's first Internet newspaper" so we definitely saw ourselves as a newspaper in many ways, but without paper, and without all the restrictions.' In other words the Huffington Post established from the outset a flexibility to its operation that perfectly meshed with the Internet age and the changing reading habits of people around the world. When I interviewed Arianna, the Post was receiving 95 million unique monthly visitors, had editorial HQs in eleven countries and more on the way, and she had secured a $315 million deal with AOL.

TYPE 4 INNOVATION: INNOVATION AS A CONSTANT MINDSET

Type 4 innovation involves not making one huge change or using what your competitors are doing to inform your thinking, but endlessly questioning your own operation and how you might improve it, what Clive Woodward calls 'doing a hundred things one per cent better'. Australian hockey coach Ric Charlesworth gave out a 'one per cent award' after every match to the player he felt had done 'that little bit extra'.

The British cycling team and then Team Sky under Dave Brailsford have excelled at this, asking every conceivable question, large and small, right down to finding out what size and type of pillow the riders sleep best on when at home, and taking the exact same pillows on the road, from hotel to hotel. For Team Sky, their favourite mattresses have followed. Anything that could legally assist performance led to questions being asked and new answers explored. Just as Matt Parker gloried in the title of 'Director of Marginal Gains' when working at British Cycling, so Brailsford's right-hand woman Fran Millar is 'Director of Winning Behaviours' at Team Sky – even business cards have to speak to the winning, innovative mindset.

Another British Cycling innovation was the 'Secret Squirrel Club', a team of experts whose knowledge could help Brailsford and his team tackle the simple but essential question: how can men and women ride faster on bikes? The club's members came not from cycling but from such sectors as aerospace, the car industry, fabrics and textiles; they were engineers, manufacturers, scientists and academics.

Their forensic focus on aerodynamics and performance led to one specific major change in the run-up to the Beijing Olympics. It had always been assumed, for obvious reasons, that the fastest way to get round the track was by taking the 'fastest line' – as close to the edge as possible. That was – and remains – the case for individual races. But the Secret Squirrel Group worked out that in the men's team pursuit, where four riders rotate the lead, accelerating and decelerating up and down the sloping bank as they do so, it would help for them to move the riding line slightly away from what everyone assumed to be the fastest line. 'We asked the question and in the answer we discovered that we didn't know something we thought we knew, and made an important winning adjustment as a result,' Parker tells me.

Another question he and Brailsford asked the experts to consider pre-Beijing led to the creation of the so-called 'hot pants' British cyclists wore. Parker explains: 'We asked the question: "What is the best temperature to give you the best physiological start, the ideal muscle-warming temperature?" They did the research and decided it was forty degrees. We then got to work with designers, academics, scientists, and developed new clothing. We can look back on that as a major successful product of our approach to innovation.' Each change in itself may not have been earth-shattering, but together they proved a powerful combination.

MARRYING INNOVATION TO LEADERSHIP AND STRATEGY

If British cycling is an inspiration for those looking to adopt the marginal gains approach to innovation, it also offers a warning. The range of issues the team tackled – from racing strategy, to bike design, to the pillows cyclists slept on – was a very diverse one. In the hands of a less focused team, these could have become uncontrolled distractions rather than opportunities for improvement. All too often, when groups of people or organisations look to up their game, they do so by embarking on an ill-thought-out programme of 'innovation' in which small groups of people working on completely different things end up getting in each other's way and competing for attention and funding. Sainsbury's former CEO Justin King calls it 'throwing mud innovation'. He says: 'It's not about trying anything. It's about knowing what you're trying to achieve. How you behave when innovation fails will tell people all they need to know about

whether you're serious about innovating or not.' He said he sought
to build a culture of innovation based on three principles: '*celebrate*
it when it is successful; *reward* it when it is successful; and *learn
from failure* by not making the same mistakes twice'.

Anyone seeking marginal gains, therefore, needs to start with
a clear idea of what they're seeking to improve and how it ties in
to the overall objective and strategy. And in this context simply
chanting the vague mantra 'We want to be better' is not enough.
Matt Parker insists innovation has to be given clear parameters.
'Just saying you want to win the Rugby World Cup or win the
Tour de France doesn't provide the necessary contextual framework
for innovation,' he argues. 'You have to come up with subsets of
goals beneath that which are tangible and which you can control.
This is the key part but it's often skipped over. When we set out
to be the best in the world at track cycling we knew that would
mean being the best in the world at aerodynamics: this gave us an
area which was clear and measurable, and we could innovate around
a specific performance objective. What are the numbers we are
required to hit to achieve this and then what performance improvement tools, new and existing, can give us this?'

> '*Celebrate* it when it
> is successful; *reward*
> it when it is
> successful; and *learn
> from failure* by not
> making the same
> mistakes twice.'
> **JUSTIN KING**

As my psychiatrist friend Nassir
Ghaemi points out, innovative people
often tick slightly differently from
others, possessing a high sense of self-
worth that helps see them through
the failures they will inevitably experience on their way to ultimate
success. Brian Millar, director of
strategy at Sense Worldwide, which
has some of the biggest, most established and seemingly most conservative brands on its books, says part of
their approach is to bring in 'oddballs, freaks, kids, the marginalised,
to find out how they're thinking'. For her part, Martha Lane Fox
is disarmingly honest about the close relationship between innovating

and failing. 'If you're an innovator focused on big bold things, it means you have to be prepared to screw up. I have screwed up so many times. Big things like backing ventures I should never have backed. Or like the time I sent an email by mistake to the whole company, which contained everyone's salary and a list of the people we were planning to fire.' She is also, however, remarkably robust. 'I make mistakes,' she says, 'but the key is not to do it again. Take the immediate hit, learn and move on. Do not let making mistakes put you off coming up with new ideas for innovation.' Such robustness – and the self-confidence that goes with it – makes innovators such as her very adaptable; by the same token it also means that they may not always be easy to work with. Of course, if the key innovator is the person in charge as well, their often very different way of viewing the world shapes the whole organisation. 'I am ludicrously overoptimistic,' says Charles Dunstone. 'I don't believe if I have an idea that I can't make it happen, and I believe it will work. I am also really stubborn.' When the innovators are part of a wider team, however, it is essential to establish a very clear sense of what their role is and what they are seeking to achieve.

Alex Ferguson offers a textbook example of the ability to maintain a clear sense of direction while innovating. On the one hand he had views and principles that were pretty much unshakeable. On the other, he was always open to new thinking if it didn't contradict or undermine his fundamental stance. So when a club doctor suggested using sports science to shape training, Ferguson saw the potential straight away: all he asked for was specific ideas and some kind of 'convincing' proof that it would help the players. 'It was unusual for me,' he recalls, 'because I was learning with the team, but as long as someone could prove a new idea could improve performance by 1 per cent, I would go with it.'

A similar instance of command from the centre is apparent in the highly successful and innovative research, polling and data techniques used by Obama's team in the lead-up to the 2008 presidential campaign. Whether or not Obama is a particularly digital person I'm not sure, but he grasped that, like every other organisational function, innovation required leadership, even if he wasn't himself an expert in the strand of innovation being employed. Certainly, leaving innovation outside the main tent is almost invariably a mistake. Obama's campaign manager David Plouffe said that their opponents tended to see digital as a separate part of their campaigns. Hillary Clinton's team, for example, 'had a traditional structure with digital sort of "over there somewhere" with no senior person cross-department'. In his view, this inability to integrate, the belief that you could simply tack on new methods as an adjunct to old techniques, was an important factor in gaining Obama the Democratic nomination, one he also exploited against John McCain when the presidential election itself came.

Obama's lack of personal expertise in this area is typical of many leaders today, and should not be regarded as a problem. Tony Blair did not even have a mobile phone until he left office, and his computer skills were rudimentary to say the least (mine were non-existent until I left Downing Street). The fact is that most organisations are now so complex that very few leaders can be expert in every area of them. Once upon a time, a great manager like Bill Shankly would put out the cones, coach a session, pack away afterwards, and then get in his car to watch a player he was thinking about signing for Liverpool. Today, if you visit Pennyhill Park to see the England rugby team at work, or St George's Park where their footballing counterparts train, or an ECB coaches meeting, you will be overwhelmed by the number of staff you come across. There are experts for everything. Mike Atherton, former England cricket captain turned brilliant sportswriter, recently mused in his *Times* column that cricket coaching was no longer 'a one-man job, where that man was expected to be a specialist coach for every player', and suggested that a new England coach would need to be 'an accomplished strategist, he must be able to develop a winning culture; he must be an outstanding communicator and man manager, and he must be an organiser who can put in place structures to help to develop a world-class team and world-class players and individuals'. Note that Atherton says nothing here that is specific to cricket, and indeed posits the idea that a Ferguson or a Woodward could manage a cricket team. Leadership in such settings becomes more about setting the conditions for excellence in all areas than providing the expertise yourself.

If failure to set clear parameters for innovation, and embed it in the heart of a team or organisation, is frequently a problem, so is the tendency to confuse means and ends. All too often people will hit on a new tool to achieve something and assume that that in itself is the innovation that will make the difference. In fact it is usually merely the means by which something new might be achieved.

Obama's 2008 approach to polling shows both the risk and the answer here. Back in 1997, when Philip Gould did his first brilliant polling analyses for Labour, the data available was relatively restricted. Today, by contrast, there is virtually no limit to what we can find out about the attitudes and behaviour of the public. It would therefore have been very easy for Obama in 2008 to assume that simply because his team had the technology to gather an astonishing wealth of data about the electorate, that was sufficient. As Plouffe made clear to him, though, it was merely the beginning. The fundamental point about social media is not the technology behind it or its data-gathering ability, but the fact that it connects friends and like-minded people via such platforms as Twitter and Facebook. My analysis of the genius of Facebook is that it lies in the concept of the 'friend'. People today trust politicians, professionals and the media far less than they used to, and rely more and more on the views of their families and peers, 'friends'. So if the Obama team could track and identify its supporters, it could turn them into activists who would then become ambassadors for the campaign. The team went to work on finding the people who 'liked' him, and then got them to get their friends to 'like' him too. This, not merely the fund-raising, is what made their social media strategy so bold and so effective. Simultaneously, Joe Rospars, founder of Blue State Digital, key architect of the Obama digital strategy, led the way in using the Internet to profile and segment voters so that campaigning tasks and funds could be allocated in the most efficient way possible.

'As the campaign progressed,' Plouffe recalls, 'we had their addresses, we knew if they were fund-raising or donating themselves, we knew the policy issues they were passionate about, we knew their level of activity and other interactions. We knew if they had attended or hosted an event.' In this way, the campaign could reach out to voters personally, and the digital operation allowed them to do this in a manageable way. 'If someone is passionate about education, you make sure they see everything Barack Obama is saying on that. If McCain or Romney screws up on education, you make sure they know what we're saying about that. If you know they're not so interested in foreign policy, don't clutter their in-box with everything.' This segmented approach applied to small donation fund-raising too; as Rospars explains: 'If you made three donations in the past we would derive a suggested amount to ask you for based on a formula of your second highest contribution minus an ageing factor, we had a whole lot of data for that. It's getting easier to automate that kind of thing.'

So the innovation was not their use of the Internet and social media per se; it was recognising the value it could add to the campaign and how to exploit it, by marrying all the elements of political campaigning in a systematic but segmented way. Not only did it give them the opportunity to run targeted campaigns across states but it gave them the opportunity to profile and target voters in very specific ways.

Rospars tells me that in each battleground state, there were four groups of people they were particularly interested in:

(a) people very likely to vote, but undecided who for
(b) people very likely for Obama, but not necessarily likely to vote
(c) people very likely for Obama, but not registered to vote
(d) people very strongly for Obama, but who wouldn't necessarily volunteer or donate.

Most campaigns tend to be myopically focused on group (a), he says, the undecided who are likely to vote. 'But in some states, groups (b) and (c) might compose a much bigger percentage and therefore that would influence our efforts in that state.' Likewise, I can imagine that group (d) might easily be overlooked. But the Obama team had an ultra-sophisticated operation to target them, and turn their political support into financial support too.

One particularly successful innovation was an intimate dinner for four people with Obama. To have a chance of being one of the four, you had to chip in a few dollars. Hundreds of thousands did so, and the campaign raised around $10 million each time. It also meant the Obama team had all their details and could go back to make more asks. They used celebrities like George Clooney and Sarah Jessica Parker to host dinners, and to make financial appeals by email, and they even polled on which of their top celebrities would be more likely to get a positive response from a certain demographic. Rospars said the difference between 'our best-performing message and our worst-performing message' could be as high as tenfold on any given day. But the approach overall raised tens of millions over the eighteen-month campaign.

The other crucial point to make about the Obama digital campaign was that it was embedded in his overall strategy and message. By background a community organiser, Obama wanted a message that said at heart he still was, and he was reaching out to every individual. 'These digital relationships gave people power and ownership of the campaign and made individuals feel their preferences and opinions were valued,' Plouffe says. 'When we were taking on Hillary, she had a lot of the big party people and a lot of the big donors, so the only way for us to do it was to build a grass-roots network and he was on board with this because it fitted with his message and his background as a community organiser.' There is little doubt that the Clinton campaign, as she runs for president again, will have learned from Obama's superiority in this field.

It's important to emphasise the achievements of Plouffe and

his colleagues, because in today's digital world people all too often assume that by virtue of having an online presence they are being innovative and cutting-edge. After all, the statistics are pretty impressive. YouTube has more video content uploaded each month than the three main US networks broadcast in fifty years, reaching more US adults aged eighteen to thirty-four than any cable network. LinkedIn, with over 200 million users, had two people joining every second between 2012 and 2013. Pinterest grew from 200,000 users in early 2012 to over two million in 2013. Instagram had 150 million global users in late 2013, representing an increase of 15 per cent in just two months. Ninety-three per cent of marketers use social media for business. It took the telephone seventy-five years to reach 50 million users, the radio thirty-eight years, TV thirteen years. It took the Web four years. It took the Angry Birds space app thirty-five days. One way and another, digital media is a very powerful tool, but only if used properly. You need to know what you want to do with it and how to wield it. Plouffe and Rospars did, and helped Obama considerably

Above all, though, everything comes back, as ever, to strategy. If you don't have that in place at the outset, attempts to innovate will be muddled and potentially self-defeating. Obama's innovative approach to electioneering worked because the changes were embedded in a distinct world view. All those clever step changes made in British cycling worked because people understood how each one interlocked and what the overall aim was. Strategy is a team game. Innovation is a team game.

Shona Brown and Kathleen Eisenhardt in 'The Art of Continuous Change' suggest that innovative organisations operate at the edge of chaos, and continually balance present and future. Managing the process and the individuals is therefore a difficult task. Innovators need to be clear about what they're doing and how they plan to achieve it while being in a state of flux. They need to be organised and disorganised at the same time. They need to manage the setbacks and processes and goals and objectives. Innovation becomes a process of management.

MARRYING INNOVATION TO TEAMS

As I've pointed out, pursuing innovation within an organisation or a team almost invariably causes tensions. The natural tendency of many people is to prefer the safety of the status quo. What's more, if they're very experienced – and so valued members of the team – they may actually be sceptical of alternative world views. Expertise can be a two-edged sword in this way. Thirty years' experience of doing things the wrong way isn't much good to anyone. Every organisation needs experience, but it can sometimes blinker people, persuading them that they have mastered their area so completely that their current perception is the only one worth considering. Such people may not be able to make that mental jump that leads to a breakthrough. History is littered with great ideas that were pooh-poohed by the 'experts'. Twitter looks so obvious now, but when the germ of the idea was first presented to an Odeo workshop by two of its co-founders, Biz Stone and Jack Dorsey, it bombed; or, as Stone put it: 'On the whole, the project wasn't very well received.' People thought it was too simple, which was kind of the point.

'With all our faults and vulnerabilities,' Stone relates in his book, *Things a Little Bird Told Me*, 'our small team was going to create something the world didn't know it needed until it arrived.' Therein lies a wonderfully innovative mindset. No wonder he subtitled the book 'Confessions of the Creative Mind'.

'Opportunity is manufactured,' he says. In other words, the entrepreneurial spirit – be that a business entrepreneur or a social entrepreneur, or anyone who wants to make change happen – comes from the insight that to make change, you have to decide to make change. To innovate, you have to think anew, ask new questions, get new answers. It means shifting from the idea that opportunity is something that may or not come your way to the view that opportunity is something you can bring about yourself.

Jim O'Neill told me that as head of asset management at Goldman Sachs, where they were big on research and asking the right questions, he could have his pick of some of the brightest and most educated minds in the world. However, 'I preferred to recruit from those who hadn't come through the typical finance path and worked at other big banks because it became very easy to become institutionalised by these organisations.'

> 'Opportunity is manufactured.'
>
> **BIZ STONE**

This is precisely why great teams, with strong leadership in place, often look outside themselves for new ideas – and have the confidence to do so. In the sports arena – to take just a few examples – Woodward was happy to hire Humphrey Walters with his sailing background, Brailsford brought in Rampton psychiatrist Dr Steve Peters and swimming coach Tim Kerrison to help British Cycling and Team Sky, and baseball legend Billy Beane hired Harvard economics graduate Paul DePodesta as assistant general manager, all demonstrating that you don't have to be immersed in a particular field to make a contribution. Indeed, the chances are that you'll probably make more of a contribution in an area where your expertise is less familiar because you'll view everything with fresh eyes and take nothing for granted.

Kerrison, who joined Team Sky in 2009 ahead of the official launch, spent his first year out on the road, often asking very basic questions – like 'why do you do that?' – of riders, coaches, *soigneurs*, mechanics, sports scientists, dieticians, anyone who might have a role in improving or weakening the performance of the athlete and the team. 'What I liked about getting someone from outside,' says Brailsford, 'was that he had real expertise in physiology and elite athletes, and he was questioning all the deep-rooted assumptions that had built up within the sport and within the team. Some of those assumptions were right. But some were just habit, and actually, seen with an outside eye, totally illogical. Whenever we have a problem we try to approach it from an angle that no one has ever approached it from before.'

Brailsford saw in other professional cycling teams how easy it was for institutionalisation to take hold. 'Most of the other teams just got stuck in a certain way of doing things – ex-rider gets put in a managerial, coaching or supporting position and he's been exposed to a particular way the sport has worked, namely how it worked for him. His experience would be solely based on his own unique experience and he might see other potential experiences through the same lens. Steve Peters gave us a totally new lens on the athletes' minds, and Tim gave us a new lens on the systems we were using. Their analysis was terrifically insightful and refreshing.'

Brailsford goes so far as to say he doesn't understand why people wouldn't relish taking on board new ideas and trying to apply them to their own competitive setting. 'New ideas are invigorating – every year a few of us leaders in sport get together, cycling, rugby, NFL, NBA, Formula One and lots more, and I take down loads and loads of notes. You can always learn and if you have the mindset to incorporate that information into your own setting then you have a major advantage.' Indeed, the first time I met Billy Beane was at just such a conference where he and Arsène Wenger were discussing the role of data in the transfer market, and how to evaluate more human elements alongside it, like motivation, background and so forth.

Sebastian Coe's experience with his father – and coach – Peter Coe was a similar case of trusting someone without fixed preconceptions. Coe Senior, an engineer, though with self-taught expertise in physiology, had no previous experience as a coach or an athlete, but Coe Junior reckons that gave him an edge. 'My father had one great advantage over most other coaches – who, practically without exception, were all former runners – in that he brooked no specious or imagined thresholds simply because it was commonly held belief, or had been personally experienced. And while he discounted nothing out of hand, set-in-stone dogma and old wives' tales got very short shrift. If it made no scientific sense, it was consigned to the bin.'

One of the most inspiring examples I have come across of this kind of cross-fertilisation is at Passmores school in Harlow, which came to national attention on the Channel 4 programme *Educating Essex*. Here the head teacher Vic Goddard explicitly cites Brailsford's marginal gains on the school website as its guiding approach and is an advocate of the mantra of establishing a firm framework before innovating (in Brailsford's words 'It is no good innovating around the edges if the heart of the operation is failing'). Goddard first gave the staff structure ('a seven-part lesson that they had to work by'), then set them a stretching exam results target ('If our expectations of the kids are low then the kids' expectations of themselves will be low'), and then went about bringing doubters round. He talks of 'radiators and drains – radiators give out energy, drains suck it in'. But while fully prepared to get rid of people who were intransigent, he also went out of his way to keep those he regarded as talented but sceptical on board. In the case of one particular teacher, this meant talking to him before anyone else about a planned change ('I need a bit of advice. I need a sounding board,' he said to him), winning his approval and then using it to bring in others.

One of the marginal gains he is proudest of is a toilet block at the centre of the school, which emerged from asking the children what they least liked about the school, and being shocked that so many mentioned the toilets. He then involved them in the design of the new block, which has led to a huge decline in incidents of bullying and fighting.

Of course, not all sectors are so open to outside influence or ideas. Business people who have been invited to involve themselves in the political sphere, for example, often find the experience deeply frustrating and emerge from it defeated (though there are certainly exceptions: former Sainsbury's chairman David Sainsbury was a brilliant science minister who successfully brought his experience of innovation in a world he knew well, and applied it to a world where he had to learn fast). And businesses themselves can be snooty and suspicious about inviting outside help. But there are signs of minds prepared to be a little more open. Justin King sought to learn from the world of sport, and, like Metro Bank, turned to Humphrey Walters. He also told me that 'At Sainsbury's we had a specific recruitment programme targeted at the armed forces with a fast-track programme to store management to tap expertise from elsewhere.'

CREATING AN INNOVATIVE CULTURE

As I've said, there are powerful counter-forces to innovation in many teams: individuals who fear or are suspicious of change; others whose very expertise in a particular sector makes them sceptical of a proposed innovation. Such people can't be ignored. American entrepreneur Eric Baker, the tough right-winger who developed viagogo, the world's largest ticket marketplace, nicely identifies two stages in the development of a group. During the first phase, when the group is starting out, the analogy is with sport. 'The great thing about sport is that it is cut and dried,' he tells me. 'You are out there for a couple of hours and there is a winner or a loser or a draw. Simple. When you are innovating, you need the mindset that says "I am going to win", and you treat it like a ball game. However, as the team becomes more established, the analogy moves from sport to politics. 'You have to persuade people to your position and you have to do it on an ongoing basis. The second you win an election, you have to start thinking about the next one. And that means you need to be able to communicate. Make it simple. "Yes we can." "Change, change, change." And you ask the people what the change is and they don't know but "hey, I like the sound of it because that guy can sure as hell communicate".'

For his part, Brailsford sees the embracing of new ideas as having a huge impact on the types of management and leadership teams it is possible to create. 'You've got to get people to buy in to what you're trying to do and explain to them how you expect to do it first and foremost. What I like are the guys you ask to go away and think about something – give them some simple tools and methodologies – and then they come back with ideas. They are proactive and don't have to be led in instigating change.'

The real challenge comes in the management of innovation, developing the culture and conditions that encourage continuous improvement around a set objective. 'For us in rugby,' Matt Parker says, 'it's pointless all the coaches sitting around talking about changing processes on the pitch if we're not going to involve the players. When they are involved, they better understand why things are changing and are therefore more likely to comply with change. If you give competitive athletes ownership of strategy in the right environment, you will generally get positive results. This is down to the culture and the coaches being brave enough to give them responsibility.' Similarly, Clive Woodward gained a real advantage in getting the players to understand the reasoning behind what they were doing and feels it's something underdeveloped in other sports. 'To be honest, in football I was shocked at times at how the players were just expected to sit there and take instructions, without really being involved in the thinking.'

Brailsford talks with real enthusiasm about an idea he is currently putting in place. 'I realised how important it was for me to be on the ground and understand what the *soigneurs*, mechanics and riders are feeling as they travel around racing and on the bus from day to day. We are putting in an ideas box at the back of the team bus and any employee can put a suggestion in for how we can improve on any area, however small or large.' And no idea should be ignored, no matter how ridiculous it seems, as long as there are efficient filtering processes in place to make sure time isn't wasted on ideas going nowhere. 'With innovation you need to be going outside your own sphere and you have to remember that ideas have got value, they haven't got rank.' He qualifies this with a crucial point. 'If you want people to give you ideas then you have to genuinely show that you take them seriously even if you say no. Now if these ideas go two weeks without response then we are disrespecting those people and we are destroying the culture. In an innovative culture, you just don't know where the next idea is coming from.'

In the words of Deborah Dougherty, management professor at Rutgers Business School at the State University of New Jersey: 'Organising for innovation has to be the default option . . . as opposed to bureaucracy.' In order to innovate you have to choose to innovate, and you need an organisational structure that places innovation at its core – not as some separate task that can be performed by others. 'In an innovative set-up, everyone should be encouraged to innovate,' says Arianna Huffington. 'I want ideas to come from anywhere, whether it is me or the intern.' HuffPo's 'editor at large' programme, their mentoring scheme and coding education for staff have all come from ideas first mooted by people fairly well down the staff pecking order.

INNOVATION WITHOUT END

'One of our slogans is that "we zig when the world zags",' says Charles Dunstone. 'We are always looking to go against things that others are doing.' Given that the world is in a constant state of flux, there is rarely, if ever, a point at which anyone can say 'job done'.

The problem, of course, is that you rarely 'own' any innovation for long. All too soon your competitors imitate or surpass, and that brief advantage you enjoyed disappears. As José Mourinho puts it, in the context of sport, 'There is no copyright to new ideas.' Spotting trends and keeping yourself ahead of the pace of change is a precondition for success. 'There is so much on TV, so much technology, everyone knows everything about everybody,' he tells me. 'Everyone has access to what a small number of people produce in terms of new ideas. If you have the idea to play with a left-footed player on the right and a right-footed player on the left, it does not have copyright. Zonal defence at corners, no copyright. Someone can produce something, a new idea, which then becomes fundamental and there is no copyright. So you must innovate all the time. You must always be thinking of where things are changing.'

What this means, of course, is that constant progression, whether of the radical or marginal gains variety, is essential. And simply copying someone else is not enough because while it might briefly level the field, it won't take you ahead. It's a permanent battle in every walk of life.

> 'We zig when the world zags.'
> **CHARLES DUNSTONE**

The last FIFA World Cup was a classic example of the dangers of complacency and tiredness stifling innovation. Spain had dominated world football for over six years. Many countries tried to copy the Spanish model: focusing on possession and rotating of possession as a feature of attack and defence. But by 2014 those teams that followed the Spanish approach – including, of course, Spain itself – came unstuck. Germany, by contrast, had moved on, adopting more open, high-energy, counter-attacking football. No doubt the naive will now try to copy the German model. But successful countries will move on, keep adapting, keep innovating, and make sure the strategies of the national team and the national league remain aligned.

There are poor and fruitless imitations in politics too. I think one of David Cameron's weaknesses has been to portray himself as 'heir to Blair', without understanding New Labour was not primarily about communications – effective though hopefully the communications were – but about policy and strategy and a genuine programme of change. Business has countless examples of spectacular imitative failure. Richard Branson mentioned his problems taking on Coca-Cola. But what about when Coca-Cola took on Coca-Cola, putting 'new Coke' out there as a rebrand of the world's most popular and famous soft drink? In the backlash that followed, almost half a million complaints were logged.

By contrast a company such as Inditex has achieved its extraordinary success by very virtue of the fact that it hasn't imitated its competitors. It may not be a familiar name to many – it doesn't believe in advertising – but it is the world's largest fashion retailer, making 18,000 fashion design changes a year for its Zara chain, another 12,000 for its seven other brands, and has made its founder, the reclusive Amancio Ortega, the third richest man on the planet, according to Forbes, with $64 billion to his name.

'Our business model is the opposite of the traditional model,' Pablo Isla, the group's chairman and chief executive, told the *Financial Times*. 'Instead of designing a collection long before the season, and then working out whether clients like it or not, we try to understand what our customers like, and then we design it and produce it.' For more than a decade, the group opened at least one new store somewhere in the world every day. Now bigger than Gap, they are in eighty-eight countries, with 6,400 stores, selling 900 million items a year, and plenty more online. A simple innovation: ask the customer what they want, then design, rather than the other way round, and do it with speed.

As a mindset, innovation is the attitude that never assumes everything is going to stay the same forever but, instead, that everything is likely to change, and the winners are the ones who will best read and respond to the rhythms of change, so that instead of being driven by change, they lead it. So you have to lay the foundations for innovation, you have to think afresh, take risks, be prepared to fail, be able to deal with pressure and setbacks, be able to manage sometimes complex processes of innovation. Or, as Arianna Huffington puts it: 'Innovation is never seeing yourself as a finished product. It is understanding that you are always work in progress. It is about disrupting your own operations and looking at how they can improve. You must be your own disrupter.'

WHAT DOES GOOGLE DO? WHAT WILL GOOGLE DO?

When Microsoft's Satya Nadella took over as CEO from Steve Ballmer, nobody could miss his focus on innovation as the central message and purpose. 'The first thing I want to do and focus on is ruthlessly to remove any obstacles [to] allow us to innovate, every individual in our organisation to innovate. And then focus all that innovation on things that Microsoft can uniquely do.' And as if people didn't get the message about the I-word, he added: 'Our industry does not respect tradition – it only respects innovation.'

But how, other than through words, does a company ensure innovation is in the DNA of the brand? I ask D-J Collins, a former colleague in government who went on to work for Google and now runs his own firm with Prince Charles's former adviser Paddy Harverson, the principles that lie behind Google innovation. His response is that it is less the funky office space, the hang-out zones, the free food and drink everywhere, the time allocated to 'thinking' than these very clear and hard concepts: 'First, expectations culture:

there is a very, very high expectation about what problems techs can solve. The bar is set high. Larry Page leads from the front on that. Nobody gets away with crap work. Second, hiring: they only hire the absolute best engineers. It has more computer science PhDs than any other tech firm. Third, everyone is involved: there's no separate "innovation" team, everyone is expected to lead on innovation. Seriously. Fourth, investment: the company invests massive amounts into R&D and always has. Fifth, the focus on long-term: the company invests for the long-term and doesn't worry too much about short-term margins.' Collins's final point about Google is what he calls 'restlessness', adding: 'The feeling is that you should never ever be satisfied, that there is always another idea or product out there that can improve things.'

> 'Innovation is never seeing yourself as a finished product.'
> **ARIANNA HUFFINGTON**

He draws my attention to the founders' IPO letter, written by Larry Page and Sergey Brin to would-be investors, modelled in some ways on Warren Buffett's annual letter to Berkshire Hathaway shareholders, when Google moved to public ownership in 2004. 'Google is not a conventional company. We do not intend to become one,' it begins. Innovation is mentioned repeatedly. 'We have implemented a corporate structure that is designed to protect Google's ability to innovate and retain its most distinctive characteristics.' In addition to the focus on the long-term, even warning investors to expect a fall in share price, the importance of a clear leadership structure, able to make big decisions quickly, is emphasised.

Virtually all the business people I have spoken to will talk about Google when asked to nominate a great innovator, highlighting the encouragement – freedom they would call it – to Google's employees to have thinking time. Collins, though, also nominates Bill Gates as a hugely successful and innovative businessman, who has perhaps not received the recognition he deserves for boldness.

'His ambition was staggering. It's not like building an app, he set out to put a PC in every office and every home. Amazing. The great technology innovators don't set out to build products, they set out to see very difficult problems. So whether Gates with universal PCs, or Jobs wanting to make it easier to enjoy music, it's as if they look at the world and think it's wired in the wrong way, and that they can rewire it. That's what I found so inspiring about working for Google.'

But how long can innovators keep innovating? Inevitably in the case of companies such as Google, Facebook and Amazon, the jury is out – it's simply too soon to know whether they can sustain the vigour of their early years. Charles Dunstone points out the possible pitfalls: all three companies are now very large – with the potential, therefore, to be less agile – and all three were set up by powerful individuals without whom continuing future success cannot absolutely be guaranteed. He argues, for example, that Apple is not the dynamic force it was in Steve Jobs' time: 'Apple has not produced anything as revolutionary as when he was there.' Justin King similarly argues that continuous innovation cannot be about just one or two powerful individuals.

Certainly, there are some danger signs. Dunstone's suggestion that as start-ups expand they become less innovative is arguably borne out by Google's decision to buy YouTube and others, and Facebook's purchase of Instagram and WhatsApp. 'Other terrible examples,' says Dunstone, 'would be News Corp buying MySpace and AOL buying Bebo.' It's interesting to note in this context that Richard Branson has a habit of splitting his companies and keeping them in silos to try to avoid Virgin becoming too corporate.

Another trap once great innovators sometimes fall into is that of becoming imitators. True, as Justin King argues, there can be advantages to being a 'second mover'. 'People can learn from the mistakes of others, make their version more practical, or customer-facing. Think of BSB versus Sky in the early days. Microsoft versus IBM. Kodak versus digital. Even Apple versus Samsung is an interesting fight.' But, as Charles Dunstone would counter, 'Bing was a

very late poor Google, Zune was another late, worse, iPod.' It's
never safe relying on what others are doing to point the way.

And contemporary politics clearly shows the risks of a non-
innovative culture. The belief that the last win is less important than
the next one, the insight that if you stay the same, others are bound
to improve, is hard to discern in too many of today's politicians.
Just as the hedge-fund guys know they have a bad image, but can't
be bothered to do anything about it, so a lot of politicians know
they have a bad image too, but seem incapable or afraid to make
the scale of change needed to give themselves the best chance of
improving it. They absorb rather than challenge the negativity
surrounding them. In constantly seeming only to attack each other,
they tend to give justification to attacks upon them all as a breed.
The systems appear archaic, because they are, but nobody seems
to know how to modernise them without offending their own tribe
or adding to the sense of disengagement from the public. What's
more, when change is made it's all too often carried out with no
reference to an overarching strategy. It's change for change's sake.
In education, for example, headmaster Vic Goddard argues: 'The
government doesn't really know what it wants for students and a
lot of schools take that lead and are unable to develop their own
vision. Without a vision you can't expect to implement change
successfully because for those implementing the change there will
be confusion about how and why.' It is not a happy scene.
Fortunately, in other walks of life, people have a more creative and
disciplined attitude to change, closer to Google than to government.

13

DATA

'Scientific knowledge is based on data – the advice doesn't have to be taken but it shouldn't be attacked just because it is data or science. People see science and scientists as arrogant but knowledge is above everything else.'

BRIAN COX

WHEN FACTS AREN'T FACTS

The question the expert faced was a stark one: were the documents genuine or were they forgeries? There was plenty there on which to base a judgement: sixty volumes of handwritten material, plus a wealth of accompanying letters, memos, notes and reports. Various avenues of inquiry were therefore open to him. He could scrutinise the handwriting and decide whether it looked the same as the real thing. He could check the content to see whether it seemed accurate and plausible measured against what was already known about the author. He could assess whether the archive seemed coherent or whether there was anything in it that seemed out of place. He could ask questions about how the documents had been found and assess whether what he was being told rang true.

In the end he did all these things, studying the material closely for an hour and weighing up the pros and cons, before coming to his conclusion. Then he gave his answer. The material, he declared, was indeed genuine – and therefore of enormous historical importance.

Unfortunately, he was completely wrong. The documents in question were not an invaluable, previously unsuspected historical archive, but the forged Hitler diaries. Some of them had been written just a few months before the historian Lord Dacre made his inspection.

Gathering information is a relatively straightforward task, particularly today when, thanks to the Internet, such vast quantities of it are being generated and stored. But, as Lord Dacre found to his cost, information is not the same thing as knowledge. And while amassing data is essential to success, knowing how to handle it and which traps to avoid is just as important.

The mistakes Lord Dacre made are telling. Firstly, because those who had asked him to authenticate the diaries had paid a lot of money for them, they put him under pressure to come up with a clear-cut opinion, quickly. He came to his conclusion within an hour, when surely he should have spent days, weeks, sifting the evidence. Secondly, the sheer quantity of documents threw him off balance. He made the dangerous assumption that no forger would risk creating so much material. And because there was so much that appeared to be the real deal, when he did come across something that didn't quite fit, he ignored it in favour of evidence that confirmed his gut feeling. Much later, when the diaries were conclusively shown to have been faked, he realised that one document he had seen – a letter *from* Hitler – would, if genuine, probably not have been among 'Hitler's' papers at all but among those of the person to whom he had sent it. At the time, while he noted the anomaly, alarm bells did not ring loudly enough.

Lord Dacre's error of judgement is a good example of confirmation bias: to an extent he saw what he wanted to see, in an environment where many others wanted to see the same thing too. Of course, confirmation bias can also operate to affirm a minority opinion. Scientist and broadcaster Professor Brian Cox points to the controversy in the UK over the safety of the MMR vaccine as an instance of confirmation bias, when scientist Andrew Wakefield – and sections of the media – in arguing that there was a link between the vaccine and the incidence of autism, took up a stance contrary to overwhelming expert opinion. He also says that current debates over climate change are littered with instances of confirmation bias, where climate change deniers look only for data that appears to support their preordained view. It's an all too common occurrence among humans. 'You have to be absolutely brutal to train your mind not to be swayed by a bias that fits your own view. You have to be completely loyal to the principles of statistics and suppress your desire to find things that aren't really there.' He adds that the risk of misinterpretation can actually increase as more data becomes available. 'The more data you've got, the more there is to choose from to fit your own perception and this is something you need to guard against. In particle physics we spend all of our time guarding against that.'

Data, then, it goes almost without saying, needs to be handled with care. Individual facts may be objective, but the very act of putting them together requires human intervention and therefore involves a greater or lesser degree of subjectivity. That in turn leaves the door open for misunderstandings and mistakes. And the sheer volume of available data, and the fusion of news and comment in both mainstream and even more so social media, means that the supposedly objective world of facts can get distorted very quickly. Take, for example, the findings of a survey conducted in 2013 by Ipsos MORI and King's College London in which British citizens were asked basic questions about their own country. Time and again, the answers they came up with were hopelessly wide of the mark. Asked how many teenage girls get pregnant before they are sixteen, survey respondents estimated that figure was nearly 1 in 6; in fact it is closer to 1 in 200. They thought that a quarter of the population is Muslim when in fact it is 5 per cent. A third thought that the government spends more on Jobseeker's Allowance than on pensions, when pensions actually take up fifteen times as much budget. When we interpret evidence, we do so on the basis of certain fundamental assumptions. But what if our assumptions are wrong – and we have persuaded others to accept them too?

'The thing about conventional wisdoms is that they are almost always wrong,' says Obama strategist David Axelrod. That may be a slight overstatement, done for rhetorical effect, but, as Axelrod himself has found, it is often the case that even when the facts overwhelmingly point in one direction, people will take refuge in preconceptions. Thus, for instance, during the 2008 Obama campaign, Hillary Clinton's people were convinced that their attacks on her rival – and, in particular, their criticisms of his inexperience, and some of his tactics – were valid and must therefore be hitting home. They, and the media, were also highly critical of the thrust of Obama's campaign, which focused on a handful of key states. The extraordinary quality of the data that Obama's team was gathering, though, showed that the criticisms were misplaced, and gave them the courage to stick to their guns even when, as campaign manager David Plouffe recalls, 'Hillary [Clinton] was way ahead in the polls and for months the conventional wisdom was that we had blown it.' As I've mentioned before, the 2008 campaign hit new heights in terms of the personal connections that a campaign was able to make with individual voters, and the feedback the Obama camp measured was largely positive. Campaign leaders relied on data and were prepared to make judgements based on the quality of that data.

> 'The thing about conventional wisdoms is that they are almost always wrong.'
> **DAVID AXELROD**

Joe Rospars of Blue State Digital says: 'Through the interaction with individuals on the campaign website we knew so much about them. A digital ad they clicked on, an offline event they RSVP'd to, a donation they made after a particular moment in the campaign. This all gives us a profile of the individual and makes campaigning less generic.' This meant that when they engaged with members of the community through phone or email or in person, there was a real personal element to the campaigning, and they could trust the data more. Plouffe says: 'The data helped us focus resources. Of course the candidates are hoping for support every-where, but ten states decide the outcome, so you put more resources and energy in those. Then you really try to drill down, you have your general messages at the top, but you want to know which part of your campaigning an individual voter connects with because that then helps you plan further interaction.' The Clinton campaign, by contrast, relied more on gut instinct, their own attacks and previous track records – and got it wrong.

INTUITION AND OBJECTIVITY

The people who make the best use of information tend to have two distinct skills. On the one hand, because they are steeped in what they do, they have a strong and immediate sense of which data is likely to be relevant and which will probably turn out to be white noise. Intuition, in short. On the other hand, because they are also able to be dispassionate, they don't allow gut instinct and emotion to get in the way if what they're looking at doesn't fit with what they were expecting to see.

'Intuition' is a word that you'll often find used by and about highly successful people, but it's a word that needs to be approached with a degree of caution. There may well be intuitive geniuses around, and great moments of intuition, but in most cases 'intuition' is no more and no less than the result of such deep knowledge and study that thought processes are almost instant and so seemingly miraculous. So when Garry Kasparov says to me, 'A chess player who didn't rely on intuition at all would be paralysed and decisions would either take too long or you'd be unable to act and actually make a decision at all,' I'm very conscious that his intuition has come from years of practice; indeed, Kasparov immediately goes on to talk about the importance of constant analysis. 'Looking back at your decisions to analyse their correctness and their source is very important. Why did you do what you did? Did it reflect instinct, calculation, emotion? People tend to be either overcritical or over-flattering when they do this sort of thing. You have to move beyond an emotional response of regret or boastfulness and into a useful analysis you can work with.'

José Mourinho ticks in a similar way. A highly intuitive manager, he also makes full use of all the information to hand. Take a tactical change – he might call it strategic – he made in the second leg of the Champions League quarter-final in 2013 when Chelsea overcame a two-goal deficit to beat Paris Saint-Germain late in the game. He adopted a substitution strategy, partly 'intuitive' but also based on prior opposition analysis, which showed that in the French League PSG were very rarely subject to direct attacking play. 'I brought off a fullback and a midfielder for two strikers and we went more direct and we won the game. It was instinct but it was based on knowledge.' This is his way of answering the question of whether he is a data or intuition person. He is saying that he is both, that he needs to rely on his instinct, but often this is subconsciously influenced by data he has learned and understood. It is hard-earned intuition.

Sam Trickett, considered one of the best all-round poker players in the world, with tournament winnings alone well over $20 million, is another example of a great practitioner who has acquired his apparently extraordinary speed of thought through practice. He left school at sixteen, with no significant mathematical or statistical education, yet he has a reputation for – and results that demonstrate – application of strict logic under pressure; and in speaking to other respected professionals from that world it is clear he has an ability to go against the obvious 'standard' play and balance quantitative and qualitative information because of his deep understanding of game theory.

A turning point for Trickett came early on in his poker career when, despite really good results, he overreached his desire to be the best and compete at levels both his bank balance and ability were not ready for. He spent time teaching poker to ensure at least some guaranteed income, but found the experience had a much greater benefit. 'It was definitely the catalyst for me in going from good to very good,' he says. 'I used to think about poker very one-dimensionally and then when I was teaching I'd have to really think through every stage of the thought process because I'd have to communicate the information. I couldn't just say this is right because it is. Going through the process of asking exactly why I was doing what I was doing was huge for me. It made me realise that I actually thought I knew what I was doing but when I had to explain the logic and evidence behind it I didn't. Then I taught myself to make sure I did.'

He – like other good strategists – is also possessed of that other key data-crunching skill: objectivity. He approaches every situation afresh, judging it entirely on its own merits. This means, for example, he doesn't fall into the classic trap of assuming that because he has encountered a similar situation before, what he did then will work this time. 'Most players are making too many decisions based on a robotic or almost fixed model,' he argues, 'but the weakness is that it presumes that the other players are playing like robots.' He is very aware that even a game as structured as poker offers endless variety. 'No hand is the same, but people try and base a decision on an easier one they've seen before.' It's an entirely understandable human tendency, he says, but 'it's a flawed way to make the decision'. Trickett, in other words, possesses that deep knowledge that makes it look as though he is playing intuitively, but he never allows complacency to creep in. 'You really have to understand the fundamentals and that is the definition of a winning mindset to me. I always know exactly why I am making the decision I am, I'm not just thinking to myself this feels right so I'm going to go with it. There is always a sense of logic behind it.'

ASKING THE RIGHT QUESTIONS

According to Daniel Kahneman, the Israeli-American psychologist and Nobel Prize winner in economic sciences, who has spent a lifetime studying the psychology of decision-making, human beings have a tendency to ask a question that they think they may have the immediate answer to rather than risk the more difficult one that might ultimately prove to be more revealing. In his book *Thinking,*

Fast and Slow, he shows how our problem-solving instincts prefer System 1 thinking – instinct based on assumption – to System 2 thinking – a slower, more thoughtful and analytical approach. A football manager might, for example, think: 'We played this team last year; the left back was poor, so we'll target him.' In so doing, however, he has replaced the tricky question 'How are we going to win this year?' with the much easier one 'How did we win last year?' There are therefore twin dangers with this initial question. If you ask too easy – too comfortable – a question, the answer probably won't tell you much. And if you don't ask a clear question, muddle is almost bound to follow.

Given how much data there is on just about every conceivable topic – and how relatively easy it is to gather it – where do you actually start? According to virtually every leading figure I've spoken to, you start by asking the right questions.

Obvious, you might think, but it's extraordinary how often people set off with a vague idea of 'finding out' about something, with no clear idea of precisely what it is that they want to know.

> 'We asked different questions and got interesting answers.'
> **BILLY BEANE**

My experience has been that it's those in elite sport who are most forensic about posing the key initial question. In part, one could argue, it's because the goals they're seeking to achieve are more clear-cut than they are in, say, the political sphere. But even if that's the case, the fact remains that, time after time, their initial self-discipline, and their insistence on an answer that will help them win, can plainly be seen to pay off further down the line – an object lesson, perhaps, for others.

Look at the Team Sky cycling team and the Tour de France. When they started out as Sky Pro Cycling in 2009, all their research stemmed from the initial question they asked themselves. Not the vague 'How do we get better?' Or the unspecific 'What improvements have there recently been in cycling we could learn from?' But, according to Dave Brailsford, the very targeted question, 'What

does it take to have a British winner of the Tour de France?' Because
no British team had ever won it, it was a widely held view that no
British team ever would. But by setting the clear question, the team
made sure that the mass of data they were about to accumulate had
a clear purpose and a defined potential benefit. The question sounds
obvious, but it is the questions you then ask of the data available
to you that will decide if your objective can be met.

'We know that the winner of the Tour has to climb as well as
the best climbers in the race and time trial better or vice versa,' says
Brailsford. 'So the team set to work on looking at data that would
tell them what physiology was required, what demands the course
made, what characteristics top riders and previous winners displayed,
and so on. The purpose was to map a power curve – power on the
y axis, time on the x axis – most likely to match the Tour winner
for that year, and see which of their own riders got closest to it.
'For every rider and every ride,' Brailsford recalls, 'we would monitor
the maximum average power they could sustain for one second, five
seconds, one minute, three minutes, five minutes, fifteen minutes,
thirty minutes, one hour, three hours, five hours, etc.' It became
clear that Bradley Wiggins was the closest, and all training interventions were then geared around the gaps in that modelling. 'We looked
at Bradley and we knew if he bought into this, and trained to fill
the gaps, he could get there. He was the best time trialist, very good
over thirty minutes to an hour, but we might need to make training
interventions around his five- to ten-minute power output so he
could cope with attacks and changing intensities in the mountains
and his three-hour average power output if he was going to be able
to handle the really long mountain stages with lots of climbing and
little rest.'

All this carefully organised data then fed into the provision of
a really clear coaching structure, giving them the analysis they needed
to work out who *could* win, namely Wiggins, and a training plan
geared to ensure that he *might*. A plan developed over time was
executed day in, day out during the race, with a large team playing
its role to perfection. Winning it once, in 2012 with Wiggins, was a

huge achievement. Winning it the following year too, with Chris Froome taking over as lead rider, was remarkable, but in its own way unsurprising, given that the fundamental process had by now been proved to work. They had focused on the essentials and cut out anything that was just 'noise'. They mastered the data; they didn't let it master them.

Oakland A's manager Billy Beane achieved his extraordinary level of professional success by displaying a similar approach to data. Having asked himself the broad question, 'What is required to win baseball matches?' he followed up with a tighter second question, relevant for a club that was not exactly rolling in money, 'How do I get better value for money from my recruitment strategy?' What then began was a ruthless focus on data that correlated to a player's ability to score or prevent runs. 'What we did was kind of obvious, just that nobody else was thinking that way,' he tells me, making it all sound so simple. 'We just used data that had been there for years and years and tried to accurately correlate it to performance on the baseball pitch.' Previously, old-fashioned scouts had given qualitative opinions, based on what they saw, rather than looking more deeply at data that could help predict the number of runs a player was going to score or prevent in the future. Beane asked himself a question that set him on the road to interrogating the data in a way that yielded answers that were free from the taint of received wisdom.

INTERPRETING THE DATA

If getting that first question right is difficult and requires immense self-discipline, so is the sifting of data that follows. Here, Beane makes an important distinction between statistics and analytics. 'Stats,' he says, 'are pieces of information to tell the fans something about the game.' They are snippets of information that are valid in themselves but have no wider utility. José Mourinho provides a specific example from his own sphere. 'If a player has 90 per cent pass completion but they are all over two yards under no pressure, it doesn't really tell us anything.' Analytics, by contrast, take raw statistics and determine which ones are just noise and which have a practical application. For Mourinho, a valuable piece of analytical work would involve looking at *how* a team loses the ball, because that will inform strategy. 'Do they lose it in the first phase with a short pass from a central defender to midfield? If they do, then we intensify pressure. With Vincent Kompany [Manchester City defender, seen as one of the best in the world], you assume he will bring the ball out well, pass it OK, so less pressure on him, more on where he will pass to.'

For Beane, analytics involved moving beyond the old standard of batting averages as the key measure of a player's batting performance, to a new standard called 'on base percentage' – in other words, how often a batter gets to the next base. The old batting-average approach didn't allow for factors that were beyond the batter's control – poor fielding, for example, or poor pitching. 'On base average', by contrast, focused on the performance of the individual, looking at all the ways in which he could get on base. 'I wouldn't say the raw batting average is a completely useless stat,' Beane says, 'but it doesn't tell us a lot about whether that player will be able to produce a high consistent batting performance in the future. That is an example of a stat, whereas on base percentage was analytics.'

Earlier I mentioned the success of Netflix in taking a $100 million-dollar bet on *House of Cards*, which helped garner 17 million new subscribers, and has opened a new era in viewing habits. But Kevin Spacey explains that they did so in part by understanding the difference between data and analytics. Spacey is scathing of the Nielsen ratings. 'One box on one TV set recording what you watch is supposed to represent half a million people's viewing habits and on such nonsense TV ratings and advertising rates are worked out. Netflix records what people actually watch, when, how, how long for, how often they pause, so that gives an enormous amount of data. But then the analytics comes in asking questions. So before buying *House of Cards* they would survey viewers and ask them, "Do you like Kevin Spacey films? Do you like David Fincher movies?

Are you into political dramas? Did you watch the British *House of Cards*?" Data lets you know what people are watching. Analytics gives you the judgement on what they are likely to want to watch in the future. They asked the questions and the answers made them confident *House of Cards* would work for them, even before we had started shooting.'

Statistics, then, have a somewhat passive quality to them. They're the sort of things that pundits love to trade ('That was the sixth time someone called Alan scored in the Merseyside derby'). By contrast, good analytics must have, as professional sports gambler Matthew Benham puts it, 'predictive utility'. Statistics will tell you which political party is ahead in the polls at a given point, but since they're framed around the question 'How would you vote if there was an election tomorrow?' – and except on the eve of the poll there won't be one – they have little predictive utility. Detailed qualitative research about people's views and what they feel about their lives, on the other hand, has an analytical quality to it and so may have predictive utility.

Benham is a master of this skill, a man who has made himself extremely wealthy – wealthy enough to buy outright the club he supported as a child, Brentford – by using statistical modelling that is highly analytical. He operates on the insight that not just the punters, but also pundits, and indeed top players and managers, know less than they think, because rather than look at hard data, they rely on instinct, emotion, media talk and David Axelrod's 'conventional wisdoms which are almost always wrong'. His advantage, he says, is that sport is now surrounded by noise twenty-four hours a day, globally, and punters, media and betting firms are constantly misled by their own views and by statistics that have little relevance to the future. If a top striker goes several games without scoring, he says, those few games cannot give you a sample size sufficient for predictive utility. When pundits say a club has gone five games without scoring at home, they are repeating facts that are of no statistical relevance. It doesn't automatically mean the chances of them scoring in the next game are reduced, if for example in the previous game they hit the bar three times. Likewise, when a pundit says 'they've just got a new manager so I fancy them to win', they are believing 'noise'.

The 2014 World Cup offers good examples of just what Benham means when he says he sees the pundits as allies, because many of them talk so much nonsense. These would be the pundits who constantly peddled the conventional wisdom that Brazil would win the World Cup because they were at home (not as relevant as you might think, although Benham pointed out that refereeing bias towards the host is genuine), that it was 'their time' (totally irrelevant), or that Argentina would win it because Messi was the best player in the world (relevant but insufficient). Few pundits predicted that Germany would win, yet any strategic analysis combined with data analysis would certainly have put them up there. In other words, there was little statistical support for majority views. But they nevertheless had an impact on the market.

One of the biggest bets Benham ever made – he is coy about the exact sum but it was huge – was on Spain to beat Italy in the final of the 2012 European Championships. While the market had Spain as slight favourites, he thought they were undervalued. In the semis, Italy had beaten Germany who were the in-form team with two wonder goals (wonder goals stick in people's minds). However, in that game Germany created a lot of chances. Spain on the other hand had been winning narrowly. 'In fact, using our model, Spain's level had not dropped across four years. The reason they were seen as boring by the media was because they were so effective at keeping the ball away from dangerous areas. Additionally they were creating around eight very good chances every game but just hadn't been scoring that much.' It was a classic example, he says, of his model being far superior to the conventional wisdom dictating the market. Spain won 4–0. He won handsomely too.

Billy Beane, a soccer fan as well as a baseball genius, uses a soccer example to illustrate just how important it is to make qualitative distinctions between pieces of data. Statistically, he suggests, a goal is just a goal, but, for the purposes of analytics, there is all the difference in the world between a tap in from two yards after a goalmouth scramble and a spectacular overhead kick from thirty-five yards. 'The score sheet judges them exactly equally,' he points out, before going on to outline how an analyst would study what they have to reveal. 'Now if you're using past goals to predict goals in the future then you have to start to weight the contextual elements of the goals. You have to account for the pressure of the situation. Then there is the quality of opposition – three goals against Bayern Munich carry more weight than three goals against Hertha Berlin – and also the difficulty of the chance and the frequency of that type of chance.' There are many thousands of individual actions taking place in a match. All have impact, but some have more impact than others. 'What proper analytics can do is allow you to apply proper weighting to each action or series of actions. That then lets you know if you are strong or weak in a particular area. Managing a team, I want to invest in the talent that creates the opportunities or performs the events that have a strong link to winning.' What is clear is that you can't make decisions about which talent you are investing in and why until you have really delved into the correlation of events in the game to winning. Benham's statisticians, working in front of banks of TV screens and computers at his HQ in north London, incorporate all sorts of complex factors into their modelling such as the quality of the chance (area of the pitch, pressure on the ball) and the quality of the opposition (how impressive it was in creating the chance).

So just how far can analytics take you? Billy Beane's view is clear. 'When you have done both intuition and data, I don't believe you'll ever go back to intuition. You can't tell me that it makes more sense to make emotional judgements in a vacuum when you have information that can clearly have an impact on the decision you're making.' That's not to say that he rules out other ways of making a judgement – in his own sphere, for example, he talks of the value of 'all the possible research avenues to establish things like preparedness and work ethic, concentration and focus, competitiveness and self-confidence'. But offered a binary choice between statistical analysis and gut instinct, he would opt for the former.

Matthew Benham offers another Kahneman insight: whenever humans have an opinion, our natural thought process is to convince ourselves it is 100 per cent right with utter certainty even if we're not sure where the opinion has come from or what exactly it is based on. Daniel Kahneman's point is that you can never lose that feeling. Humans have an extraordinary ability to convince themselves of a fact or correlation that might be wrong.

Brian Cox, not surprisingly, concurs. 'People like to think they exercise judgement and have strong intuitions for which decisions to make and I think that is entirely wrong. It's ridiculous not to gather all the data you can and respect it and mine it because the answers are there. It's a very liberating experience to use facts to justify your decisions.'

Beane holds up Warren Buffett as a supreme example of master analyst. 'I love how people think he is an example of emotional judgement overriding data. He is not. He is a rational contrarian. He just doesn't go around shouting about using data.' He recalls the aftermath of Hurricane Katrina in 2005, which caused the

> 'When you have done both intuition and data, I don't believe you'll ever go back to intuition.'
> **BILLY BEANE**

deaths of 1,833 people and around $108 billion of damage. It was the third successive year there had been a hurricane in the region, the most hurricane-intense period since records began. Beane said Buffett decided it was a mathematical aberration. 'There's all the "noise". No one was willing to insure anything in the region so the only company that did was Buffett's. He just ignored the "noise" and looked at it rationally, taking account of the regression to the mean. They haven't had a hurricane since. He didn't know for sure, but his reading of the data pushed him that way.' It's another brilliant example of the famous Buffett dictum: 'Be fearful when others are greedy and greedy when others are fearful.'

THE HUMAN ELEMENT

The digital and technological advancements of the last ten to fifteen years have, of course, made data easier to compile and more accessible to analysis. As my conversations with people such as Benham and Beane suggest, though, when you delve deep into the success stories, the true winners are not the data geeks who crunch numbers all day every day and do it without any deep understanding of the history and logic of what they are studying. More than ever the true winners are capable of weighting different pieces of contextual information in order to make a decision when it really matters. In other words, it seems to me that those who have been most successful with data have included their own knowledge – and scepticism – in the mix, a blend of intuition (however acquired) and objectivity.

Without that human element, the risks of skewed analysis are simply too great. The financial crisis of 2007 and 2008 offers a casebook example of this. By 2007 the models used by many banks to judge lending and risk had become so complicated that few bankers actually understood them. This lack of understanding extended to the rating agencies who were supposed to be monitoring the lenders. Standard & Poor's, for instance, told investors that when they rated a collateralised debt obligation (CDO) at AAA (the highest rating), there was only a 0.12 per cent probability that it would fail to pay out over the next five years, when, as it turned out, around 28 per cent of AAA-rated CDOs defaulted. No one, it seems, was prepared to ask the very simple and basic questions that would have shown what a house of cards had been created. After all, however sophisticated the data, if the assumptions and generalisations underlying the model are wrong, then the data will not calibrate in the right way to make reliable predictions about the future.

To a large extent, then, there's a careful balance of the human and statistical to be achieved – and these two standards operate on a sliding scale. At one end, I've been struck by how data-driven supermarkets tend to be. But then they have a very clear sense of what their goal is: to profile customers in order to match what they are offering with what people want. As Sainsbury's ex-CEO Justin King puts it: 'Retail businesses are data businesses. Data allows you to do so many things you couldn't do before. Just look at the maths. Sainsbury's have 25 million customers a week buying between them 500 million things in ever-changing combinations. There are 40,000 items per store and customers choose an average of fifteen. So there's a lot of data there.'

Yet, at the other end of the scale, you only need to consider what makes people successful in what is (to outsiders at least) a chance-and-numbers activity – poker – to appreciate the human element, and to recognise that here, as in so many areas of life, the strengths and failings of individuals mean few things can be predicted with absolute certainty. Explaining how top-level poker works, Sam Trickett points out that because people are emotional and that because significant sums of money are at stake they tend not to play poker in a uniform way. Arguably there is nothing more pressured than having to make decisions where you can personally win or lose millions of pounds in front of others in a matter of minutes, when those decisions are completely in your control but you are dealing with imperfect information. 'It all comes back to game theory, and game theory is far from an exact science.'

At one level, according to Trickett, it's all about data analysis. 'You've got to break down the tough situation into the pieces of evidence that have a direct impact on what is happening in this hand or this moment, not try and base it on a similar hand against a different type of player some time ago. I always get to a tough decision and think right back to the start of the hand or even any history we've got between each other. And then you break down the hand from start to finish.' But it's also about confidence, about inferring information from the way other people appear and react. 'You have to assess every single piece of information possible. Sometimes a lot of hands are played in a vacuum and you've got no obvious social pieces of information in front of you and no history between you and the other player and therefore it comes down to understanding basic fundamentals of the game. However, other times there may be a really obvious piece of information such as he's looking at the pay jumps in the tournament or he's obviously aware of the fact that you're playing with confidence and therefore more likely to be bluffing. Sometimes decisions can become pretty exact once you've broken down the game theory. I see a lot of really good players make terrible decisions because they ignore some crucial social information. They fail at the whole meta-game and game-theory element of poker and think about it too much from a mathematical modelling standpoint. I feel like I excel at the meta side of the game and I'm very good at extracting and weighting information in a given situation.'

An awareness of the need for a balance between data analysis and human judgement is apparent among others I've spoken to. Head teacher Vic Goddard talks about the value of looking at post-codes and parents' background in framing expectations for pupils, but also says: 'Data is always only a conversation starter.' There are, he argues, simply too many variables for a purely statistical analysis of current and likely future performance. Businessman Charles Dunstone similarly feels that statistics alone do not give you the big picture. 'We have a call centre in Stornoway. Apart from the government I think we're the biggest employer there. We were making some changes and it was recommended we close it down. But the data only tells you part of the story. This was Stornoway. It would have been devastating, but on an Excel spreadsheet it just says 120 jobs, same as 120 jobs anywhere else. Also these people had become specialist in the really difficult calls, bereavement, that kind of thing, they were a cut above your average call centre. You don't get that from data alone. We kept it.' Interestingly, he is critical of the way many in business view data: 'They don't drill down enough to inform leadership.' This is not an argument for disregarding the use of data. It is an argument for understanding the data and how it should inform strategy and leadership. This is something he feels those in the political sphere handle better.

But for me perhaps the most fascinating case study of analytics comes from former Goldman Sachs executive Jim O'Neill, an economics winner with a place in history thanks to his prediction that Brazil, Russia, India and China (the BRIC countries, as he styled them on the fateful morning of 11 September 2001) would be the fastest growing economies of the first decade of the century. He was right – though he views such a data-strewn field as economics as prone to error. 'The key with any economic data is to be consciously aware there is a reasonable chance that you are going to be wrong. I trained myself, influenced by past successes and failures, that if I am right 60 per cent of the time – however measured – I would be happy. To kid yourself that you can be right more frequently than this is an error.'

O'Neill's starting point was to focus on a small number of data points, thereby avoiding initial over-complexity in what would, inevitably, become a very complicated model. So his research team paid particular attention to two long-term drivers of economic growth: a country's labour force size and development, and its productivity. At the same time, the team sought to incorporate into the modelling inevitable areas of uncertainty. And in particular, they considered the two key issues in any statistical study, correlation and causality.

Now there may be many things correlating to successful economic growth, but that is very different from the issue of causality. There happens to be, for example, an almost perfect positive correlation between US spending on science, space and technology and suicides by hanging, strangulation and suffocation, but that doesn't mean (and clearly can't) that there is any causal link between the two. Yet the problem with every model is that the more data you add, the more likely you are to see patterns where there are none, and correlations where none exist. John Browne, the former CEO of BP, who is now closely involved in making huge private equity investment decisions, argues this is precisely the reason why you need to understand a sector fully if you are to engage with it successfully: 'There has to be a basis of causality that you understand and this comes down to having a real deep understanding of the markets you are in and the progression and trends of the markets. You can never get away from that and data cannot teach you that.'

For O'Neill, the issue of separating correlation and causality was particularly acute when it came to considering productivity. 'If countries with large and young working populations can find and/ or be encouraged to do things to improve their productivity,' he says, 'they are going to be economically large. It is as simple and as complicated as that!' He goes on to elaborate. 'The labour force part is relatively straightforward as that doesn't change so quickly, at least over a twenty-year period, but the productivity effect is more tricky, as it is influenced by many variables, possibly as many as twenty significant ones.' The more variables involved, the more uncertainty enters the equation.

And this is where human understanding, rather than statistics, comes in. Faced with all the complications and potential ramifications of the data he was looking at, O'Neill arrived at a fundamental insight. And it was one that did not stem from economics but from politics. Quite simply, it became clear to him that all the BRICs wanted to engage more on the world stage. Whatever their past, whatever their politics, they were determined to be part of the globalisation process, and as winners not spectators. Throughout his career O'Neill had highlighted inflation targeting as essential to improving productivity. 'People need to know what money can buy. If they can't trust prices, they won't do anything to invest or improve their future. Without giving people the sense that whatever they earn and save is going to have value, no politician can talk seriously about sustained growth.' And what struck him was the observation made by one of his Brazilian economists, that when he was a teenager, inflation on a daily basis was what it is today on an annual basis. Attitudes had begun to change in the late 1990s when a new set of political leaders set about bringing inflation under control and improving the country's fiscal health. 'By placing the control of inflation at the centre of macroeconomic policy, it seemed the government was giving the country a chance of reaching its productivity potential and exploiting its young working population.'

O'Neill's insight is a great example of intuition founded on deep knowledge. The data crunching therefore rested on a very firm basis.

As with the global economy, so at sea, and when I ask Ben Ainslie what is more important, the ability to analyse the data or the ability to make decisions, he is clear. 'It is the mindset to be able to get big decisions right under pressure. There are lots of sailors out there who are very savvy with the data and can absorb a lot of it, but if you can't use it to make a split-second decision based on that data in a competitive environment, then there isn't really much point to it. You have to be able to assess a few data points that are relevant, but at the same time just stick your head out of the boat and make a judgement about the weather or the water and decide.'

Billy Beane has a very colourful way of describing how these two vital forces – data and intuition – come together in this way: 'You evolve to the point where you get the data that has the best predictive utility. But in trying to find this out you have started a process that allows dissection whereas if you use intuition alone there is no dissection. You can't go back to create the event to find out why it was wrong. Every event with instinct is a linear event. Data gives you a road map that allows self-correction because you become a human algorithm.'

14

TURNING DATA INTO BOLD INNOVATION: FROM FORMULA ONE TO NARENDRA MODI

'World-class performance comes by striving for a target just out of reach but with a vivid awareness of how the gap might be breached. Over time, through constant repetition and deep concentration, the gap will disappear only for a new target to be created just out of reach again.'

MATTHEW SYED

When I was growing up, the big name in motor sport was Scotsman Jim Clark, who won two world titles before dying in a crash during a Formula Two race in Germany in 1968, aged just thirty-two. It's a salutary thought that his Lotus car of the sixties, driven to full potential over a single lap, would come in over thirty seconds behind the F1 cars of today – and bear in mind that regulations are significantly more restrictive than fifty years ago.

Today improvements are measured in milliseconds, as are the gaps between winners and losers. At the Singapore Grand Prix in 2014, for instance, the difference between first and tenth place was seven-tenths of a second. It's not surprising, then, that just as speed has increased over the past few decades, so has the number of engineers working to achieve it. 'Formula One has gone through big change,' Paddy Lowe, executive director of the Mercedes team, tells me. 'In the seventies it was a back-of-the-shed thing with a lot of trial and error. These days the engineers come from the best engineering schools across Europe and top engineers want to work in Formula One. In the seventies the entire team would fit in a small van. Now we have twenty engineers and sixty operational staff just at the race.' In fact, today's Mercedes team comprises 700 people, of whom 250 are engineers.

I ask Lowe who is more important to the operation: him leading the vast team of engineers, or the driver in the car? 'It's probably fifty–fifty. You can't have a great car without a great engineering team. But the car needs a great driver. This year is a good example. The car is very fast, but you only have to look at the grid to see that Nico [Rosberg] and Lewis [Hamilton] are exploiting it to the limit in very tense situations in qualifying or in a race.'

Two things struck me on my visits to Silverstone, and to the team factories of both Mercedes and McLaren. The first was the obsession with constant improvement – I never once heard someone say, 'We're doing fine.' In fact when it comes to the 'marginal gains' philosophy espoused by Dave Brailsford and others, I think few are as single-minded in its pursuit as the top teams in Formula One. 'I can't tell you how much pleasure we get from spotting a change we could make,' says Lowe, 'researching it, testing it, assessing it might take two-tenths of a second off the lap time, then the driver delivering that two-tenths. That's what we live for.'

And that leads me to the second observation I made. In its quest for constant improvement, Formula One is obsessed with gathering and interpreting data. 'In the old days,' says Lowe, 'the drivers could bullshit you, say this felt wrong, that felt wrong, the car is crap. There's no room for bullshit today because we can see what's happening with every part of the car. When I started, we recorded eight channels of data and now we have 16,000 from every single parameter on the car – and we derive another 50,000 channels from that data. There's nowhere to hide. Equally, every single engineer knows the tangible standards we're looking for and that the car needs to reach the benchmark data points we've outlined.'

While Lewis Hamilton does a test drive round the Silverstone track, where days earlier he won the British Grand Prix, I stand at the back of the garage as thirty or so engineers stare at computers and analyse various elements of his car's performance. Another group of engineers is doing the same back at the Mercedes factory in Brackley. The tyre engineers are monitoring readings of how worn the tyres are and how they're responding to different parts of the track. The brake engineers are looking at the responsiveness of the new brakes they've been working on since Hamilton's latest triumph. Then when the car comes back in, the driver gives his own feedback.

On a visit to the factory a few weeks later, Rosberg having meanwhile won in Germany, with Hamilton third, and Mercedes consolidating their grip on the Drivers' and Constructors' World titles, it becomes clear that the trackside data analysis I'd seen is just one tiny part of it. Here is the heart of the operation: a race analysis room where all data, over either a testing period or a race weekend, is analysed and potential changes considered. More than four hundred parts of the car, all newly manufactured and pre-tested before the race in Hockenheim, are now being retested after the event. As in the aviation industry, each component is part of a process called 'lifing', where every mile it completes is rigorously monitored and its degradation over the course of the race measured. The engineers explain that they are operating on the edge of the performance/reliability trade-off: they are seeking to get the maximum performance they want out of the car, where it's pushed to its absolute limit; but they also have to make sure that it doesn't actually break down, and that while the parts endure huge stress, the car as a whole continues to perform to its maximum potential.

They have a model of how degraded they feel each part should be for it to have achieved maximum performance. If a part has broken, then obviously it's been under-engineered and they need it to be tougher and more reliable the next time. However, if a part comes back exactly as it went on the car, then the marginal gains mindset tells them it was over-engineered and minor adjustments to save weight and space probably need to be made. Components such as wheel bearings are run to approximately 50 per cent of their potential full life before being replaced, as well as being monitored throughout for excessive loads during their operation which may affect their durability. Other components will be run to near 90 per cent of their maximum life before being replaced.

'In a very simple sense,' says Lowe, 'you are always having to balance downforce and drag. If you can increase downforce without it being accompanied by extra drag then you have a major performance gain. Performance in Formula One is about trade-offs, and improving downforce without being accompanied by extra drag is the most important efficiency concern. Anyone proposing a change in the design of the car will look to demonstrate this gain first and foremost. However, after that you have to look at the information coming from all the different engineers and departments and make decisions about different trade-offs and the impact any changes made to one part may have on the rest of the car.'

A good example comes in the development of cooling systems. F1 cars use their motion through the air to cool the engine. Generally, the better the engine can be cooled, the more power it develops; but the bigger the cooling requirement, the higher the penalties in terms of weight and aerodynamics. So it's about finding the right trade-off between aerodynamic performance, weight, engine power and engine life – and balancing these for the best possible lap time over the duration of the race. Then the package needs to be adjusted for local factors, like the temperature at each circuit. Incidentally, imitation of innovation in F1 is very difficult. 'It's not just about mimicking an idea and bolting it onto your car,' says Lowe. 'All cars are different and you have to find a way to make new ideas fit with the DNA of your car. That's why, to win, you need genuine innovation, not imitation.'

Much reliance is placed on a modelling software technology called CFD (computational fluid dynamics), one of the biggest computer simulation systems in the world. According to Lowe:

'In CFD you can see the flow in 3D and from there we'll decide whether it's worth taking to the wind tunnel. Then you test it on the driver in the loop simulator, and the track. It might be aerodynamically the best available option but does it have the characteristics to do well on the track?'

'To win, you need genuine innovation, not imitation.'

PADDY LOWE

Lowe sees CFD as a significant advance as it has allowed Formula One more detailed, data-driven analysis of aerodynamic developments. 'It started in about 1990 but only by about 2005 or 2006 was it starting to become a mainstream part of development. Before it was just a few blokes in the corner and the other guys said either "that's interesting" or "it's a load of bollocks". Now it's completely mainstream; you won't put an idea in the wind tunnel without first evaluating it in CFD. It allows us to filter the ideas we want to take further very quickly.' Those filtered ideas are then evaluated in the wind tunnel, a complementary development platform where a model 60 per cent of the size of the actual car is tested on what must be the fastest treadmill in the world.

The loop simulator is perhaps the most dramatic example of F1's attention to detail. This allows the driver to 'drive' with the new car parts on an exact simulator of Grand Prix tracks around the world. While it is partly about getting feedback from drivers, its main purpose for the engineers is to get data on exact race simulation and how the car responds to various parts of the track. 'Any change we make to the car we can make it on this simulator,' says Lowe. 'We also have a development platform called a seven-post rig which can simulate the contours of any track in the world to test the suspension. Telemetry data gathered during track running is used to reproduce its characteristics on the rig, so that we can optimise the ride and handling of the car by tuning the suspension characteristics.'

These simulations are all the more important because of the rules limiting testing on real tracks to three pre-season and four mid-season, with no testing of new parts on the track outside that. 'Part of the value of a test is working out what, how and why to test next,' says Lowe. 'If I had one word to sum up our approach to innovation, it would be iteration. There is constant iteration at every phase in the process and this keeps things moving. We have pressure sensors on the car and on the model so we can see if a new part produces the same output on the track as it does in the tunnel. The analysis may then come from the race engineers about how it worked on the track and the suitability for the driver in practice, because their subjective "seat of the pants" feedback also matters. At every point information is being fed back to the development team, so this gets our minds working for the next thing – if it worked, or if it didn't I'm asking why it didn't and we either fix it or develop an alternative. The faster and more accurate we make these loops – we call it the cycle time – the faster we can deliver the next potential developments.' Twelve performance developments were made after the German Grand Prix, for example, and up to twenty can be made on a car from one Grand Prix to the next.

The risks of data overload are clear: the team is handling everything from historical data within the sport, through testing and race data, to data gathered by the driver in the loop simulator, wind tunnel data and data produced by a CFD. This is where leadership and judgement come in: knowing which data to use to frame expectations and benchmark points for performance of the car. But the dominant mindset is that the data tells the story, and they have to hear it. 'It's so complex it is at times beyond comprehension,' says McLaren supremo Ron Dennis. 'You might be looking at the performance of twenty, thirty components and between them establishing how to take milliseconds off a lap time.' 'The data is what drives the process of innovation rather than stifles it,' says Lowe. The truth is that the wealth of data allows them realistically to frame expectations, but not from the narrative of 'this is what we need to maintain' but rather 'this is how much we can potentially improve'. Or, as Ron Dennis puts it, 'The data points are like musical instruments, and the driver is conducting the orchestra based on how he listens to the music.'

This receptiveness to data makes F1 astonishingly flexible and innovative. 'I see myself as innovative within the sport,' Lowe says, 'because I have to be. You can design something and be racing it four days later. The other teams are doing the same. It's unbelievably competitive.' It's an intensity that Lowe clearly feels is not matched in other fields. 'In this business when someone says "We're on it", it really means that. Our culture is relentless. Sometimes we work with companies from other sectors, or academia, and you meet up and just think they're not "on it", they are light years away from how quickly we move. You go into a meeting and we say "Let's do it this afternoon", and they say "No, we can't do it until next month", and you realise it's a totally different mindset. The big figures who were influential in the development of Formula One were real "we're on it" people. Frank Williams, Patrick Head, Ron Dennis [all of whom Lowe worked for earlier in his career]. Ron was classic. He was always asking why the process couldn't be quicker. I'd say "I think we can make this change for the next race" and he would say "What's wrong with this one?" Cultures change through the attitudes of leaders and those guys made this industry what it is.'

> 'If I had one word to sum up our approach to innovation, it would be iteration.'
>
> **PADDY LOWE**

Lowe explains that some of his brightest minds are already thinking about the car for next year, and one or two are thinking about the one after that. An engineer explains that the reason why one team might emerge from a mid-ranking position to being dominant is because of 'game-changing innovation', adding: 'It comes from the designers thinking about the dimensions they've got to work with. You'll have a part of the design office just working on completely new ideas. [Ross] Brawn running a double diffuser won them the championship in '09, and Red Bull's period of dominance was consolidated by the perfection of the exhaust-blown diffuser which has now been outlawed. This is where the designers in Formula One really are among the best in the world. They have brains that can see the future and not the past.'

An example of a winning innovation for the Mercedes engineering team was the turbocharger design they came up with for the 2014 season. 'When we began working on this project,' Lowe says, 'we knew that there was a big advantage to be found from working as one unit with our engine colleagues from the very beginning. All the way through, the question wasn't "what delivers most power?" or "what is the best solution for the chassis?" but "what gives the biggest lap-time benefit?" We had the same mission. By splitting the turbine and compressor at different ends of the engine, we unlocked performance and packaging benefits that our rivals haven't been able to emulate.' To achieve this required not only deep understanding of the data, but superb team work, both in the execution and in that initial decision to go ahead – after all, the team bosses have so many ideas put in front of them that they need to be confident that the handful they pursue will justify the effort and expense.

Driver Nico Rosberg underlines the extent to which it is a team game. 'We are making improvements to the car all the time, and as drivers we are always working with our engineers to get the most out of them. We have new components every two weeks which we need to understand and adapt the car to take account of; that's a constant process we need to be successful at with our engineers. This sport is all about building good relationships with your co-workers and using all their inputs to go faster. It's a massive team effort where every item is so important for the race weekend.'

It's also a sport where fortunes can change almost overnight. Ron Dennis, for example, ruefully talks about McLaren's recent record and the loss of driver Lewis Hamilton. 'McLaren was a winning machine, and now we're not. That's hard. This is a hero to zero sport. Mercedes knew they wouldn't have a competitive car last season so they put all their effort into this season, they adapted to rule changes well, and now they're dominating. The mistake we made was that, in trying to grow, we diversified, and we lost that focus and commitment you need. We moved away from the focus being on the core, Formula One.' The margins, though, are tiny. 'One per cent hero to zero. Look at Apple, gets hit by software problems, shares move at 4 per cent and wipe off billions. Four per cent for us you would be on the back of the grid. One second off and you're twelfth. You cannot hide. A public company in the US does monthly reports, UK quarterly. We have to go out every two weeks and show what we have. Here we are, running between fourth and eighth, and people are saying you're history and out of it, and there is no magic switch – when you don't have a competitive car, climbing into competitiveness is so difficult.'

Losing Lewis Hamilton was clearly a setback, but not the reason for McLaren's recent relative decline. 'These things happen. Lewis had committed to drive for the team in the future but there were things going on in his private life, he was not fully settled in his head, less than perfect in his thought processes for that time. We had terms and conditions agreed, he was leading the Grand Prix, the fuel pump failed – it was actually a Mercedes part – and he didn't finish the race, which took away his chance of winning the World Championship. Niki Lauda [non-executive chairman of Mercedes] went to him that night in his hotel room, got him at the right moment, offered him a lot of money and he went. I had mixed emotions obviously. I took him at twelve, financed his career, guided him, but he did great job for us, maybe it was the time to move. Last year we were having a bad year, and he has hit the sweet spot.'

The governing body also plays an important part in ensuring that complacency never sets in. 'The rules are changing all the time,' Lowe explains. 'Whenever you are looking to innovate to get ahead, the FIA are attempting to stop it because they don't want the teams to get too far ahead of each other and that is part of the challenge. The enjoyment of any benefit is brief – so you have to keep moving on to the next thing. To me that is the core reason why Formula One is such an innovative industry. You need to get every drop of performance out of the car within a very tight framework. You can't skirt round problems. You have to solve them.'

In 2014, for instance, there were new rules on the maximum amount of fuel teams were allowed to use during the race and a restriction on the fuel flow rate to the engine – in part a response to demands from outside for a more sustainable approach to racing. So as well as improving cars, Mercedes scrutinised the fuel they were using, developing an oil that is thin at low temperatures and thick at high temperatures, and therefore more efficient. It's a good example of a challenge forcing innovation. Over time, the innovation in question will filter down to improve the efficiency of road cars.

More generally, such is Formula One's extraordinary skillset that it is finding applications in sectors well beyond the world of motor racing. McLaren Applied Technology, an offshoot of the F1 team, now employs 250 people. When I visit McLaren HQ in Surrey, I notice, alongside the lines of old F1 cars, a beautiful bike, ridden by pro cyclist Mark Cavendish, part designed by McLaren. And the system known as Marple, which guides decision-making on when a driver should come in for a pit stop, is now being adapted for use by air traffic control at Heathrow.

Peter van Manen, McLaren Applied Technologies vice president, is clear about the value F1 can bring to other sectors, from aviation to toothpaste! 'Motor racing, and especially Formula One, demands nimbleness of thought,' he says. 'It requires not only innovation but improvisation too. Big business tends to struggle with both those processes.' What guides their pit-stop teams is the old saying: 'more haste less speed'. 'The pit crew of a top Formula One team can perform a complete four-wheels-off-then-four-wheels-on pit stop in just 2.3 seconds, in the middle of a fraught and frenetic Grand Prix, and to do that the guys have to adopt a fast-but-not-hurried approach. Working with GlaxoSmithKline, we've adapted that approach and tailored it to improving speed and efficiency on GSK's toothpaste production lines. As a result, instead of a change-over [from one toothpaste packaging line to another] taking thirty-nine minutes, all of which was "dead" time from a productivity point of view, a changeover is now down to just fifteen minutes. In turn, the entire mindset of the people on those production lines has changed. They're now embracing responsibility and accountability. And they're now becoming increasingly alert to ways in which they can innovate and improvise.'

Compare the F1 mindset grounded in innovation and using data to drive it with the political parties who like to greet every local or by-election result as showing 'we are on track', or the business which greets disappointing quarterly results with the explanation that they were 'to be expected given the climate'. As for my most hated political phrase, 'the problem is . . .', you won't hear it from Paddy Lowe and his team. 'This is a sport that likes problems because we're here to try to solve them, not walk away from them,' he says.

I sometimes feel in talking to entrepreneurs or innovators in other walks of life that many see the data as being somehow separate from the innovation. The data is nuts and bolts. The innovation is all about ideas, which come from elsewhere. If data is used in decision-making processes at all, it tends to be to confirm existing prejudices, not to suggest new directions. But what is clear from the way the current winners in Formula One use data, is that far from restricting ambition and innovation, it has led the process of encouraging and creating them. Every piece of information is measured with quantitative analysis and this means that everything that is tested and every element of performance has tangible outcomes and can be compared against past or expected performance. This forces those within the teams to think about how to change all the time in order to reach the maximum possible performance levels. There is nowhere to hide and giving subjective opinions to defend poor performance won't wash because so much evidence is there in black and white. The more subjective evaluation you have – and politics is even more awash with it than sport or business – the easier it is to hide and therefore the easier it is to say you don't have to change, you don't need to force improvement, no need to innovate, let's muddle on through. Perhaps it's the 'nowhere to hide' element in data-rich F1 that has created the 'We're on it' mindset that Paddy Lowe regards as an integral part of the culture. And that, ultimately, is why figures as impressive as Brailsford, Woodward and Ainslie – who is recruiting from F1 for his Americas Cup challenge – all look to Formula One with mutual respect and admiration.

There's another name – strangely enough, given what I've just said, from the world of politics – that I would add to that list of great, data-driven innovators: Narendra Modi, the man who, in May 2014, became prime minister of India on the back of a huge 13.77 per cent swing to his Bharatiya Janata Party (BJP), crushing the dominant Congress Party to forty-four seats, their worst ever general election result. It was a victory of bold strategy and superb execution; a victory for innovation, and for use of data.

> 'This is a sport that likes problems because we're here to try to solve them, not walk away from them.' **PADDY LOWE**

The boldness came not least from the personality of Modi himself, the sixty-three-year-old son of a grocer from Vadnagar, a Hindu nationalist, and member of the BJP's once banned parent organisation Rashtriya Swayamsevak Sangh (RSS). For many he's a controversial figure, who came to international attention during the Gujarat riots in 2002, when his administration was criticised for doing too little to stop the violence between Hindus and Muslims that followed on from the burning of a train filled with hundreds of Hindu pilgrims at Godhra. The passage of years did little to soften critical views of him. He was barred entry to the US, while the UK and the EU refused to deal with him. It was only as he headed to power that boycotts were lifted.

During the run-up to the campaign, Modi was polling 20 points ahead of his party, suggesting that, whatever the international view, he was making a big impact on domestic opinion, and so he took the calculated risk to make it 'all about me'. He understood that to win, you must make the weather; and to make the weather in politics, you must get noticed. That means saying and doing interesting things. It means working hard. It means not just enduring but enjoying attacks from your opponents, because they present two opportunities: the opportunity to fight back, and the opportunity to be the centre of debate. I cannot think of a parliamentary election, anywhere, ever, that was so much about one person.

So creating Brand Modi was a deliberate strategic choice. In a country where leaders can sometimes be coy about their ambitions, Modi left nobody in any doubt about his objectives. He wanted to move from being a regional to a national figure; he wanted to lead the BJP campaign, he wanted to lead it in his way, with his team; and he wanted to win big. Setting the objective so clearly allowed him to frame the strategy to meet it. The boldness of ambition and the determination he displayed inspired others to want to be part of the team, at whatever level.

'Modi successfully created the impression that in him the public would be backing a winner. Without being triumphalist, Modi's talk and walk were that of a winner from the day he was nominated by the BJP as their prime ministerial candidate,' says Manoj Ladwa, a British-born lawyer and long-time friend of Modi, who worked as his communications director in charge of research, analysis and messaging.

In a country as vast as India, building the team to match the scale of his ambition was essential. He surrounded himself with some of the best and brightest brains in India, from all walks of life. He persuaded CEOs, entrepreneurs, lawyers, lecturers, accountants, to take sabbaticals and help him win.

Jyoti Shiralee, a marketing professional from Mumbai, who took some time out from her career to join the campaign, says: 'What inspired me was his missionary zeal and commitment to building a strong and vibrant India and that he achieved what he did through merit and hard work, against insurmountable odds and despite very humble beginnings. He is probably the only politician who has this rare ability to connect with an aspirational India through simple yet profound messages, and balance bread

and butter issues like sanitation, employment, inflation or corruption with larger national issues of nation building, development,
good governance and gender issues.' She adds that his direct
appeal to women when saying 'India can never progress if 50 per
cent of her population lags behind' or that 'Women should not
just be homemakers but nation builders too' were 'path-breaking
thoughts . . . I can't think of another leader who is at once a
decisive leader, a master politician and strategist and a superb
communicator.'

According to respected and popular columnist Ashok Malik,
who is known to be close to the BJP leadership, Modi successfully
capitalised on three long-term trends that came together at the election. First, a population getting younger and younger, with no fewer
than 12 million people entering the workforce each year. Second,
the creation of an urban-centric economy, with 60 per cent of GDP
coming from cities and towns, meaning that many more than just
the one in three Indians who are full-time residents of urban India
were dependent on the urban economy and worried by two years
of slowdown. Third, the media explosion that saw TV, and to a
lesser degree social media and the Internet, create new pan-Indian
trends, consumer habits and news phenomena. Modi became the
beneficiary of these trends, by making himself the answer to the
questions that lay behind them. Malik explains: 'He succeeded in
presenting himself as the answer to the economy's problems and to
the job deficit; he was the tough, no-nonsense (and sometimes angry)
man from the "real India" – not Delhi – who represented the social
underdog and empathised with his or her aspirations; and he was
the news phenomenon who cleverly created made-for-television
events that the media couldn't ignore.'

To do all that, though, Modi knew the campaign was not just
about the people at the top table. Obama-like, he motivated a vast
army of volunteers to take his messages to their friends, families and
communities. Social media and mobile telephony were used as never
before to reach out and build networks of activists.

He led from the front. 'Nobody worked harder than he did,'

says Manoj Ladwa. 'Five thousand events, he spoke at 450-plus rallies, he travelled 300,000 kilometres, he never stopped, he never rested, he fought like his life depended on it, even when people were saying it was in the bag.'

The policy messages were fairly simple, focusing on economic development, the need to control inflation, help create jobs, tackle corruption, deliver good governance, and women's safety. But it was the reach of the message, and the discipline and innovation with which he carried and communicated it, that made the campaign so successful, making it one of the biggest mass mobilisation efforts anywhere on earth, ever. Bear in mind that this is a democracy so vast that more than 120 million – equivalent to the entire population of Japan or Mexico, the tenth and eleventh largest countries in the world – were voting for the first time. It was these younger people who helped create the biggest single electorate of all time.

One of the most dramatic innovations was the use of 3D technology, normally associated with the entertainment industry, which allowed Modi to address a rally live and in the flesh in one part of the country, while the same message was being carried to huge crowds by a totally lifelike hologram. It is estimated that Modi 'directly' reached in the region of 100 million people, face-to-face at his rallies or via his hologram.

Modi's team worked with Musion, a London-based company whose 3D holographic technology had allowed singer Mariah Carey to 'perform' in five cities at the same time, and who had also 'digitally resurrected' the murdered US rapper Tupac, which led to 15 million YouTube hits within two days. But the scale of their Modi operation dwarfed any of this, and the new Indian PM's campaign has a place in the Guinness World Records for the most hologrammed event. That was on 26 April, when 'Modi' spoke simultaneously to 128 audiences totalling more than 1.5 million people. Through the campaign, Musion used more than 30,000 square metres of holographic projection foil, 200 projectors, 500 satellite dishes, 5,500 metres of trusses, 1,300 lights, 500 audio speakers, 200 sound mixers and power amps, and 14,000 metres of speaker and power cables.

The staff involved travelled between them more than three million miles.

Ahmedabad was the HQ for the campaign; here (and on a smaller scale in Delhi) Musion built studios from where most of the speeches were delivered, and where the campaign team could also see exactly what the audiences at the various venues around the country were watching. A GSM camera car at each location beamed back images of the venue construction and the speech in real time, which was simultaneously displayed on a massive screen at the HQ. Given how campaign morale can rise and fall according to what is happening out on the road with the candidate, I can only begin to imagine the positive mood all this generated inside the Modi camp, and the anguish it was causing to his opponents.

Logistically, it was a huge and expensive operation, requiring teams of experts to be on top of the detail and the technology at every venue, with others on standby able to fly to a venue at a moment's notice. Musion flew out twenty-five of their own people to oversee the project and train two thousand people who then helped to deliver it. But Modi's team knew that if it went well, it would take the campaign forward on many levels. At its simplest, it was a way for vast numbers of people to 'see' and hear Modi direct, so it allowed him to get his message out. The media carried the message more readily because the medium was so interesting and innovative. As thousands flocked to hear him speak, teams of supporters combed the crowds to establish who they were, what their interests were. This data was used to get those people more active and involved, but also to shape the messaging of the rest of the campaign. It was through such people-to-people contact, for example, that the Modi team realised the BJP traditional strength – national security – was less important in the eyes of supporters and non-supporters alike than youth unemployment. 'It just came through again and again and again,' says Manoj Ladwa, 'and we tailored the campaign, the message and the policy work accordingly. The more we brought people into the campaign, the more we felt their influence.'

This innovation and sense of urgency also helped Modi capture that often intangible but hugely important campaign asset: momentum. He became an irresistible, unstoppable force. Success bred success. As he persuaded outsiders to join him, and they were able to help deliver results, so others wanted to join. When he was able to show that seemingly harsh personnel decisions were reaping rewards, it meant he was able to make more, and get the team he wanted. As his stature grew, so his appeal grew. As his appeal grew, so a sense of inevitability developed that he would win. It was the perfect campaign storm, created by him, working in his favour, reducing his opponents to a sense of defeatism which in turn began to have a negative impact on their morale and thus their operational effectiveness. It reminded me of something Sebastian Coe told me after the 2001 UK general election, in which he was working as chief of staff for Tony Blair's opponent William Hague. Both the athlete and the politician in him were speaking when he said: 'There is no worse feeling than being in a contest that you know deep down you are going to lose.' It was how Modi's opponents felt long before the polls opened.

It was, of course, an enormous team effort, but as leader, and as the human brand in question, Modi must take most of the credit. A key member of the team was Piyush Pandey, chairman and national creative director at South Asia Ogilvy & Mather India. 'Nothing can become a brand if a product is not so great,' he says. In other words, when Modi spoke, people had to want to listen, and they did. 'Modi is both a great product and a great brand. When I say "great product" what I mean is that he has intrinsic differentiators such as strength of conviction, decisiveness, transparency and accountability. When I say "great brand" what I mean is that people see him as both an icon of development and a leader they can trust. Not only is he dedicated and hard-working himself, but he also has the natural ability to motivate people around him to come together and give their very best to the task at hand. It was a privilege to lead the advertising campaign for the BJP. In over three decades in the business, I have never had a greater, more challenging learning.'

As the brand developed, it did so in all sorts of different directions, some planned, some spontaneously taken on by others. Among the planned was a 48-page comic book, *Bal Narendra*, portraying stories of Modi's childhood and youth, including the one of him swimming in a crocodile-infested lake in Gujarat. He takes a baby crocodile home, but his mother makes him take it back, explaining how children hate to be parted from their mother. Modi stated in the book that its purpose was to inspire young people 'to dream of doing something meaningful, rather than merely becoming someone'. We can only imagine the cynicism with which such an exercise might be greeted if attempted by an American or British candidate. But it worked for Modi. So did the street plays, and the animated cricket-themed films in a country obsessed by the sport.

One of the more dramatic unplanned parts of the brand was a superhero animation, *Nation in Motion*, made by a Modi fan club. To Western eyes it looks like the stuff of satire, Modi in a black-and-maroon cape, a giant M where Superman has his S,

> 'Nothing can become a brand if a product is not so great.'
> **PIYUSH PANDEY**

and as he flies over India, darkened cities and villages light up, roads are paved, dried-up dams start flowing with water, and our Superhero defeats bad-guy terrorists whose bullets and weapons just bounce off his honed chest and six-pack. 'The opposition had been banking on painting Modi's personality as dictatorial. It backfired, and in fact, Modi's strong and no-nonsense image became a rallying call, especially for BJP's target youth and women voters,' says Manoj Ladwa.

If it all sounds a little cultish, then that is merely another sign that his OST were effective. Modi masks, Modi mobile phones, Modi video games, Modi kurtas, Modi saris – if you could put a face on it, Modi's face was there. All of this contributed to the sense that he really was the only show in town. And now in power, the legend grows to the next stage, with a Bollywood biopic on the way from actor Paresh Rawal, who contested the elections for the BJP in Ahmedabad East.

All these activities – planned and unplanned – were the product of strategy. Modi prepared the ground for his candidature carefully. He built the inner team painstakingly, and showed steel in doing so. The messages were honed and refined. The attention to detail was clear. The planning was meticulous.

'Modi thrives on the big canvas,' says Manoj Ladwa, 'but the detail, every bit of it, matters. He spends a lot of time thinking things through, often in solitude, and garnering ideas and suggestions from multiple sources. He patiently listens to presentations and will ask both pointed and open questions. He is always fully engaged. These are qualities I have not seen with such intensity in any other political or indeed business leader.'

When the elections were announced, voters were blitzed with print, television and radio advertising that emphasised the themes Modi had been promoting for some time. He recorded messages which were sent to over 100 million phones, another innovation for India. His Twitter following rose past 5 million. He had 10 million 'likes' on Facebook. This was a highly organised and well-prepared multi-media campaign. When finally he won, his tweet that 'India has won, good days are ahead', was the most retweeted in Indian history, just as Obama's 'four more years' picture of himself and his wife had been the most retweeted American tweet. India may not be as developed as the Western democracies when it comes to social media and campaign techniques, but Modi's team took existing communications and campaigning models and adapted them to deliver a truly groundbreaking campaign which any American or European leader would be wise to study in detail, in terms of the reach he managed to extend to in such a massive country. Indeed, Arvind Gupta, who headed the BJP information and technology team, says without any hesitation that they did 'better than Obama'. 'Mr Modi has always been fascinated by technology and deploying it for governance and political purposes. This is a trait he has demonstrated in Gujarat as well. He pushed the technology drive in this campaign by setting the big-picture goals, but leaving the execution to domain specialists.' Modi's 'social

media evangelism', he says, 'was the key to the ground-up movement of support'.

He goes on: 'The use of analytics in this election was much
more complex but as targeted and refined as that by the Obama
campaign in 2008. At the moment, no other party in India has
woken up to analytics in the manner Mr Modi and the BJP have.
Politicians study group psychology and mass communication. They
strive to reach large numbers together. Yet, social media, email and
the smartphone are promoting individuals, empowering individuals
and equipping direct communication with individuals. We combined
analytics with mobile technology for personal communication and
message to the highest number of voters ever in Indian election
history.'

In one analysis of the election I read, I saw this interesting
observation from Prathap Suthan, managing partner of the Indian
creative and ad agency Bang in the Middle.

> It is not uncommon in the world of marketing for a brand
> to become not only bigger than its creator but also to
> revitalise and rejuvenate it back. What iMac and iPod did
> to Apple Inc. is what Narendra Modi has done to the BJP.
> Prior to Modi, the BJP brand was on the brink of irrelevance
> for what it stood for. Its Hindutva identity resonated deeply
> with the partition generation but its effect had weakened
> for the successive generations.

Modi turned that around. Of those 120 million first-time voters, the
BJP secured 39 per cent support, Congress 19 per cent. A rout.

In addition to the hologram 3D technology adding reach, the
rallies themselves were better than anything India had seen before:
LED screens to give everyone a clear view of Modi, speakers at key
vantage points to ensure good reaction from the crowd, live feeds
for TV, live streaming on the Web. An *Indian Express* reporter wrote:
'Narendra Modi rallies have become fully-fledged stage productions
involving light, sound, carefully chosen music, stage design and sky

cameras – all intended to enhance viewer experience and build the Modi brand.'

He not only set the agenda, he became the agenda. He turned the election into a referendum on him. This in turn fitted into an unstated but clear message in those areas where MPs or candidates were not popular. You are not voting for them, you are voting for me. They did.

Ashok Malik says: 'In adapting to the new trends as he did, he became an all-India political leader in a very innovative manner – without a famous surname, without the advantage of having been a "national" or Delhi-based political figure for years, without a legacy to back him. He created a model for a bottom-up, rather than top-down, national leader. This meant voters identified with him, rather than with his party's local candidate. In that sense it was a very personality-driven appeal and a very personal mandate.'

His opponents played to his strengths. He was not afraid to attack; and he was not afraid of being attacked, because it allowed him to control the terms of debate. With outgoing Prime Minister Manmohan Singh clear that he wouldn't be staying, the Congress Party made an error in announcing that though Rahul Gandhi would lead the campaign, they would fight it without saying who would be prime minister if they won. This too played to Modi's hands, making him the only person that voters knew for sure was standing to be PM, a tactical error by Congress, making the election all about him.

The crowds he generated reflected the personal appeal to the masses. But he had most of the big business leaders, including steel giant Ratan Tata, Gautam Adani and the billionaire brothers Mukesh and Anil Ambani, and tacitly the overwhelming majority of Indian business lined up in support, adding credibility to his economic message.

As for the fears that the deaths in the 2002 riots would lead to him being portrayed as authoritarian and megalomaniac, he and his advisers did something else that would be difficult in the US or the UK: they largely avoided the subject. They said there was nothing more to say, so they said nothing.

His transformation from a regional, ideological and thus controversial politician to leader of the world's largest democracy, courtesy
of this extraordinary campaign mixing old and new, was truly extraordinary. From overall strategy to media and comms, from organisation to fund-raising, Modi built the teams that enabled him to meet
the 272-plus seat objective with a fair bit to spare. The scale of his
victory is the reason why strategists from parties around the world
are flocking to India to ask and find answers to the question: 'How?'
The answer, again looking through the OST prism, lies in a very
clear strategy and superb execution through tactics; but it was also
another triumph for boldness of ambition, brilliance in innovation,
and in the gathering and use of data.

PART 4

CHANGING SETBACKS INTO ADVANTAGES

15

CRISIS MANAGEMENT

'If leaders do not stay focused on the big picture, stay focused on the strategy, everyone else wanders off pretty quickly.'

BILL CLINTON

CRISIS? WHAT CRISIS?

Judging by the newspapers of the time, New Labour spent its entire existence lurching from one crisis to another. Tony Blair had a 'worst week yet' (according to the cuttings from Sunday newspapers I used to file in my top drawer for my own amusement) on average every four weeks in the first term, three weeks in the second term, and two weeks in the third. In our first year in office, the words 'government' and 'crisis' turned up in headlines 202 times; in year two the figure was 376; by year four it had climbed to 418. 'Blair' and 'crisis' were far more common. For a while, I collected crisis headlines, and here is a selection from one month: A&E crisis, airline industry crisis, air traffic control crisis, army crisis, ash cloud crisis, asylum crisis. That's just the 'A's. At the other end of the alphabet we had a teacher shortage crisis, tourism crisis, university crisis, waste crisis, youth hostel crisis, youth jail crisis and a Welsh musicians crisis. Apparently there was a Viagra crisis too.

Here is the thing, though: few if any of these were genuine crises. They were problems. Of course, because most took place in the political sphere and so in the full glare of media and public scrutiny, they may sometimes have seemed like crises, just as the difficulties that any organisation encounters may feel to those on the inside like total disasters at the time. But a distinction needs to be made. These days I'm often called in to help with corporate crisis management, and more often than not, the conclusion I reach is that what I've been asked to advise on is not a crisis at all. Crises are relatively rare in sport too, whatever people say to the contrary. If a top team loses three matches in a row, the media will label it a crisis. It is not. It might be a difficult period. It might be the point at which the board decides they need a change of manager, in which case it becomes a personal crisis for the manager and his family perhaps, but it is not a crisis for the club, which has the opportunity of a fresh start with a new leader.

So what does a real crisis look like? Well, I could choose from one of the five (yes, only five) full-blown, 24-carat, no-doubt-about-it crises in which I was involved in Downing Street: 9/11 and the subsequent war in Afghanistan, Iraq at several points, the Kosovo intervention, the fuel protests of 2000 and the foot-and-mouth epidemic of 2001. But instead I want to look first at an event that on the surface, far from being an earth-shattering problem affecting the lives of millions, was a little local personal difficulty.

If you say 'Bill Clinton' and 'crisis' in the same breath, for most an image of a dark-haired intern called 'Monica' flits across the mind. It always will, to his death and beyond, and he knows that. What started out as a sexual transgression, though, quickly mushroomed. He had form in this area, and his enemies smelled blood. The Republicans saw the chance to see off a formidable opponent. The politically motivated prosecuting counsel Kenneth Starr perhaps sensed his place in history, and had virtually limitless funds and investigative powers to go after the leader routinely described as the most powerful man in the world and yet who, as he admitted to me when I talked to him about it several years later at the Ritz Hotel in London, felt anything but. 'I was the president of the United States, and I was sleeping on the couch.'

This gets to the heart of what a crisis is: it's not something that has simply gone wrong – after all, things go wrong all the time and are usually fairly easily corrected; it's an event or situation which threatens to overwhelm you if the wrong decisions are taken to deal with it. The Lewinsky scandal certainly met that definition. For some it may have appeared a purely personal matter to be settled between Bill and Hillary, but the fact is that Clinton could quite easily have been driven from office, his reputation shredded for all time, and with the country plunged into political crisis to boot. What is more, even if he had made all the right decisions – which he didn't, not least when he lied in a TV address, claiming 'I did not have sexual relations with that woman, Miss Lewinsky' – he might still have been driven out.

Similarly, for New Labour, while the foot-and-mouth outbreak of 2001 and the fuel protests may not have been crises on a global scale, they were crises nonetheless, not least because in the early days both gave off signals that the government had lost control and had no answers. Even for non-control freaks, that is quite scary. For control freaks, it is a nightmare. I vividly recall the day, at the height of the fuel protests, when the prime minister had to leave Hull several hours ahead of schedule because the police advised us that protesting hauliers were encircling the city and there was no guarantee that the roads could be kept open. In my diary for 12 September I recorded just what all this could mean.

> By the time I got back to the office the full horror of the situation was mounting. We weren't far off a crisis in the basic infrastructure of the nation. Fuel shortages leading to food shortages and an inability to run public services. There was some movement of tankers but not enough to change things. We were now looking to step up military options as well as putting pressure on the oil companies. I left for home just after midnight. TB's last words that it would get a lot worse before it got better.

Food shortages! Public services closing down! Needing the military to keep the country moving! Now you really are talking crisis.

Obviously, no two crises are identical, but they tend to have certain underlying features in common. The same goes for strategies to cope with them.

Crisis *objective*: bring the crisis to an end (emerging stronger is a bonus).

Crisis *strategy*: depends on the crisis.

Crisis *tactics*: depends on the strategy.

CRISIS STEP 1: STAY FOCUSED OR ELSE LOSE THE PLOT

If the Lewinsky scandal reveals the nature of a crisis, Clinton's overall handling of it has elements of a masterclass. One particular day comes to mind: 6 October 1998, the day the Starr Report was published. One can only imagine what Clinton must have been going through during the preceding twenty-four hours. He had little idea what Starr was going to say or do. Every news organisation in the world was waiting to gorge on his sex life. His wife was still angry with him, as I had witnessed at the White House, when she would paint on the First Lady smile in public, only to erase it pretty quickly when the crowds and the cameras went away.

But as he was waiting for the Starr report to land, the president was on the phone to Tony Blair (I was one of a small number of UK officials listening in), and he was totally focused, not on Starr, but on Russia, and some difficult issues concerning the decommissioning of nuclear weapons. He barely mentioned his problems, other than when Tony said 'Good luck today' at the end of the call, and Clinton said 'Yeah, we'll see'.

Later I asked him how he was able to block out what was happening to him that day, and how he had managed to get through the whole sorry episode. 'I had a very simple objective – survival,' he replied. 'My strategy was to get on with the job, focus on those things that only I could do, because I was the president. And my tactics were to make sure the American people knew that's what I was doing. They sustained me throughout.'

When his autobiography was published, I interviewed him for UK television, and the same focused message came through – however bad things were, he had stuck to the OST rule that is at the core of a winner's make-up. 'I was still president. The people gave me that job. I swore an oath to do it, and frankly I preferred to think about that, because that was something I could have an impact on. There was absolutely nothing I could do about what Kenneth Starr did and about what the press said about it. There was nothing I could do about that but I could do my job every day, and so I got up and concentrated on the things that I could impact instead of being consumed by things I had no impact on.'

'How lonely did it feel?'

'Oh, sometimes it was lonely but, you know, I was lucky, my family and my friends, my staff, my cabinet, they all stayed. Nobody bolted. Most of the Democrats, almost to 100 per cent of them in Congress, stayed, and they stayed in the face of this unrelenting kind of self-flagellating press coverage, you know. They just never quit. Until we won the '98 election and Kenneth Starr came out with his report and it was obvious that Congress was going to go forward with the impeachment anyway for purely ideological and spite-filled reasons. Then the press finally began to change and shifted back to a more balanced point of view, but we had a couple of years there where it was just horrible. And I just got up and went to work every day. I kept saying, I have two choices here: I can be all upset about this and focus on those things that I can't have any impact on; or I can wake up every day and realise this is a tiny part of life, I can be grateful for my blessings, grateful that I have a chance to do this job and focus on things that I can have an impact on.'

Clinton's ability to concentrate on what really mattered helped him keep some sort of perspective on the Lewinsky affair. He knew he'd done wrong. He also knew, though, that the campaign against him was overdone, and he trusted the public to see that too. 'The fact that there was so much politics involved made it a lot easier for me to fight, so I just got up every day and fought it.' That in turn ensured that his approach was thought through, not panicked. 'I realised that if I spent all my time answering questions about Kenneth Starr, my personal life or whatever charge anyone wanted to ask, then that's immediately what the media would show on television at night and then the voters would believe that's all I was doing, even if I spent ten minutes a day on it. So I just didn't talk about it. I allowed myself to be publicly defended by other people and I only spoke to the media and therefore to the American people about my job, and they could make up their minds about all the charges that were flying back and forth, but – I wanted them to see that no matter what happened I was doing my job . . .'

> 'I had a very simple objective – survival.'
>
> **BILL CLINTON**

Clarity of focus on OST, then, is the first rule of crisis management, and yet frequently it's the first victim. In those moments of panic that come as a problem unfolds, the natural inclination is to charge off in all directions in a desperate attempt to fix things. It's all too easy to forget that you have to decide exactly what it is that you want to achieve before you try to fix it. In government we used to devise slogans – essential both for internal and external consumption – which we endlessly repeated to hammer home what our OST was. During the foot-and-mouth crisis, for example, after some early fumbling it became 'We will do what it takes to knock out the disease, then rebuild the countryside'. That may sound obvious, but given the furore that was going on, it would have been very easy to have mixed the two objectives together and achieved neither. For Kosovo, it was 'Our troops in, his troops out, refugees go home'. When it came to the fuel protests, our internal message was a stark one: 'End the protests because government cannot be held to ransom.' This very effectively concentrated people's minds.

Such focus also helped block out the white noise around us. In any crisis there will be many on the outside – the media, in particular – more than ready to offer their views and unsolicited advice. But these cannot be allowed to hold sway. As Bill Clinton puts it: 'All of us in public life are too willing to let momentary press coverage define our reality'; and once this powerful outside voice gets in, 'it becomes everything in our lives'. He goes on: 'You have to give someone permission to destroy your positive outlook on life, to destroy your determination to be a better person today than you were yesterday, to destroy your determination to use a job in public life to make life for the public better, and I just decided not to give them that permission.'

Arsène Wenger feels the same way. When disaster strikes, he argues, ignore the hysteria and focus on what matters. After all, what can you say when your team has lost 8–2 against your fiercest rivals, Manchester United, as Arsenal did in August 2011? The answer: in the immediate aftermath, not a lot. Let the headlines scream crisis for a day or two, let the players feel the pain, then regroup. 'We were titanically bad,' he admits, 'but we managed to get the boat over the iceberg. We come back to values and ideas, because nobody can predict a football game . . . When I go through a difficult period, I think "How can I improve the results?" but my checklist is more "Am I in line with what I think is important in my job?" That's why I think it's important to not just think about winning the games but also think about what is important to me in this job, in the way I see the game. Because when you go through crisis periods, that is what will help you survive.'

In handling that particular horrific defeat, he consciously took a long-term view. He didn't panic or turn on the team. 'Anything you say in that moment could be even more detrimental.' He spoke individually to people, gave them two days off, and then started afresh on Monday. 'The drama is strong enough at the weekend that you don't have to add any more to it, you don't need to say they were absolutely disastrous, they know it. And I believe as well that the big results don't have that much significance in the long term. They have an emotional significance, but not great footballing significance . . . I know that this team is not as bad as the result was.'

Arsenal won eight of their next nine matches.

Remembering the underlying strength of the team brings to mind a political equivalent of an 8–2 defeat which we suffered on 16 May 2001, the day we launched our election manifesto for a second term. First Tony Blair gets harangued by a member of the public outside a hospital, to the delight of the media. Then Home Secretary Jack Straw is slow-handclapped by the Police Federation, so the chances of any coverage for the manifesto are fast disappearing. And when Deputy Prime Minister John Prescott punches a voter in the face, those chances are gone. All in the same day, perhaps the most important day of the campaign apart from election day itself.

I told Tony about the Prescott punch as we got into the car after a TV recording. He did his Bambi look, a 'what the fuck?' expression that somehow combines anger, panic and disbelief. But Terry Rayner, the driver, and the Special Branch protection officer sitting alongside him in the front passenger seat both laughed heartily on hearing my description, their reaction very different to Tony's. That gave us a strong indication as to where real public opinion, as opposed to media frenzy opinion, would be on this, and we ended up laughing too.

> 'All of us in public life are too willing to let momentary press coverage define our reality.'
>
> **BILL CLINTON**

By the morning, the media were in full cry, the broadcasters were playing the punch on a continuous loop, and the airwaves were filling with voices saying John had to go. We sat around for half an hour at campaign HQ in Millbank, agonising over how exactly Tony should handle questions on John at the morning press conference. We had agreed he wasn't going to sack him, so the question was what convoluted form of words to use to explain why not. But when it came to it, two little words popped out of Tony's mouth, instinctively, and the words, and the manner in which he said them – a slight shrug and the hint of a smile – defused the situation brilliantly. 'John's John.' It didn't stop the frenzy in the media, but it somehow settled the issue with the public, as was clear when Philip Gould called in with focus group reports later. What's more, it clarified things: what we were experiencing was a frenzy, not a crisis, and it remained nothing more than a frenzy because we didn't let the media define our reality. Our 8–2 defeat became a setback. Of course, had we overreacted it would have become a crisis: losing your deputy prime minister and one of your best campaigners at the start of an election campaign, forcing a Cabinet reshuffle and a change of your campaign plans – that sounds closer to a crisis to me.

CRISIS STEP 2: BE HONEST WITH YOURSELF

When things go wrong, the natural human tendency is to hope, firstly that it's not your fault and secondly that it will all simply go away if you shut your eyes for long enough. Both hopes are wrong, and they cause untold damage. Take the Murdoch empire during its crisis over phone hacking. At the individual level, much pointless energy was spent trying to avoid blame. At the corporate level, similar quantities of pointless energy went into creating a 'heads down' mentality which hoped that the crisis would work itself out. As a result, News International never took the initiative until it was too late. Had senior executives accepted that there was a problem they had to deal with, they could have launched their own investigations, instead of putting their heads in the sand and thinking they could bully and bluster their way through it. As a result, it was left for others to set up inquiries, and the Murdoch empire was thereby placed in a position in which it was impossible ever to recover the initiative. The reputational damage has been enormous.

It's worth contrasting this approach with another media scandal: that concerning Jayson Blair who resigned from the *New York Times* in 2003 when it emerged that he had made up and plagiarised some of his news stories. Once alerted, those at the top took charge, investigated thoroughly and even opted to cover the affair as the big story it undoubtedly was. They knew they had a problem, and they admitted it themselves. There's no doubt that in the longer term it did their credibility a lot of good.

Or compare the action taken by General Motors when thirteen deaths were linked to a faulty ignition switch in one of their cars and that taken by Malaysian Airline's flight MH370 which went missing somewhere between Kuala Lumpur and Beijing in March 2014. The former problem was very much the fault of General Motors, but while they did a lot wrong in the lead-up to the crisis, when it broke they were honest with themselves and realised that they needed to recall 2.3 million cars. The latter disaster does not appear to have been irrefutably Malaysian Airline's fault, yet their hesitancy in grasping the reality of what was going on ensured they took the blame. Fair? Unfair? Irrelevant – handle it badly and you will get hammered. Handle it well, and perhaps you won't get hammered as much as you deserve to.

One of the reasons I admire Charles Dunstone is that on the one occasion when things went seriously wrong for him, he was honest about the problem and his company's shortcomings. TalkTalk had launched their broadband service, and had been overwhelmed by demand. 'It was meltdown,' he recalls. 'We were so naive, so overoptimistic. We just had no idea how big it would go and we couldn't cope. We had people going into stores because they couldn't get through to the call centres, but the people in the stores couldn't get through to the call centres either. So many people wanted to join that we looked like absolute idiots. That was the downside of my excessive optimism. It felt terrible, really terrible, the most miserable time of my life without a doubt. But we kept plugging away and I remember telling the board, "Right, things are improving, we are now only as bad as everyone else. We've caught up with the mediocrity everyone else offers up." We really had been useless. Our HR guy said it was like eleven-year-olds playing football; everyone just ran around where the ball was. I like to think we're a bit more grown-up now.' That admission – 'We really had been useless' – is both refreshing and rare.

CRISIS STEP 3: BE HONEST WITH OTHERS

I've said how well Bill Clinton handled the Monica Lewinsky crisis, but he did, of course, make one monumental blunder. For perhaps understandable human reasons to do with saving his marriage as well as his career, he lied about the affair, which caused him enormous subsequent problems. He admitted that waking up Hillary, on the sleepless night when he finally decided to tell her the truth, was one of the worst moments of his life. Yet it was also in a way the turning point. He told me that once he knew she knew the truth, and decided she was not going to dump him, he felt he was able to begin fighting the allegations on his own terms, as the formidable campaigner and communicator he is.

The hope that things won't emerge into the cold light of public scrutiny is an understandable one, but almost invariably everything ultimately gets out. New Labour experienced the truth of this very early in our time in office over our handling of what almost became a full-blown crisis: the controversy over a £1 million donation to the Labour Party by Formula One chief Bernie Ecclestone. Defending massive donations is never easy. This one was particularly difficult because it came at a time when we were changing policy on tobacco companies' sponsorship of sport and it looked as though Formula One might be getting special treatment. The reality was not as simple as that, but the perception was a potential disaster area and my advice had been that the only way to deal with it was to get everything out in the public domain before it was dragged out of us. Tony initially agreed, and while he chaired an Anglo-French summit with President Jacques Chirac at Canary Wharf, I slipped out to dictate a briefing note with all the facts, and a handling plan, the secretary whistling through her teeth when the 'million' word passed my lips. Tony then had his mind changed by others, including Gordon, who was also at the summit meeting. And from that moment facts were gouged out like bad teeth, slowly and painfully. We only brought the frenzy to a close after two weeks of dreadful media coverage and political attack by putting Tony up for a difficult interview, to take the heat and use up political capital which would have been better used elsewhere, and could have been, had we got onto the front foot earlier.

By contrast, although we mishandled the early days of the foot-and-mouth crisis, we did manage gradually to get our act together. At the time, the media reported that the public had no confidence in the government's handling. But post-crisis polling suggested this was not the case and that farmers were among those who had actually felt the government did OK in difficult circumstances. A key moment in winning over the farmers came when we decided to be much more open, using, for example, the government chief scientist to set the context for the public. Of course, we should have done this earlier. During the fuel protests, part of the process of bringing things under control was a daily appearance by the prime minister simply to say what the situation was, and what we were doing about it. The feedback we got was that these were the most important parts of our strategy and that for all the public cynicism about politics, people do listen to political leaders at times of crisis.

It's worth bearing in mind one further complication when seeking to disseminate the truth: most people dread a problem, but there will always be some who revel in it. From his considerable experience of crisis, airline boss Willie Walsh made an interesting observation to me that chimes with my own experience. 'Crisis is horrible, you're caught up in it day and night, but sometimes people enjoy that. And there is a danger then that people create crises, possibly even subconsciously, because they want to have a crisis to deal with.' This creates a dangerous environment, one in which reality becomes smoke and mirrors, and it makes it even more important to establish the truth and ensure it is broadcast and understood.

CRISIS STEP 4: ORGANISE AND CHANGE QUICKLY

Because the way a crisis plays out is so unpredictable, you cannot assume that what you already have in place will deal with it. The

NATO campaign against Serb leader Slobodan Milošević over his ethnic cleansing of Kosovar Albanians is a case in point. There was no doubt who was militarily superior, or who had the expertise to ensure regular briefings to the media: thanks to its role in helping to keep peace throughout Europe following the Second World War, NATO had what communications strategists call 'an A-grade brand'. But what it had not fully bargained for was a dictator who played the media game according to very different rules in a very different age. NATO was a collection of democracies whose leaders had to explain and often justify, via the indefatigable spokesman Jamie Shea, the decisions they were making – in some countries in the face of deep unpopularity. Milošević's Lie Machine, by contrast, could pump out whatever it wanted, true or false. When the Milošević news agency, Tanjug, made a claim which turned out to be false – 'NATO has dropped napalm on a primary school' for example – it just moved on to the next one. When NATO made mistakes, as sadly happens in all conflicts, it was held – understandably – to far higher standards. In other words, there was no equivalence in the way Milošević's and NATO's conduct was reported.

The turning point, which led to Clinton demanding a shake-up of NATO comms, and me being seconded to Brussels to oversee it, came when a NATO plane bombed what the pilot believed to be Serb troops but was in fact a convoy of refugees. This was a terrible, tragic blunder. What it also confirmed was that the status quo could not be sustained. As criticisms rained down and the media storm grew, various parts of the US administration and various countries within NATO all started saying totally different things about what had happened, and who was to blame. It was a classic case of teamship breaking down when times get tough. The reality was, of course, grim, but in political terms we somehow conspired to make it ten times worse.

That convoy tragedy dominated the media around the world for a fortnight, a long time in media terms. It was only really brought under control when we got the man who had led the mission, a central casting square-jawed airman in bomber jacket named Dan

Leaf, to come to Brussels and do a second-by-second explanation to the world's press of what went wrong. Then, with the backing of Clinton, Blair, NATO General Secretary Javier Solana and – crucially – military commander General Wesley Clark, we put in place new centralising structures of coordination, planning and rebuttal, largely based on what we had developed in Number Ten. We set up a new twenty-four-hour media operations room with instant access to all capitals. Speeches, press conferences and interviews with the main leaders were organised so that they were not happening at the same time, but they were all pushing the same messages. We had twice-daily conference calls between NATO, the US, UK, France, Germany and Italy, with lines out to all other NATO capitals. Moreover, because we now had round-the-clock liaison with the military, they were able to focus on their own prime function – winning the war – rather than having to divert time and energy to dealing with the politics and managing the media.

The foot-and-mouth epidemic called for even more drastic reorganisation of existing bodies. At the outset, we were too influenced by the Ministry of Agriculture's claim that they could deal with it, and that their authority would be diminished if the centre took over. In fact, we should have listened to Canada's wily prime minister, Jean Chrétien – we were with him in Ottawa as news of the first case of FMD came through – when he urged Tony to get right on top of it, because it was 'one of those issues that can really do you damage'. It really did.

Again, centralisation proved to be the answer, just as it was later with the fuel crisis. This time we experienced one of those classic problems where the various people involved claimed it wasn't their responsibility. The Treasury insisted it was not a taxation issue, but a security one. The Home Office said no, this was a transport problem. The Transport Department said it was all about tax. Round and round we went. Meanwhile, the oil companies, so used to competing with each other that they seemed incapable of cooperation, kept their heads down, knowing the government would take most of the heat. It was only when everything was brought together into one command structure that the tide started to turn. That single command structure also meant that everyone gave consistent messages. There's nothing worse in a crisis than different people pitching in with different accounts and excuses – such uncoordinated responses undermine both effectiveness and trust.

CRISIS STEP 5: GIVE A CRISIS A HUMAN FACE

When people are panicking and scurrying for cover, the hardest thing is to find people prepared to stick their head above the parapet. Yet so often merely the act of doing this can help calm things down and ensure that they are properly managed. For those at the eye of the storm, there is now a leader, someone they can turn to and, equally importantly, someone who will keep them in the loop rather than leaving them to rely on gossip or outside information – even a daily staff email is better than assuming they know what's going on. For those on the outside, the spokesperson is physical evidence that the problem is being taken seriously and will be dealt with.

Big organisations, it has to be said, are not good at this. BP's handling of the Deepwater Horizon oil spill, for instance, was almost a textbook example of how not to handle a crisis. Leaving aside the question in my own mind of whether this huge oil corporation had ever done any meaningful crisis scenario planning at all (an oil spill at sea, I would have thought, might have been on its list of 'foresee-able unforseeables'), when the crisis actually occurred the company gave the impression of lurching from one misspeak and misstep to the next. John Browne, whose successor Tony Hayward was in the hot seat when the spill happened, is characteristically polite, but his assessment is also pretty clear. 'You got the sense the lawyers took over and got in the way. When a crisis happens there is a tendency to go to corporate-speak when actually what is needed is the human face. Crisis is the time for more humanity not less.' He faced a similar experience himself in 2005 when the Texas City refinery exploded, killing fifteen and injuring 170. 'How to balance big advice with human activity is really difficult. People have died, but lawyers are saying "if you say that, boss, they'll come after you, so best not to comment". Having a human face without the lawyers running the company is very important in these tragic situations.'

In the case of Deepwater Horizon disaster, it's questionable whether BP chose the right man to be their spokesman. In government, of course, the buck invariably stops with the PM or president, but in other walks of life it doesn't necessarily have to be the top man who fronts things up. Tony Hayward is a very clever man and in many ways was a good CEO. However, he is not a communicator, and his very British wit and manner did not play well with an angry American audience. Somebody should have suggested – before the disaster – that in the event of a crisis, it might be worth having someone other than him as spokesman. It just wasn't his strength. Every comment – one or two of them, unfortunately, rather unguarded – was pounced upon and torn to pieces. By the time he was in front of hearings in Congress, it was like a blood sport.

A good communicator will be on tap twenty-four hours a day, sending out fast and overwhelming responses. If a false perception arises, they will rebut it with speed and aggression. Remember the old saying about a lie being halfway round the world before the truth has got its boots on? Rebuttal is not just about refuting false claims. It is about establishing the factual base for an argument. So you decide the key facts you want communicated, or the key messages, and make sure they are put over. If you allow repeated falsehoods to take hold, they become political truths. Silence becomes an admission of guilt. Defensiveness gets punished.

And yes, actions speak louder than words. When volcanic ash from Iceland led to great swathes of European airspace being closed down in 2010, Willie Walsh of British Airways, having decided that government caution had become overreaction, opted – bold this – to defy them by taking a 747 carrying just him, two pilots and an engineer out over the Irish Sea to do tests and show that it was safe to fly. He had been involved in difficult and often bitter meetings and calls with government ministers and officials, and he decided to follow his impulse. 'On day one I understood why they did what they did. On day two I didn't, and I felt we had to do something to show up the lack of any actual clear reasoning behind a decision that threatened to cripple the industry. So on day four we took off. We had to do something to show this was nonsense, that the government had closed airspace without any clear criteria to decide how to open it again, and I felt we had to challenge them. So we did. I thought it wasn't enough just to send experts. There had to be visible, physical signs of leadership.' The extent of the boldness was underlined by a comical moment when the pilot asked air traffic control for permission to change direction. 'Standby, I'll check,' came the reply. When reminded this was the only plane in the air, he said, 'Oh yeah, I forgot, go where you want.' The next step was to order twenty-eight flights in from various parts of the world, despite being told by government this was 'illegal'. By the time they got to Heathrow, the airport was open for business again. Crisis over.

CRISIS STEP 6: COVER ALL THE BASES

This is perhaps the toughest challenge. Crises have a way of lurching in unexpected directions. You think you're dealing with the core problem, only to find some other problem looming. In reality, it's likely to be a logical extension of the central crisis, but at the time it may not feel like that, and it's another reason why people so often panic rather than focus when firefighting.

During the fuel protests, for example, we started off thinking we had a problem with particular hauliers. But then newspapers started to predict panic-buying of fuel, and in so doing immediately created a self-fulfilling prophecy: the haulage problem spread to the entire population. And now broadcasters who could have used their bulletins to set out how much fuel was left in stock instead chose to interview panic-buyers, so pushing more panic-buyers to join the queues, driving stocks ever lower. The crisis only came to an end when Health Secretary Alan Milburn warned us that we were two days away from being unable to deliver basic health care. We mobilised nurses, doctors and others around that message and the mood started to turn against the protesters.

With the foot-and-mouth outbreak, we thought we were dealing with an entirely domestic issue. But then we started to get the message that the endlessly repeated shots on American TV of burning pyres under the headline 'BRITAIN ON FIRE' were creating a tourism issue too as people and businesses cancelled flights. So focused had we been on the crisis in hand, we failed to foresee this related secondary crisis coming along. Rather belatedly we put together a communications strategy aimed at reassuring our main tourist markets that it was safe to visit Britain. The damage, however, had been done.

We did show a strong ability to think laterally after the 9/11 terrorist attacks, though. It's worth recalling the pandemonium and uncertainty of that day. Nobody could be sure initially what was happening. Was the attack on the first of the Twin Towers a freak accident? Did the attack on the second tower mean that this was a US crisis or was an attack somewhere else imminent? World leaders found themselves operating in the same time frame and with the same basic information as anyone watching the TV news channels. Nobody saw it coming, at least not that day, and not in that way. At a very parochial level, the first decision we had to take as the Twin Towers fell from the New York skyline was whether Tony should go ahead with his planned speech to the Trades Union Congress in Brighton. After one tower fell, we decided he would. After the second fell, we decided he wouldn't. Instead we headed back to London for a series of meetings in COBRA, which sounds like the villain's lair in a James Bond movie, but is, rather prosaically, Cabinet Office Briefing Room A. Ministers, police, intelligence services and transport chiefs gathered to make an assessment of what needed to be done. A lot.

Even before those meetings, on the train back from Brighton, I made a list based on notes Tony had scribbled on a lined A4 pad, and the discussions we had, going through all the issues he wanted to address when we got back to Downing Street. This was it.

- Meetings needed today.
- Security briefing (foreign and domestic).
- Implications for UK airspace. Do we shut down? Restrictions?
- Policing on streets.
- Key buildings. Liaise with big firms and economic institutions. Stock Exchange. Bank of England. Canary Wharf.
- Security at Jewish sites.
- British victims. Minister in charge.
- Parliament – do we recall? Statement or debate?
- TV and press, key messages and format. Press conference when?
- Link to rogue states/WMD.
- Palestine/Middle East peace process.
- Own diary in next few days. Travel? Where?
- When speak to Bush? Which others first?
- EU response. UN response/special meeting? International agenda to fill vacuum. G8.
- US feeling beleaguered – need to help and support.
- Will US lash out? And where? Probably Afghanistan. What will happen re Libya? Iran? Iraq?
- Prepare a paper as if we were US? What will Bush be getting advice on? Need to get inside Bush mind.
- Putin re Chechnya, saying 'told you so'.
- Oil supplies.
- Where are troops that may become relevant? MoD.
- Reassure British Muslims. Outreach. Minister in charge.
- Analysis of Islamic fundamentalism.
- Intelligence re perpetrators – almost certainly al-Qaeda.
- Bind in Musharraf.
- Taliban analysis.

In retrospect, I think this is a pretty thorough summary of the problems and challenges we were to face in the aftermath.

Operating in a very different sphere, Willie Walsh, then with Irish carrier Aer Lingus, similarly had to deal with a whole set of challenges. 'First,' he recalls, 'it was about finding out if the airline had any people killed or injured. Then we had to check where all our flights were as US airspace was closed. One had just taken off from Dublin, so we could call it back, two had gone too far, and we were having to find places to land in Canada, but of course so was everyone else, the airports were filling up, and you're worrying about whether they have enough fuel to get to where they need to, and can they land when they do, it was terrible, the whole thing. You're sitting in the crisis centre and you get the call saying one of them is running out of fuel, then the sense of relief when it lands. Then the next stage it becomes a financial crisis. At the time 50 per cent of our revenues came from transatlantic business, and that virtually disappeared. There was a real risk we could go out of business.' If ever there was an embodiment of a crisis – an event or situation which threatens to overwhelm you or your organisation unless the right decisions are taken – it was 9/11.

Of course, really great organisations and leaders have this uncanny ability to plan for the unexpected. For every BP that appears not to have anticipated a likely scenario, there are examples of people and companies which have. Here again, a healthy dose of paranoia can come in handy to make them alive to potential missteps, think ahead, or see how some incident they've seen reported somewhere could so easily have happened to them. The obsessive Clive Woodward is a case in point. When he was overseeing travel arrangements for the 2003 Rugby World Cup, he made sure that the players and staff were well looked after and then made an allocation for a lawyer, the QC Richard Smith. Why? Well, it's Woodward's natural tendency to plan for the worst, but he also recalled what had once happened to England football captain Bobby Moore: he had been arrested on suspicion of shoplifting en route to the Mexico World Cup. 'To be honest,' recalls Woodward, 'I could see us being set up, I could see all sorts of things going wrong, I didn't know what they would be – at the back of my mind I was thinking someone might try and plant drugs on one of the players – but I felt we needed a top lawyer on hand. Richard is a rugby fan, and was really up for it, and I am glad he came. We needed him.' As indeed they did: during one match, England briefly and accidentally had sixteen players on the pitch – obviously a breach of the rules – and disqualification suddenly loomed. Thanks to the advocatory skills of Richard Smith, England got away with a £10,000 fine, and a two-week touchline ban for the fitness coach Dave Reddin. A potential disaster had been averted. 'Everyone came out of that hearing knowing that Richard had been absolutely brilliant,' says Woodward. 'He justified his presence for the whole tournament on that day alone.'

A CRISIS CASE STUDY: MELTDOWN AT HEATHROW

In recent times, whenever I have been asked for examples of good and bad crisis management in the business sector, I give the Deepwater oil spill and News International's handling of phone hacking as bad, Willie Walsh and BA's handling of the fiasco that became the launch of Heathrow airport's Terminal 5 as good. Now, today T5 is seen as a success. But when I actually talk to Willie Walsh I realise I was wrong in thinking that he had been rolling out some carefully prepared crisis-management scenario plan. 'It was kind of making it up as you go along,' the CEO of International Airlines Group, then head of British Airways, tells me. 'We had planned for a few operational problems, but not for everything going wrong at once. We had no plan B, no plan Z, nothing.' To be fair to him, 'making it up as you go along' is at least a leadership/head-above-parapet point, but the journey he took was not as I envisaged.

T5 was all planned as a wonderful breakthrough moment, for the airport, BA and Britain's transport needs. The Queen had done the official opening, and the world's media had been invited to witness the birth of a project which had already won plaudits for its architecture and was now set to become the answer to the problems besetting Heathrow as the world's (then) busiest airport, and show that the UK had not lost the knack of delivering big, complex logistical projects. 'I'm afraid we started to believe our own publicity,' he says. Instead of the plan being seamlessly delivered in front of an excited media pack, they had a live 24/7 disaster area to report upon, and relished the task.

It was sometime between 4 and 5 a.m. on opening day, 27 March 2008, that Walsh sensed things were going wrong, and within another hour, 'totally off the rails'. A workaholic who knew how big a day this was, he had been there from 3 a.m., his main role to see off the first departing passengers, and welcome in the first arrivals, being flown – nice touch – by a female pilot. At first, he noticed a few small things suggesting all was not well – for example staff not being sure where they were meant to be stationed. Some people were also arriving late because there had been problems with car park signage. Then the first IT problem emerged: staff logging into computers in the baggage handling department discovered that the password they had been given did not allow them in. After three failed attempts they were blocked, unable to do their jobs. 'The IT people had misaligned two columns, ID login and password, so nobody could get into the system,' Walsh explains. 'Because it was happening to everyone, we realised something was wrong and they worked it out fairly quickly and we managed to sort that one, but we lost an hour or so, and people were getting a bit nervy.'

The second IT problem was much more serious, and it took several days for it to be established. 'Off the rails' was now becoming 'virtually unmanageable'. 'When we had been testing all the systems, we were trying to do it as though for real, but of course the bags were not actually going anywhere, so the IT guys put what is called a patch in the system, which meant the bags were moved around within the airport, but obviously no messages were sent on to foreign airports, because no bags were actually leaving. And even though we had asked whether this patch had been taken off for when we went live, and we were told yes, in fact it turned out no, it hadn't, but we didn't realise that until the Sunday, four days after the opening. We had all these little problems going on, you expect that at any new terminal or airport, but that was the big one. I'd say 80 per cent of the crisis was caused by these IT problems, particularly the patch. To think something as simple as that could cause such havoc. If it had been the only thing, maybe we would have got there quicker, but combine it with ten, twenty smaller things going wrong and you're in trouble.'

Of course, a crisis throws up difficult choices and one was whether to let the planes depart without bags – they did – and another was whether to tell the passengers before they landed – they didn't. Before long, thousands of bags were heading to the delivery points for the planes, being rejected three times and so ending up in the early bag store. 'It was absolute total chaos. The tag on the bag would be saying "I am going to Miami" but the system would say "no you're not", because this patch was restricting its movement so it didn't actually leave the airport building. Nobody could figure it out. Before long we had seven thousand bags that we knew were not going to arrive with their owners.'

Walsh says he felt 'physically sick' as he grasped the scale of the problem on day one. 'I have never been angrier in my life.' He felt he had been let down by people who had assured him these systems would work. But interestingly, given the mega-high-profile role he would play in subsequent days as the crisis was brought under control, one of his first decisions was to go home. 'I realised I was becoming part of the problem. I was so angry I was worried I was going to start thumping people. So I thought, "Right, I'm doing no good here, I'm making things worse, I'm leaving it to the operational guys." I'm pleased I was able to do that. I think it was the right call.'

> 'If it had been the only thing, maybe we would have got there quicker, but combine it with ten, twenty smaller things going wrong and you're in trouble.'
>
> **WILLIE WALSH**

He was worried that merely by being there he was undermining those whose job it was to deal with the problem. This was similar to how we had reacted when MAFF were worried that a centralising approach to foot and mouth would undermine them. We let it drift for days. Walsh reversed his stay-away decision the next morning, and was clearly now relying on instinct.

'I went home and I just thought, "What do I do?" The team called me and they said they were looking at having to cancel half of all flights tomorrow. I said, "No way, you cannot do that, call me back with a different plan when you've thought about it properly." They called back and said 20 per cent. I pressed them: "Are you sure we need to do that?" and they were and we went with it. Then the next day I went in, I was in by five, and I said to Julia [Simpson, media adviser, formerly a member of AC's Number Ten team] that I was going to go over there and talk to the media. Not surprisingly she asked me what I was going to say. I said, "I don't know but I'll know when I get there, I just know I have to do this." She was advising me to wait till we were clear, but I felt there was a leadership vacuum. Also, people were saying "these guys were all available when things were going well and now they have disappeared off the face of the earth". The media felt they had been sold a pup and they were really going for us. The first interview I did was Tom Symonds of the BBC. His first question was "Whose fault was this?" and I said straight out, instinctively: "Mine, this was my decision to do this, I take responsibility and now I'm taking responsibility for fixing it." And I could tell by the look on his face he was surprised. A couple of the other journalists there started to laugh because they could see he was a bit thrown. I hadn't planned to say it, but it felt the right thing at the time.'

He went out to the BBC radio car to do an interview for the *Today* programme and the sound man who had heard his previous interviews said: 'That was a very brave thing you did there, taking responsibility like that. I don't think I've ever heard a CEO do that.' 'That got me worrying whether I had done the wrong thing,' Walsh recalls. 'But I thought there had to be physical evidence of leadership in a crisis, and as the person at the top of BA, that had to be me. I might well have been leading a disaster, but I had to show that I was visible, taking the flak, and above all saying what we were doing to fix things. In truth the specific things that had gone wrong were not our fault but Heathrow's, and one or two of our people thought I'd made a mistake putting BA out front like that, but I felt I had no choice. Nobody was interested in blame, the public just wanted it fixed. I figured out if I put my hands up it would allow everyone to say "I got this wrong, I got that wrong", so I said internally we will find out whose fault it is after, but for the moment let's say it's my fault and now fix it.'

My memory of Walsh from then on is that he was barely off the TV screens. 'There was hardly any other news anywhere,' he recalls. 'Once I'd decided to front it, I knew I had to do that till the crisis had calmed. The first four days were the worst time of my life, without a doubt. Day five we started to feel we were slowly getting there. By day ten, I felt we were operating as I would have liked to have done on day one. Reputationally it took a lot longer, maybe six, even twelve months before it was no longer the thing most people associated with the Terminal.'

THE CRISIS ARC

The events at Heathrow Terminal 5 offer a cautionary tale, but ultimately an impressive example of good crisis management. And they also display the classic crisis pattern: the crisis itself; the moment of panicked incomprehension; the first attempts to sort things; subsidiary problems feeding in and exacerbating it; the crisis getting worse before it gets better; final resolution, then (sometimes) lessons learned.

When you're in the thick of things, it's hard to recognise the truism that things get worse before they are better as being in any way comforting. But it's an important truth to hold on to because that knowledge should supply an element of consistency to problem-solving. Or, as Jack Welch puts it, 'Try to remember in the heat of it that the flames will die down.' There is a danger in a crisis that people dealing with it imagine this is what their life is going to be like forever. But however bad you think it is at the centre, it is not as bad in the real world. It may end with you losing your job, losing an election, losing battles. But it ends. And with every one survived you learn a little more about the next one. Rereading my diaries about foot and mouth, I can feel even today the various, often horrific, emotions as the crisis arc unfolded. The first case, 22 February, slow to react. Four days later, the first feeling this is a potential crisis. Too slow to centralise. By 1 March, the sense that the ministry is becoming 'overwhelmed'. Prince Charles critical of our handling (we could have done without that). Councils call for a delay to local elections (which meant delaying the planned early-May general election too). 14 March, the first signs of a tourism crisis. 17 March, TB 'panicking'. 18 March, we start to centralise and grip properly. Election delayed. TB begins a series of visits around the country to take the heat. Dither re vaccination. Statistical chaos. Military called in to help get on top of the massive logistical operation of burning thousands of cattle. Then a surreal episode as a campaign begins to save a single calf called Phoenix. Then slowly the sense of crisis subsides. 8 May, we finally launch the campaign for the general election. Eight days later, our 8–2 disaster with the Prescott punch. It is remarkable what can be survived, and there is no doubt that once you have known full-blown crisis, you will learn from the experience for the next one.

GETTING GOOD OUT OF BAD

Since all crises ultimately come to an end, it's essential to have someone working on your return to normal strategy once the crisis is over. This is something New Labour didn't do well. We tended to take the best people and involve them in dealing with the crisis in hand. Indeed, one of the most impressive aspects of Walsh's leadership during and after the Terminal 5 fiasco was that he decided that, if anything, they had lacked ambition in the potential for how good T5 could be. As the crisis unfolded, he realised it should be used as the opportunity to make further improvements beyond merely bringing everything back under control. In the immediate aftermath he made some personnel changes, and two directors left the company ('They were very good people, but I had lost confidence'). He also acted quickly in putting one of his brightest people, Robert Boyle, into post-crisis strategic re-entry, so that he could focus on what BA would do after the crisis rather than be sucked into the day-to-day management of it. 'It upset some people, but I was clear we needed that separation.' BA also changed their advertising campaigns, spending money that would have otherwise gone on their traditional glossy ads to spell out, in real-time adverts at the airport and in the media, how many flights were moving in and out of T5, their punctuality, and crucially how many bags. But more importantly, 'we reset targets out of failure'.

He explains this maximalist approach to crisis management. 'Great things can come if you are prepared to learn from mistakes. People shouldn't worry about making mistakes, so long as it's not the same mistake again and again. I wouldn't will that kind of feeling on anyone, when anything that can go wrong feels like it is going wrong, but I do believe that T5 is a great place now, and in part because we lived through those days. When Denver airport opened they had baggage issues for six months. We had ten days of hell and then we got going properly. Was it as bad as it looked at the time? Definitely. Did we ultimately exceed our own ambitions? I think we did.' His pride is obvious.

It is the same when tragedy and horror strike, and bring with them the potential for crisis. The question is whether you allow it to overwhelm you, or build from the setback. One of the low points of our time in government was the Omagh bombing, deliberately timed and designed not just to kill and maim people, but to kill and maim the whole peace process. We had secured the Good Friday Agreement, new political structures were being formed, then bang, the bomb explodes on 15 August 1998, twenty-nine die, 220 are injured, and all the talk is of crisis, hammerblow, back to the bad old days. The reactions of the politicians – not least those who had previously supported terrorism and now claimed to be turning their backs on it, like Sinn Fein leaders Gerry Adams and Martin McGuinness – were key. They said and did the right things. But the really powerful statements came from the families of those who had lost their lives, that they wanted this to be a spur to peace, not a reason to give up hope that progress was possible. Tony Blair interrupted his holiday in France to visit Omagh in the immediate aftermath, and received that message loud and clear. Later, the dust having settled a little, he visited again, this time with his wife Cherie, taking Bill and Hillary Clinton with them to this devastated community. It made a lasting impression on the Clintons, Hillary telling me as they left Northern Ireland, 'this process can work because those people so want it to', and the president telling me, in an interview some years later, that he felt the bombing had been an important turning point in the right direction.

'We reset targets out of failure.'

WILLIE WALSH

'We went to Omagh to see the victims of the bombing and for them that bomb represented the importance of the peace process. They didn't say "OK, they took my loved one away, now I want to be vindictive and take five of theirs away and we've got to go back to the way it was"; not a single soul said that to us, and that's when I knew – it's a terrible thing to say, but in the awful ashes of Omagh is when I knew that the Irish peace would not die.'

Compare that head-above-parapet approach – of both leaders and citizens – with the dominant attitude in the banking sector in recent years: a case study of how not to do it. First, the banks appeared not to see the global financial crisis coming. Second, their initial reaction was to imagine the best-case rather than the worst-case scenarios. Third, if they had planned for such a crisis, it was not apparent from their response. They did not appear to have a plan at all. Fourth, they did not get their heads above the parapets; instead they looked to others for leadership, hoping the storm would pass. Political leaders had no option but to get involved. It was a crisis with the potential to destroy the world economy. As Obama,

Brown, Merkel, Sarkozy and others stepped up to the plate, the bankers seemed to deliver a collective 'phew' – the same response as oil company leaders in the fuel protests.

Then something else happened for the bankers – one of them emerged as the leading symbol of their greed and incompetence, Sir Fred Goodwin of RBS. Horrible for Goodwin and his family. Great for the others, who pulled their necks in even more tightly. But the problem with a strategy of 'sit tight, let others take the heat, all this will pass' is that in a genuine crisis, it is never going to be enough. Andrew McNally, who worked through the crisis as UK chairman of the German bank Berenberg, and is now trying to fashion a new approach to capitalism, founded on equity not debt, and with a greater commitment to social purpose, fears many in his profession have learned nothing from the GFC. 'Because it feels like we're through the worst, some of the banks are just going back to the status quo ante, like nothing really happened,' he tells me. 'In fact it's an opportunity to change, and if we don't take it, there will be another crisis and there will be far more victims. Part of me worries that the moment may have passed us by already, that even if we change to the extent we should, we're still facing another crisis down the track, because people don't wish to face up to the scale of change required: change in regulatory systems and working practices, change in values, change in attitudes. Too many people are thinking "the storm passed, OK, it wasn't great but we're still standing . . . let's go back and do it all again". Surely if a crisis is to have any value at all, we need to learn from it.'

For me, perhaps the supreme inspirational sporting example of a determination that some good should come from bad is the aftermath of the Munich air crash of 1958, in which eight Manchester United players were among twenty-three people killed when their plane skidded off the runway. That was certainly a crisis. And yet such was people's insistence on keeping going that, with a team predominantly made up of reserve and youth team players, Manchester United went on to fulfil every fixture for the rest of the season, remarkably making the FA Cup Final, when they lost to

Bolton Wanderers 2–0, and beating AC Milan at Old Trafford in their first post-Munich European tie before losing 4–0 in the return leg at the San Siro. Indeed, Munich, as much as anything else, created the identity of Manchester United as a club that never gives up and always shows resilience. They use the crisis as a strategic and motivational driver to this day. Manager Matt Busby, who had the last rites read to him twice but miraculously survived, and later Alex Ferguson, always instilled into their players that the club's past was a part of the here and now. In 1968 Manchester United won the European Cup at Wembley, beating Benfica 4–1, with a new team of young superstars – George Best, Denis Law and Brian Kidd – becoming the next generation of the Busby Babes. Their youth and energy was supported by the experience of two Munich survivors, Bill Foulkes and, captain on the night, Bobby Charlton. When Gary Neville took to the field for the Champions League Final in 1999, he said the Munich crash was in his mind, though it happened almost two decades before he was even born. So out of tragedy and existential fear came something inspiring and enduring.

What Bill Clinton did in the Oval Office with Monica Lewinsky doesn't get close to Munich in terms of heroism. But there are similarities nonetheless. Catastrophic as it was, ultimately it made him stronger. Today he is one of the best-known and most-liked people alive, his record viewed with considerable nostalgia; he remains a major player, the man Barack Obama turned to when he needed his own re-election campaign fired up, a man whose presence and counsel are sought by public and private sector organisations all over the world; and who might even be back in the White House soon, making more history as the first ever male 'First Lady'! Every leader who complains about the media in a crisis should commit to memory what Clinton says about not giving 'permission' to critics to destroy, and ask themselves, every time it gets bad: 'Was it worse than this for Clinton?' It was as bad as it gets, and he got through it not just alive but thriving. Crisis? What crisis? Indeed.

16

RESILIENCE

'Do not judge me by my successes, judge me by how many times I fell down and got back up again.'

NELSON MANDELA

Of all the world leaders I have met, Nelson Mandela is the only one who, virtually every time I was in his presence, prompted a slightly accelerated heart rate and the hair on the back of my neck to stand to attention. The first time I met him, I was a journalist on the *Daily Mirror*, he was not long out of jail and the anti-apartheid movement stalwart and Labour MP Dick Caborn asked me if I could persuade publisher Robert Maxwell to sponsor the tribute concert being planned at Wembley to celebrate Mandela's release. Maxwell agreed, but on condition that Mandela came for a lunch or dinner at the *Mirror* HQ penthouse in Holborn. He arrived by Maxwell's helicopter, and all who met him were blown away by his charm, grace and humour. Maxwell, however, proceeded to give Mandela a lecture about 'the art of negotiation', including this priceless line: 'Nelson, the single most important quality you require in a negotiation is . . .' (pause for effect) '. . . patience.' Cue intake of breath by all around the table, with the exception of the man who had spent almost three decades patiently hoping for release from prison, who smiled and said without rancour: 'Bob, I think I know a thing or two about patience.' In the league of setbacks and irritations he had endured, a bombastic newspaper owner was well down the table.

Whatever lessons Maxwell might have thought he could teach

Mandela, one of the many things Mandela teaches all of us is the extent to which a truly resilient mindset can turn most setbacks into positive opportunities. Here was a man who used his several trials as a platform to express himself and publicise his goals at a time when the media were barred from printing speeches or articles by ANC figures. He turned confinement in prison into an opportunity to talk with other leading members of the ANC, something that the authorities had made virtually impossible when he had been 'free'. And he determined that the appalling state violence of 1990, when South Africa was virtually collapsing beneath the weight of its contradictions, should be met by non-violence from the ANC, thereby forcing the government into talks and turning the setback of countless civilian deaths into a route out of the armed struggle tactic that so many in the ANC supported.

Consider, too, the many other hurdles in his way that he had to live with and overcome. He lived in a society where a Land Act of 1913 had deprived blacks of 87 per cent of the territory in the land of their birth, where the Urban Areas Act ten years later had created slums and where the 1926 Colour Bar Act had banned Africans from practising skilled trades. In his early days Mandela and the ANC Youth League ran foul of the 1950 Suppression of Communism Act, causing him in early 1956 to be restricted to Johannesburg, subjected to a five-year ban on attending meetings, and forced to abandon his law firm with Oliver Tambo. A few months later he was arrested for 'high treason'.

Setbacks came from his 'own side' too, in particular from the Pan-Africanist Congress formed in 1960 by extremists unhappy with the Communist links of the ANC and its tactic of defiance (it wanted a more aggressive and violent approach). While Mandela and his comrades welcomed anyone brought into the struggle against apartheid, the role of the PAC was almost always that of a spoiler for the ANC: it would divide people at critical moments; it would ask people to go to work when the ANC called for a mass strike; it would make misleading statements to counter any pronouncements of the ANC. In the end, the heavy-handed approach of the PAC forced the government to declare both the PAC and ANC as illegal organisations on 8 April 1960, where, overnight, being a member of the ANC became a felony punishable by a term in prison and a fine; furthering its aims was punishable by ten years in prison.

In 1962, Mandela was finally caught late at night en route from Durban to Johannesburg. He was sentenced to three years for inciting people to strike and two years for having left the country without a passport. Nine months into that five-year sentence, Mandela and other members of the ANC were charged with sabotage, and he was sentenced to life imprisonment (the death penalty had been a very likely possibility).

Life on Robben Island was not easy for inmates, especially not for Africans who were treated like animals: they were given pap (maize brewed in hot water) for breakfast and dinner, could wash themselves only with sea water, and were forced to work long hours in the lime quarry. Mandela used his legal and political skills to fight for better rights for political prisoners, but it would be more than a decade before they were permitted to read newspapers, have study time, allowed the same clothing as other prisoners, and given better meals. Mandela was supposed to be able to see his wife Winnie every six months, but the authorities conspired to ensure that these visits happened once every two years. As anyone who ever saw Mandela with his huge extended family knows, he was a family man, yet he had to endure the loss of both his mother and his eldest son while in prison, and was not allowed to attend either funeral.

Events outside would have a direct impact on Mandela's treatment inside. Attacks by ANC fighters on South African police forces would see Mandela facing further punishments. Yet through it all, he only rarely allowed his will to falter; he focused less on his own setbacks and suffering and more on how to end their root cause – the apartheid system of government – with an understanding that evolved over time that it could only happen if somehow he was able to develop meaningful relationships with those responsible for his treatment, both within the prison and, more importantly, within the political system. This capacity not only to engage with but also to forgive his oppressors is what made Mandela a truly wonderful human being, and it was part and parcel of his extraordinary ability to connect with people. I remember once asking him to sign a copy of his book, *Long Walk to Freedom*, for Monica Prentice, one of the few black people who worked in Downing Street. He took a while to get the top off the fountain pen, open the book at the right page, and start to write, slowly and deliberately, in an old-fashioned and neat hand. He was halfway through 'To Monica' when he looked up and said 'Hold on, it's not *that* Monica, is it?' And then the smile, and then the laugh. I asked him: 'Mr President, how were you able to forgive the people who did what they did to you and your people?' His response was simple: 'By understanding that if all you have is bitterness, you can never be free.'

'I've lost almost three hundred games. Twenty-six times, I've been trusted to take the game winning shot and missed. I've failed over and over and over again in my life. And that is why I succeed.'

MICHAEL JORDAN

Few of us, of course, possess Mandela's equanimity or his resilience – and few of us live lives that require those qualities to the same extraordinary extent. But all of us, not least those who strive particularly hard to achieve, will experience disappointment or setbacks at some point. At such moments we can gain reassurance by remembering we are not the first to have faced adversity; and strength can be drawn from reflecting on those who have overcome far worse. It is also vitally important to remind ourselves that we cannot allow a setback to destroy us.

Even a one-off event can threaten to derail. Take, for example, David Beckham's miserable experience when he was sent off during the match against Argentina in the 1998 World Cup, having momentarily lost his cool and kicked Diego Simeone. Suddenly, one of the heroes of English football found himself being viewed as one of the villains. In his autobiography he describes the excruciating moment when the rest of the team trudged back in, defeated on penalties, after the match. 'Nobody breathed a word to me,' he recalls. 'There was almost complete silence. I could feel my stomach tightening even more. I gulped, breathed in, and gulped again. I was in a packed changing room, but I had never felt so lonely in my life. I was isolated and afraid.' In the aftermath he was sent dog faeces in the post and Beckham effigies were burned by fans.

But then a turning point, both in terms of the moment and in some ways his life, in the form of an approach by England teammate Tony Adams, at the time captain of Manchester United's biggest rivals, Arsenal. 'He put his arm around me. It was a strong embrace. I could feel that he meant it; that he could see how much I was suffering; that he wanted to take away some of the pain. "Look, son, everyone makes mistakes," he said. "Don't let it get you down. You are going to come back stronger and better."'

Adams's remark may sound a reassuring platitude, but there is an essential truth to it. When I was in Downing Street, I kept a postcard listing ten little acronyms in my inside pocket (in fact, I still do). The seventh read GGOOB (get good out of bad), a good rule in crisis management, as Bill Clinton and Willie Walsh showed, and not a bad one in life more generally.

Craig Bellamy, the Australian rugby league coach, puts it this way: 'As a rule I believe you learn more from a loss than a win, and the same applies to periods of adversity.' Or this from Colm O'Connell, the Irish coach of Kenya's top runners: 'The winner is the loser who evaluates himself correctly.'

I learned a lot from talking to baseball's Joe Torre about the importance of leadership, teamship and the right mindset. But I learned a lot about resilience too, and when he opened up, it was pretty clear where his had come from. Torre is a real GGOOB man. 'I grew up in an abusive home, where my dad hit my mom a lot and as a child you just feel helpless, and you blame yourself. I think that's partly what gave me some of my drive as a player, getting away from that, and proving myself. And as a manager, I think it helped me understand the feelings of players better, the pressures they were under. I've seen with a lot of players, especially maybe some of the minorities, how their competitiveness comes from the fight for survival, a real necessity.'

Today he and his wife run the Joe Torre Safe at Home Foundation, which helps children who are growing up in violent homes, and he has created a dozen domestic violence resource centres – 'Margaret's Place' – in his mother's honour. As Torre says: 'It is using my celebrity to try to help kids deal better with this than maybe I did. It took me years to stop blaming myself. I only resolved it as an adult when I went on a four-day self-help course, and I realised I was not born with these feelings, they were the result of all the things my dad brought into the house.'

> 'The winner is the loser who evaluates himself correctly.'
>
> **COLM O'CONNELL**

You also sense that his propensity to self-blame, albeit born in horrible circumstances, was something he used as a positive. 'As a player I was always so hard on myself, probably took too much of the blame, but then I would use that, try to improve. I would always be analysing what I could have done better. There is so much disappointment in our sport, and what it teaches you is that the easiest thing in the world would be to quit, so you don't quit, you don't give up. I was never good at failure. If I failed as a player, I beat myself up. If we failed as a team, I beat myself up.'

His period as Yankees manager was under owner George Steinbrenner, known for his tough style, and his rapid turnover of managers if they failed to deliver. Torre didn't exactly get off to a great start, with the New York press nicknaming him 'Clueless Joe', before he turned things around, and lasted over a decade there. 'George sure was a tough boss but nobody was tougher on myself than I was, so that kind of helped too. I was there twelve years and at the end it was almost like nobody knew how to say goodbye.'

Torre quit the Yankees, but he had been fired from previous jobs, and here too resilience was key. 'Getting fired is never good.

I remember the time I was fired after my second job and I was pretty low, and my wife said "How are you going to be remembered?" and I said "Maybe as the guy who failed to live his dreams" and she said "Why – are you dead?" And of course the people who are winners, the people who are successful, they are resilient, they fail, they learn how to deal with setbacks. So I was down when I said that, but I got myself up again. Babe Ruth had it so right – "It is hard to beat a player who never quits." That was my mindset and the mindset I encouraged in my players. Some days you will fail, you will come up empty, but if you keep going, keep working, stay resilient and determined, you can come through, you can get there. And when you get there, the important thing is staying there, and staying there is not about staying the same, it is about improving. You must never lose that perspective.' Ric Charlesworth puts it even more sharply: 'The only real defeat is death, for it ends our capacity to adapt and change and improve.'

This reflects not just a 'get good out of bad' mindset but also a certain bloody-mindedness, and that's something I've found in many other successful people too. In NFL, they don't come much more successful than New England Patriots quarterback Tom Brady. One of the sport's superstars, with three Super Bowl rings and two Most Valued Player awards, he is spoken of in the same tones as his childhood hero, Joe Montana. But his success owes a lot to a setback which to this day can reduce him to tears (you can see this for yourself on YouTube, if you look up 'Brady 6' interviews). Back in 2000, he was passed over again and again in the NFL draft, finally scraping in as pick 199 out of 200 in the sixth and final round, with no fewer than six quarterbacks – the Brady 6 – ahead of him. In the interview, he describes how he went for a walk with his parents, unable to follow the process on TV any longer, and confronted the notion that his professional football dream was over. But when he arrived at the Patriots, he sought out owner Robert Kraft and told him: 'I am going to prove to you I am the best quarterback.' Kraft says there was something about the intensity in his eyes as he said it that made him feel he would.

Often called 'king of the comebacks' – itself a sobriquet that suggests the ability to respond to setbacks – his first two Super Bowls were won by individual pieces of Brady brilliance in the last moments of the game. He denies, as is sometimes said of him, that he has a chip on his shoulder, but admits he is driven by 'the feeling that nobody wants you'. He recognised he was not the fastest, not the fittest, not the most gifted. But he still felt he could be the best and that feeling of rejection from 2000 spurred him on. 'I want to earn it every single day.'

It's perhaps that 'what doesn't kill you makes you stronger' truism that also explains a man such as Ade Adepitan, Paralympian basketball player turned broadcaster. His early life was certainly tough. Born in Nigeria, he contracted polio at fifteen months. Then when he was three he moved to the UK, which meant separation for some time from his sister, who has Down's syndrome, because the family could not afford for everyone to come to Britain. His parents had to fight to get him into a mainstream school where he was one of only two black children, and the only child with a severe disability. He was headhunted to play wheelchair basketball, but this led to a family rift and his father not speaking to him for a decade, because his parents preferred him to use calipers rather than a wheelchair. His mother first knew he was playing international sport when she accidentally caught sight of him on TV.

So far so misery memoir, you might think. But what is remarkable, and truly inspiring, about Adepitan is when he says this: 'I don't recognise anything in my life as a setback at all.' Failures and rejections, including his repeated failures to be accepted for Team GB before finally he made it, were in his eyes merely steps on the road to a life he was determined should be one of success and fulfilment. His attitude – which echoes almost word for word that of a Brailsford or a Jordan in able-bodied sport, or a Branson in business, is founded on the idea that obstacles only exist if you allow them to. 'I don't see obstacles. I see objectives, and I see opportunities to meet them.' It is an attitude which made him a natural choice to present Channel 4's award-winning coverage of the London 2012

Paralympic Games, themselves a watershed moment in terms of attitudes to people with disabilities.

'As a kid, the only time I felt disabled was when I walked past a mirror and saw myself walking differently to everyone else. Even today I don't see myself as a disabled person. In my opinion disability is in the mind and all you can do is focus on the best you can get out of yourself. Everyone has some kind of disability, because nobody is perfect.' More than that, he believes that his disability made him more inventive, keener on setting himself big challenges. 'Walking the mile to school every day was more of a challenge for me than others but I always embraced that challenge. It made me stronger.'

He loved football, but accepted he couldn't compete on the same basis as outfield players, so turned himself into a goalkeeper. One breathtaking save became a life-changing moment, when he realised that he had suddenly earned respect for something he showed he could do, rather than sympathy or scorn for the things he couldn't do. He has a house full of medals and trophies but says: 'What is more valuable to me than the medals or the achievement is the journey I've had to go on to get there because that's what makes it an achievement.'

> 'I don't see obstacles. I see objectives, and I see opportunities to meet them.'
> **ADE ADEPITAN**

The one area where he accepts that his disability may have had a direct impact on his early rejections was in the area of teamship. 'The main reason I was always attracted to sport was because when you play sport it means you are fit and when you are fit you don't need to rely on anyone but yourself. Having trained myself to become so independent it was difficult for me to learn teamship; I think that's genuinely difficult for a lot of disabled athletes. A wheelchair basketball team is one of the toughest teams to be in. You've got athletes who have come out of the most difficult situations and this can create tough personalities, tough characters and huge egos. Persuading these people that you have to sacrifice everything for the team is difficult.

Myself and the captain Simon Munn never really got on, but after I was dropped, he was the one who decided I needed to get called back and after that I had massive respect for him because he had put our differences aside for the good of the team.'

Adepitan says he takes the same qualities he used in sport to his new challenge in broadcasting. 'I now care about my broadcasting as much as I did about my sport. So I prepare. I think about the team. I look for the next challenge. I set goals. I focus on the big moments. I got told I was presenting the 2012 Paralympics in October 2011 and I looked at it in a sporting context: what do I need to do to be ready for it? What do I need to know, the interesting stories, the medal hopes, the rivals, the international athletes? Then I broke my day down accordingly in preparation. I used exactly the same approach to scheduling as when I was training and it worked for me. The skills I learned from sport I use every day in any other working environment.'

Many of the same themes come up in the life and attitudes of Britain's most famous and decorated disabled athlete, Tanni Grey-Thompson. 'I have no memory of being able to walk, so I don't think about it. I hate it when people go on about how brave I must be, or how I "suffer" from spina bifida. I have it, that's it. I am in a wheelchair, that's it. So get on with it. Being in a wheelchair has given me more mobility, not less, it has given me the life I had as an athlete. You would never find me complaining about being in a wheelchair, but I have complained plenty of times about the life of a wheelchair athlete, being treated as second class compared with the able-bodied guys, and I still do.'

Inevitably people's own circumstances dictate what they think and feel about the world. When I think of Kosovo, I think of politics, of the military, of Milošević's ethnic cleansing and the current government's attempt to win recognition as a nation-state. But when Tanni Grey-Thompson mentions Kosovo, it is to say that the country could become 'a threat' to developed countries like the UK in Paralympic sport 'because they have so many amputees'. That is the Paralympian winning mindset at work. GGOOB.

I find her and Adepitan's example inspiring. Their struggles were long and hard fought. For others, hard-won success after a setback hasn't brought with it the powerful sense of achievement you might expect. Adversity can be debilitating, however well it has been overcome.

And in this context Australian surfer Layne Beachley has an extraordinary story to tell, one which demonstrates the power of resilience, but which is certainly not unambiguously upbeat. In her case, the challenges started very early on. As she puts it to me: 'My determination and competitive spirit came from the moment of conception.' Quite a dramatic statement. It is when you learn more about what that moment entailed – an act of rape by a young man who would not take no for an answer when Beachley's teenage biological mother tried to struggle free – that you perhaps understand why, in our very first exchange in a long interview, she identified it as such a defining moment in her life.

Her natural mother, Maggie Gardner, whose family had moved to Australia from Scotland when she was a child, was forced by her parents to give her away for adoption. Beachley's adoptive mother, Val, died of a brain haemorrhage when she was seven, leaving her father Neil to raise her as a single parent. He and his natural son Jason were tall. She, who had weighed just five pounds at birth, and spent the first six weeks of her life in intensive care, was tiny, often taunted at school by kids asking why she looked different to the rest of her family, prompting her to ask one day: 'Am I adopted?'

When finally her father confirmed she was, the information triggered an extraordinary determination in her. 'When my dad told me, yes, you're adopted, that awakened something inside me, made me decide, so clearly, that I was going to be a world champion at something. I was going to be the best in the world, it didn't really matter what it was, but I was going to do it. I was sure that was how the love and the respect I wanted would come my way. I would be the best in the world, I would be loved, and being the best would make me worthy of it.' This moment of complete clarity is not unusual among successful people. Arnold Schwarzenegger says he knew he was going to be a successful actor and politician long before he was. Mick Jagger knew he was going to be a rich and famous rock star the moment he picked up a microphone and saw a crowd react to his voice. Layne Beachley may not be as well known around the world as the Rolling Stones – though she is now married to a rock star, Kirk Pengilly of INXS – but in surfing she is revered.

Beachley's determination remained constant through all the setbacks that followed – defeats in her sport, financial struggle, bouts of severe depression, low self-esteem, crippling self-doubt, fear of failure, fear of success, fear of commitment, fear of abandonment, late development, failed relationships, heavy drinking and repeated suicidal thoughts. There was always something inside her that made her sure she would make it.

The fact that the 'something' she would master became surfing was an accident of geography, as she was growing up in Manly, near Sydney, and she loved the sea and the surf from the moment Neil Beachley introduced her to it. But it was complicated by her parallel and often turbulent race to establish where she really came from, and find out why her parents had given her up. Eventually, aged twenty-seven, she met her biological mother, having already discovered in an earlier phone call with her the truth about the circumstances of her conception, which 'hit me like a hammer to the head'. So here is a young woman who has been given away by one mother at birth, loses her adoptive mother aged seven, speaks to the birth mother for the first time in her twenties and learns over the phone that she was the product not of love, but of rape, and when finally they meet it sets off a relationship that is both complex and sometimes troubling. Add in her adoptive dad later getting married to Christina, someone Beachley would initially not get on with, and who would also die prematurely, from breast cancer, and clearly, as a psychiatrist might say, there is a lot in there to unbundle.

She did her unbundling in the ocean, which became the place she felt most at home, where she felt both release from her realities and the ability to define her own self. She had to work harder than most. She lacked the physique and the natural talent of rivals. She had to take up to six part-time jobs to fund her travel to tournaments, first around Australia, then all around the world. In her first competition, she came last, but recorded in her diary that it just made her more determined. 'Every setback fired me up more.' She decorated her walls with motivational sayings, such as 'From adversity comes greatness', 'What you put your mind to, you can achieve', 'Life's battles don't always go to the stronger or faster woman; sooner or later the woman who wins is the woman who thinks she can.'

Beachley has kept a diary since she was ten, and it tells a warts-and-all story of a remarkable sporting and personal journey. Amid the determination and the motivation, that same diary is full of doubts about her own abilities, her own character, about whether she will ever make it. When finally she does, and wins her first world championship in 1998, she fails to share in the sense of joy and euphoria others are feeling on her behalf. Instead she is straight on to the next challenge she sets herself – to win it by a record margin – and then the next, to go one better than previous world champion Lisa Andersen's four world titles in a row. Of that first world title, Beachley wrote in her diary:

> I've spent so long preparing for this day that its impact isn't as great as it would be for someone who hadn't spent so much time and energy getting here. It will mean more to me in the future than it does right now, because I knew this day would come, it was just a matter of time. Even though I've accomplished this great feat, it seems like the moment of completion isn't as exciting as the anticipation of the event. I'm still excited about the prospects for the future and sometimes I stop and think, 'Fuck! I did it.' So many different emotions to be experienced but most of all I'm relieved.

This reminds me once more of Tiger Woods, who chastised his wife Elin for suggesting they should have a special celebration when he won the first tournament he competed in after their marriage, as other golfers she knew and worked for had done. 'E – we're *supposed* to win,' he told her. 'Tiger never allowed himself to be satisfied, because in his mind satisfaction is the enemy of success,' coach Hank Haney says. 'His whole approach was to delay gratification and somehow stay hungry. It's the way of the super-achiever: the more celebrations, the less there'll be to celebrate . . . Any accomplishment was important only as a reference point for future improvement, not a pleasurable moment to dwell on.' This is another common winning trait: focus on the next win, not the last one. But in Beachley's case, it was because she had a particular outlook. 'I had developed this mindset that goes: "I have shown I can succeed through struggle, and so this means the *only* way to succeed is through struggle." That was how it was for me. Everything *had* to be a struggle. So whether it was training like a maniac at five thirty in the morning, or running up the sandhills when I had flu, I just pushed myself so hard because there had to be struggle. And I'm sure that all comes from the very start, the fact I had to struggle to stay alive when I was born, I was so weak and tiny, the fact that I had all these other things then coming at me. I learned to operate and succeed in survival mode, and that is why I was never really content.'

Even when Beachley won the fifth world title in a row, beating Andersen's record, and then her sixth, setting yet another record, there was still no sense of joy. On the contrary, one of the lowest periods of her life seems to have come after that sixth title win. Though now indisputably the greatest ever woman surfer, it was still a man's world. She eventually broke all ties with Billabong, one of the commercial giants of the surfing world, when her business partner discovered that despite the impact she was having on sales and the sport's growing media profile, she was being paid a lot less than the top men. Walking away from them was a big step to take, one most of her friends and colleagues advised her against, but she did it. 'It was an issue of respect,' she says. Author Michael Gordon wrote in the book he did with Beachley, *Beneath the Waves*:

Layne had taken many risks in her life, most of them in the water, but in the bravery stakes this was surely the biggest of them all: to reject the biggest pay cheque of her career [almost $400,000 a year] from one of the biggest players in an industry dominated by just three companies. Whatever fears she harboured on the inside, she projected raw courage to those around her, including those who questioned the wisdom of her decision.

It was certainly bold, and given it coincided with a period in which she had been asking Maggie Gardner not to try to get too close, it led to a spell of considerable emotional turmoil. One charged diary entry, for 16 April 2004, shows her struggling with those emotions.

All I want to do is run into my mother's arms and cry and feel protected and secure, away from the harm of the world. Life gets harder as you get older. Sure, I'm a fear-confronter, a lover of challenge, but at the moment I just don't have the energy or the strength, so all I want to do is run and hide. I'm scared, tired, exhausted actually, unorganised, wanting to give it all up and leave this place. Not that I would ever hurt myself, for that would be such a selfish act. But that seems to be a reasonable and desirable solution. Leave all my problems behind and let someone else sort my problems out . . .

And then you see the setback-as-opportunity mindset kicking in . . .

Then I reach a level of sanity and perspective. Life really isn't all that bad. I have a wonderful, loving boyfriend who brings me such happiness and comfort, a supportive and loving family, a bunch of friends who all believe in me and value my presence in their life, as I do theirs, four houses, the opportunity to create a successful business and, on top of that, I have an amazing ability to lift and inspire people, to motivate themselves and bring their dreams to reality, all by example. My perseverance, determination, dedication, commitment, passion, enthusiasm etc. are human qualities we all possess but sometimes we allow our brains to get in the way, much like mine is now.

Now she is going off-track again . . .

I'm currently making the choice to be scared, unhappy, tired and upset. I'm a product of my choices. We all are. We all have choices, like the quote I read today: 'If you have the choice to walk down two different pathways, always choose the hard one.' I've definitely done that.

Back on track . . .

I'm lucky that I find such solace in surfing. So I guess I should be more thankful than scared. I'm human. I choose these emotions. Everything happens for a reason. Every mistake is a learning experience. There is no right or wrong. It's just a journey we call life. It's time to go surfing for the love of it. Remove the mind, the expectation, the pressure, the desire to win. Replace it all with the desire to experience joy, the joy and the relaxation of being in the solace of the ocean, enjoying the intoxicating power of the waves, the laughter of my heart and the clarity of my mind. It's one of the few times in my life when I wish to have a mother.

It's clear from this and subsequent entries that she was entering a period of bad depression. Fast flow the suicidal thoughts, the feelings she has made the wrong choices, taken the wrong turn, is ostracised within the industry, out of her depth. Ten days after an entry in which she said she had 'lost the will to live', she lost her world title. At that moment, six in a row, in anyone's eyes an astonishing achievement, counted for nothing. All she felt was a pain in defeat not compensated for by any previous joy in victory.

Yet as the depression lifted, so the hunger to get her title back returned, and she trained harder than ever. But then more setbacks, a period of injury and illness and several months, enforced absence from the water, a time which forced her to reassess once again. Many considered her a spent force. From 1998 to 2003 she had been unassailable. But first one and then a second much younger surfer had taken the title of world champion away.

So when she returned in 2006, now thirty-three, expectations were fairly low. No wonder then, as she won her title back and, for the first time, really enjoyed it, she called number seven 'the sweetest win of all'.

'It took me all that time to get to a stage where I could come out of the water feeling happy, regardless of the result,' she tells me. 'That's why the seventh win was so important because it was the first one that I truly enjoyed. I had come to realise that I didn't have to struggle to be successful, I could just do what I was good at and enjoy it. People may think this is really weird, I mean how can you not enjoy winning and being the world champion for six years doing the thing you love more than anything else you do? But no, that seventh title really was the first time I experienced that sense of real pleasure, real joy in winning, and it was wonderful, really one of the best things in my life.'

'But all the success you can look back on, and which has now given you a great life, you wouldn't have had that without the struggle, the survival mode?' I suggest.

'Almost certainly not. That's where my competitiveness came from, seeing everything as a struggle for survival. I think there's something in the Australian psyche on that, the whole convict mentality, needing to prove something. We have a lot of very good sports people and I think a lot of Australians do feel that need to prove ourselves to the world.'

She doesn't know where her real father is, has no desire to

meet him, and her fame has led to some rather strange approaches by men claiming to be him. Her relationship with Maggie Gardner is clearly complicated, and has its ups and downs. Now in her early forties, Beachley is a regular on the speaking circuit, with her own business and property interests and her own charity, the Layne Beachley Aim for the Stars Foundation, which enables young girls and women to invest in their future and fulfil their potential in all endeavours, even producing several Olympians. I ask her if she ever reflects, given her view that her fighting spirit dates right back to conception, that some of her good qualities might have come from someone most of us would assume to be a bad man. She shakes her head. 'No, I don't think of him in those terms at all. I have learned to accept me for who and what I am. I feel very content. I am probably in the best place I have ever been. I still surf every day, because I just love it, every wave is different, I love what it does for my mind, body and soul. I love the freedom and solitude but also the social side. The ocean is still the place where I feel free, where I find solace and comfort, where I can best express myself.'

'That's where my competitiveness came from, seeing everything as a struggle for survival.'
LAYNE BEACHLEY

She says she has never had a desire to have children. She tells me the story of a time in the UK in 2012, when she had a short break with a friend and his wife and children, after she had completed a stint as athlete liaison officer for the Australian team at the London Olympics. 'I was exhausted after the Games and these girls were just giving me such a hard time, "Why have you never had kids, why don't you want kids?" on and on, and I was so tired and eventually I just snapped and I said, "You know, I just don't like kids," and later I went and sat down on my own and asked myself "Why did you say that?" And I decided it wasn't true, it wasn't that I didn't like kids but that I didn't *want* kids. And the reason is that I don't want to sacrifice the life that I have to another entity. I love this life and I am determined to keep it that way. I am 100 per cent aware of my own selfishness in this.'

She is bringing the same single-minded approach to her own happiness that she once brought to the pursuit of world titles, which gave her little happiness until the final title was won.

Her marriage seems to be a good one – she and her husband were recently snapped by paparazzi in a very public display of affection. They were married far from the ocean, in a valley, at a time chosen by her rock-star husband, ten past ten, on the tenth of the tenth of the tenth, 10 October 2010. Not, as I had imagined when she told me, as a reminder of those times when Beachley scored 'the perfect ten' for the perfect ride, but because in Chinese numerology it means everlasting love and happiness. Her amazing winning career behind her, she thinks she can now find it.

17

THE WINNING SPIRIT OF AUSTRALIA

'We have a lot of winners. It's about where we come from.'

SHANE WARNE

Back in mid-Victorian times, Tom Wills, the son of a wealthy Australian family descended from convicts, was sent to Rugby School, where he played an early version of rugby football. On returning to Australia he captained Victoria Cricket Team and in 1858 called for the formation of a 'foot-ball club' to keep cricketers fit in the off season. Keen to push for something that Australians could call 'our game', blending aspects of football and rugby, he wrote this now famous letter to *Bell's Life in Victoria and Sporting Chronicle* (which became the *Australasian Post*):

> Now that cricket has been put aside for some few months to come, and cricketers have assumed somewhat of the chrysalis nature (for a time only 'tis true), but at length will again burst forth in all their varied hues, rather than allow this state of torpor to creep over them, and stifle their new supple limbs, why can they not, I say, form a foot-ball club, and form a committee of three or more to draw up a code of laws?

He put forward another practical argument too, which would horrify the groundsmen of today:

If a club of this sort were got up, it would be of vast benefit to any cricket-ground to be trampled upon, and would make the turf quite firm and durable; besides which it would keep those who are inclined to become stout from having their joints encased in useless superabundant flesh.

He believed that, rather than copy games from England, Australia should have its own sport: Aussie Rules. This approach explains in large part its early hold on the Australian psyche, and the vast attention the big games attract today, according to 'Player of the Century' Leigh Matthews. 'It has stayed our game. People know about it around the world, but really it's only played here. Because it started as a way of keeping cricketers fit during the winter, it means it's played on cricket ovals, so already you're limited to countries that play cricket. At the MCG [Melbourne Cricket Ground] you're talking 160 metres long by 120 metres wide, and you need real speed and stamina. There's no offside rule, no line of scrimmage, and that means it's always been a player's game, more than a coach's game. It's a great team sport, and it needs a lot of these qualities that we Australians like to have: fitness, physical and mental resilience, being in a team. In the southern states it's basically a religion, the dominant sport bar none.'

It's also a very tough sport, as became clear to me from two incidents that Matthews describes. One occurred when he was head coach at Collingwood, and took personal charge of a fitness test on Alan Richardson who had broken his collarbone just a fortnight before the 1990 Grand Final in which he was desperate to play. The test took the form of a gruelling ordeal as Matthews repeatedly tackled Richardson, hammered him to the ground and then, as the player thought it was over and they were heading off to the dressing room, shoulder-charged him in his chest, grabbed him, threw him to the floor and landed his full weight on him, targeting the collarbone area. 'I know it sounds brutal but it was important that if he was going to break down he did it before the match, not in it.' The other incident involved Nigel Lappin at Brisbane Lions, who in another pre-Grand Final fitness test was passed good to play despite a recent broken rib. He played, helped win the match and only later learned he had done so with a punctured lung suffered during the fitness test. 'It seems hard to believe,' says Matthews, 'but it shows how much he wanted to play, and the price people will pay to succeed.'

Given the dominance of Aussie Rules, it's perhaps not surprising that this is the tough environment where Shane Warne – described in 2000 by cricket's bible, *Wisden*, as one of the five greatest players of all time – cut his sporting teeth. He explains to me that in part it was the physicality of the sport, and the regular brawls, that drew him to it. 'Growing up, I lived for Aussie Rules. That was always my dream, to play for St Kilda.' But it was not to be. 'The nearest I got was a game for the reserves. I played at a good level for three years, but I wasn't tall enough and I wasn't fast enough. I had a great kick, but just lacked that bit of speed.'

So Warne turned to cricket – not without reservations. 'I actually found cricket a bit boring, certainly compared with Aussie Rules. Those guys are the best athletes in the world. They run 27k over two hours, they hit, no padding, they kick. I don't think there's another sport like it.' But then cricket started to take over. 'When I realised AFL wasn't going to work out as I hoped, I ended up playing cricket more, '87–'88, then '89 I went to England, played in Bristol, by '90–'91 I was a first-class player and then '91–'92 playing for Australia. I only went to England really because some mates said it was fun and I was doing some pretty dire jobs. In 1988 I was working in a jewellery factory, I was delivering beds for a bedding company, working in a pizza shop Friday night. I did an accountancy course in Melbourne for a year, that was pretty boring, so I left for England. I had started to work a bit harder on my cricket, played at the Academy, bowled and bowled and bowled at my brother, so I was trying to do my best. Eighteen months later I was an international cricketer. It all happened so fast, it was crazy. Once I had that it really made me so focused, I decided I was going to give it 100 per cent, 24/7, this was going to be my thing. AFL had been the plan, didn't work out, so it was going to be this. I was determined to improve and keep improving.'

Warne's experience is not untypical of many first-rate sports people, but, as his flirtation with Aussie Rules suggests, there is something very 'Australian' about his career path. And there's also – to my mind – something very 'Australian' about his experiences of and attitudes to sport, traits clear in Tom Wills's letter to *Bell's Life*, and which stretched back to Britain using Australia as a dumping ground for 165,000 convicts in the eighteenth and nineteenth centuries. 'We have a lot of high achievers, and I think you can go right back to where we came from, how we started out as a country, all the slaves and the convicts, and the idea we were somebody else's rejects,' he says. 'There are three things that are really Australian to me: we have the "never give up" attitude; we like being in the thick of it; and we're not afraid to fail. Not being afraid to fail is a huge part of this. "Come on, mate, I'll have a go," and maybe it works and maybe it doesn't, but you'll never know until you try. Some countries don't try things the same way we do because it's hammered into them that they cannot fail. That's a hopeless way to go about things to my mind. "Never give up" are the three most important words in the language.'

Of course, it's very dangerous – and wrong – to claim that everyone in a particular nation ticks in a particular way, but when I talk to people like Warne or Layne Beachley or Leigh Matthews I'm aware of certain attitudes they seem to have in common with many other Australians I know – attitudes that, taken together, mark them out a little from other nations, or, at least, give Australia part of its distinctiveness. This 'never give up' and 'be prepared to fail' mindset is certainly one element, and while it may seem an obvious quality to embrace, and one that is certainly found among other cultures, its Australian version is slightly different from what I've encountered elsewhere. It's more akin to that trait you see in entrepreneurs for whom risk is much more closely associated with gain than it is with loss.

It is the same mindset that has helped Johnathan Thurston

become the world's best rugby league player, as confirmed by two Golden Boots and three Dally M 'Player of the Year' awards. 'Growing up I was always told I was too small; I couldn't tackle properly. When someone tells me I can't do something, it's like someone is having a dig at me and I just want to prove them wrong.' He's been doing it all his life. 'I always knew I was better than the person in front of me. But I would always train harder, do the things others were not doing or not prepared to do.' The day before I interviewed Shane Warne, I was in France, and watched as his compatriot, cyclist Michael Rogers, won his first ever stage of the Tour de France. As he dismounted and fell into the waiting arms of his support team, he was weeping, and later explained that the reason he found it all so emotional was because he had made a conscious decision to change his mindset: he was no longer afraid of failure, he said, and it was that changed outlook that had made him go all out to win.

'There you go,' says Warne when I tell him what Rogers said. 'If you're not scared of losing, you go for it, you want it more. We're not afraid of messing up, of taking risks and then knowing that if it doesn't come off your teammates will say "well, the guy tried something different there, it didn't work but no worries". I've never cared if I stuff it up. Give me a crack at anything. The more aggressive you are, the more luck you get. If you're in doubt, attack. If you're not sure, attack. What's the worst thing that can happen?' So fear of failure is there, and helps spur them to excel. These Australian stars, though, seem to accept that things don't always work out the way they'd hoped, and what drives them is their wholehearted 'never give up' attitude that puts a positive spin on failure and enables them to handle it. At seventeen, Johnathan Thurston 'put all my eggs in one basket', relocating to Sydney to pursue a potential career with the Canterbury Bulldogs.

> 'We have the "never give up" attitude; we like being in the thick of it; and we're not afraid to fail.'
>
> **SHANE WARNE**

Failure was never discussed. 'I washed cars from 7 a.m. to 3 p.m. then trained from 4 p.m. until 8 p.m. at night for about a year. I would write my goals down. Everything I was doing was to achieve that dream of playing rugby league. I didn't like waking up every morning at six to go and wash cars but I knew that was what I had to do to play football so that is what I would do.'

Warne is definitely on to something when he says that English cricket has 'a much more conservative approach, more reserved'. He is convinced that had he, fast bowler Glenn McGrath and batsman Steve Waugh – three stars of one of the greatest Australian sides of all time – been English, they wouldn't have had the same chances so young. 'We were all thrown into Test cricket early, I'd only played half a dozen first-class games, Glenn and Steve not much more, but they took a risk on us, they saw something and decided to give it a go.' 'But what if you'd failed?' I ask. I'm thinking of a Burnley goalkeeper, Billy O'Rourke, thrown in at the deep end as a teenager in a rare televised match at Queens Park Rangers in 1978, which Burnley lost 7–0. He left the pitch in tears and his career never recovered. But Warne says: 'I did fail. I had a really poor start. My first test was a disaster. I got dropped a couple of times. But nobody wrote me off. I had to fight and show I could improve. When my third chance came, I took 7 for 52 against the West Indies, and really felt I could be something special.' He contrasts the English tendency to hold back with his belief in taking a chance. 'I think if you see talent you give it a go. Imran Khan saw Wasim Akram practising in the nets and he said, "Hey, why is this guy not in the Pakistan team? He's something else." I'm not sure England would do that.'

Warne's 'Come on, mate, I'll have a go' seems, then, to be a standard Antipodean response to a challenge. And it's given an extra Aussie force in the use of the very distinctive and egalitarian word 'mate'. It explains the sentiment of a reader's letter to the Australian *Daily Telegraph* in 2000, explaining why some Australians booed American athletes at the Sydney Olympics.

Australians love people who are humble, down to earth, almost embarrassed by their own successes. We love [swimmer] Ian Thorpe, who is not only a decent young man, but who can just get on with the job without all the pomp and ceremony that Americans love to employ. We don't boo Yanks because we think they are better than us. We boo Yanks because they think they are better than us.

Again, this attitude – a refusal to be cowed or too easily impressed – seems to go back to the earliest days of European settlement. Because members of the convict class were not able to achieve a civic position and were discriminated against in the distribution of land grants, even though they made up nearly half the population, they developed a hatred of 'superiority' that evolved into a promotion of equality. No more 'sirs' or 'lords' or 'ladies', just 'mates' and 'mateship'. As Francis Adams wrote in the 1884 book *The Australians*: 'This is a true republic, the truest, as I take it, in the world. In England the average man feels that he is an inferior, in America that he is a superior; in Australia he feels that he is an equal.' I sense that every time I go there, as true today as it was in the nineteenth century.

The curious relationship with the UK, and in particular England, has had an important bearing on Australia's development as the more meritocratic nation. Take cricket, for example: in England, the sport was used both to reflect and to cement class and social structure, with 'gentlemen' amateurs and working-class 'players' who could take money for their labours. The gentlemen and the players might be in the same team, but they used different entrances and changing rooms. All because they went to different schools and had different accents. The working-class professionals tended to be bowlers, because this was a form of labour, whereas batting was far more befitting of the style of the gentleman. In Australia, by contrast, all of this was – is – anathema. Fast bowler Dennis Lillee, when being introduced to the Queen at the Centenary Test in 1977, asked her for an autograph; four years later, when introduced to her again at Buckingham Palace when being awarded the MBE, he offered his hand with the words: 'G'day, how ya goin'?'

It is only when you understand the centrality of egalitarianism to Australian culture that you realise that the Antipodean interpretation of the 'tall poppy syndrome' – defined by *Sydney Morning Herald* journalist Peter Hartcher as 'the tallest flowers in the field will be cut down to the same size as all the others' – is not the same as, say, the British one. In Britain there can be an element of envy in cutting people down to size.

> 'In England the average man feels that he is an inferior, in America that he is a superior; in Australia he feels that he is an equal.'
>
> **FRANCIS ADAMS**

That's less the case in Australia. 'It isn't success that offends Australians,' Hartcher said. 'It's the affront committed by anyone who starts to put on superior airs.'

I'm not saying Australia is perfect – there is still too much casual sexism and racism – but the spirit of 'mateship' has, to my mind, various very positive ramifications. In the first place it means that people are more likely to be judged by what they can do rather than by who they are or who they know. As writer Donald Horne said in his 1960s classic, *The Lucky Country:* 'There are no possibilities in Australia of determining status by simple inspection. You can't place a man in a social scale by listening to his accent or what he talks about or by looking at his clothes or observing his manners.' To this day, the Department of Foreign Affairs website defines Australians as 'people who believe in the principle of giving people a *fair go* and standing up for their *mates*, the disadvantaged and the underdog'.

Such mateship also encourages a team spirit. Ric Charlesworth tells of a meeting of the Australian women's hockey team, the Hockeyroos, several months before the Sydney Olympics. 'A home Games,' he says, 'that was a big thing, a huge opportunity, especially for the star players.' But what particularly struck him was that well before the tournament began, 'they agreed that any money they made would be shared, including among the players who didn't make the final selection'. His conclusion: 'As their coach, I knew from that moment we were going to do well.' They went on to win gold.

Thurston, who requires just one more Dally M 'Player of the Year' medal or Golden Boot to become on paper the greatest player of the modern era, is more obsessed with his team role than the individual glory that has come his way. 'I have high standards and expectations so I try to bring that out in the players around me, especially the younger boys, the ones who are new to it all, who are living the dream. I make sure they're being the best they can be, as we need a squad. You have the seventeen best players – thirteen to start the match and four for the interchange – and then you need another eight who can come in to do a job. The best clubs get the best out of their seventeen to twenty-five. I try and work with those boys so that if they get that opportunity they don't let the team down. I've been able to win all those individual awards, but that's not what drives me, it's to win the premiership with the [North Queensland] Cowboys, or the World Cup with Australia.'

And if Australia's belief that the egalitarian spirit of mateship sounds as though it might not help the competitive instinct, actually it may increase it. In his book *Battlers and Billionaires*, Dr Andrew Leigh compares the English Premier League and the Australian Football League, Manchester United winning twelve titles out of twenty, no AFL team winning more than three. Leigh argues the reasons are structural. English football operates much like modern feudalism: those at the top get the most TV money, then spend the most to get the top players, maintain their power, and the wheel keeps turning, favouring the few at the expense of the many. In the more egalitarian AFL, TV revenue is shared out evenly among teams. Players enter the game via a draft, in which the lower-ranked teams get the first pick of promising players, and the team's total salary bill is capped at around Aus$9 million, the equivalent of a few weeks' work for Wayne Rooney. Australians still want to win. But they have a sense of companionship that helps their teams excel.

Another striking aspect of the Australian psyche – and, again, I think this is part of the whole mateship phenomenon – is what Dame Edna Everage likes to call a bit of 'spunk': a determination to see a challenge as an opportunity; the love of a fight, allied to an optimism about the fight. Nor is it confined to men. Layne Beachley has it. Athlete Cathy Freeman has it. Cyclist Anna Meares has it. Former Prime Minister Julia Gillard had it when she made her brilliant speech against misogyny in the Australian parliament.

Spunk is not just fearlessness on a Shane Warne scale; it includes the sort of courage Nelson Mandela was thinking of when he said: 'the brave man is not he who does not feel afraid, but he who conquers that fear'. Perhaps its elevation as a particular Australian virtue stems from the First World War when, as life was being taken from so many on the beaches of Gallipoli, it was being given to the legend of the Anzacs (Australian and New Zealand Army Corps) and their qualities of endurance, ingenuity, good humour, mateship and courage.

Warne is in no doubt that his reputation as a team player, and his dedication to the team ethic, comes not just from his personality but also from his background in Aussie Rules. 'A team has all sorts of personalities, different dynamics, people with different mindsets,' he says. 'Sure, you might have some more selfish than others, but I didn't like playing with selfish players. If Glenn McGrath was on fire and I was just bowling a few overs to give him a breather and dry things up at the other end, I was happy, because if Glenn was on fire, it meant we were on top. My mindset was always "can I help the team?" If I get five wickets great, but if I get three or four and the guy at the other end is taking more, even better. I think when you start out the thing is you don't want to make a fool of yourself, then when you realise you might be pretty good, you step up, you can go from good to outstanding, but it's always about the team. I can honestly say I never had the mindset that says "as long as I do OK, as long as I get my wickets, that's fine". Never.'

To have an eleven full of such mindsets – Ricky Ponting as leader, McGrath, Waugh, Damien Martyn, Justin Langer – ensured

Warne was that very special phenomenon: a truly great player in a truly great team. 'There is nothing better than the feeling that right through the team, you have strength and quality,' he says. What all these players had was natural ability, a will to win, an understanding of teamship, a positive 'never give up' mindset, which combined together to give them that vital commodity: confidence. 'I always wanted the ball. Once you get a reputation, opponents worry, and that can be an asset to the team, when the batsmen see the captain throwing you the ball, and they get a bit nervy. I loved turning games most of all, I loved being in the situation where we needed to change the momentum of the match and I get the ball and take a couple of quick wickets, feel the game turning. That is when I loved it the most. All I had in my mind, whatever I was doing, was winning. If we were falling behind I would be thinking "give me the ball, I can take a hat-trick, we can win this", even if it felt like we were losing.'

The resilience Warne showed in the early days of his career has proved necessary at several points since. He has experienced plenty of setbacks and crises, not least for some of the off-field scrapes he's got himself into, both personal and financial. 'The highs and lows are what make you what you are,' he says. 'You have to experience both. There is nobody out there who has never made a mistake. Nobody who hasn't done something and gone "Jeez, why did I do that?" Remember, cricketers are away nine months of the year, you get family problems sometimes, nothing to do with the game. Players get up to stuff. There is no school that teaches you this kind of thing apart from the school of life and you have to learn from it, all the time trying to improve yourself as a person and as a player. I look back and I have no regrets. I would be in a straitjacket if I spent all my time thinking about stuff that I could regret. The way I look at it is that I have had a lot of opportunities and a lot of luck, I appreciate all the chances I've been given and I think I've repaid the people who gave me those chances in full.'

When I ask him what the worst setback was, he doesn't hesitate. 'Ah, no doubt about that one, mate. It was 2003, so towards the end, I guess. I was a bit chubby, triple-chin time, and my mum gave me some pills that she was taking for weight loss. So I tried them and the next thing I know I'm getting done for using a banned substance. What the fuck! I have never done drugs, never been interested, and in fact as a leg spinner I'd have made things worse by taking banned stuff, not better. To be doubted like I was, after all I'd done for the game and for Cricket Australia, I felt very hurt and let down, it was a huge blow. It meant I was out of the game for a year. My tests had always been the same, never in doubt, but they didn't want to believe me and that really hurt.'

But he bounced back, turned the setback into opportunity, got good out of bad. 'It worked out OK because I had the year out, I got a decent rest, and so I probably got three/four years more cricket than I would have done.' This period included what he described – to my surprise given all he had won before – as 'my greatest achievement of all'. He was referring to the Rajasthan Royals winning the first series of the new Indian Premier League Twenty20 contest, which he said surpassed even the 5–0 Ashes win against England with which he ended his Test career, or his Man of the Match performance in the 1999 World Cup Final.

> 'I would be in a straitjacket if I spent all my time thinking about stuff that I could regret.'
> **SHANE WARNE**

'Winning with the Royals was without doubt the most satisfying thing I have ever done. Nobody expected us to win, we were bottom favourite, the cheapest franchise, but I had that mindset – we can win.' Royals owner Manoj Badale says: 'I have never encountered a winning mindset quite like Shane's. What he did was incredible.'

Such resilience is apparent everywhere among Australian sportsmen and women. Take, for example, the remarkable success of Nova Peris, the first Aboriginal to win an Olympic gold medal, as part of Ric Charlesworth's hockey team; she then switched to sprinting and won Commonwealth Gold; and later to politics, becoming a senator in the Northern Territory, and the first Aboriginal woman elected to the Federal Parliament in 2013. 'If I want to do something,' she says, 'I block out all the negatives that say I cannot do it. I am going to do it because my mind tells me I want to do it and I have to do it.' She reflects on her roots. 'There are a lot of reports based around Aboriginal people that say you should be incarcerated; your life expectancy should be this, your numeracy and literacy skills should be that – for me, it has always been about my dream and my vision in life. Whatever card you are dealt in life you just have to deal with it.' There is still too much discrimination against Aboriginals, she says –'it is wrong and makes me angry' – but she sees her role in part as showing that, through resilience and determination, it can be overcome.

She has a neat explanation of the difference between winning in sport and winning in politics, but the qualities required are in many ways the same. 'In sport it's like climbing mountains – that's the feeling . . . all the hard work, then reaching the top of the mountain and screaming out a big YEAH. In politics the challenge is not about climbing the mountain, it's about moving the mountain, especially in Aboriginal affairs. I believe I can do this, but I'll do it stone by stone. That's the challenge I'm faced with. I'm not deluded by the fact it's a bloody big job and being the first Aboriginal woman in Federal Parliament is a big thing, but having a whole heap of firsts under my sleeve has enabled me to wake every day and rise to the challenges.'

If mateship is part of Australia's national DNA, it's certainly paid off in the sporting arena. For the last twenty-two Olympic Games, Australia, with its relatively small population, has finished in the top ten of nations thirteen times. It is tenth in the all-time Olympic medals table, even though many of its top athletes perform in non-Olympic sports. Team GB had a fantastically successful 2012 Olympic Games in London, but in the medals per capita table it nevertheless finished ten places below Australia.

Yet, as elsewhere in the stories of winners throughout this book, setback and resultant innovation have played important roles too.

The 1950s and 60s had been a golden era for Australian sport: fifteen out of nineteen wins in the Davis Cup, thirteen golds at the 1956 Melbourne Olympics. *Sports Illustrated*, the leading American sports magazine, on comparing thirty-four nations, declared Australia number one on a per capita basis, calling it the most 'sports-playing, sports-watching, sports-talking, altogether sports-minded' country's population ever, a land 'inundated with athletes'. But then came the disastrous Montreal Olympics of 1976, from which the team returned with just one silver and four bronze medals. National soul-searching followed. Ric Charlesworth, the star player in the men's hockey team which had secured Australia's one silver medal, recalls: 'We felt like the last of the real amateurs. Without change we understood we were slipping backwards.'

Montreal shone a light on national identity, and the role sport plays in defining Australians. 'Sport was the first form of Australian foreign policy,' said Donald Horne, in his book *The Next Australia*. 'Until the British got into some wars to which the Australians could send volunteers, it was the only way in which Australians could prove they were the best.'

It was clear, though, that the world had caught up. Eastern bloc countries wanted what Australia had. And, because they could not apply a cultural approach in the short term, they opted for a structural one – a so-called 'medal factory', whose methods, legal and illegal, delivered the success they craved as sport became an important weapon in the Cold War. However questionably devised, their strategy was paying off. Australia's response had to be to professionalise: not just take its natural advantages for granted, but exploit them properly.

'We will no longer let the rest of the world pass us by,' said Prime Minister Malcolm Fraser on Australia Day 1981 as he opened the Australian Institute of Sport (AIS). Funding jumped from $8.4 million to $18.7 million and then $24.8 million between 1980 and 1983. Australia's next prime minster, Bob Hawke, introduced further changes: re-establishing the Department of Sport, Recreation and Tourism; expanding investment in the AIS to include swimming complexes, sports science and sports medicine facilities; recognising the economic potential of sporting events through investing in infrastructure like Adelaide's Formula One track; encouraging more participation at amateur level; setting up the Australian Sports Commission to increase international competitiveness.

When multimillionaire Alan Bond's syndicate won the America's Cup in *Australia II*, despite only a tiny fraction of the country's population participating in the sport, the nation rejoiced. Hawke, visibly excited, declared on national television: 'Any boss who sacks anyone for not turning up today is a bum.' The *Australian* newspaper declared it 'a turning point, not just part of the lift in the nation's mood as the drought broke and the economy improved but a moment that made Australians more confident on the world stage and marked the start of a new international engagement'.

It took more than a decade to reach the top ten of the Olympic medals table again, at the 1992 Games in Barcelona. 'People think that sports science was the catalyst,' says Ric Charlesworth, who played a vital role in the country's sporting turnaround. 'It was not. The AIS did four things: it built facilities; it employed coaches; it provided money for athletes; it allowed them to compete internationally and overcome the tyranny of distance.' When I tweeted that I was writing about why Australia produced so many sporting winners, and asked for views, I had a huge response. These two tweets from Labor MP Tim Watts, the Federal Member for Gellibrand, tell the story particularly well: 'Reasons [for success] have changed over time. Wealth and outdoor culture up to Montreal Olympics. Govt $ since then. Montreal is key though'; 'As for WHY we fund it now why do the French subsidise cheese? It's a part of our national self-image.'

Beyond Australia's new-found urgency to succeed was the strategic thinking that made such success possible. In OST terms, it could be expressed as follows:

Objective: produce winners
Strategy: centralise excellence and investment

Tactics: build world-class facilities; develop world-class coaches; increase access to international competitions

The following decade proved one of the most successful in Australia's sporting history, with success at the Olympics inspiring success elsewhere. At one point Australia were world champions at cricket, rugby, tennis, women's hockey, men's and women's surfing, and on a per capita basis the top Olympic Games winner too. Almost all of the 240-strong team at the Barcelona Olympics had either attended the AIS or been supported by the Australian Sports Commission.

Former Prime Minister John Howard believed that 'sport makes the Australian nation tick'. Current PM Tony Abbott made it an election pledge to get sport 'back on the front pages where it belongs'. So you can understand why there might be a correlation between national identity and a desire to win. As to how the two become aligned, Ed Smith, England cricketer turned author, has a plausible explanation.

Structures are easy to copy; cultures are far subtler. When is success structural and when cultural? If you are aiming to emulate a winning team, it's a crucial distinction. Take West Indian cricket in the 1970s and 1980s. Certainly, their cricket was strong at the roots – far stronger than when the Test team declined in the 1990s. But surely the more decisive factor was cultural. Here was a loose confederation of islands collectively throwing off the yoke of colonialism. There was a score to be settled – against England, against the white world. The West Indies honed intimidation alongside self-expression. It was a party with a purpose.

Australia's success too, Smith suggests, is cultural: retaliation for an inferiority complex created through colonialism known (since the 1950s) as 'cultural cringe'. Sport has helped them overcome that, and it is above all sporting success – clear from the highly visible sporting infrastructure, from the volume of coverage in the media – that defines

Australia's winning profile. Its central place in the national life was shown too in the way the whole country was in mourning over the death in November 2014 of batsman Phil Hughes at the age of twenty-five, killed by a bouncer, some paying tribute by organising cricket matches in their workplace, thousands more taking part in a spontaneous 'put out your bats' campaign, leaving bats and caps in public places in tribute.

For a country of just 23.5 million, Australia also does pretty well in being seen as a serious economic and political power. And it's a country whose politics and political campaigns get noticed, and whose leaders tend to be far better known and more influential than leaders of much more populous countries. It is a member of the G20, by a long way the smallest country population-wise to be so. When the global financial crisis was at its peak, it was largely the partnership of Australia's prime minister, Kevin Rudd, and Britain's Gordon Brown that led to the G20 taking a prominent role. It's a country that is listened to by other Western powers, while increasing its influence with China and the rest of Asia.

There is, then, something about the Australian psyche that engenders dynamism and a desire for success, seemingly in every walk of life. But I think it's in the sports arena that it's most apparent – or, at least, easiest to measure. As we've heard from many winners, though, getting to the top is one thing, staying there another. At the 2014 Commonwealth Games, Australia's old enemy, England, topped the medals table in Glasgow, knocking the Australians off the top for the first time since 1990. (Australia has still won the Games on twelve occasions to England's six and Canada's single triumph on home ground in 1974.) Glasgow was far from being a 'Montreal moment', but Australia is Australia, a nation expectant of and demanding success, so what now?

Important steps have already been taken. Winning Edge, launched in 2012, aims to take the country to the top five Olympic rankings by 2022, through focusing on the sports most likely to yield most medals, and with a programme of innovation, backed by investment in sports science, research and talent identification. OST. The

AIS Centre for Performance Coaching and Leadership was launched a year later with Darlene Harrison at the helm.

Interestingly, they are now applying business techniques to the recruitment of coaches. 'The answer is not always within sport,' Harrison explains. 'There are a lot of high-performance environments to borrow and steal thinking from and tweak for your system – that's where the innovation comes from. For the profiling work we've done, we use a leadership profile that's used extensively in business. Big firms invest in the process of recruitment maybe as much as 10 per cent of their overall HR bill. This should apply to sport so we would learn to be more predictive: what we might get as opposed to what they did before; not just past performance as the indicator for success, but evidence that they can do it again.'

The purpose is to allow for winners to be identified earlier, for gaps in necessary skills to be identified and worked on. It also leads to the possibility of longitudinal studies. What if you could track a manager or a coach over the period of their career, the highs and the lows, and see if aspects of their 'winning' profile altered at various times? And could the same approach be applied to other fields, politics for example?

The AIS has produced a manual, 'Success Profile for High Performance Coaches'. Take out references to sport and form your own view as to whether this could apply to a CEO of a multinational or a prime minister.

> **Experience**: sustained performance at international level; devising and executing long-term plans; working within high-performance environments.
> **Knowledge**: understanding key-levers for high-performance delivery; how to use support; up to date with trends.
> **Competencies**: interpersonal (compelling communication, building partnerships, influence); leadership (leading change and developing others); business/management (building talent, establishing strategic direction, operational decision-making).

Personal attributes: passion for results, elite disposition.
Personal style: self-belief, competitive/driven, strong
ambition for athletes, clarity of thinking, team player,
commitment/persistence, passion/enthusiasm, honesty and
integrity, disciplined, listens, curious, adaptable.

Almost half of the places on the AIS Centre for Performance
Coaching and Leadership course are allocated to CEOs. Almost 90
per cent of the teachers are former athletes. Work supporting the
profiling of eighty-five coaches showed traits shared by high-
performing coaches and business leaders: high adaptability in their
expression of leadership style; high ability to self-analyse (mirror
test); high degree of communication style at a very personable level
and an ability to adapt this style with situational demands, including
moderating their voice tones and accompanying messages. Where
both showed the need for development was in the area of strategy
and leading change.

'Our driver at the moment is the coach as a performer in his/
her own right in training and competition,' Harrison explains. 'How
does their performance impact on overall performance? We might
look at coaching as talent as we look at an athlete as talent and then
think about attracting talent, recruiting talent, managing talent and
identifying talent going forward.'

Ric Charlesworth says Australia still 'punches above our weight'
but that Glasgow must serve as a spur to the next steps of change
and innovation. His mantra, learned from an old surgeon who trained
him as a doctor, has always been 'the price of life is eternal vigilance'.
That, he says, is the mindset Australia has to adopt if it is to remain
a winning nation, in sport, business and much else besides. History
suggests they will.

18

THE QUEEN: A VERY BRITISH WINNER

'The Queen will become a business-school case study in the management technique of rebooting.'

TRISTRAM HUNT, MP

A big part of me believes that the royal family is the pinnacle of a class system that holds Britain back by preventing it from becoming a true meritocracy, and that given all the advantages the royals are born into, they can hardly go wrong. But a bigger part of me has developed a huge admiration for the Queen, not least her skills as a leader. In challenging times, she has secured the monarchy for at least another generation and, given the way Prince Charles and the younger princes have developed as part of a concerted strategy by 'The Firm', probably much longer than that. Into her seventh decade on the throne, she is one of the most respected and most popular people alive. She is surely the oldest fashion icon. And she must be the most recognised woman on the planet, her face the most reproduced image of our age, not least on over 300 billion stamps and hundreds of millions of coins and banknotes around the Commonwealth. I mentioned earlier the show-of-hands game I did for Rupert Murdoch in his native Australia, where his reputation was low. The same audiences gave a near full house of raised hands for the Queen's high reputation. If you can see off republicanism in Australia, you can see it off anywhere.

She wins plaudits closer to home, too. John Browne, for

example, says: 'She ticks a lot of the boxes on leadership. She is clearly good at strategy, instinctively. She definitely has one, and she is good at executing it. She leads a team which is integrated into the strategy. She has adapted, slowly, over a long period of time, while pursuing broadly the same strategic principles, and she has never lost the plot, when there has been plenty of pressure to do so.'

There have been thousands of bad headlines, many setbacks and some crushing low points during her long reign, but the monarchy is in as strong a position as it is possible to imagine any institution to be in our modern culture of negativity. Parliament's esteem has fallen, and the stature of government with it; the reputation of business has been damaged by the behaviour of the banks and a lack of social purpose among enterprise more generally; the Church no longer commands such a central place in our lives; the media isn't trusted, nor public services given the respect or benefit of the doubt they once were; the military remain valued but cuts and controversies have reduced their standing; virtually alone among the major institutions, the monarchy has bucked the trend, and much of that is down to the Queen. One of her closest advisers says, modestly: 'We got our crisis in early, before the Internet really changed the terms of trade.' I think there is a lot more to it than that.

Historian turned Labour politician Tristram Hunt agrees with the self-deprecating royal adviser, but adds: 'Something changed about the Queen. She went from being seen as a figure not necessarily in control of the family and the institution to a different place, above it all. Maybe it was the public response to the series of disasters or perhaps the post-Diana moment, where there was criticism yet also an appreciation of some of the decisions and challenges. I think the public felt they went too far and yet she remained the same.'

As something of a lifelong republican, I'm surprised to find myself saying this but she and the institution more generally constitute a good case study for many of the issues I have been examining in this book: boldness, innovation, adaptability, resilience, long-termism, crisis management, turning setbacks into opportunities. They are fascinating, too, in relation to strategy. The word itself is effectively banned by the Queen and the Duke of Edinburgh, who once complained to an official that 'the only two people who talked more about strategy and planning than you were Hitler and Stalin'. The Queen sees monarchy as an antidote to politics, and in so far as she allows herself to contemplate a sense of strategy, it is in 'being the Queen' and viewing monarchy as a values system. But she did lead and allow the building of a new team which, whether she and Prince Philip liked it or not, most definitely strategised for their adaptation to a world of change, responding to a sense of the institution losing its way, and losing its goodwill from government. This was at its height in the 1970s when political opposition to the monarchy was growing, Parliament forced changes to the Civil List, and Prime Minister Jim Callaghan later wanted to make the royal household a Department of State.

Seen through a contemporary lens, with the Queen unassailable, Prince Charles in a stronger position than at any time since his first marriage began to go wrong, Prince William and his wife showing off their new baby to huge adoring crowds in New Zealand, it is easy to forget just how battered the royals were. For the Queen, the personal nadir was 1992, her '*annus horribilis*', that very phrase coined to convey how many awful situations she had had to deal with, as well as an appeal for some sympathy

'She [the Queen] ticks a lot of the boxes on leadership. She is clearly good at strategy, instinctively. She definitely has one, and she is good at executing it.'
JOHN BROWNE

from her subjects. If it was the low point for the Queen, it was the high point for modern republicanism. She and the family were frankly reeling from a succession of personal disasters that saw their standing and popularity fall. 'People began to question what the institution was for,' says one of her advisers. 'We were descending into a rather grisly soap opera, and just when you thought we were coming up for air, something else would come along and drown us out again. It was truly horrible.' Andrew Morton's book, *Diana, Her True Story*, which was told with the Princess of Wales's active cooperation, kept global focus on the private life of Prince Charles, this in the same year that Princess Anne divorced her husband and Prince Andrew separated from his wife. It didn't help that a few days before her '*annus horribilis*' speech, the Queen caught a dreadful cold which made her sound weak and hoarse when she delivered it. And it was the year Windsor Castle caught fire. The fire was described to me by an adviser who was with her at the time as 'without doubt the lowest point of all. This was her home, and I can remember standing in the quadrangle, and this woman, who never lets anything faze her, never puts her emotions on display, had the look of someone who just felt everything was going wrong. She looked destroyed.' He said the only time he ever saw her make a speech with tears in her eyes was when the castle was restored and she hosted a reception for, and awarded medals to, around a thousand people who had helped with the restoration.

Just how low the monarchy had fallen in public esteem was underlined by the response to Prime Minister John Major's announcement that the government, rather than the royals, would pay to repair the damage. There was an immediate outcry and the powers that be therefore had to back-pedal, promising that some money would be raised from savings within the existing grant-in-aid, while other funds would be generated by charging for entry to Windsor Castle and by opening and charging for entry to Buckingham Palace as well. These were huge steps for the royals to take, not least because forces of conservatism as powerful as the Queen Mother were totally opposed.

So how did the royal family get from such a low point to one, barely fifteen years later, when – at a time of austerity – a global audience of billions enthusiastically watched the grand wedding between Prince William and Kate Middleton?

Her advisers tend to clam up whenever asked directly if the Queen herself felt the monarchy was in danger, but the fact that some of them do suggests she might have had such fears too. One member of her team told me, somewhat dramatically, that the appointment of David Airlie as Lord Chamberlain in 1983 was 'the single most important moment in her reign'. To this day, those he then brought together to help the Queen through a difficult period of her rule do not know if that appointment was made knowing that, for all his aristocratic background, Airlie would be something of an agent of change. 'The Queen has a penchant for tall handsome men,' the aide tells me. 'David Airlie is one such. But he was a businessman, chairman of Schroders, chairman of General Accident, and he brought a business eye to the household, and frankly saw that it was running out of money, losing the respect of government, and was stuck in the mire.'

Helped by KPMG accountant Sir Michael Peat, who would later become a key adviser both to the Queen and Prince Charles, he presided over a report of 1,383 pages, with 188 recommendations, which amounted to what they called 'privatisation' of the household.

'The whole plan,' one courtier explains, 'was to take back our own destiny from the government and to do that we had to have control of the finances, a proper management structure and then recruit people who were more in tune with the modern way of life.' That required cultural and mindset changes too, not easily implemented in an essentially conservative organisation.

Two parallel bodies were set up, the Lord Chamberlain's committee, made up of advisers, and the Way Ahead Group, chaired by the Queen, with the Duke of Edinburgh, their four children and other minor members of the family also present. It says something for their relative efficacy that the Lord Chamberlain's committee still exists, whereas the Way Ahead Group met infrequently, decided little and was eventually disbanded. The broad outlines of a forward vision flowed from a paper written post-*annus horribilis* by private secretary Sir Robin Janvrin, a key hiring of the Airlie era and one of a small number of officials who worked with the Way Ahead

Group, which suggested the ordering and planning of the family's activities beneath four key planks of strategy: identity, continuity, recognition of achievement and service. The Lord Chamberlain adapted his role from being primarily ceremonial to becoming more like a chairman of the board, with the Queen as CEO.

To an extent, the monarchy's ability to focus on the long term – something that is denied to politicians, businesses and sports managers who have to worry about the next election, the next quarterly results, the next big match – helped this reforming movement. 'The Queen refuses to accept she needs a strategy; but she does have a vision,' one leading player in her team tells me. 'It is to do with values, familiarity, certainty, continuity and leadership; much stronger forces than thought or strategy.' He quoted the words of American essayist Ralph Waldo Emerson that the Earth endures and the stars abide. 'The Earth and the stars don't have a strategy. They just are. The Queen just is. That is how she sees herself. Her year is a season. Her day is a mini-season. She moves at the same pace, does the same things.' Viewed from one perspective, this sounds like a justification of the status quo. But the Queen, looking ahead to her 2002 Jubilee, and aware that the public support that is so essential to their survival had wavered, knew that if she was to secure the long-term future of the institution she needed to make changes to win back the affection that the royal family had clearly lost. 'Is it really about affection?' I ask one adviser. 'Yes, because the opposite is disaffection. If you have a disaffected public, you have no monarchy. That was always understood, and they were becoming disaffected, and parts of the media were fuelling that for all it was worth.' In fact, the regular polls that the Palace conducted showed that even when parts of the media were in full cry against them, the basic support for the institution, and especially for the Queen, never fell below 60 per cent. But given it was the next generation that was causing most of the negative headlines, the worry as she and the Queen Mother aged was that once they went, that support would fall quickly. Their strategy had to be based on making the institution of the monarchy relevant for the modern age. It had to maintain and develop the Queen's enduring strength and popularity, but 'rescue' the standing of her children, especially Prince Charles.

Back in the first chapter, I made the point that strategy is the place to have arguments, not avoid them. For the royal family, the arguments began in earnest in the late eighties and early nineties, but because strong opposing views were held, a compromise had to be forged, with 'resisters' (who felt that the storms would pass and that there was no need to 'over-react') tending initially to hold the upper hand, but with Airlie and his team bringing in more outsiders. For her part, the Queen would allow the debate to develop and at various key moments sided with change. 'She genuinely doesn't have views or ideology. That means she actually can adapt when she has to. She's not someone naturally inclined to change but she knows sometimes she has to, and she's not worried about loss of face,' says an adviser. It would be wrong to characterise the debate as being between 'traditionalists' and 'modernisers'. It was more a debate between resisters and evolutionaries, and during the early stages, the evolutionaries had to be patient. 'Often, it was one and a half steps forward, one step back, sometimes two steps back, so we had to bide our time,' said one.

> 'The Queen just is. That is how she sees herself. Her year is a season. Her day is a mini-season.'
>
> **FORMER MEMBER OF THE QUEEN'S TEAM**

At each moment of setback, the 'modernisers' – another banned word – would accelerate the process of what they called 'loosening'. As one of them explains: 'Royal Collection, big bridge crossed despite huge opposition from the Duke and the Queen Mother. [Paying] Tax – huge bridge crossed (helped by Charles). Opening up Windsor, bit of a bridge crossed. Opening up Buckingham Palace, huge bridge. But what was really loosening things was that we were getting in very good people, dispensing some of the old retainers, which wasn't easy, but building a more cohesive team who were capable of adapting to the change.'

There's no doubt that Diana's death in 1997 sent a profound shock through the institution. 'For a couple of days that week,' says one former adviser to the Queen, 'there was real fear, because we just could not fathom why the public were turning on a grieving family trying to console two young boys. We felt like we had lost our point of connection, lost our bearings, and that was a scary feeling.' That observation chimes closely with the definition I set out earlier of what constitutes a real crisis: an event or situation that threatens to overwhelm you or your organisation unless the right decisions are taken. And there's no doubt that Diana's death did for a day or two lead to a sense that they might be overwhelmed. 'It did feel like nothing we had felt before. There were certainly moments when we felt we were losing control. We were behind the game.' For those Palace officials at the forefront of the push for evolutionary change, it was proof that things had not changed enough. As one of the architects of the reforming strategy says: 'It was as though the *thinking* happened in the late eighties/early nineties; then 1992–1997 was like stage one of implementation, slow, but with the sense of direction clear; post '97 the pace accelerated because the resisters caught up with what was already happening.'

Tony Blair was asked by Lord Airlie to help the Palace with their preparation of Diana's funeral, and I was involved in the Buckingham Palace planning meetings with a couple of Number Ten colleagues. So big were the crowds in the Mall that the only way to get from Downing Street to the Palace was on foot, and as the week between death and funeral wore on, as the crowds and mountains of flowers grew, so did the mood of ugliness. But I think it's possible to pinpoint precisely the moment when the potential crisis started to subside. It was when the Queen finally came down from Balmoral Castle, and she and the Duke of Edinburgh spoke to some of the crowds mingling outside the palace, at the same time as Princes William and Harry went to talk to others elsewhere. You could literally feel the pressure on them subside.

Difficult issues remained to be resolved, however, for example which of the family would walk behind the coffin, with the Duke of Edinburgh clear that Charles should not walk alone, and that his sons should be with him, and details being ironed out to the last minute. One of the most tense discussions between traditionalists and reformers concerned the issue of whether the flag at Buckingham Palace should be flown at half mast, traditionalists arguing it should not, reformers very clear that it should. The Queen's own strong instinct was that it should not, given Diana was no longer a royal. Her equally strong instinct had been that she should stay at Balmoral to comfort her grandsons. 'She is opposed to anything kneejerk, and she felt it was kneejerk to rush back,' one courtier tells me. 'She is good at considered change, but so anti-kneejerk that perhaps it makes her less good when precipitous action is called for, because she doesn't do that, her strength is steadiness, not being ruffled. But as the public anger grew, she accepted the advice of Charles and others to return, and to lower the flag. She operates on instinct and a desire to get things right.' Her altered stance certainly worked, since the public mood quietened. Broadcaster David Frost turned to one courtier on leaving Westminster Abbey after the funeral service and – in echo of what is so often heard said of such moments – observed: 'You will emerge stronger from this, I am sure of it.' Yet days earlier, the same courtier was pondering whether the scale of hostility meant that 'skipping a generation', straight to Prince William after the Queen died – which would certainly have been in line with Diana's strategy – might be needed to win back popular support.

The crisis over Diana's death might have panicked some into a wholly new direction, but those at the centre of things after 1997 were careful not to lose sight of the fundamental values the monarchy stood for. What therefore followed was not exactly modernisation – though some officials said they drew lessons from what had happened in politics in recent years – and it certainly wasn't revolution. It was, if you like, urgent marginal gains. One adviser says that throughout the process he had in mind *The Leopard*, the classic Italian novel by Giuseppe Tomasi di Lampedusa. It tells the story of changes in Sicilian society during nineteenth-century Italian unifi-cation, and contains the line: 'everything needs to change, so every-thing can stay the same'. 'We wanted people to notice change without us shouting from the rooftops about it,' one courtier tells me. 'It was very different to what a politician or a business has to do. As a royal, "show not tell" is easier.' Given the microscopic media attention paid to the royals, it was never difficult to get attention, but it did require buy-in from key members of the family, and everything that would be interpreted as change had to be signed off by the Queen. 'She approaches everything with a very pragmatic view. It's a kind of ruthless common sense. She is very uncomfort-able if you try to suggest she does something that is not authentically her, but she does understand even institutions like the monarchy must change and adapt. For it to remain a symbol of continuity, it has to evolve, every day move it forward a click. There is the Queen in a headscarf still out walking with the corgis and there is the picture on our Facebook page or an announcement of something she is doing on our Twitter feed.'

Various patterns of incremental change can be detected after 1997. There was a review of the monarchy's relationship with virtu-ally every institution of service in the land, 'from the Women's Institute to the SAS'. A key one involved the way in which the royal family interacted with the public. Officials had noted the multiracial nature of the crowds that had mourned Diana, so now there was a very deliberate attempt to associate the family, and particularly Prince Charles, with ceremonies for new UK citizens, rather than merely emphasising traditional British identity. The royal family also engaged more actively in promoting tourism. And they made more imaginative use of the palace at the time of major celebrations, allowing Brian May of rock band Queen, for example, to stand on the roof and play 'God Save the Queen' on his guitar.

Throughout it all, though, the Queen remained centre-stage. As one of the people intimately involved with royal matters throughout this period puts it: 'Only one person can be the Queen, and that is the Queen; only one family can be royal – so be royal.'

He considers her visit to Ireland in May 2011 a high point. 'She is literally the only figure in the world who could make that visit. That was the kind of thing that was lost when the focus was on the family as a soap opera.' Her handshake with Sinn Fein's Martin McGuinness, once a member of an organisation that had killed a close member of her family, Lord Mountbatten, and for years had had her on its target list too, was a defining moment, planned only at the last minute. And at the sixtieth anniversary of the Normandy landings in 2004, when Iraq remained a source of contention between the politicians who attended – George W. Bush and Tony Blair on one side of the argument, Jacques Chirac and Gerhard Schroeder on the other – it was the Queen who made sure the day was not derailed but remained a commemoration. 'Not only was she out of the politics but she was from the period being remembered, and as she stood there, you got a real sense of the specialness of her and of the position. Only she could do that.'

Perhaps the most extreme example of this policy of continuity and change was the opening ceremony of the London 2012 Olympics. When the organisers first mooted the idea of a scene with the Queen and James Bond actor Daniel Craig, they assumed the best they could hope for was her permission to use a lookalike. According to Sebastian Coe, when it was put to her by David Cameron in their weekly audience, she said yes, and that she would 'play' herself in the palace but perhaps have a lookalike in the scene where she jumps from a helicopter . . . 'We were aiming very, very high,' says Coe. 'We were stunned when she agreed.' But it fitted the covert strategy perfectly. Her instincts gave it the go-ahead. It was an extraordinarily 'modern' thing to do – the Queen and James Bond in the opening ceremony. Yet the film was packed with tradition, with minor roles for the corgis, footmen, Big Ben, Winston Churchill's statue in Parliament Square, Tower Bridge, black cabs, red buses, the Thames and the Union flag – alongside more modern elements, like the London Eye and a group of schoolchildren being shown the Throne Room. Of course, a sense of humour is often cited as a key element of Britishness; the Queen showed hers in taking part, and in keeping her role secret even from Princes Charles, William and Harry, who first knew when they saw it unfold in the stadium. But if you look carefully at how she plays her role, there is no acting. She remains the Queen. It was one of the highlights of the ceremony, and guaranteed her an even more rapturous reception when she, as opposed to the 'Queen' in the helicopter, took her seat – still unsmiling – in the stadium. 'She signed off every element,' says one of her team. 'It was a great moment for us, because she was in her mid-eighties by then, her standing was totally secure, and what that did was show a truly global audience not just that she had a sense of humour, but that the *British* public had huge affection for her, and recognised her unique place in their lives.'

Perhaps the difference between the 'old' royal family and the 'new' is best shown in the much more proactive media approach, particularly with regard to TV. The Queen certainly understands the power of television – after all, she was the one who pressed Churchill's government to have her Coronation filmed and broadcast live. But she has never given a real interview – it's a reflection of her desire to maintain a sense that the monarch is different. True, back in the 1970s, she did do a 'walk and talk' with BBC racing commentator Peter O'Sullevan, and she was once close to doing something with Clare Balding for the Horse Show, but in the end decided the 'no interview' rule had served her well, and it became a lifelong vow. It led to a wonderful moment of culture clash in the press office when *Larry King Live* was told that no, the Queen would not be accepting his invitation to be interviewed live. 'Oh no,' came the reply. 'Does that mean she's doing *Oprah*?'

In recent years, though, the Queen has agreed to a new strategy focused on granting greater – though often very controlled – TV access, giving permission for a succession of projects with which the Palace would to some extent cooperate. Under the guidance of Paddy Harverson, brought in from his role as communications director at Manchester United, Prince Charles has done even more. The old ways – 'never complain, never explain' – were over.

Projecting themselves via TV may sound obvious. But as one

courtier tells me: 'You have to remember that for decades "never complain, never explain" *was* the strategy.' And of course in the Charles and Diana years, TV played a big part in stirring controversy – the Diana *Panorama* interview and the Prince Charles Jonathan Dimbleby film were almost like acts of war in a brutal PR battle. 'They felt scarred, really scarred, and they had to be persuaded this was the way to go,' an adviser says. In addition, the whole household could still be reduced to cringing wrecks if anyone mentioned two previous attempts at major television productions: the 1969 *Royal Family* documentary, filmed over a year, which showed them talking to each other, having a picnic, watching TV, and generally trying – and failing – to appear 'normal'; and the *It's a Royal Knockout*, a not so regal version of a popular TV show. The *Royal Family* film in particular, which had been recommended to them by a friend in the TV industry, was used again and again by 'crustier' elements of the household to argue against allowing greater media access. They considered it an unmitigated disaster that 'opened the floodgates' to a more intrusive and prurient media – and that those floodgates should be slammed shut again.

The new openness to the media, which the Queen approved, showed very clearly that lessons from the past had been learned. As one of Charles's team said, it was agreed that media access should be allowed, but that it was essential 'to move the focus from the personal to the professional'. Previously, Charles in particular had been the subject of relentless personal scrutiny, journalists focusing on his first failed marriage, his relationship with Camilla, his out-of-control young sons not on the right path, behind-the-scenes staff issues and personality clashes, murky goings-on below stairs, spending, gifts. 'There was so much attention on all that, it was unignorable. So we had to close down the media focus on the private side and start to open up the other, what the royal family actually does as royals. We could not have done one without the other.'

Broadcasters were therefore invited in to discuss specific ideas, with three basic conditions before a project went forward: there had to be relationship of trust with the broadcaster; there had to be a context – an anniversary or a special interest, it could not just be TV for the sake of it; and there had to be an agreement to ring-fence the project so that there was a clear and defined focus. Neither the Queen nor Charles was going to change as a person, so the key was finding new ways of projecting them. It required a new approach and a new mindset, not a revolution.

Little by little, Prince Charles saw the benefits as he cooperated with a film on gardening with Alan Titchmarsh, which received good ratings and reviews, then a film on the thirtieth anniversary of the Prince's Trust, with a set-piece interview with Trevor McDonald, then a major (modern) concert event and, coinciding with that, an interview with the three princes, Charles, William and Harry, by popular presenters Ant and Dec. There were one-off interviews and specials with Charles on art, on his painting, on antiques, on the countryside, on the Welsh Guards, on Dumfries House, on composer Hubert Parry. He presented an archive programme about his mother, and, more recently, he read a weather forecast to mark the sixtieth anniversary of BBC Scotland. Arguably, Charles stood to gain the most from this approach to TV, but other members of the royal family also became involved. Journalist Robert Hardman's three-part series on the monarchy, for example, focused more on the Queen.

For the Prince of Wales, the aim was to use a series of smaller projects to build up to a landmark documentary for his sixtieth birthday by John Bridcut, and it was considered a triumph in St James's Palace, a whole hour focused on who he is, what he thinks and what he does for the country – and Princess Diana was not even mentioned.

They then started to take the same strategy abroad. They agreed to a profile by CBS's *60 Minutes*. One of Charles's team says: 'They set the whole piece up as "you think you know Prince Charles but you don't", and then sort of rolled out all our positives about him.' Charles has now cooperated for programmes with all the established US networks.

Meanwhile the young princes were being brought into the same strategy. Their view of the media will always be coloured by what happened to their mother; there is no getting away from that. They do blame the media in a way for what happened to her, but they decided if you work with someone you trust you can do a lot. And, of course, given his future role, William knows that he cannot be in a state of permanent warfare with the media.

Both have therefore worked closely with television. For his part, William has appeared in a documentary about the work of the Tusk Trust of which he is patron. Prince Harry did his first full-length interview for a programme with Tom Bradby on Lesotho, *The Forgotten Kingdom*, in 2004, in which he spoke about hoping to make his mother proud. The programme helped raised over half a million pounds. He has appeared in a number of films, often focused on the military and surviving extremes. In the process, his image as a wild-child clubber dressing up at parties as a Nazi has been transformed into one of a prince who may still go clubbing, but who runs with Usain Bolt, organises the Invictus Games for injured service personnel and is particularly popular among younger people.

From top to bottom, what the Firm began to see was the benefits of being on the front foot, creating your own narrative, rather than on the back foot constantly being forced to react to the agenda of others. 'Once we showed a new approach could deliver, we started to take command of things much more,' says someone involved in devising the strategy. 'So when the tenth anniversary of Diana's death was looming, we got out with our own plans. Six months ahead, we announced a concert and a memorial service, so before the media had even started to think about it we were out there and the boys were saying "this is our mother, our memories, discount everything else". We were front foot, less reactive.'

Courtiers also point to two very different women who made a big change, one by accident, the second by design: the actress Helen Mirren and Charles's second wife Camilla.

There was nervousness when the royal household heard a feature film was being made about the Queen and her relationship with Tony Blair in the aftermath of Diana's death. Those at the Palace and at Number Ten who were asked to give background information all, so far as I know, declined to help on the grounds that to say yes might lead the film-makers to claim that the script was in some way 'authorised' and therefore wholly 'accurate'. To be honest, we all assumed that a hatchet job was being planned. In the event, however, Helen Mirren played an idealised version of the monarch. 'There was a new wave of interest in the Queen, and a new wave of popularity,' says one of her team. 'It was a piece of luck in a way, but it was a piece of luck that ran with the grain of our strategy. I really do think it was a big thing, a massive moment.' The Palace is always coy about whether the Queen has seen it, and what she thought of it. My sense is she has, and that she liked what she saw.

'It made everyone see how far we had come. The anger over the flag – that was a time of real concern. We all felt very vulnerable. The film was such a sympathetic portrayal of the Queen, and I do think it made people feel differently, and that presented us with a new opportunity to take the new strategy forward.'

As for Camilla, courtiers seem universally to credit her with a big role in improving things for Charles. 'There was a lot of worry before the marriage, about whether they would ever be accepted as a couple,' says one of his team, 'but in the event media coverage has been almost uniformly positive.' She brought happiness to him, stability to the family, legitimacy to the relationship, the Queen was pleased, and it started to feel like a new world almost. It was like lancing a boil. It was definitely a turning point.

'She used to have to come in through the back door – not a good image. Suddenly they could go on tour together, and instead of Charles seeming a lonely man, he had company and laughter. She also always talks to people more comfortably than the natural-born royals. She had seen it all, she knew the way the media worked, her son was a writer/journalist, she had been around Charles when the mess was happening, and she learned from it and got him to learn from it too.'

It used to be a treasonable offence to imagine the death of the monarch. Given her age, it seems reasonable for us to think of the world beyond the Queen. Charles wouldn't be human if he hadn't thought about it many times, increasingly as they both aged. His team is clear that he will be different to her, and different to how he has been himself as Prince of Wales. 'There is no defined role for heir to the throne; there is a defined role for the head of state. But equally, no two monarchs are the same. He will bring continuity, but also change,' says someone who has worked closely with both over many years. 'He's had lots of time to think about it. The Queen started so young. He will be much older. He will bring wisdom and experience. He knows he'll have to rein himself in a little, but he won't be silent. He knows they are in a good place but they won't take it for granted, won't sit around saying "great job". Nothing will take away from her being one of the defining figures of our age. Her death will be a remarkable moment, a vast moment of history, time to take stock, to realise a whole set of new challenges have come along.'

In other words, having learned the benefits of being more proactive and strategic, the next phase for the royal family is already being planned. 'Of course they do,' says one of the Queen's advisers, when I ask if mother and son talk about 'life beyond the Queen'. Polling shows the Queen is by far the most popular and respected royal, and that William comes ahead of his father. They also know, having had so many ups and downs, that it would not take many mistakes to get the media mood to turn again. But they definitely seem to realise that is less likely to happen when they are applying a proper strategic approach to all they do.

That the institution of monarchy should be in such a healthy state at this transitional moment owes much to the Queen herself. People say of her that, though possessed of a strong personality, she radiates a sense of calm, and doesn't let things get to her. She reads or at least looks at, all the daily papers, and when she travels she does the same with the national media wherever she may be, but even when coverage has been hostile she has never complained. 'She's seen it all really,' a former member of her press team tells me, 'and I think it's getting through so much that gives her this sense of calm when things are not going terribly well.' Of course, as I've said elsewhere, calmness in a crisis is the mark of a good leader. She's not a big blamer either. 'She does bollock you, and you can feel it from a single look of her eye,' says one member of her team, 'but only when you deserve it by not paying attention to detail.' She also has a powerful sense of duty. When King Juan Carlos of Spain abdicated in 2014, it was made clear that she would never consider doing likewise. 'She would be mammothly opposed to something like that. It is not a job. It is a vocation. She took a vow of service,' says one of her courtiers.

He goes on: 'I know you're against the whole hereditary principle, but let me tell you why it works with the monarchy. It is about humility. You and I, or anyone else who gets anywhere in life, we get there on some kind of merit. We might be clever, we work hard, we climb the greasy pole, and then we make our own decisions about what to do and when to stop, when to change what we do. The Queen and the Prince of Wales are not in doubt for one moment that they did nothing, nothing at all, to deserve to be where they are. They were just plonked there. They are accidents of birth. There was no interview, no selection panel. And that has made them very humble about those positions, and very focused about doing the right thing, and disciplined about duty. To me, that is one of the secrets of her success.

'I do not believe people want a communism of wealth or lifestyle. They like her riding to the opening of Parliament in a gold coach, or driving to a hospital in a Rolls-Royce. But people do want a communism of humanity. She has always understood that instinctively. They know she is different, but they also know she is the same, eats the same things, breathes the same air, understands them and wants them to understand her. That is the communism of humanity, and her understanding of that goes a long way to explaining why even with your views, you see her as a success and a great leader.'

I can honestly say I have never before lumped communism and the Queen in the same thought, but he may well have a point. Whatever way you look at it, she has outlived communism, and seen off republicanism too. She is a very special, and very British, winner.

Conclusion

THE ART OF WINNING

'If you can't win, what is the point?'

HAILE GEBRSELASSIE

This book has partly been about role models, and the things all of us can learn from people who have been hyper-successful in their chosen fields. I will never be a billionaire businessman, but I subscribe to Richard Branson's newsletter because he almost always has something relevant to say about something that I'm involved in. I will never be as good a footballer as Diego Maradona, but he turned me on to the power of visualisation. I can take Dave Brailsford's marginal gains as an outlook and apply it to how I prepare for a new challenge. I have seen statesmen and stateswomen very close up – from Margaret Thatcher onwards – and am not sure I could do their job, but I do know it is possible both to emulate and also to avoid some of the qualities I saw in them.

Researching Warren Buffett, I came across a transcript of a fabulous discussion that took place between him and Bill Gates – America's two wealthiest men, with $84 billion between them at the time – in front of 350 students in Seattle in 1998. Despite the generation gap and Buffett's technophobia, which meant for years he resisted even having a computer, they are close, and their friendship has led to one of history's biggest acts of philanthropy, with Buffett deciding to sign over almost all of his billions to the Bill and Melinda Gates Foundation. As the students in Gates's home town listened in, Buffett had a great piece of advice to offer about role models.

I have one little suggestion for you. Pick out the person you admire the most, and then write down why you admire them. You're not to name yourself in this. And then put down the person that, frankly, you can stand the least, and write down the qualities that turn you off in that person. The qualities of the one you admire are traits that you, with a little practice, can make your own, and that, if practiced, will become habit-forming.

Buffett, one of the most extraordinary communicators of the last century, went on to say this beautiful sentence, which I subsequently discovered came from the pen of Samuel Johnson: 'The chains of habit are too light to be felt until they are too heavy to be broken.' He explained:

At my age I can't change my habits, I'm stuck. But you will have the habits twenty years from now that you decide to put into practice today. So I suggest that you look at the behavior that you admire in others and make those your habits, and look at what you find reprehensible in others and decide those are the things you are not going to do. If you do that, you'll discover that you convert all of your horsepower into output.

If I do the Buffett exercise, I find it hard to pick out just one person to admire, and find myself making lists. Mandela is often first, but in a way he is too saintly, his qualities so great that it feels wrong even to think one could start to emulate him. The same goes for Lincoln. Buffett and Branson, whose names keep coming up as role models for business people, feel closer, their qualities more attainable for mere mortals, even if most will never get near the success they have enjoyed.

But as I scribble lists, cross names off, write new ones down, I see that sport is where I have found the 'winningest' winning mindsets. I know as well as anyone just how hard politics is, that no business or sport venture is as complicated or multifaceted as a government, that no CEO or manager faces quite the pressures a president or prime minister is under. That does not mean politicians cannot learn from sport and business, and one of my hopes for this book is that people in politics will see just how much they can learn from elite sport in particular. Whether looking at strategy, teamship, leadership, resilience, innovation, data, handling failure, there is so much to take from what the best in sport – and also business – do well. Too many politicians pay lip service to sport. They know the public passions it can arouse, and what it can do for the national mood, yet they fail to see how much value the best of sports practice could actually bring to their own performance and operations, just as they fail to appreciate the lessons they can learn from great entrepreneurs or business leaders.

A name that is always around when I am reflecting on what Buffett said to those students, and thinking about role models of my own, is Ethiopian athlete Haile Gebrselassie. He is a wonderful runner, and a wonderful man. I first met him at the Great North Run in the early 2000s. Brendan Foster introduced us and they both said if I really wanted to experience an incredible mass participation event, I should go with them to Addis Ababa for the Great Ethiopian Run. So I did, in December 2003, and saw that Gebrselassie was a living legend there, something of a role model to an entire nation.

The run was without doubt one of the most joyous things I have ever done. It started on a vast boulevard and when Gebrselassie fired the starting gun he sparked an explosion of energy and happiness as a sea of men, women and children set off, in identical green, red and yellow T-shirts. At the time I was writing my series on greats in sport for *The Times*, and I interviewed him the following day. I asked him what lessons he drew from his own sporting success, and there was a simplicity and clarity to what he said. Lesson 1, use your background. Lesson 2, if you have talent, use it. Lesson 3, love doing what you do. Lesson 4, have role models. Lesson 5, have a good team around you. Lesson 6, always maintain discipline.

Lesson 7, stick to your schedule. Lesson 8, always prepare properly. Lesson 9, always focus on the next win, not the last one. Lesson 10, see the broader significance of winning.

Sound familiar? Yet what makes Gebrselassie so relevant in applying them to the themes of this book is that he can speak about them in relation to the three main areas of activity I have been examining: sport, business and politics. Gebrselassie has ticked the sports-winner box many times over, with golds in the 10 kilometres at successive Olympics in Atlanta and Sydney and four successive World Championships, as well as sixty-one national and twenty-seven world records, including one for the marathon which he set aged thirty-five, long past retirement age for many athletes. He has also ticked the business box, with his portfolio of hotels, property, a coffee plantation and a car distribution franchise with Hyundai – not to mention the schools he has built as part of what he calls 'putting something back' – making him one of his country's most successful business and social entrepreneurs. Yet he sees these two phases of his life as something of an apprenticeship, and is now planning to tick the politics box too, with the same ambition to reach the top. If Albania's Edi Rama is the only current national leader to have represented his country at sport, Gebrselassie could be the next.

So I went to interview him again, to find out if those same lessons were still in practice.

Back in 2003, in Lesson 1, when Gebrselassie talked about using his background, he meant that in a country with no golf courses, few pools or tennis courts, he was never going to be a golfer, swimmer or tennis player. Running was all he had. It was the way to get around, he loved it, and had a talent for it. Living at altitude, in a country full of good runners, also helped. His father, though, a subsistence farmer, was not keen for him to be an athlete, feeling it was unlikely to help with the finances for a poor family of ten children growing up without a mother, who had died when Haile was seven. Today it is his background as an established, successful, wealthy national hero that he will use as the base for his political career. Where once the role model was 'Yifter the Shifter', Ethiopian runner Marius Yifter, now it is Mandela. Where once his coach was the core of the team, now it is his 1,500 staff. He tells me: 'I am not doing this to be more famous, I have enough of that. I am interested in doing what I can to help my country.' Haile Gebrselassie is a man who has set himself big objectives, and then shown he can master both strategy and tactics in meeting them. OST. He gets it.

'So in a race,' I say, 'when you let an opponent go, then reel him back in, then let him lead again, then pull him back by outsprinting him at the end, that is a tactic, yes?'

'Yes, that is a tactic. I used that.'

'So what can you learn from that now, how can you apply it now?'

'I can apply it a lot. For example, when you are in a stadium, thousands of people, let's say for a 10k race, twenty-five laps, if you decide to go from the beginning and everyone knows you are going to win, they stop watching you, it is boring, unless maybe if you have said it is for a world-record attempt. So you go side by side with others, you are showing there is competition, and at the end you show how good you are. Same in business, people need competition. Something the same in politics, if you are out too far, the competition will become boring. Why are elections in your country and in America so interesting? Because mostly they are neck and neck, it is a race.'

There is one other advantage he believes a life at the top in sport gives him over others with more conventional political experience, and that is what he calls 'honesty'. Not honesty simply in terms of 'telling the truth', but the honesty that goes with understanding, as Ron Dennis said about F1, 'there is no hiding place in public competition'.

'You have to show up and show how strong you are. You cannot shrink away,' says Gebrselassie. 'In politics there is a lot of weaving in and out, people can hide. In sport there is nowhere to hide, it is fair, you see what you see, and the judgement is easy. For me, when we talk about democracy, it is not just fair elections but to show everything is clear and transparent afterwards. I think coming from sport helps in this. It is a way of thinking.'

Gebrselassie, accustomed to playing cat and mouse with rivals over the course of marathons, is also playing the long game in politics. When I saw him at another Great North Run a few years ago, he told me he was planning to enter parliament in the 2015 election. But now he tells me he has decided against it. Why? Not because his ambitions have stalled, but because, as he frankly admits, sporting metaphor as ever to hand, 'I need more training. Like a marathon, if you are not prepared enough, you lose. I am not ready for the next election, which means I need more preparation.' Nor, he suggests, is the politics of the country ready. At the last election, the ruling Ethiopian People's Revolutionary Democratic Front took 499 of the parliament's 547 seats; forty-six went to allied parties, and just two to opposition and independent candidates. Both the US and the EU were highly critical of the way the election was conducted. Regional elections were even more one-sided, the EPRDF winning all but one of 1,904 council seats.

'In these conditions how can you go and make a difference?' he asks. 'It is hard, so you wait. I could win a seat, but then if I am on my own, what change can I make? I am just protesting. I am not saying our politics will become like yours, it may take ten or twenty years, more, democracy can take a long time to develop, but it will change.'

'What if it doesn't?'

'It will.'

So, now in his early forties, he is thinking one, two, even three decades ahead as he imagines a time when he can put what he has learned in sport and business to broader use.

He says that many of his great races were won not on the track or the road, but on long, lonely training runs in his hills of Ethiopia. 'You might be training hard, it is hurting, and that day's training is what gives you the extra, the fitness and drive, that comes on the day of the race. So when you train, you worry not about the race but about the preparations, do you see the difference? A twenty-mile training run all alone, out in the hills – that may be the run that wins the race, so that run is as important as the race itself. If you

do not train enough, you will lose. If you train well, you give yourself the chance to win. I feel the same about politics. You cannot
just go from one to the other, you have to upgrade yourself, so I
have to educate myself more, read, really find out what it is that
the people need. When I was competing as a runner, it was about
me, my performance, and winning. In business, it is about what I
want to happen, how I make that happen, but I need many people
to help me. Politics is about what other people need. It is different.
You do not run alone.'

There is no surprise in what Gebrselassie says is the most
important thing that links sport, business and politics. 'You have to
win. In sport, it is clearer what that means, you win the match, you
win the race, you win the trophy or the medal. In business, you
want to be number one, and it is about profits; no profit, you lose.
Less clear, but still fairly clear. In politics, you must win the election, but then winning is about what you do. The real winners win
their elections, and then raise their country from what it is to what
it can be. If they are number two or three, you want to take them
to the front. If you are at the back, you bring them up. Unless you
do that, you cannot really say you are a winner.' He adds that how
you win can be as important as whether you win. So Lance Armstrong
has shown he has a winning mindset, but 'he is a big loser, man'.
There must always, he says, be integrity in winning.

'I believe everything we do is in some way about politics. I have
done something for my country in running. But the best way to do
something for your country is through politics because that is how
you can change your country for the better. I would love to do that.
I would do it with the same determination, the same desire, as I do
with my running.'

To walk around Addis Ababa with Gebrselassie is to see a man
loved and revered by Ethiopians young and old. He tells me of the
moment when he realised he had a very special talent for running,
and the effect it could have on people. 'It was 1988, and I won my
first 1500 metres at my school. The director of the school took me
onto the podium in front of two thousand students and said "Here is

the athlete who won" and everyone was clapping and I thought "Wow, did I do that?" I have never had an atmosphere quite like that since, even big races like Olympics, it was so special, just my own local high school. There were lots of boys who were bigger and more handsome for the girls, nobody really recognised me till then, but I got the attention, it was like "Hey, is this what happens when you win?"'

> 'If you do not train enough, you will lose. If you train well, you give yourself the chance to win. I feel the same about politics.'
>
> **HAILE GEBRSELASSIE**

I suggest to him that if politicians get adulation, it comes in small doses, and tends to evaporate with the hard choices of power, because in politics you must disappoint as well as please. 'I know,' he says. 'So are you not worried that the moment you become a "proper politician" you'll no longer be seen in the same way, you won't be so popular, and so won't maintain support?' Gebrselassie replies with nothing more than the smile that has lit up race tracks and podiums all over the world for more two decades. His Dutch manager, Jos Hermens, is more forthright. 'That's why he's waiting. If he did it now, he becomes a lone voice, and he cannot make happen the things he wants to happen. But he will. He is a born leader.'

When talking of great leaders, Gebrselassie puts Winston Churchill in much the same league as Mandela, and considers that his ejection from office 'after saving your country from something terrible' was as dramatic a sign as can be imagined of the fickleness of people when it comes to their politicians. 'They always want more, they always want something different,' he says. It is why he believes people are being unfair in suggesting Barack Obama has been a disappointment. 'He is trying so hard to raise his country up – look at his greying hair and see how hard he is trying.' He shares my positive assessment of Angela Merkel and thinks that if Hillary Clinton becomes US president, 'women may well show men they can do things better because they take a different kind of approach, more flexible, more balanced'.

Some of the attributes you hear commentators bestowing upon leaders in a race – boldness, courage, stamina, tactical cleverness – are those we like to see in leaders of bigger and more complicated ventures. Gebrselassie says that when he was controlling a race, he felt like a leader. 'To me, leadership is all about taking responsibility. When you become a leader you are the one who has to lead people to do things they don't know they want to do. You are the responsible person. That is the same in business and politics.' Again, his sporting experience has been part of his apprenticeship.

'If I am doing a race, let's say the Berlin Marathon [he won it four times], where I set a world record, and in the build-up, people are saying "he is the number one", I start to think "I have to do something special", and I don't sleep, I worry, I am determined to run a great race. If I was number two, I would be more relaxed, I would be thinking "oh well, I want to win, but the pressure is all on the number one". I have to show something, win well, break a record. So it is about wanting and embracing responsibility. And that experience in sport helps me now. My business gives me a lot of headaches, I worry, sometimes I don't sleep well because of a problem, and I think about all the possibilities and it reminds me of when I had a big race and I would be sleepless the night before, what if this happens, what if that happens, what if my tactics are disrupted by someone knocking me off my stride, these worries are part of the preparation. It is pressure and I feel it as a responsibility. Same in politics; if the president or prime minister is prepared and he knows everything in a perfect way, he is fine. It is all about preparation, all about responsibility.'

He knows that nothing is certain about his political ambitions. 'I am almost done in sport. I am doing in business. I will do politics, and we will see.' But just as he – not to mention his father – could never have imagined the fame and wealth his running brought him, so growing up in Assela, he did not imagine that one day he would command the range of successful businesses he runs today. The lessons he learned in sport he took into business and now the lessons from both will be taken into politics. It is why he is a worthy final interview to the book. We can learn from others. But if we are able to look at ourselves openly and honestly, we can learn a lot from ourselves and our own experience too. Winners never stop learning, from their own successes and failures, and from the successes and failures of others.

Indeed, running through this whole book, I hope, is the notion that whatever walk of life we are in, we can learn from others. During my life, in the media, in politics and in the more varied life I lead now, I feel privileged to have met as many winners and studied as many winning mindsets and winning operations as I have.

It has been inspiring and also humbling to immerse myself in the lives of the many exceptional people who agreed to talk to me. Inspiring because that is what so many of them are, whether a José Mourinho or a Ben Ainslie who so clearly live, breathe, sleep the desire to win and to keep winning, a Richard Branson or Jimmy Wales or Arianna Huffington because they want to change the world, and are doing it, or a Garry Kasparov with a brain the size of a planet, or a Layne Beachley whose story was in some ways the most inspiring of all. Humbling because, though I like to think I have many of the attitudes and qualities required for a winning mindset, I have heard and learned from people – especially in sport and business – who take the winning mindset to ever higher levels.

I think the most consistent lesson of all from those I have met is this: however good you are, you can always be better. Perfection doesn't exist. It's why Romanian gymnast Nadia Comaneci told me that her reaction on being awarded 'the perfect ten' at Montreal was to enjoy the moment, but tell herself the judges were wrong, because she had done better in training, and could do better again. Once we have reached perfection, where else is there to go?

Or listen to what Kenyan runner Paul Tergat says about his own place in athletics history. Had Gebrselassie never existed, Tergat, one of twenty-three siblings from a polygamous father, would be first on many people's lists of the greatest long-distance runners of all time. But unlike Gebrselassie, he never won Olympic gold, coming second behind the Ethiopian in the 10k final at Atlanta and at Sydney, where the margin of defeat was nine-hundredths of a second – even closer than in the men's 100 metres final. Life-changing stuff.

So when I ask him what it takes to be a great winning athlete, he says: 'I am not qualified to answer.' This is a man with five world cross-country championships and a stack of world records and medals to his name, but he says: 'I've achieved more than most athletes, but great athletes get Olympic gold medals, and I only have silvers.' On that basis, he feels he should not be included in the list of great winners. Yet it is precisely because of that attitude that in my view he should, just after Gebrselassie; because that story illustrates this central lesson about room for improvement, seeing one success as the stepping stone to the next, never losing the hunger for more. It is without doubt a key part of the winning mindset. So many of the people interviewed spoke of feeling almost let down when they actually won something they had set their hearts on. That feeling is born in the 'responsibility' Gebrselassie spoke of, the extra pressure that comes from being 'the leader'. Like Leigh Matthews, who felt that he could never fully enjoy the winning feeling to the full, because within moments of the match ending his mind was turning to the next one. Like Dave Brailsford being criticised by his staff for never wanting to celebrate. Like Tiger Woods chastising his wife for thinking a victory called for a special gathering for friends and family – because winning is his business, it is what he is meant to do. To the sportsman, greatness is what you reflect on when you're retired.

This ability always to focus on the next challenge, and then the next, leads me to something Alex Ferguson once said, when encouraging me to make sure that Tony and I, and other key members of the 1997 campaign team, were taking care of our diet, exercise, sleep and general well-being. 'People underestimate the importance of energy,' he said. 'In high-pressure situations, in leadership positions, you're always having to think, adapt, make decisions, communicate;

these all require energy.' And, of course, energy is not a limitless resource.

Sometimes, the difference between winning and losing is the ability to summon up extra reserves of energy you didn't know you had. That is all too apparent in the sports arena, and what makes the final moments of a close contest so dramatic is that often we are witnessing human beings dig deeper than we or they thought possible. We see the ones who can keep going beat the ones who cannot. In sport, this doesn't happen by accident. Brian O'Driscoll has described to me how in the latter stages of his rugby career, his coach Joe Schmidt focused on 'training while fatigued. So many matches come down to the last moments. Joe would get us tired through endurance work, and then practise on skills, and there were various times it paid off, where we had that little extra in the closing moments.' But this discovery of latent energy can also happen when a business is preparing for an important launch, or going through a crisis, and people know that there's still work to be done and they cannot stop until it's completed. If I recall the times when Tony Blair kept negotiating through the night in Northern Ireland, and somehow the other parties and their teams managed to keep going too, and several of the big breakthrough moments happened in that way, I am reminded of what reserves of energy the most unlikely people have when they are made to look for them. I have also known that feeling – often with a week to go before an election – when something stirs inside you, usually fear of defeat, and you are able somehow to push the exhaustion to one side, keep going, one more hour, one more idea that you put into action, one more attempt to galvanise the troops and get them to feel the same surge of energy. This is not a healthy way to live, and it cannot be done every day, but it's a great feeling when it happens, when you dig deep, and find that, yes, there is something left in there. It comes from a deep desire to win, a desire to make a difference, real belief. It is what Gordon Brown summoned up late in the Scottish independence referendum campaign.

And in this context I remember one of the many inspiring remarks made by Vince Lombardi, coach of the Green Bay Packers, a remark that applies not just to sport but to all ventures: 'I firmly believe that any man's finest hour, the greatest fulfilment of all that he holds dear, is that moment when he has worked his heart out in a good cause and lies exhausted on the field of battle – victorious.'

To Lombardi, the 'good cause' was winning a football game. It was as important as the battles that Churchill led in war. It mattered. This is something else that links the people in this book. They believe. They care. They are passionate. They have found what they love doing, and they have been determined to do it as well as they possibly can. I have gone fifty-seven years of my life without really understanding why Formula One can arouse the passions that it does. But then I spend time with the people at Mercedes and McLaren who devote their lives to it – who really believe that who goes past that chequered flag first in that Grand Prix is the single most important thing happening anywhere in the world at that time – and it comes alive for me, because suddenly I can see the dedication, the sacrifice and the absolute focus on being the best they can possibly be. There is something wonderfully noble about that, not least when the dedication and sacrifice are coming not just from those who get fame and glory, but the ones whose names we will never know, who are just 'doing their job' as part of the team.

So here is another key lesson: either winners *are* a great team, or they *have* a great team. Nobody in this book – from the Queen and Mandela down – has done it alone. What winners do is get the right people, motivate them in the right way, and maximise their potential to the benefit of the individual and the team. This is where politics falls down all too often, and I wish there was an obvious answer as to why, beyond ego and ambition, which are both essential winning attributes, but not if used to the detriment of your own side. So much of the animosity in politics is within teams rather than between them. It is so wasteful, of energy and talent. Imagine if, in Germany's World Cup-winning team, Philipp Lahm had refused to pass to Bastian Schweinsteiger, or André Schürrle had refused to cross the ball if it meant Thomas Müller might score . . . yet all too often that is the reality in politics, and frankly it is pathetic. They should heed the words of Brian O'Driscoll when he says: 'There is no greater feeling than when a team clicks, when I'm waiting there at number 13, the pack is doing its job, the ball is coming out, 9 to 10, then out to us in the centre, and I know we're going to do something special. When every cog in the machine works, it is the best feeling there is, but you will only get that feeling if the whole team is doing its job.' Or the words of Johnathan Thurston, who says 'there is no better feeling' than working hard with a team, then winning as a team, and 'no worse feeling' than losing. 'Winning brings so much joy and happiness. I just want to win, win, win, and I know the processes I need to do throughout my life to do that.'

Many of the people I have talked to are wealthy, a consequence of their success. Yet real winners really do care more about winning than they do about wealth. I don't think naivety is one of my weaknesses, and I totally believed Branson and the other business people when they said their own wealth was not their main motivation: having ideas and making them work was. Jim O'Neill says: 'I have met lots of billionaires but none who started out with the ambition to be one.' Warren Buffett lives in the same house he bought for $32,000 many years ago. Branson tells me: 'I can honestly say I have never gone into any venture saying "The purpose is to make money". I go into a venture saying "Can we provide something people need and want, and can we be proud of what we create?" And if you do that, the money comes. Whenever I talk to young entrepreneurs I always say to them "Can you honestly say you are adding value to people's lives with your idea? If you can, then you have the start of a successful proposition."' Now, he says, he is taking the same approach to non-profit work, whether trying to come up with clean fuel for airlines, or turning island states into carbon-neutral areas; he has businesses around the world producing wealth that he is using to meet new bold challenges in the public and political arena.

Dave Brailsford once had no more than the bags and the bike

and the small savings he took to France as a young man to try to make it as a cyclist. He struggled, but he learned. He now has a Bentley, a knighthood and, more importantly for him, a reputation among his peers as a leader and innovator in sport. Tiger Woods and Rory McIlroy could put their money in the bank today, and earn more from the interest than most of their fans would earn in a lifetime. Yet still they work, on to the next thing, and the next, wanting to be the best and stay the best at what they do, also thinking of new challenges and of legacy, what lasting influence they may leave on their sports and the wider world. Even Floyd 'Money' Mayweather – I am refusing to let his 'middle name' defeat my thesis that winners put success ahead of money – trumpets his wealth as a symbol of his supremacy in the business of boxing. If all he cared about was being super-rich, he reached that objective many years ago, and could have been long retired by now.

So what other final thoughts and lessons do I take from analysing winners as I have? Some of these are blindingly obvious, but worth stating nonetheless.

Winners work hard. The effortless rise to the top is a myth. The work ethic is fundamental. Practice and pain are essential.

Winners make sacrifices. Whether it's the girlfriendless Gary Neville, the home-leaving Brailsford, the six-jobs-to-pay-for-her-sport Layne Beachley, the seven-days-a-week working life of businessmen and women, and effective politicians, they do the things they have to do, and often do without the things that others take for granted. The training regimes required to reach and stay at the top, the need to focus on diet and rest, are now of an order that frankly few could live with. They may get the rewards, but only if they make the sacrifices too.

Winners don't just take focus and concentration for granted. They work at it. The most extreme example may be Tiger Woods, but there are different approaches. Usain Bolt enjoys lie-ins and parties and 'messing around' with girls. He admits having dabbled with marijuana in the past and he loves junk food, once eating a hundred chicken nuggets in a day (while competing in the Olympics).

Yet given Bolt is the fastest man on earth, nobody can dispute that he's a winner. His charisma and his evident love of people have also made him one of the most popular sports stars in the world. The difference with Woods is stark. It shows it can take all sorts to win. But amid the fooling-around image and the amazing natural talent, it is possible to find points of connection.

Bolt loves winning, hates losing. He knows that he needs others to push him, and made sure to find the right coach for him, Glen Mills, who became like a second father. He learns from mistakes. He has learned to endure physical pain in training and in competition. He has learned to use setbacks as opportunities. He only started really to flourish when he stopped caring about what people thought, and realised he had to toughen up, the turning point being the time a Jamaican crowd booed him when he pulled up in a race with a hamstring injury.

Winners do OST. As my conversation with José Mourinho shows, there can be different interpretations of the words, but on this I think we agreed: you have to set a winning objective. You have to be clear what that means. You have to be clear about the basic plan that you intend to execute. Once you have that, you can be endlessly tactical, but you should not deviate from your core strategy unless, as Garry Kasparov said, there is fundamental change to your environment.

Winners innovate. This is part of the same mindset that refuses, as Arianna Huffington puts it, to take success as an end point. It is also a recognition that any meaningful sporting, business or political activity takes place in fiercely competitive circumstances, nothing stays still forever, and, as José Mourinho puts it, 'If you stand still, you get left behind.' I was struck by Mourinho's point about there being 'no copyright'. As the world becomes more open and transparent, ideas don't stay secret, or belong to one person or one team alone. To stay ahead, you have to focus not just on your own performance, but on those trying to win against you. And that requires the mindset that understands it is possible to stay true to a core strategy while also adapting to changed circumstances around you.

Winners take ideas from others, and as well as having their own ideas, learn from the success of others too. As former Tesco CEO Terry Leahy said in his book on management: 'Competitors – and the act of competition itself – are great teachers . . . My strongest competitors are the best management consultants there are: I look at their operations, their products or simply visit their website to find out about their thinking, research and planning – for free.'

Winners must adapt as the clock ticks away. So many top sportsmen and women face serious issues of mental health when they stop competing. I had similar issues when I left Downing Street. It's not easy to go from something full-on and meaningful to trying to shape a new life. But other challenges open up that allow you to take the talents you have in a new direction. Swedish table-tennis legend Jan-Ove Waldner, once the second most recognised Westerner in China (behind Bill Clinton), had to retire like all sportsmen do, but now uses that phenomenal fame, calling the world's biggest and most table-tennis-obsessed country in the world 'my main market-place'. I spoke to Brian O'Driscoll a few months after he retired on a high in 2014, winning trophies to the very end, and he admitted he felt disorientated. 'Being a professional athlete is all I have known, and in sport, when you're done, you're done. I miss the routines and the dressing room and the sense of being part of a team. I know that nothing is going to replace the thrill of playing in front of 70,000 people, or the euphoria of winning a big match. Anyone who tells you they prefer their post-playing life is a liar, but I also know I have many years ahead of me and I have to work out what to do.' Brendan Foster did not want to stop running. But he had to. So he went into the business of sport and has presided over the biggest mass participation run in the world. Seb Coe was a top athlete, one of the best ever, and could easily have rested on those laurels. He didn't; he took the talents he had and adapted them to business, to Parliament, and then to leading the remarkable success of the 2012 Olympic Games. It is something in his character that drives him to want to be the best at what he does, whatever it is.

Winners are resilient, and Coe has shown that in so many

ways. On the track, not least recovering from the setback of unexpected defeat. In politics, being part of a losing Tory team, but bouncing back in the politics of sport. Today his stock is so high that people forget that even when he was a winner in sport, he often had a hard time from the media which now eats out of his hand. The press could be vile about him. When he won his second 1,500 metres gold, in Los Angeles in 1984, as he crossed the line he immediately looked up to the press box, real anger in his eyes, and yelled: 'Who says I'm finished now?'

> 'If you stand still, you get left behind.'
>
> **JOSÉ MOURINHO**

'They deserved it, some of them,' he tells me. 'It was the nastiness of it. The *Mail* did a big piece on my so-called dysfunctional family, horrible stuff. Someone did a piece on us being a classic two-child family, which was a bit odd because I'm one of four. Some of them came very close to saying I had Aids. So it was a good moment, giving some of it back. Maybe it was an overreaction, but it was how I felt.'

It was also because, as a winner, he had learned how to use anything and everything that happened around him as a form of pressure, a motivation, a spur to better performance which, ultimately, was all he cared about. Winners use emotion, but also know when to control it.

Winners think big and bold. They are ambitious.

Winners have a plan and where possible they stick to it.

Winners pay attention to detail, know it is in the implementation and constant iteration of planning that winning objectives can best be met.

Winners never give up. They embrace pressure and they embrace setbacks.

Winners turn disappointment into progress. They learn from mistakes.

Winners always want to improve and the desire to improve is what leads to innovation.

Winners feel special. This is not universal, but I was struck by how many of the people I met acknowledged feeling from a young age that they would be more successful than others.

Winners focus on the next win, not the last one.

Winners have the will to win, and know that it is not the same as wanting to win.

Winners know the mental and the physical are always connected.

Winners care about their reputation and know that building it never stops.

Winners respect experience, but not if someone keeps doing the wrong thing.

Winners hate talent being wasted.

Winners hate losing.

Winners win, because they have to.

INDEX